The Crisis in
Youth Mental Health

Recent Titles in Child Psychology and Mental Health

THE CRISIS IN
YOUTH MENTAL HEALTH

Critical Issues and Effective Programs

Volume 4

Early Intervention Programs and Policies

Norman F. Watt, Catherine Ayoub, Robert H. Bradley, Jini E. Puma,
and Whitney A. LeBoeuf

Volume Editors

Hiram E. Fitzgerald, Robert Zucker, and Kristine Freeark

Editors in Chief

Praeger Perspectives
Child Psychology and Mental Health
Hiram E. Fitzgerald and Susanne Ayres Denham, Series Editors

PRAEGER

Westport, Connecticut
London

KH

Library of Congress Cataloging-in-Publication Data

The crisis in youth mental health : understanding the critical issues and effective programs / editors Hiram E. Fitzgerald, Robert Zucker, and Kristine Freeark.
   p. cm. — (Child psychology and mental health)
Includes bibliographical references and index.
ISBN 0-275-98480-X (set : alk. paper)—ISBN 0-275-98481-8 (v. 1 : alk. paper)—ISBN 0-275-98482-6 (v.2 : alk. paper)—ISBN 0-275-98483-4 (v.3 : alk. paper)—ISBN 0-275-98484-2 (v.4 : alk. paper) 1. Adolescent psychopathology. 2. Child psychotherapy. 3. Youth--Counseling of. 4. Community mental health services. I. Fitzgerald, Hiram E. II. Zucker, Robert A. III. Freeark, Kristine. IV. Series.
RJ503.C76 2006
618.92'8914—dc22   2005030767

British Library Cataloguing in Publication Data is available.

Library of Congress Catalog Card Number: 2005030767
ISBN: 0–275–98480–X (set)
        0–275–98481–8 (vol. 1)
        0–275–98482–6 (vol. 2)
        0–275–98483–4 (vol. 3)
        0–275–98484–2 (vol. 4)
ISSN: 1538–8883

First published in 2006

Praeger Publishers, 88 Post Road West, Westport, CT 06881
An imprint of Greenwood Publishing Group, Inc.
www.praeger.com

Printed in the United States of America

The paper used in this book complies with the Permanent Paper Standard issued by the National Information Standards Organization (Z39.48–1984).

10   9   8   7   6   5   4   3   2   1

2/8/07

CONTENTS

SERIES FOREWORD

The twentieth century closed with a decade devoted to the study of brain structure, function, and development that in parallel with studies of the human genome has revealed the extraordinary plasticity of biobehavioral organization and development. The twenty-first century opens with a decade focusing on behavior, but the linkages between brain and behavior are as dynamic as the linkages between parents and children, and children and environment.

The Child Psychology and Mental Health series is designed to capture much of this dynamic interplay by advocating for strengthening the science of child development and linking that science to issues related to mental health, child care, parenting, and public policy.

The series consists of individual monographs, each dealing with a subject that advanced knowledge related to the interplay between normal developmental process and developmental psychopathology. The books are intended to reflect the diverse methodologies and content areas encompassed by an age period ranging from conception to late adolescence. Topics of contemporary interest include studies of socioemotional development, behavioral undercontrol, aggression, attachment disorders, and substance abuse.

Investigators involved with prospective longitudinal studies, large epidemiologic cross-sectional samples, intensely followed clinical cases, or those wishing to report a systematic sequence of connected experiments are invited to submit manuscripts. Investigators from all fields in social and behavioral sciences, neurobiological sciences, medical and clinical sciences, and education are invited to submit manuscripts with implications for child and adolescent mental health.

Hiram E. Fitzgerald
Susanne Ayres Denham
Series Editors

ACKNOWLEDGMENTS

This project began at a lunch meeting when Norman Watt, Robert Bradley, Catherine Ayoub, Jini Puma and Hi Fitzgerald concluded that there was a great need for a book that summarized the benefits of early intervention. Shortly after agreeing to pursue such a book, Deborah Carvalko, acquisitions editor at Greenwood Publishing Group, contacted Hi to inquire if he knew anyone who would be interested in editing a series on the Crisis in Youth Mental Health. Bingo! This four-volume set is the result and volume 4 is that original lunch time project. The volumes represent a product forged from the labor and energy of an editorial team composed of long-time and current research and professional colleagues: Catherine Ayoub, Robert Bradley, William Davidson, Hiram Fitzgerald, Kristine Freeark, Whitney LeBoeuf, Barry Lester, Tom Luster, Jini Puma, Francisco Villarruel, Norman Watt, Robert Zucker, and Barry Zuckerman. Each editorial team drafted an extraordinary set of researchers who collectively frame the parameters of the crisis in youth mental health, provide cogent analyses of effective evidence-based preventive-intervention programs, and draw attention to policy implications of their work. Volumes such as these are labors of professional and personal love because the rewards to be gained are only those realized by the impact that words and ideas have on current and future generations of scientists, parents, and policy makers. No one has more passion for bringing science to bear on the problems of society than Lou Anna K. Simon, President of Michigan State University. In her commentary, she eloquently and forcefully articulates the need to forge campus–community partnerships, using evidence-based practices to both understand and resolve community-based problems.

Editors and authors provide the grist for anthologies, but there are many millers that grind the grain and bake it into a final loaf. First to thank is Deborah Carvalko who provided the opportunity to even imagine the project. Lisa Pierce, senior development editor at Praeger Press made sure that this host of contributors met their deadlines. Apex Publishing, assisted by four extremely meticulous and energetic copy editors (Ellie Amico [vol. 1], Bruce Owens [vol. 2], Caryl Knutsen [vol. 3], and Carol Burwash [vol. 4]), moved everyone through a tight time frame for copy editing and page proofs, assured cross-volume uniformity in format and style, removed split infinitives, identified missing references, and translated academic language into a more common prose. Finally, at Michigan State University, Vasiliki Mousouli was the diligent project manager who maintained contact with more than 60 editors, authors, and publishers, organized and tracked all of the manuscript activity, and made final format corrections for APA style. In her spare time she managed to complete her doctoral program requirements in school psychology and successfully defend her doctoral dissertation.

What began as lunchtime table talk, resulted in four volumes that collectively summarize much about the crisis in youth mental health. All involved have our deepest respect and thanks for their contributions.

Hiram E. Fitzgerald
Kristine Freeark
Robert A. Zucker

SPECIAL COMMENTARY: UNIVERSITIES AND THE CRISIS IN YOUTH MENTAL HEALTH

Lou Anna Kimsey Simon
President, Michigan State University

There are at least two key reasons why universities are concerned about the crisis in youth mental health. First, increasing numbers of students matriculating at colleges and universities have mental health problems. Because social and emotional well-being is paramount to academic success and to the ability to negotiate the demands of the workplace, universities must be concerned about student social-emotional health. Second, understanding the causes and life course progression of mental health problems relates directly to the scholarship mission of the university, especially those with historical ties to the land-grant system of higher education. Land-grant universities, established by the Morrill Act of 1862, were founded to allow all citizens access to higher education and to bind together the scholarships of discovery and application. Thus, land-grant universities are about values and beliefs regarding the social role and social responsibility of universities with respect to ameliorating the problems of society.

In 2005, Michigan State University celebrated its 150th anniversary as an academic institution, and in 2012 it will celebrate its 150th anniversary as the first land-grant university. We have been actively engaged in a campus conversation concerning the role of land-grant institutions in the twenty-first century, and much of that conversation has focused on renewing the covenant between higher education and the public that higher education serves. When land-grant institutions were founded, the focus of that covenant was on agricultural production and the mechanical arts. Today, the covenant extends to the broad range of problems in contemporary society, not the least of which are those associated with the causes, treatments, and prevention of mental health problems.

Professional and public documents increasingly draw attention to the pervasive problems affecting children throughout the United States and the world. Considering all forms of mental illness, recent studies indicate that half of the population will experience a mental health problem sometime during their lives. In the United States, 1 in 10 children and adolescents suffers from mental illness severe enough to cause some level of impairment, but only 1 in 5 receives treatment. Most mental health problems are transitory and relatively easily resolved by brief interventions, including support from mental health professionals, friends, family members, or other individuals in one's social support network. Epidemiologists report that approximately 6 percent of the population experiences profound mental health problems and may require psychotropic medications and intense psychotherapy to maintain manageable levels of adaptive behavior. However, an increasing number of individuals deal with mental health problems at a level of severity that lies between the ordinary and the profound. The number of children with learning disabilities, speech and language handicaps, mental retardation, emotional disturbances, poor self-regulatory skills, aggressive behavior, substance abuse disorders, and poor school achievement is increasing at alarming rates. Seventeen percent of all children in the United States have one or more developmental disabilities; 20 percent of all school-age children have attention problems; the age of onset of drug use, smoking, and sexual activity continues to spiral downward (Fitzgerald, Lester, & Zuckerman, 2000; Koger, Schettler, & Weiss, 2005).

Collectively, students enrolled in higher education represent the rich spectrum of U.S. ethnic, racial, political, gender, religious, and physical diversity. If higher education does its job well, students will be challenged to examine their personal beliefs and values against this diversity, arriving at deeper understanding of their own values as well as those of others, both of which are implicit to sustaining a free, democratic, and diverse society. For many students, such free-ranging discussion and debate is exciting, provocative, and enriching. Other students may encounter diversity that is beyond their prior experience, and public discourse and challenge to their personal beliefs may provoke anxiety and distress. The mental health crisis among America's youth directly translates to a mental health crisis on America's college and university campuses. Increasing numbers of students report suicide ideation, feelings of hopelessness, depression, anxiety, and a sense of being overwhelmed (Kadison & DiGeronimo, 2004). Increasing numbers of these students come from broken families, and many come from stressful neighborhoods and communities. The crisis in youth mental health contributes to the crisis in college student mental health, and both challenge university capacity to provide the depth of support necessary to help students maintain psychological and behavioral health in the context of pressures for academic success.

The good news is that prevention specialists from many different disciplines have developed evidence-based programs that not only have positive impacts on child behavior but also have positive impacts on families and communities. This four-volume set was designed to affirm principles underlying the importance of prevention and the view that individual development is best understood within the framework of systems theory. Systems theory begins with the premise that from the moment of conception, the organism is embedded within an increasingly complex array of systems (family, neighborhood, school, community, society) and that all components mutually transact to shape development over the life course. The contextual embeddedness of mental health problems, therefore, requires perspectives from a broad range of social, behavioral, economic, and biomedical sciences as well as the arts and humanities in order to understand behavior in context. Thus, universities are uniquely positioned to make significant contributions to the understanding and remediation of mental health problems because universities are the repositories of all of the disciplines and can provide the means for interdisciplinary, systemic research and the development and assessment of prevention and treatment approaches. Moreover, from a land-grant perspective, such research and development activities gain even greater authenticity when conducted within the context of campus-community partnerships for health and well-being.

Resolving the crisis in youth mental health is essential for maintenance of a mentally healthy society, because youth comprise society's future policy and political leaders. Universities contribute to the resolution by providing a range of wrap-around supportive structures and services and by building stronger campus-community partnerships in health. Equally important for universities is a commitment to search for causal factors that shape developmental pathways that generate mental health problems, to develop biomedical and behavior treatments, and to discover successful ways to prevent or ameliorate mental health problems early in development. The chapters in *The Crisis in Youth Mental Health* focus attention to each of these objectives.

REFERENCES

Fitzgerald, H.E., Lester, B.M., & Zuckerman, B. (Eds.). (2000). *Children of addiction: Research, health, and policy issues.* New York: Garland.

Kadison, R.D., & DiGeronimo, T.F. (2004). College of the overwhelmed: The campus mental health crisis and what to do about it. Boston: Jossey-Bass.

Koger, S.M., Schettler, T., & Weiss, B. (2005). Environmental toxicants and developmental disabilities. *American Psychologist, 60,* 243–255.

INTRODUCTION: TRANSFORMING THE VILLAGE THAT RAISES OUR CHILDREN

Norman F. Watt and Robert H. Bradley

Sometimes evidence in favor of a particular scientific theory or social policy comes from the unlikeliest of places. One would not expect evidence in support of interventions for impoverished children to come from behavior geneticists, but a recently published piece by Turkheimer, Haley, Waldron, D'Onofrio, and Gottesman (2003) does just that. Usually, behavior geneticists can be expected to search energetically for, and document evidence of, genetic inheritance of traits and behaviors, but these investigators employed highly sophisticated analytical methods to demonstrate the opposite: how environment shapes human intelligence in impoverished children.

The subjects for their study were 319 twin pairs drawn from a massive sample in the National Collaborative Perinatal Project, who were studied from birth through age seven. Their twin sample comprised 114 monozygotic (identical) and 205 dizygotic (fraternal) pairs that spanned the entire spectrum of parental social class, which was measured, as usual, by parental education, occupational status, and income. The behavior of principal interest was intelligence, as measured at age seven by the Wechsler Intelligence Scale for Children (WISC).

The conclusion of their study (for technically sophisticated professional audiences) was this: "Results demonstrate that the proportions of IQ variance attributable to genes and environment vary nonlinearly with socioeconomic status. The models suggest that in impoverished families, 60% of the variation in IQ is accounted for by the shared environment, and the contribution of genes is close to zero; in affluent families, the result is almost exactly the reverse" (Turkheimer et al., 2003, p. 623).

This arcane conclusion can be translated for educated lay readers into much simpler language: *Most* of the measured intelligence of *privileged* children at age seven can be attributed to genetic inheritance, and *little* can be attributed to behavioral experience in their social environment after birth. That is because most privileged children receive sufficient support for their intellectual development either at home, at school, in peer groups, or via other combinations of settings. By contrast, *most* (60%) of the variation in the intelligence of *impoverished* children at age seven is accounted for by social experience in the environment they share with their siblings, and almost *none* of that variation ("close to zero") can be attributed to their genetic inheritance. What is the implication of this finding? Change what happens in the lives of poor children and you change their prospects for a productive and satisfying life.

WHAT IS THE CRISIS IN MENTAL HEALTH AMONG OUR CHILDREN AND YOUTH?

Let us begin by stipulating what we consider to be the crux of the crisis in mental health among children and youth and how that guides us toward some urgent transformations in the policies and practices of modern society so that the "village" in which every child lives can adequately support the well-being of those children. It starts with a relationship between basic economics and human health:

> Useful insights come from studies of the relationship between income equality and life expectancy in wealthy societies (Wilkinson, 1992a & 1992b). These studies show that the proportion of national income being received by the least well-off families (after taxes and transfers) in each country is a strong positive correlate of life expectancy differences between them. Those countries with relatively equal income distributions are healthier than those with relatively unequal distributions. Furthermore, those countries that were able to preserve or increase their level of income equality during the 1970s and 1980s enjoyed greater gains in life expectancy than did those countries with increasingly unequal income distributions. Wealthy countries with the largest income gap from richest to poorest do show improvements in health status over time, but their gains are smaller than among wealthy countries with narrower income gradients.
>
> The validity of this relationship has been challenged (Judge, 1995) based upon concerns about the comparability of data on income distribution between countries, the arbitrariness of the income cutoffs used, and problems in reproducing the results. But these concerns have largely been answered by the work of Kaplan, Pamuk, Lynch, Cohen, and Balfour (1996), who compared income distribution and life expectancy among the

50 U.S. states and found that those with higher levels of income equality had populations with longer life expectancies. Because this study was done within one country, income data for each state came from a common data source. Also, the design passively controlled for national level effects. The observation that relative income equality predicts improved population health status serves as a valid starting point for understanding the determinants of health in wealthy societies. (Hertzman, 1999, p. 23)

Granted that life expectancy is only one facet of health (albeit a convincing representative!), why should we in the wealthiest, arguably healthiest nation in human history be concerned about that fact of public health? Consider some telling economic facts about our recent national history (Table 1). Those sobering figures only tell the story of the United States until the turn of this century. Happenings in the past five years portend an even more pessimistic future for poor children in the United States. Specifically, there is no longer a large budget surplus, one that may have supported the implementation or expansion of services for poor children.

Table 1
Resource Disparities and Immobility across Generations

- Inequality of income fell sharply in the early 1940s when wage and price controls were imposed during World War II, but high-wage earners did not begin to regain their advantage until 30 years after the controls were removed (p. 8).
- Real annualized family income growth in the postwar era was evenly distributed across social class levels (slightly favoring the poorest families) from 1947 to 1973 but grotesquely favored the most affluent from 1973 to 2000 (p. 6).
- From 1973 to 2000 family incomes in the United States grew enormously, but hardly any of the increase went to those below the average in society (p. 6).
- Hourly wages of the average male high school dropout declined from 1973 to 1999 by 28%; the average high school graduate earned 16% less; whereas workers with advanced college degrees earned 20% more (p. 4).
- From 1973 to 1998, 94% of the growth in average income went to the top 1% of U.S. population (p. 7).
- Since 1974, pretax income of the wealthiest 20% of Americans has risen from 40.6% to 47.7% (of the total) but has declined for the poorest 20% from 5.7% to 4.2% (p. x).
- By the early 1990s, the top 1% of wealth holders in the United States owned 34% of the nation's wealth vs. 20% in Sweden and the United Kingdom (p. 10).
- Intergenerational correlations in income reveal that the United States has less mobility than most countries. Fathers' and sons' earnings correlate .40 or higher in the United States, .23 in Canada, .34 in Germany, and .28 in Sweden. Only South Africa, scarred by apartheid, has as much income immobility across generations as the United States has (p. 10).
- During the last half century, the United States has become a more polarized and static society, one in which children have become the most disadvantaged age group (p. 11).

Source: Heckman & Krueger (2003).

Moreover, congress enacted a set of quite regressive tax reforms that will do little to increase the spendable incomes of poor families. In effect, poor families are not likely to get richer under the new tax policies and neither are they likely to get new forms of government support to offset the negative consequences of poverty.

THE IMPACT OF POVERTY ON CHILDREN'S LIVES

The socioeconomic status (SES) gradient for health in the United States affects almost every aspect of well-being. It begins at conception and continues to death (as the life expectancy data show). Not only are the prevalence rates for most illnesses and types of injuries greater among the poor than the affluent, but the likelihood of comorbidities is greater as well. Poor children are exposed to more conditions that bode ill for their well-being (e.g., teratogens, violence) and to fewer conditions that support wellness (e.g., good health care, stimulating experiences, social networks with ample resources).

The impact of poverty on adaptive functioning is pervasive. Consider just one aspect of cognitive functioning as illustrative. "[L]ike most other high-level cognitive capabilities, children's early mathematical capabilities show a considerable degree of differentiation by social class during the years when the neurological circuitry on which they depend is showing its most rapid development.... [W]e have shown that a well-designed early intervention program can have powerful effects, providing it is targeted at the central conceptual structures that children will need for their subsequent learning and development" (Case, Griffin, & Kelly, 1999, p. 148).

The social class gradients are sharply reflected in both international and national studies of literacy. Countries and provinces with high overall literacy standards are especially successful in educating youth from less advantaged backgrounds. "Gradients persist because parents with more economic and social capital do things differently" (as shown in this volume by Risley and Hart). "On average, they are more likely to talk more with their children, read to them more often, buy them more educational toys," and generally enrich their home environment (as documented in this volume by Bradley). Individual differences in parental behaviors that affect developmental outcomes begin during pregnancy with choices about nutrition, smoking, and the use of alcohol and drugs (as featured by Olds in this volume). "Schools and schooling systems can vary considerably in their effects on children's outcomes, and ... their effectiveness depends on their social context" (as argued passionately by Rusk in this volume). "Three of the most important features of that context are the norms and expectations established by school staff, the disciplinary climate of the school, and the support of parents and the wider community. The steepness of the gradients therefore depends on the extent to which children from differing socioeconomic backgrounds have equal access to supportive school contexts" (Willms, 1999, pp. 89–90).

> Longitudinal studies with repeated measurements from birth to adulthood clearly show that most seriously antisocial adolescents and adults had behavior problems during childhood. The origin of these behavior problems can be traced back to fetal development and infancy. Preventive interventions over the first 3 years of life for at-risk families clearly reduce the prevalence and the seriousness of behavior problems. It appears clear that money invested in well-planned early preventive efforts with at-risk families will give greater payoffs than money invested in later preventive efforts with the same at-risk families ... it is clear that the prevention strategy will, within a 20-year period, reduce substantially the relative amount of resources needed for corrective interventions in education, health, and justice systems. (Tremblay, 1999, p. 71)

The SES gradient, as it pertains to children's health, obtains throughout the entire spectrum of the income distribution. "Children in deep poverty fare more poorly than children just at or above the poverty threshold" (Brooks-Gunn, Duncan, & Britto, 1999, p. 121–122). Federal programs in place in the United States do not raise all children out of deep poverty (i.e., at 50% or less of the poverty threshold), and more of our children live in deep poverty than in other Western countries, in part because we support families less generously than do other nations, such as Canada, France, Sweden, Italy, and Germany. Absent more generous transfer payments, tax policy changes such as the Earned Income Tax Credit, or improvements in minimum wages, the social class gradient in the United States will remain steeper for our children than for those in other countries, with the resulting risks for developmental health in America.

CAUSAL PATHWAYS THAT MAY CONNECT SOCIAL CLASS WITH DEVELOPMENTAL HEALTH

To have any hope of offsetting the pernicious impacts of poverty means that policy makers and practitioners need to understand in considerable detail the mechanisms that create these effects. Hertzman (1999) offered the following four causal hypotheses to account for the striking correlation between social class and developmental health:

- *Individual lifestyle.* In this account, the health habits and behaviors of those in different subgroups lead them to have different risks of particular life-threatening and/or disabling conditions. In particular, health-promoting behaviors may tend to be practiced more frequently among those in higher socioeconomic groups, and health-damaging behaviors, the reverse.

- *Physical environment.* Differential exposures to physical, chemical, and biological agents at home, at work, and in the community lead to differences in health status in this explanation. This category would include all the diverse influences of the built environment on health.

- *Social-economic-psychosocial conditions.* This includes the effects of access to material resources, social isolation, civil society functions, income distribution, and the panoply of psychosocial stresses of daily living.

- *Differential access to and/or response to health care services.* This encompasses differences in health status that are related to differences in care-seeking behavior, differences in the quality of health services and access to them, and differential outcomes for a given treatment. (p. 27)

Whether offering explanatory analysis or intervention, every chapter in this book addresses one or more of these root causes of the health crisis we confront, and, at least implicitly, every chapter is predicated on the sad conclusion of Heckman and Krueger (2003) that ours "has become a more polarized and static society" in recent history "in which children have become the most disadvantaged age group." That said, the chapters offer a convincing case that early environment not only matters but, within certain biological boundaries, it is sovereign. It can be shaped and reinforced, both constructively and otherwise. Where environmental supports are absent or deficient, they can be replaced or improved. Where environmental hazards are present or even virulent, they can be removed or mitigated.

Fortunately, the accumulating evidence of effective solutions is encouragingly compelling, as summarized by Keating (1999):

- The key necessities for supporting healthy child development can be relatively easily identified: income, nutrition, child care, stimulation, love/support, advocacy, and safety.

- Given what we know, our societies have underinvested in development between conception and school age, compared to what we invest thereafter. In fact, our institutional arrangements are (unconsciously) based on the presumption that early development is the least important, not the most.

- Improving the quality of human development requires paying attention to all levels of social aggregation: family, neighborhood, school, civil society, and the national socioeconomic environment.

- Collecting ongoing evidence of systematic variation in cognitive and behavioral development across communities and understanding its

determinants is crucial for positive change. (p. 339; see also Ramey &
Ramey and Zill & Resnick in this volume)

If *effective* interventions are possible to redress the social inequalities
cited previously, when is the optimal time to intervene, how should it best
be done, for whom, and at what cost? The answers in these pages will
address those questions in depth.

THE ORGANIZATIONAL PLAN FOR THIS BOOK

Chapters for this volume have been organized according to the following four rubrics:

- The role of society in promoting health, opportunity, prosperity, and
  education.
- The role of the home and family.
- Child care and preschool intervention.
- Prevention and promotion at preschool age and beyond.

The first three chapters by Heckman, Duncan and Magnuson, and Rusk
are written by economists and policy experts who analyze public intervention on a macro level, placing the remaining three units in a larger context
with an emphasis on the costs, benefits, obstacles, and remedies as they
intersect with public policy. A Nobel Prize in economics (2000) should
command our attention to the data and the cost economic analyses of
James Heckman. What should not be overlooked, however, is his breadth
of sophistication about the published literature on child development and
on education. There is no more forceful advocate for the view that early
intervention is more efficacious and more cost-economical than later
(especially remedial) intervention.

If a blue-ribbon committee or task force is appointed to study poverty
or large-scale interventions to reduce poverty, it is very likely that Greg
Duncan and/or one of his apprentices will be appointed as a member.
He was trained as an economist, but he is equally at home in the science
of human development. Like Heckman, Duncan and Magnuson argue
strongly for the cost-economic advantages of early intervention, especially
to promote academic success. Drawing on his participation in the "Neurons
to Neighborhoods" project (Shonkoff & Phillips, 2000), however, Duncan
broadens the causal justifications to capitalize on special neuropsychological and biobehavioral critical periods, so-called windows of opportunity
that, once bypassed, may be closed forever, such as the exquisitely timed
mechanisms for imprinting that expire within a few hours after birth.

We expect the provocative policy challenges of David Rusk to elicit the most heated controversy in this volume. His credentials in government and public policy stand on their own, quite independently of those of his world-renowned father. As a state legislator and mayor of Albuquerque, New Mexico, and with many years of experience consulting in urban planning, he personally created many innovative "metrics" for assessing community progress (and regress) in integration of housing and success (or failure) of schools, which are remarkably illuminating. Many readers may argue that interventions at school age may be "too little and too late," as indeed Risley and Hart argue with persuasive documentation in this volume. Nevertheless, few circumspect observers would argue that school-age interventions can be neglected because "not much happens after age five." (Freud made that mistake a century ago.) Much indeed happens in our schools, and they are very influential in shaping adult outcomes both academically and in characterological development generally.

The next three chapters by Risley and Hart, Bradley, and Ayoub focus particular attention on the influences of the home and parenting in shaping early childhood development. Many readers may be introduced for the first time in this book to the startling findings of Hart and Risley in the Juniper Gardens program, which has all the makings of a classic in developmental research. Notwithstanding her modest claims to just being a simple child care teacher, Betty Hart deserves to be recognized as a heroine of U.S. psychology for her extraordinary patience and persistence in recording, transcribing, and coding more than 125 million words of family conversation—occupying 30,000 pages of transcription—in the homes of 42 families during monthly visits over two-and-one-half years. Todd Risley insisted on her recognition by listing her as first author on their two coauthored books.

Why do we characterize their findings as "startling"? Consider the concise selection of empirical findings reported in their two books (Table 2). Children of working-class parents heard twice as many words addressed to them each hour as did welfare children, and children of professional parents heard three-and-one-half times as many words as welfare children! Furthermore, those ratios approximated their relative vocabulary size at age three. The authors extrapolated from these averages that professionals' children would have 48 million words addressed to them at home before age four, working-class children 30 million, and welfare children only 13 million.

The nature of parental communications to their children also differed sharply. Children of professional parents heard expressions of encouragement or approval more than six times as often as welfare children did, but they were scolded with expressions of disapproval less than half as often. Such interpersonal transactions are bound to have profound effects

Table 2
Summary of Social Class Differences in Language Development

	Welfare (n = 6)	Working Class (n = 23)	Professional (n = 13)	Overall Mean (N = 42)
Average utterances per hour addressed to child before age 3	178	301	487	341
Words spoken per hour to child before age 3	600	1,200	2,100	1,393
Recorded vocabulary size (number of words) of parents expressed to child by age 3	974	1,498	2,176	1,633
Recorded vocabulary size (number of different words) expressed by child by age 3	525	749	1,116	831
Measured IQ score of child at age 3 (Wechsler Intelligence Scale for Children)	79	107	117	106
Average hourly exposure to encouragements by child before age 3	5	12	32	17
Average hourly exposure to prohibitions expressed to child before age 3	11	7	5	7
Encouragements vs. prohibitions: difference in hourly exposure before age 3	−6	+5	+27	+10

Source: Hart & Risley (1995, 1999).

on children's self-esteem and confidence. In effect, welfare children were invalidated by their parents twice as often as they were endorsed, whereas professionals' offspring were personally endorsed six times as often as they were scolded. The cumulative psychological effects of such experience at home are unlikely to be reversed by more equitable treatment at school or on the playground.

Perhaps most disturbing of all are the longitudinal correlations reported by Hart and Risley. The volume of parent-talk to their children *before* age three accounted for almost *all* of the variation in the children's intelligence (except for measurement error) at age three (r = .78) and also the size of their vocabulary at age nine (r = .78). It would appear from these findings that most of children's intellectual and linguistic development is largely determined before they even enter preschool at age three or four.

The chapter by Bradley provides a useful complement to the decisive work by Hart and Risley. It broadens the focus to include a diverse array of social and physical features of children's early environments, with particular attention to how these features are implicated in children's development. It is generally the exception rather than the rule that such a study is done *without* including the HOME scale that he developed with Bettye Caldwell (Bradley, 1994). The chapter is organized so that it showcases the various means by which parents affect the development of children. Thus, it could serve as a primer for parent education of high school students throughout the country. The focus is on the direct activities of caregiving. Thus, it would allow teachers/parent educators to simply provide some meaningful illustrations regarding particular developmental goals, then invite discussion. Catherine Ayoub extends the purview on parenting, drawing on her diverse background as a nurse and forensic psychologist, to include the miscarriages of parenting and the abuses that usually take a heavy toll on healthy child development and on families as a whole.

The next four chapters by Olds, Raikes and Emde, Schweinhart, and Reynolds and Temple report on four landmark interventions that capture the interface between the home and extramural agencies—most of them quite explicitly with doctrine that espouses bridging that interface as an integral and necessary part of effective early childhood intervention. One could plausibly quibble with our choice to align the Nurse-Family Partnership program of David Olds with the chapters on child care and preschool intervention, which typically transpire *outside* the parental home, whereas Olds's intervention takes place primarily *inside* the parental home. Actually, the partnership probably belongs in an intermediate category by itself for two reasons: (1) it focuses predominantly on health issues of pregnancy and infancy, and (2) it deliberately intends to bring extramural professional influence *into* the home. We chose to align it with child care and preschool intervention for its emphasis upon professional services from sources outside the home.

Little needs to be said to identify the Nurse-Family Partnership. It started as a pioneering program, one of a kind, and it has proved so successful that variations of the program have been adopted in states throughout the United States and abroad. It is noteworthy that David Olds was trained in developmental psychology at Cornell, which many consider to be a wellspring of knowledge and advocacy for systems theory (Bronfenbrenner, 1995), so we might assume that the originator of the Nurse-Family Partnership was

well schooled early on in the theoretical nuances delineated in this volume
by Bob Bradley.

The authorship of the chapter describing the Early Head Start experiment
is itself symbolic of a cardinal feature of that program. It was written by
Helen Raikes, a federal program officer in the Administration for Children
and Families since the inception of the program in the mid-1990s, and
Robert Emde, a prominent psychiatric authority on early childhood development. The collaboration between "the feds" and the scientists has been
a uniquely successful feature of the National Early Head Start Research
Consortium. Emde might be characterized as "triple-dipping" in that he
served on the planning committee that drew up the plans for the program,
then served as a principal investigator for the Colorado research site, and
ultimately was elected as the program coordinator for the last three years
of follow-up research on the national cohort of subjects.

High hopes have been invested in the Early Head Start program, not
only for the intrinsic interest in the "downward extension" of the Head
Start model but also for its potential to deflect the criticisms of the lack in
systematic demonstrations of the efficacy of the larger Head Start program.
For that purpose, it was considered important to employ a randomized control design for credibility, as explained in the chapter by Raikes and Emde.
There are serious risks when taking an experimental intervention "to scale"
from the outset, and, as principal investigators ourselves in the consortium,
we must confess some surprise at the abundance of research findings that
have emerged in the first decade of Early Head Start's existence. Much is
still expected to emerge from the research analyses in progress, and, fortunately, most of the data collected will be available for public use in the very
near future.

The High/Scope program also needs little introduction. Beginning with a
modest experimental intervention in Ypsilanti, Michigan, it has expanded
to a veritable juggernaut of child care intervention and training, to which
many people ascribe much of the credit for the continuous legislative
reauthorizations of the national Head Start program, despite the regret-
tably weak documentation of Head Start's effectiveness. We were sad-
dened by the passing of David Weikart shortly before the planning of this
volume began, but we are pleased that Larry Schweinhart was able to step
forward and tell the story of the remarkable tradition that was inspired
originally by Weikart. We should perhaps mention that High/Scope is
distinguished—among the programs represented in this volume—by its
national leadership in systematically improving the educational quality of
preschool interventions.

The scientific presentation of the impressive results of the Chicago
Child-Parent Centers is especially noteworthy for the unique marriage of

expertise in developmental science and economics. David Olds and the Rameys have also presented important cost-economic analyses of their respective programs, but Arthur Reynolds and Judy Temple have made the return on social capital an especially prominent feature of their analyses in this volume.

The last three chapters examine a longitudinal interface between preschool interventions and school-age development and beyond, even into the college years. Again the transitional interface is treated doctrinally as an integral part of effective early intervention, looking toward the ultimate goal of healthy and prosperous adulthood. It is often pointed out that parents are the first teachers almost every child encounters. Lest we forget, our educational systems (through college and beyond) present most of the important successors in that role, and education (as Watt and Puma point out) is the most important tool for leveling the playing field for *subsequent* generations.

THE CURRENT PLACE OF CHILD CARE AND EARLY CHILDHOOD INTERVENTIONS

The scholars and child advocates who sat around tables during the early to mid-1960s planning the early phases of Head Start could only dimly envision the paths that research, policy, and funding for early childhood programs would take over the ensuing 40 years. Human actions are hard to forecast with more than moderate accuracy. Nonetheless, three things can be said about the experiments in early education represented in this volume. First, they have set standards for how to conduct potentially convincing policy studies. Second, they are the studies (there are a few others as well) that researchers, policy makers, and child advocates cite when addressing key questions about the effectiveness of early childhood programs. Third, they make clear what well-grounded and well-implemented programs can accomplish with regard to improving the lives of poor children. These studies have been part of the corona of social consciousness that has moved just ahead of a massive comet of social change regarding the early care and education of young children living in conditions of poverty.

The High/Scope experience (see Schweinhart in this volume) is particularly valuable for state-level planners who are considering what their states should do regarding prekindergarten programs. The High/Scope model focuses on three- and four-year-olds. It offers a well-integrated curriculum based on research in human learning and development. The evaluation design used for the High/Scope model is exemplary, and the evidence for long-term impacts on child (and adult) well-being is compelling. Importantly, from the standpoint of policy development and program implementation, the High/Scope Educational Research Foundation has been quite successful in supplying training and support in implementing the High/Scope model in many other states and countries. In effect, they have shown that the model is transportable beyond a research context and that its impacts are generalizable beyond Ypsilanti, Michigan, and whatever might have been fortuitous about the ecology of Ypsilanti at the time the program was first put in place.

In many respects, the Chicago Child-Parent Centers program (see Reynolds & Temple in this volume) provides a good complement to the High/Scope program. The Chicago program also targeted three- and four-year-olds but it did so within an existing very large urban school district and on a much larger scale than the original High/Scope program. Issues surrounding initial implementation and sustainability were seemingly formidable, but the mission was accomplished. Although the research design was not quite as clean as is the case for the other experiments represented in this volume (e.g., lack of a randomized control design), the quasi-experimental design is solid, and great care has been taken with analyses to avoid overinterpreting study findings. The findings themselves are impressive, showing long-term benefits of program participation. Innovations have been applied in an effort to gauge the full impacts of the program (such as scouring public records for evidence of child maltreatment). The message that emerges from the Chicago study (a message that equally flows from several of the other studies represented in this volume) is that the impact of well-designed early childhood programs typically goes well beyond just helping children to be more successful in school. One of the impacts of the Chicago study is that program participants were less likely than comparison children from the Chicago public schools to be the victims of abuse. The implications of this message are profound, but the message itself should come as no surprise based on what we know about human development and what is predictable from systems theory. What we know about human development is that changes in one domain of development often lead to changes (for good or ill) in other domains. Systems theory tells us that changes in one member of a system can lead to changes in other members of the same system. Initial change in a child could lead to a change in the parent (or vice versa); the same can be said for two siblings or between peers. Systems theory also tells us that the same input (e.g., a good early literacy program) can have various impacts downstream (e.g., better grades in reading at 2nd grade, greater likelihood of selecting higher-level math courses in 11th grade, reduced likelihood of engaging in risky behaviors in 8th grade, a tighter bond with parents in 5th grade, etc.); hence different outcomes for different people and different results at different times in life.

The other experiments represented in this volume address a slightly different question. What happens when you begin a program in infancy rather than waiting until children are prekindergarten age (three or four)? The experiments carried out by Olds and the Rameys (both discussed in this volume) approach the issue of providing services to children and families in very different ways. Olds delivered services to the family at home, using the mother as the primary target of the intervention. By contrast, the Rameys delivered services both at home and via a child care center, but greatest emphasis was on the child and via a carefully structured curriculum at the child care center during the second and third years of life. No center-based program serving infants has been more powerful in demonstrating the potential value of providing comprehensive services from child care settings than has the Rameys' Abecedarian program and its offshoots (Project CARE and the Infant Health and Development Program). The designs are tight and the long-term effects are impressive. That said, the site differences that emerged from the Infant Health and Development Program (IHDP) give rise to a cautionary note: It is not always easy to fully and faithfully implement even a well-designed program; take nothing for granted. Differential results from IHDP, favoring children with higher birth weight, leads to a caution: participants in even well-designed interventions may need to bring at least a modicum of assets to the table in order to benefit fully from the program.

A variation on this message comes from a recently published meta-analysis on parent education programs. Bakermans-Kranenburg, van Izendoorn, and Bradley (2005) found that families in better living conditions benefited more from parent education programs than families living in more adverse circumstances (the so-called Matthew effect, an allusion to the parable in Matthew 25:29, "For unto every one that hath shall be given, and he shall have in abundance; but from him that hath not shall be taken away even that which he hath").

As is true of the program of research on early education by the Rameys, the program of research on early intervention by David Olds has involved a series of trials, each expanding upon the previous. The initial implementation of the Nurse Home Visitation model took place in Elmira, New York, where the recipients were mostly small-town European American families. The next implementation was in Memphis, Tennessee, where the recipients were mostly urban African Americans. The most recent was a large-scale effort in Colorado, where the recipients were diverse by geography and ethnicity. Like High/Scope and Abecedarian, the research design used for the Nurse Home Visitation program was a randomized trial. Like those, the conceptual underpinning is strong, but the conceptual underpinning was different, drawing more from health beliefs research and less from research on learning. The long-term impacts from Olds's program have been notable. Not surprisingly, the impacts both overlap with and diverge from those reported by Schweinhart and the Rameys in this volume. As an example, the impacts on child cognitive functioning have been less pronounced for children whose mothers were involved in the Nurse Home Visitation program than for children who directly experienced enriched curricula in High/Scope and Abecedarian. It is also the case that the impacts have not been fully consistent across the three trials. The message that not all participants benefit equally and/or that participants may need to bring certain assets to the table in order to benefit also finds support in the research by Olds. Specifically, there was a reduction in child abuse only for those families for whom domestic violence was not present. The findings by Olds are notable in that they demonstrate that meaningful long-term impacts can be achieved by a home visitation approach as well as by a center-based approach. However, the findings by Olds stand largely in contrast to findings from most home visitation programs; most can present very little evidence for sustained impact, particularly on children (Gomby, Culross, & Behrman, 1999). A major reason that the Nurse Home Visitation program impacts may have been more robust than impacts from other home visitation programs is the considerable effort that went into full and faithful implementation of the program.

It is perhaps not surprising that 30 years after the implementation of Head Start, scholars and child advocates were once again clamoring for the federal government to assist children and families living in poverty. The press to offer more programs was accompanied by an insistence on improved quality and more comprehensive evaluation. Illustrative of the latter are comments made by one of the most influential experts in early childhood programs and policy, Professor Edward Zigler. He descried the lack of attention to serious research and evaluation by federal agencies ("less than .003% of the entire Head Start appropriation" [personal letter to first author]). Ultimately, the federal government bowed to these pressures by establishing the Head Start Quality Research Centers program, the National Head Start Impact Study, the National Reporting System, and the Head Start Child and Family Experiences Survey (FACES). Because of its long experience in conducting seminal evaluations of widely implemented early childhood programs, WESTAT was entrusted with conducting the FACES study (see report by Zill and Resnick in this volume). Their report details a very complex effort to determine the effectiveness of Head Start, one that was circumscribed by the necessity to evaluate programs "as is" rather than to subject them to rigorous requirements of a randomized clinical trial, such as were applied to evaluations of several of the other programs described in this volume. Despite the fact that the FACES report has been exceptionally useful to scholars and policy makers interested in large-scale early childhood programs aimed at addressing the conditions of poverty, the weaknesses inherent in the evaluation design are sharply criticized in the epilogue of this book by Zigler and Styfco. The report and the criticism continue a critical debate on national policy directed at alleviating some of the pernicious effects of poverty.

The War on Poverty (of which Head Start was a component) had been only partially successful in alleviating poverty per se or in counteracting its many adverse effects. Many poor children, despite access to Head Start and other governmental preschool programs, were still arriving at kindergarten insufficiently prepared to be successful. Moreover, research made clear how strongly brains were impacted by early experience (that is, experience prior to age three). Accordingly, the Early Head Start program was initiated in 1995. Simultaneous with its initiation, the Early Head Start national evaluation study was undertaken. Raikes and Emde in this volume report the initial findings from this study. Several things need to be said about this experiment in early education, as compared to the other experiments reported in this volume. First, like the other experiments, the design was strong (a randomized trial). Second, unlike the other experiments, no singular program model was investigated. Rather, service providers from throughout the country proposed whatever model they felt would accomplish the goals set forth under the legislation. Accordingly, the models used were quite diverse as were the conceptual frameworks that guided them. Third, unlike the control exercised over program implementation by High/Scope, Nurse Home Visitation, Abecedarian, and Chicago public schools, the control exercised by the funding agency for Early Head Start and some participant local providers was limited. A major strength of the Early Head Start national evaluation study was that it included a careful documentation of the degree to which individual providers actually implemented their program. Not surprisingly, some programs were not fully implemented. Moreover, the models actually implemented at particular program sites evolved through the course of the study. This variability carries two important implications. First, it reduces the likelihood that powerful program effects will be observed when the data are aggregated across sites. Second, the findings have considerable ecological validity; that is, they speak to the likely effects as applied to Early Head Start programs nationwide rather than to what can be accomplished by fully and faithfully implemented programs. Results, based on data collected from 17 programs in 15 sites, show significant (albeit modest) effects on both parents and children. The effects varied, depending on level of implementation, program approach, and characteristics of recipients. To some extent, the observed "impacts" can be viewed as conservative estimates of the Early Head Start program. Although there was random assignment to program or control groups, control group families often received services that were not that much different from those received by treatment group families, either from the same agency or other agencies in the community. Moreover, the study was done during the first three years in which Early Head Start services were available. Some agencies providing the service had no prior experience in providing such services and never fully implemented the planned program. If these same agencies were examined again (now with experience), the effects could well be more substantial.

To some degree, the Early Head Start program is proof that what goes around comes around. It is the 1990s version of the 1960s conviction that something must be done about poverty if children in the United States are to thrive—indeed, if the society as a whole is to flourish. Renewed concern about alleviating poverty via programs targeted to children came both from data that showed that many families remained in poverty despite the variety of governmental programs aimed at improving their life's chances and data from programs such as High/Scope, Abecedarian, and Chicago Parent–Child Centers that showed economic benefits of participation in well-run early childhood programs. These economic benefits, perhaps as much as the educational and behavioral benefits derived from good programs, stimulated states across the United States to invest more in early childhood programs over the past decade. As well, they stimulated international organizations such as the World Bank to invest in programs around the world (van der Gaag & Tan, 1998).

The coming evolution of systematic early interventions will place greater emphasis on repeated assessments of children's progress (see Zill & Resnick in this volume), more attention to the transitions that *follow* early interventions to ensure accountability and sustained impact (see Ramey & Ramey in this volume), and hopefully on promoting greater educational and vocational opportunities for *resilient* children like the Ambassadors for Literacy (Watt & Puma in this volume).

SUMMING UP

Mustard and Lipsitt (1999) draw particular attention to what may be the most important message in the present volume: "the weight of the evidence suggests that the quality of nourishment and nurturing in the early years is far reaching." They capture the most essential part of our message about intervention as well: "when societies undergo major socioeconomic change, one particularly vulnerable group is young children since they have the least political clout."

"The idea that societies need to make early childhood development a priority has been recognized at least since Plato wrote *The Republic*.

xxxiv   INTRODUCTION

Twentieth-century science has simply demonstrated the validity of this statement. The challenge is now to transform it into policy" (Tremblay, 1999, p. 71).

Love and nurturance are not attributes commonly ascribed to an entire village (though *we* might), but enlightened self-interest is probably essential if a society is to continuously adapt to ever-changing and constantly demanding external conditions. This volume is dedicated to the premise that positive adaptation of U.S. society requires devoted attention to all citizens. It is done in hopes of provoking continued support for policies and programs that benefit poor children and their families.

REFERENCES

Bakermans-Kranenburg, M.J., van Izendoorn, M.H., & Bradley, R.H. (2005). Those who have, receive: The Matthew effect in early childhood intervention in the home environment. *Review of Educational Research, 75,* 1–26.

Bradley, R.H. (1994). The HOME Inventory: Review and reflections. In H. Reese (Ed.), *Advances in child development and behavior* (pp. 241–288). San Diego, CA: Academic Press.

Bronfenbrenner, U. (1995). The bioecological model from a life course perspective: Reflections of a participant observer. In P. Moen, G.H. Elder, & K. Luscher (Eds.), *Examining lives in context* (pp. 619–647). Washington, DC: American Psychological Association.

Brooks-Gunn, J., Duncan, G.J., & Britto, P.R. (1999). Are socioeconomic gradients for children similar to those for adults? In D.P. Keating & C. Hertzman (Eds.), *Developmental health and the wealth of nations: Social, biological and educational dynamics* (pp. 94–124). New York: Guilford.

Case, R., Griffin, S., & Kelly, W.M. (1999). Socioeconomic gradients in mathematical ability and their responsiveness to intervention during early childhood. In D.P. Keating & C. Hertzman (Eds.), *Developmental health and the wealth of nations: Social, biological and educational dynamics* (pp. 125–149). New York: Guilford.

Gomby, D.S., Culross, P.L., & Behrman, R.E. (1999). Home visiting: Recent program evaluations—Analysis and recommendations. *The Future of Children, 9*(1), 4–26.

Hart. B., & Risley, T.R. (1995). *Meaningful differences in the everyday experience of young American children.* Baltimore, MD: Paul H. Brookes.

Hart, B., & Risley, T.R. (1999). *The social world of children learning to talk.* Baltimore, MD: Paul H. Brookes.

Heckman, J.J., & Krueger, A.B. (2003). *Inequality in America: What role for human capital policies?* Cambridge, MA: MIT Press.

Hertzman, C. (1999). Population health and human development. In D.P. Keating & C. Hertzman (Eds.), *Developmental health and the wealth of nations: Social, biological and educational dynamics* (pp. 21–40). New York: Guilford.

Judge, K. (1995). Income distribution and life expectancy: A critical appraisal. *British Medical Journal, 311,* 1282–1285.

Kaplan, G. A., Pamuk, E., Lynch, J. W., Cohen, R. D., & Balfour, J. L. (1996). Income inequality and mortality in the United States. *British Medical Journal, 312,* 999–1003.

Keating, D. P. (1999). Developmental health as the wealth of nations. In D. P. Keating & C. Hertzman (Eds.), *Developmental health and the wealth of nations: Social, biological and educational dynamics* (pp. 337–347). New York: Guilford.

Mustard, J. F., & Lipsitt, L. P. (1999). Foreword. In D. P. Keating & C. Hertzman (Eds.), *Developmental health and the wealth of nations: Social, biological and educational dynamics.* New York: Guilford.

Shonkoff, J. P., & Phillips, D. A. (Eds.). (2000). *From neurons to neighborhoods.* Washington, DC: National Academy Press.

Tremblay, R. E. (1999). When children's social development fails. In D. P. Keating & C. Hertzman (Eds.), *Developmental health and the wealth of nations: Social, biological and educational dynamics* (pp. 55–71). New York: Guilford.

Turkheimer, E., Haley, A., Waldron, M., D'Onofrio, B., & Gottesman, I. I. (2003). Socioeconomic status modifies heritability of IQ in young children. *Psychological Science, 14,* 623–628.

van der Gaag, J., & Tan, J. (1998). *The benefits of early childhood development programs: An economic analysis.* Washington, DC: World Bank.

Wilkinson, R. G. (1992a). Income distribution and life expectancy. *British Medical Journal, 304,* 165–168.

Wilkinson, R. G. (1992b). National mortality rates: The impact of inequality. *American Journal of Public Health, 82*(8), 1082–1084.

Willms, J. D. (1999). Quality and inequality in children's literacy: The effects of families, schools and communities. In D. P. Keating & C. Hertzman (Eds.), *Developmental health and the wealth of nations: Social, biological and educational dynamics* (pp. 72–93). New York: Guilford.

THE ROLE OF SOCIETY IN PROMOTING HEALTH, OPPORTUNITY, PROSPERITY, AND EDUCATION

Chapter 1

A BROADER VIEW OF WHAT EDUCATION POLICY SHOULD BE[1]

James J. Heckman

The purpose of this chapter is to challenge policy makers, educators, scholars, and parents to rethink educational policy in the United States, specifically to rethink how policy should foster skills in U.S. society. I think this topic is extraordinarily important. I review the principal policy issues and format that are usually discussed, and I shall explain why I think the focus and a lot of the current policy discussion is misplaced. Many of the policies that are put out on the table focus on reducing college tuition or reducing pupil-teacher ratios. Although they are well-intentioned, they are unlikely to have a substantial impact on promoting college attendance or improving schooling outcomes at current levels of expenditure. We need to think about skill formation in a way that does not assume that education is the principal source of skill in the modern society. We want to think of education as only one of many sources of human skill formation. Preschool experience, formal education and lifetime learning all are also very important ingredients.

These other ingredients do not receive the proper attention in the current discussions concerning skill-formation policy in the United States, however. First, even though policies that are directed toward younger children have a high level of efficiency, they are currently underfunded in the United States and in many other countries around the world. Second, many of our educational policies are oriented toward improving test scores, but looking exclusively at cognitive skills ignores a much broader array of skills that are very important for success in schooling and in many other aspects of life. What I am proposing is a fairly radical departure from the current policy dialogue on education. We should think more broadly about the skills-formation process. I will start with some facts about the U.S. economy during the twentieth century.

QUALITY AND PRODUCTIVITY OF THE U.S. WORKFORCE

The adage that the source of a nation's wealth is the skill of its people has special meaning for contemporary U.S. society. Since 1980, the quality of the U.S. workforce has stagnated, or its growth has slowed dramatically (DeLong, Goldin, & Katz, 2003; Ellwood, 2001; Jorgenson & Ho, 1999).

Figures 1.1–1.3, which show data from the Current Population Survey (CPS; 2000), indicate that after a half-century of progress, cohorts born after 1950 did not improve much, or at all, on the educational attainment of their predecessors. This is true for Americans of all racial and ethnic backgrounds. This has implications for productivity growth and for the performance of the U.S. economy in the next 20 years. Moreover, the stagnation in educational attainment in the aggregate is not due solely to migration. Although immigrants in general are more unskilled than the remainder of the workforce and contribute to growth in the pool of unskilled labor, stagnation in aggregate college participation is also found among native-born Americans, although immigrants contribute to the growing pool of high school dropouts (Figures 1.4–1.6).

Unpleasant as these numbers are, the official statistics paint an overly optimistic picture because they count those who have exam-certified high school equivalents (i.e., General Educational Development, or

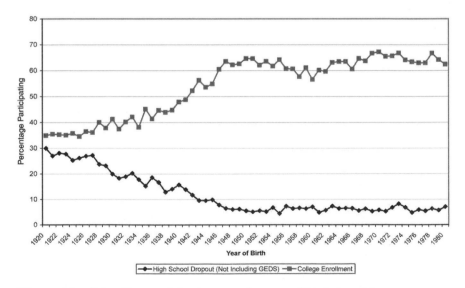

Figure 1.1   Schooling participation rates by year of birth for whites

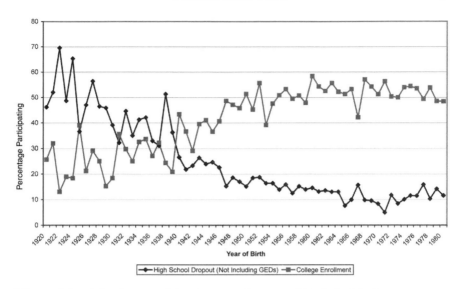

Figure 1.2 Schooling participation rates by year of birth for blacks

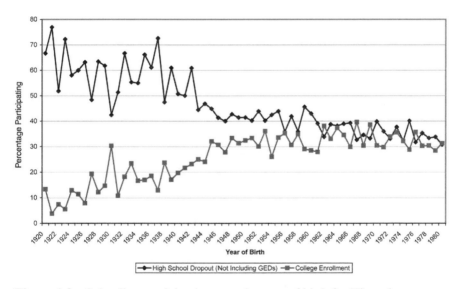

Figure 1.3 Schooling participation rates by year of birth for Hispanics

GED, certificates) as high school graduates. According to these statistics, the high school graduation rate is increasing and the high school dropout rate is decreasing (see Figure 1.7). However, there is a rise in the high school dropout rate correctly measured (see Figure 1.7). Recent studies (Boesel, Alsalam, & Smith, 1998; Cameron & Heckman, 1993; Heckman, 2005) show that those with GEDs perform the same in the labor market as high school dropouts with comparable schooling levels.

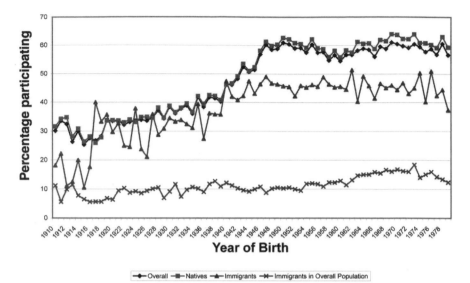

Figure 1.4   College participation rates by year of birth

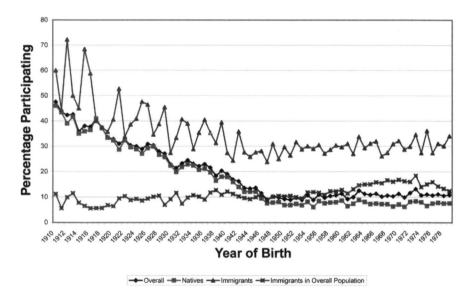

Figure 1.5   High school dropout rates (not including GEDs) by year of birth

The percentage of measured high school graduates who receive high school credentials by route of the GED is growing and is as high as 25 percent in some states (Figure 1.8). As a result, the quality of measured high school graduates is declining. When GEDs are classified as dropouts, the U.S. high school dropout rate is increasing, and not decreas-

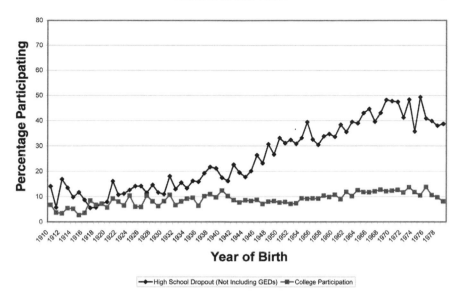

Figure 1.6 Percentage of overall educational participation rates due to immigrants by year of birth

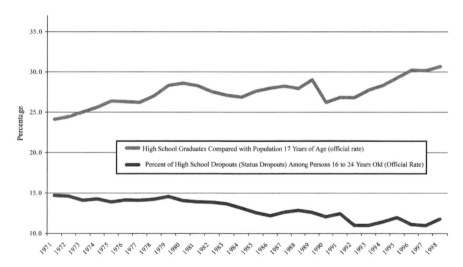

Figure 1.7 The share of high school dropouts in the United States, 1971–1998

ing, as the official statistics indicate. Figure 1.9 shows the decline in the proportion of high school graduates.

The slowdown in the growth of the quality of the U.S. labor force comes in a period of increasing wage differentials between skilled and unskilled workers and contributes to the growth in those differentials and to overall

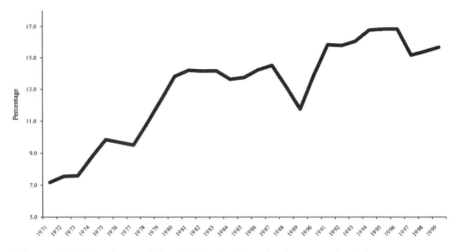

Figure 1.8 People receiving high school equivalency credentials as a percentage of total high school credentials issued by public schools, private schools, and the GED program in the United States, 1971–1999

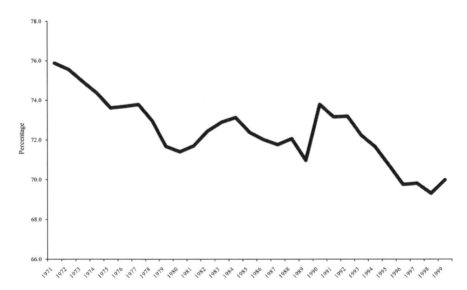

Figure 1.9 High school graduates of regular day school programs, public and private, as a percentage of 17-year-olds in the United States, 1971–1999.

Source: The Department of Education National Center for Education Statistics and the American Council on Education, General Educational Development Testing Service

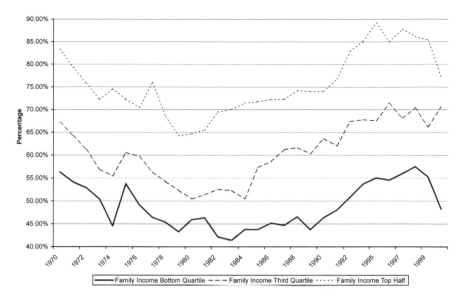

Figure 1.10 College participation among 18- to 24-year-old dependent (living at parental home or supported by parental family while at college) white male high school graduates and GED holders.

Source: These numbers were computed from the CSP P-20 School Reports and the October CPS.

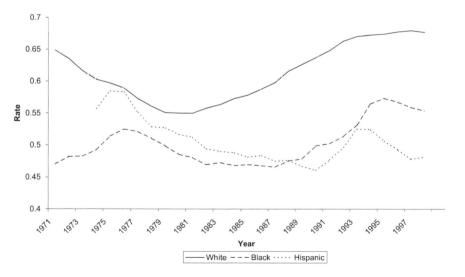

Figure 1.11 College participation by race among 18- to 24-year old male dependent high school graduates and GED holders.

Source: These numbers were computed from the CSP P-20 School Reports and the October CPS.

Note: Three-year moving averages are shown.

9

wage inequality. The measured wage premium for higher-skilled workers began to increase substantially around 1980 (Autor & Katz, 1999). In response to the economic incentives provided by the increase in the wage premium, children from certain socioeconomic groups increased their college attendance in the 1980s. This response has not been uniform across racial, ethnic, or family income groups (Figures 1.10 and 1.11), however, even though the return to schooling has increased for all groups.

FAMILY INCOME AS A SELECTIVE CREDIT CONSTRAINT

Figure 1.10 shows a strong relationship between family income and college attendance. It displays aggregate time series college participation rates for 18- to 24-year-old U.S. males classified by their parental income, as measured in the child's late adolescent years. Substantial differences in college participation rates occur across family income classes in each year. Adolescent white male high school graduates from the top half of the family income distribution began to increase their college attendance rate in 1980. Those from the third quartile of the family income distribution were less likely to attend college than those from the top half and delayed their response to the rising wage premium for skill. The response to the wage premium was even more delayed for white male high school graduates at the bottom of the family income distribution. Thus, already substantial gaps in college attendance among those from different income groups widened. Racial and ethnic gaps in attendance also widened (Figure 1.11).

Because education is a primary determinant of earnings, these differential responses to the increased market demand for skills widen racial, ethnic, and family-origin wage differentials in the next generation, making the United States of tomorrow even more unequal than the United States of today and the United States of the past. In the face of declining real wages for low-skilled workers and increasing real returns to college graduation, a greater proportion of U.S. youth are low-skilled dropouts than 30 years ago. College enrollment responses to the increasing return to schooling have been weak. Together with the decline in high school graduation, there has come a decline in the academic performance of U.S. students (Hanushek, 2003).

The problem is clear: the supply of skilled workers is not keeping pace with demand. The solution to the problem is not as clear. How should we increase the supply of skilled workers in an economically efficient way? The many fundamentally different policy proposals are difficult to compare because their costs and benefits have not been tabulated. Many recent discussions seize upon the gaps in schooling attainment by family income, evident in Figure 1.10, as a major causal factor in the stagnation of the supply of skilled workers.

There are two, not necessarily mutually exclusive, interpretations of the evidence are presented in Figure 1.10. The first, more common, interpretation of the evidence and the one that guides current policy is the obvious one: credit constraints facing families in a child's adolescent years affect the resources required to finance a college education. A second interpretation emphasizes more long-run factors associated with higher family income. It notes that family income is strongly correlated over the child's life cycle. Families with high income in a child's adolescent years are more likely to have high income throughout the child's life at home. Better family resources in a child's formative years are associated with a higher quality of education and better environments that foster cognitive and noncognitive skills. Both interpretations of the evidence are consistent with a form of credit constraint. The first interpretation is clearly consistent with the notion of short-term credit constraints. But the second interpretation is consistent with another type of credit constraint: the inability of the child to buy the parental environment and genes that form the cognitive and noncognitive abilities required for success in school. This interpretation renders a market failure as a type of credit constraint.

We argue on quantitative grounds that the second interpretation of Figure 1.10 is by far the more important one. Controlling for ability formed by the early teenage years, parental income plays only a minor role in explaining education gaps (Carneiro & Heckman, 2002). The evidence from the United States presented in this chapter suggests that, at most, 8 percent of U.S. youth are subject to short-term liquidity constraints that affect their postsecondary schooling (Carneiro & Heckman, 2003). Therefore, there is scope for intervention to alleviate these short-term constraints, but one should not expect to reduce the enrollment gaps in Figure 1.10 substantially by eliminating such constraints. Most of the family income gap in enrollment is due to long-term factors that produce the abilities needed to benefit from participation in college.

PARENTAL INFLUENCE ON CHILDREN'S ABILITIES AND ASPIRATIONS

An alternative interpretation of the same evidence is that long-run family and environmental factors play a decisive role in shaping the abilities and expectations of children. Children whose parents have higher incomes have access to better-quality primary and secondary schools. Children's tastes for education and their expectations about their life chances are shaped by those of their parents. Educated parents are better able to develop scholastic aptitude in their children by assisting and directing their studies. It is known that cognitive ability is formed relatively early in life and becomes less malleable as children age. By age eight, intelligence as measured by IQ tests seems to be fairly well set (Heckman, 1995). Noncognitive skills are more malleable until the late adolescent years (Heckman, 2000). The influences of family factors present from birth through adolescence accumulate to produce ability and college readiness. By the time individuals finish high school and their scholastic ability is determined, the scope of tuition policy for promoting college attendance through boosting cognitive and noncognitive skills is greatly diminished.

The interpretation that stresses the role of family and the environment does not necessarily rule out short-term borrowing constraints as a partial explanation for the patterns revealed in Figure 1.10. However, if the finances of poor but motivated families hinder them from providing decent elementary and secondary schooling for their children, and produce a low level of college readiness, government policy aimed at reducing the short-term borrowing constraints for the college expenses of those children during their college years is unlikely to be effective in substantially closing the gaps in Figure 1.10. In such circumstances, policy that improves the environments that shape ability will be more effective in increasing college enrollment in the long run. The issue can be settled empirically. Surprisingly, until recently there have been few empirical investigations of this topic.

The following experiment captures the essence of the distinction I am making. Suppose families participate in lotteries that are adjusted to have the same expected present value (at age zero of the child) but have different award dates. Credit markets are assumed to be imperfect, at least in part, so the timing of receipts matters. A family that wins the lottery in the child's adolescent years is compared to a family that wins in the child's early formative years. The child from the family that wins late would lack all of the benefits of investment in the early years of the child that the child from the family that wins early would receive. The child from the late-winning family would be likely to have lower levels of cognitive and noncognitive abilities than the child from the early-winning family. Although none of the data we possess are as clean as the data generated by this hypothetical experiment, taken as a whole they point in the general predicted direction.

There is no shortage of policy proposals. There is, however, a shortage of empirical evidence on the efficacy of the proposed policies. No common framework has been used to evaluate them or compare them. This chapter provides evidence on the effectiveness of alternative policies within a common cost-benefit framework.

BENEFIT-COST ANALYSES OF HUMAN CAPITAL INVESTMENTS

We analyze policies that are designed to foster skill formation in the U.S. economy. A central premise of this chapter is that effective policy is based on empirically grounded studies of the sources of the problems that the proposed policies are intended to address. Although it is possible through trial and error to stumble onto effective policies without understanding the sources of the problems that motivate them, a more promising approach to human capital policy formulation is to understand the mechanisms and institutions that produce skill, how they are related, and where they have failed.

Human capital accumulation is a dynamic process. The skills acquired in one stage of the life cycle affect both the initial conditions and the technology of learning at the next stage. Human capital is produced over the life cycle by families, schools, and firms, although most discussions of skill formation focus on schools as the major producer of abilities and skills, despite a substantial body of evidence that families and firms are also major producers of abilities and skills.

A major determinant of successful schools is successful families. Schools work with what parents bring them. They operate more effectively if parents reinforce them by encouraging and motivating children. Job training programs, whether public or private, work with what families and schools supply them and cannot remedy 20 years of neglect.

Recent studies in child development (e.g., Shonkoff & Phillips, 2000) emphasize that different stages in the life cycle are critical to the formation of different types of abilities. When the opportunities for formation of these abilities are missed, remediation is costly, and full remediation is often impossible. These findings highlight the need to take a comprehensive view of skill formation over the life cycle that is grounded in the best science and economics so that effective policies for increasing the low level of skills in the workforce can be devised.

A study of human capital policy grounded in economic and scientific fundamentals improves on a purely empirical approach to policy evaluation that relies on evaluations of the programs and policies in place or previously experienced. Although any trustworthy study of economic policy must be grounded in data, it is also important to recognize that the policies that can be evaluated empirically are only a small subset of the policies that might be tried. If we base speculation about economic policies on economic fundamentals, rather than solely on estimated treatment effects that are only weakly related to economic fundamentals, we are in a better position to think beyond what has been tried to propose more innovative solutions to human capital problems. This chapter investigates the study of human capital policy by placing it in the context of economic models of life-cycle learning and skill accumulation rather than focusing exclusively on which policies have "worked" in the past.

We use the rate of return, when it is justified, to place different policies on a common footing. For many, but not all, human capital policies, the marginal rate of return is an accurate guide for determining where the next dollar should by spent. We also compute present values of alternative policies when possible. Present values are not subject to the criticisms that are directed toward rates of return.

Figure 1.12 summarizes the major theme of this chapter. It plots the rate of return to human capital at different stages of the life cycle for a person of given abilities. The horizontal axis represents age, which is a surrogate for the agent's position in the life cycle. The vertical axis represents the rate of return to investment assuming the same investment is made at each age. What is important to note is that the rate of return on a dollar investment made when a person is young is higher than the rate of return on the same dollar made at a later age. Early investments are harvested over a longer period than those made later in the life cycle. In addition, because early investments raise the productivity (lower the costs) of later investments, human capital is synergistic. This dynamic complementarity in human investment was ignored in the early work on human capital (Becker, 1964). A central empirical conclusion of this chapter is that at current investment levels, efficiency in public spending would be enhanced if human capital

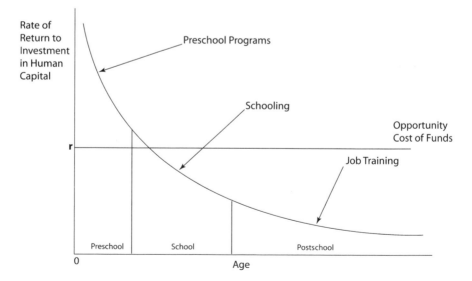

Figure 1.12   Rates of return to human capital investment initially setting investment to be equal across all ages

investment were directed more toward the young and away from older, less skilled, and illiterate persons for whom human capital is poor investment. Early interventions are more effective for the young disadvantaged populations than are later efforts at remediation.

Our analysis challenges the conventional point of view that equates skill with intelligence and draws on a body of research that demonstrates the importance of both cognitive and noncognitive skills in determining socioeconomic success. Both types of skills are affected by families and schools, but they differ in their malleability over the life cycle, with noncognitive skills being more malleable than cognitive skills at later ages. Differences in levels of cognitive and noncognitive skills by family income and family background emerge early and persist. If anything, schooling widens these early differences.

NEGLECT OF NONCOGNITIVE ABILITIES

Current educational policy and economic analysis focus on tested academic achievement as the major output of schools. Proposed systems for evaluating school performance are premised on this idea. Economic models of signaling and screening assume that cognitive ability is an important determinant, if not the most important determinant, of academic and economic success. Recent evidence challenges this view. No doubt, cognitive ability is an important factor in school and labor market outcomes. At the same time, noncognitive abilities, although harder to measure, also play an important role. Noncognitive abilities matter for success both in the labor market and in schooling. This finding is supported by studies of early childhood interventions that primarily improve noncognitive skills, with substantial effects on schooling and labor market outcomes, but only weakly affect cognitive ability. Mentoring programs in the early teenage years can also affect these skills. Current analyses of skill formation focus too much on cognitive ability and too little on noncognitive ability in evaluating human capital interventions.

The evidence presented here suggests that both cognitive and noncognitive abilities affect schooling and economic success and that socioeconomic differences in cognitive and noncognitive skills appear early and, if anything, widen over the life cycle of the child. An entire literature demonstrates that parental inputs are important correlates of these skills. Yet the policy intervention indicated by this evidence is far from obvious because the exact causal mechanisms through which strong families produce successful children are not yet well understood. Perhaps for this reason, U.S. society has been reluctant to intervene in family life, especially in the early years.

Table 1.1
Effects of Early-Intervention Programs

Program/Study	Costs[*]	Program Description	Test Scores	Schooling	Predelinquency Crime
Abecedarian Project [**] (Ramey Bryant, Campbell, Sparling, & Wasik, 1988)	N/A	Full-time year-round classes for children from infancy through preschool	High scorese at ages 1–4	34% less grade retention by 2nd grade; better reading and math proficiency	
Early Training [**] (Gray, Ramey & Klaus, 1982)	N/A	Part-time classes for children in summer; weekly home visits during school year	Higher scores at ages 5–10	16% less grade retention; 21% higher high school graduation.	
Harlem Study (Palmer, 1983)	N/A	Individual teacher-child sessions twice weekly for young males	Higher scores at ages 3–5	21% less grade retention	
Houston PCDC [**] (Johnson, 1988)	N/A	Home visits for parents for 2 years; child nursery care 4 days/week in year 2 (Mexican Americans)	Higher scores at age 3		Rated less aggressive and hostile by mothers (ages 8–11)
Milwaukee Project [**] (Garber, 1988)	N/A	Full-time year-round classes for children through1st grade; job training for mothers	Higher scores at ages 2–10	27% less grade retention	
Mother-Child Home Program (Levenstein, O' Hara, & Madden, 1983)	N/A	Home visits with mothers and children twice weekly	Higher scores at ages 3–4	6% less grade retention	

Program	Cost	Program description	Early outcomes	School-age outcomes	Later outcomes
Perry Preschool Program** (Schweinhart, Barnes, & Weikart, 1993)	$13,400	Weekly home visits with parents; intensive, high-quality preschool services for 1–2 years	Higher scores in all studied years (ages 5–27)	21% less grade retention or special services; 21% higher high school graduation rates	2.3 vs. 4.6 lifetime arrests by age 27; 7% vs. 35% arrested 5 or more times
Rome Head Start (Monroe, Morris, & McDonald, 1981)	$5,400 (2 years)	Part-time classes for children; parent involvement		12% less grade retention; 17% higher high school graduation rates	
Syracuse University Family Development (Lally Mangione, & Honig, 1988)	$38,100	Weekly home visits for family; day care year round	Higher scores at ages 3–4		6% vs. 22% had probation files; offenses were less severe
Yale Experiment	$23,300	Family support; home visits and day care as needed for 30 months	Better language development at 30 months	Better school attendance and adjustment; fewer special adjustments; chool services (age 12 1/2)	Rated less aggressive and predelinquent by teachers and parents (ages 12 1/2)

Note All comparisons are for program participants vs. nonparticipants.

*Costs valued in 1990 dollars.

**Studies used a random assignment experimental design to determine program impacts. Data from Donohue and Siegelman (1998); Schweinhart, Barnes, and Weikart (1993); and Seitz (1990) for the impacts reported here.

Source: Heckman, Lochner, Smith, & Taber (1997).

FAMILIES EDUCATE, TOO

There is a profound asymmetry in popular views about family life and schooling. On the one hand, there is a widespread belief that parents cannot make wise choices about their children's schooling. If that is true, then how can parents be trusted to make correct decisions in the preschool years, which recent research has demonstrated to be so important for lifetime success? The logical extension of the paternalistic argument that denies the wisdom of parental sovereignty in choosing schools would suggest that the state should play a far more active role in the preschool life of the child. That is a position that few would accept.

Paternalistic interventions in the early life of children in certain dysfunctional families may be appropriate. If we are to violate the principle of family sovereignty anywhere in the life cycle of learning, the case for doing so is strongest at the preschool stage (and only for some groups) and not at later stages of formal schooling, for which the argument for paternalism is most often made. Dysfunctional families and environments are major sources of social problems. Paternalistic interventions into the lives of such families may be warranted on efficiency grounds, although such interventions raise serious questions about the need to protect the sanctity of family life.

ENRICHING EARLY CHILDHOOD ENVIRONMENTS

Recent small-scale studies of early-childhood investments in children from disadvantaged environments have shown remarkable success. They indicate that interventions in the early years can effectively promote learning and that external interventions can enrich child environments. They demonstrate the value of good families by showing that interventions can remedy the failings of bad families. Early childhood interventions of high quality have lasting effects on learning and motivation. They raise achievement and noncognitive skills, but they do not raise IQ. Disadvantaged subnormal IQ children (average IQ = 80) in Ypsilanti, Michigan, were randomly assigned to the Perry Preschool program, and intensive treatment was administered to them from ages four to five. Treatment was then discontinued, and the children were followed over their life cycles. Evidence on the treatment group, who are now about 40 years old, indicates that those enrolled in the program have higher earnings and lower levels of criminal behavior in their late twenties than did comparable children randomized out of the program. Reported benefit-cost ratios for the program are substantial. Measured through age 27, the program returns $5.70 for every dollar spent. When returns are projected for the remainder of the lives of program participants, the return on the dollar rises to $8.70. A substantial percentage

(65%) of the return to the program has been attributed to reductions in crime (Schweinhart, Barnes, & Weikart, 1993).

The Syracuse Preschool program provided family development support for disadvantaged children, from prenatal care for their mothers through age five of the children's lives. Reductions in problems with probation and criminal offenses 10 years later were as large as 70 percent among children randomly assigned to the program. Girls who participated in the program also showed greater school achievement (Lally, Mangione, & Honig, 1988). Studies have found short-term increases in test scores, lower in-grade retention, and higher high school graduation rates among children enrolled in early-intervention programs. Of those studies that examined predelinquent or criminal behavior, most found lower rates of such behavior among program participants.

Table 1.2 summarizes the effects of selected early-intervention programs on student test scores, schooling, earnings, and delinquency. Table 1.3 recounts the findings of studies on the Perry Preschool program and a benefit-cost analysis of that program. The benefit-cost ratio is substantially greater than one.

Evidence on the more universal Head Start program is less clear, but the program is quite heterogeneous and is much less well funded than the Perry Preschool program. Currie and Thomas (1995) find short-term gains

Table 1.2
Perry Preschool: Net Present Values of Costs and Benefits through Age 27

1. Cost of preschool, child ages 3–4	$12,148
2. Decrease in cost to government of K–12 special education courses for child, ages 5–18	6,365
3. Decrease in direct criminal justice system costs+ of child's criminal activity, ages 15–28	7,378
4. Decrease in direct criminal justice system costs+ of child's projected criminal activity, ages 29–44	2,817
5. Income from child's increased employment, ages 19–27	8,380
6. Projected income from child's increased employment, ages 28–65	7,565
7. Decrease in tangible losses to crime victims ages 15–44	10,690
Total benefits:	43,195
Total benefits excluding projections....	32,813
Benefits minus cost	31,047
Benefits minus cost excluding projections....	20,665

Note All values are net present values in 1996 dollars at age 0 calculated using a 4% discount rate. Direct Criminal Justice System costs are the administrative costs of incarceration. Benefits from projected criminal activity (4) and projected income from increased employment (6) are excluded.

Source: Karoly et al. (1998); Barnett (1993).

Table 1.3
Outcomes of Early-Intervention Programs

Program (Years of Operation)	Outcome	Followed Up to Age	Age When Treatment Effect Last Statistically Significant	Control Group	Change in Treated Group
Cognitive measures					
Early Training Project (1952–1963)	IQ	16–20	6	82.8	−12.2
Perry Preschool Project (1962–1967)	IQ	27	7	87.1	+1.0
Houston PCDC (1970–1980)	IQ	8–11	2	90.8	+8.0
Syracuse FDRP (1969–1979)	IQ	15	3	90.6	+19.7
Carolina Abecedarian (1972–1985)	IQ	21	12	88.1	−5.3
Project CARE (1978–1984)	IQ	4.5	3	92.6	−11.6
IHDP (1985–1988)	IQ(HLBW sample)	8	8	92.1	−4.4
Educational outcomes					
Early Training Project	Special education	16–20	18	29%	−26%
Perry Preschool Project	Special education	27	19	28%	−12%
	High school graduation		27	45%	−21%

Chicago CPC (1967–present)	Special education	20	18	25%	-10%
	Grade education		15	38%	-15%
	High school graduation		20	39%	-11%
Carolina Abecedarian	College enrollment	21	21	14%	-22%
Economic outcomes					
Perry Preschool Project	Arrest rate	27	27	69%	-12%
	Employment rate		27	32%	-18%
	Monthly earnings		27	$766	-$453
	Welfare use		27	32%	-17%
Chicago CPC (preschool vs. no preschool)	Juvenile arrests	20	18	25%	-8%
Syracnae FDRP	Probation referral	15	15	22%	-16%
Elmirs PEIP (1978 – 1982)	Arrests (BB. sample)	15	15	0.53	-.029

Note: HLBW = heavier, low birth weight sample; HR = high risk. Cognitive measures include Stanford-Binet and Weshler Intelligence Scales, California Achievement Tests, and other IQ and achievement tests measuring cognitive ability. All results significant at .05 level or higher.

Source: Karoly, 2001. For a discussion of the specific treatments offered under each program, see Heckman (2000); Karoly (2001).

in test scores for all children participating in Head Start. Most of those gains decayed quickly, however, for African American children after they left the program. Currie and Thomas conclude that either difference in local-program administration or in quality of schooling subsequent to the Head Start program is at the root of the differences between the outcomes for black and white children. Ramey, Bryant, Campbell, Sparling, and Wasik (1988) note that the schools attended by the Perry Preschool children were of substantially higher quality than those attended by the typical Head Start child. In addition, the Perry program also taught parenting skills and arguably put better long-term environments in place for the children. The failure to support in subsequent years the initial positive stimulus of Head Start may account for the decline in the impact of Head Start over time and may account for its apparent ineffectiveness compared to the Perry Preschool program. Additionally, Edward Zigler would argue that results of most studies done on the impact of Head Start are misleading because they focus exclusively on cognitive outcomes instead of social-emotional outcomes, which the program has been more successful in promoting. See the discussion in Cunha, Heckman, Lochner, and Masterov (in press).

Corroborating our beliefs, it appears that early childhood programs are most effective in changing noncognitive skills, although they also raise achievement test scores. If the interventions are made early enough—and with enough intensity—they permanently raise IQ, as in the Abecedarian program, which starts at age four months. We also note that eventual decay in initial gains in test scores, like those found in regard to the Head Start program, were found for programs like Perry Preschool as well, but the long-term evaluations of these programs are quite favorable in terms of participants' success in school and society at large. The psychometric test score literature is not clear about the relationship between early test scores and success in school, graduation rates, socialization, and labor market outcomes. The fade-out effects in test scores found for the Head Start program do not imply that participation in the program has no long-term beneficial effects. Head Start may improve the lifetime prospects of its participants, despite yielding only short-term gains in test scores, which may not measure many relevant dimensions of social and emotional skills.

Head Start offers a staff of much lower quality, part-time classes for children, and limited parental involvement. The program terminates without any substantial intervention into or improvement in the home environments of the disadvantaged children. Improvements in Head Start, proponents argue, are likely to produce effects closer to those observed in more successful small-scale programs. Given the potential for success of such programs (as exhibited by the Perry Preschool experiment), more studies of the long-term impacts of various types of small-scale and broad-based early-intervention programs are certainly warranted. Provocative calculations by Donohue and Siegelman (1998) indicate that if enriched early-intervention programs were targeted toward high-risk, disadvantaged minority male youth, the expected savings in incarceration costs alone would more then repay the substantial costs of these enriched programs.

An important lesson to draw from the Perry Preschool program, and indeed from the entire literature on successful early interventions, is that the social skills and motivation of the child are more easily altered than his or her IQ, although in very early enriched programs IQ can be altered. These social and emotional skills affect performance in school and in the workplace. Academics have a bias toward believing that cognitive skills are of fundamental importance to success in life. Because of this, the relatively low malleability of IQs after early ages has led many to proclaim a variety of interventions to be ineffective. Yet the evidence from the Perry Preschool program and the evidence presented in Table 1.3 reveals that early-intervention programs are highly effective in reducing criminal activity, promoting social skills, and integrating disadvantaged children into mainstream society. The greatest benefits of these programs as a group are their effects on socialization and not those on IQ. Social skills and motivation have large payoffs in the labor market, so these programs have the potential for a large payoff.

At the same time, it is important to be cautious about the evidence from these programs. Whether they can be replicated on a large scale is an issue. Like those in the Tennessee STAR program (Hanushek, 2003), teachers in the early-intervention programs studied may have been motivated more than would be possible in a permanent large-scale program. Proper accounting for future benefits is required before strong conclusions can be drawn. The substantial gap in time between the payment in terms of costs and the harvest of benefits requires that these benefits be substantial to justify early-intervention programs. Prima facie, the benefits are there, but a stronger case would be desirable.

SUMMARY

The traditional approach to human capital policy focuses on schools, but families are just as important as, if not more important than, schools in promoting human capital. Noncognitive abilities that are often fostered in preschools, on playgrounds, and at home are pivotal ingredients for success in school and in adult life, and they can benefit from enriched early childhood environments. They are usually neglected in educational policy discussions. Public spending for investment in human capital is most efficiently directed toward young children and away from older, less skilled, and illiterate persons for whom human capital is poor investment. When opportunities for skill development are missed early in life, remediation is expensive, and complete remediation is often prohibitively expensive. Several authors have pointed out that enriched early-intervention programs targeted toward high-risk, disadvantaged, minority male youth might more than repay society for the large costs of such intervention *solely by savings in the costs for incarceration,* if they are as successful as presently indicated. The evidence for successful early intervention to address social inequality is quite encouraging, but the long delays in harvesting the benefits from human capital investments dictate both caution and circumspection in committing public resources.

NOTE

1. This research was supported by the National Institute of Child Health and Human Development (no. RO1-HD043411) and by a grant from the PEW Foundation to the Committee on Economic Development.

All figures and tables as well as a majority of the writing in this chapter originally appeared in J.J. Heckman & A.B. Krueger (Eds.), *Inequality in America, What Role for Human Capital Policies?* Cambridge, MA: The MIT Press. Reproduced with permission of The MIT Press, Cambridge, MA.

REFERENCES

Autor, D., & Katz, L. (1999). Changes in wage structure and earnings inequality. In O. Ashenfelter & D. Cards (Eds.), *Handbook of labor economics* (Vol. 3A, pp. 1463–1555). Amsterdam: Elsevier Science/North-Holland.

Barnett, W.S. (1993). Benefit-cost analyses of preschool education: Findings from a 25-year follow-up. *American Journal of Orthopsychiatry, 63*(4), 500–508.

Becker, G. (1964). *Human capital: A theoretical and empirical analysis with special reference to education.* New York: Columbia University Press.

Boesel, D., Alsalam, N., & Smith, T. (1998). *Educational and labor market performance of GED recipients.* Washington, DC: U.S. Department of Education.

Cameron, S., & Heckman, J. J. (1993). The nonequivalence of high school equivalents. *Journal of Labor Economics, 11*(1), 1–47.

Carneiro, P., & Heckman, J.J. (2002). The evidence on credit constraints in post-secondary schooling. *Economic Journal, 112*(482), 705–734.

Carneiro, P., & Heckman, J.J. (2003). Human capital policy. In J.J. Heckman & A.B. Krueger (Eds.), *Inequality in America: What role for human capital policies.* Cambridge, MA: MIT Press.

Cunha, F., Heckman, J.J., Lochner, L., & Masterov, D.V. (in press). Interpreting the evidence on life cycle skill formation. In E.A. Hanushek and F. Welch (Eds.), *Handbook of the economics of education.* North-Holland.

Current Population Survey. (2000). Washington, DC: Department of Labor, Bureau of Labor Statistics.

Currie, J., & Thomas, D. (1995). Does Head Start make a difference? *American Economic Review, 85*(3), 341–364.

DeLong, J.B., Goldin, C., & Katz, L. (2003). Sustaining U.S. economic growth. In H. Aaron, J. Lindsay, & P. Nivola (Eds.), *Agenda for the nation.* Washington, DC: Brookings Institution Press.

Donohue, J., & Siegelman, P. (1998). Allocating resources among prisons and social programs in the battle against crime. *Journal of Legal Studies, 27*(1), 1–43.

Ellwood, D. (2001). The sputtering labor force of the 21st century: Can social policy help? In A. Krueger and R. Solow (Eds.), *The roaring nineties: Can full employment be sustained?* New York: Russell Sage Foundation.

Garber, H. (1988). *The Milwaukee project: Preventing mental retardation in children at risk.* Washington, D. C.: American Association of Mental Retardation.

Gray, S., Ramey, B., & Klaus, R. (1982). *From three to twenty: The early training project.* Baltimore: University Park.

Hanushek, E. (2003). The failure of input based schooling policies. *Economic Journal, 113*(485), F64–F98.

Heckman, J.J. (1995). Lessons from the bell curve. *Journal of Political Economy, 103*(5), 1091–1120.

Heckman, J.J. (2000). Policies to foster human capital. *Research in Economics, 54*(1), 3–56.

Heckman, J.J. (Ed.). (2005). *The GED.* Unpublished manuscript.

Heckman, J. J., Lochner, L., Smith, J., & Taber, C. (1997, Spring). The effects of government policy on human capital investment and wage inequality. *Chicago Policy Review, 1* (2), 1–40.

Johnson, D. (1988). Primary prevention of behavior problems in young children: The Houston Parent–child Development Center. In R. Price, E. Cowen, R. Lorion & J. Ramos-McKay (Eds.), *14 ounces of prevention: A casebook for practitioners.* Washington, DC: American Psychological Association.

Jorgenson, D., & Ho, M. (1999). *The quality of the U.S. work force, 1948 to 95* (Working Paper). Cambridge, MA: Harvard University.

Karoly, L. (2001). Investing in the future: Reducing poverty through human capital investments. In S. Danzinger and R. Haveman (Eds.), *Understanding poverty.* New York: Russell Sage.

Karoly, L., Greenwood, P., Everingham, S., Hube, J., Kilburn, M.R., Rydell, P., et al. (1998). *Investing in our children: What we know and don't know about the cost and benefits of early childhood interventions.* Santa Monica, CA: RAND.

Lally, J.R., Mangione, P., & Honig, A. (1988). The Syracuse University Family Development Research Program: Long-range impact on an early intervention with low-income children and their families. In D. Powell (Ed.), *Parent education as early childhood intervention.* Norwood, NJ: Ablex.

Levenstein, P., O'Hara, J., & Madden, J. (1983). The mother-child program of the Verbal Interaction Project. In *As the twig is bent: Lasting effects of pre-school programs.* Consortium for Longitudinal Studies, Hillsdale, N.J.: Erlbaum.

Monroe, E., & McDonald, M. S. (1981). Follow up study of the 1966 Head Start Program, Rome City Schools, Rome, Georgia. Unpublished manuscript.

Palmer, F. (1983). The Harlem Study: Effects of type of training, age of training and social class. *In as the twig is bent: Lasting effects of Pre-school programs*, Consortium for Longitudinal Studies. Hillsdale, N.J.: Erlbaum.

Ramey, C., Bryant, D., Campbell, F., Sparling, J., & Wasik, B. (1988). Early intervention for high-risk children: The Carolina Early Intervention Program. In R. Price, E. Cowen, R. Lorion, & J. Ramos-McKay (Eds.), *14 ounces of prevention: A casebook for practitioners.* Washington, DC: American Psychological Association.

Schweinhart, L., Barnes, H., & Weikart, D. (1993). *Significant benefits: The High-Scope Perry Preschool Study through age 27.* Ypsilanti, MI: High Scope Press.

Seitz, V. (1990). Intervention programs for impoverished children: A comparison of educational and family support models. *Annals of child development: A research annual, 7,* 73–103.

Shonkoff, J., & Phillips, D. (Eds.). (2000). *From neurons to neighborhoods: The science of early childhood development.* Washington, DC: National Academy Press.

Chapter 2

COSTS AND BENEFITS FROM EARLY INVESTMENTS TO PROMOTE HUMAN CAPITAL AND POSITIVE BEHAVIOR

Greg J. Duncan and Katherine Magnuson

Social policies are often motivated by compassion or justice, but sometimes their proponents argue that they constitute worthy social "investments." Just as business decisions take into account the effect of an investment on a company's bottom line, it is useful to ask whether government expenditures that "invest" in children's cognitive and behavioral skills provide "profits" to society as a whole.

School failure is costly, not only to the children who will grow up limited by lower earnings and fewer career opportunities but also to society, which must incur the costs of additional remediation and support for individuals throughout their lives. Parent-based interventions and early-education programs are two possible ways to promote school success of at-risk children. Our chapter summarizes the evidence that shows gains associated with such programs more than offset their considerable costs.

We begin with a typology of parent- and child-focused interventions and of the logic that underlies policy-economic choices among them. Our review of parent-based strategies focuses on both direct parenting interventions and the broader questions of whether and how increasing parental resources such as income promotes children's development. We find that many parent-based interventions improve parenting (Stormshak, Kaminski, & Goodman, 2002). With few exceptions, however, program-induced improvements in parenting do not translate into improvements in low-income children's academic outcomes. In contrast, some programs for parents of children with high levels of externalizing behavior problems have been successful in improving children's behavior (Bradley et al., 2003; DeGarmo, Patterson, & Forgatch, 2004).

With regard to the "intervention" of boosting parental economic resources, recent welfare-reform experiments demonstrate that financial incentives that increase family incomes often have positive impacts on younger children's school achievement but, if anything, worsen adolescent behavior. The nonexperimental literature suggests that increasing the resources of deprived families may be more beneficial for children's cognitive development than increments to the incomes of middle-class families. Again, earlier may be better; boosting family income appears to benefit preschoolers more than older children.

In addition, we review the more promising literature on interventions that bypass parents and directly target children's human capital. A number of careful studies have demonstrated that expensive early-education interventions provide a handsome social profit. Suppose we start with a group of 200 preschoolers from low-income families. Countless studies suggest that many will not be as academically and economically successful as children from middle-class families. But suppose that we enroll half of the low-income children in an early-education program for a year, and for 30 years we track their fortunes as well as the fortunes of the children who do not attend preschool. Although it is unrealistic to expect that all of the children who attend preschool will become college-educated professionals, there still may be important differences in the attainments and well-being of the children who receive early education and those who do not. In addition, some programs that treat children's severe behavior problems appear successful (Kazdin & Weisz, 1998). All in all, child-focused programs appear more promising than parent-focused programs if the goal is to promote the well-being of children. Combining these approaches may be particularly useful in reducing children's problem behaviors.

ASSESSING COSTS AND BENEFITS

Seeking to establish whether intervention programs might indeed produce long-lasting impacts, program designers often develop very expensive "efficacy" trials, with costs exceeding $10,000 or even $20,000 per participant, and the quality of the intervention or program is much higher than what is possible in a "scaled-up" national or regional program. We very much agree with Shadish, Cook, and Campbell (2002) when they argue that informed policy requires that "efficacy" trials be followed by "effectiveness" trials in which interventions are implemented in a variety of real-world settings and with realistic levels of quality.

Even if effectiveness trials do establish program impacts, policy makers require research-based answers to additional questions. If research trials demonstrate a convincing causal linkage between intervention A and outcomes B and C, what are the costs of a feasible large-scale program that changes A and the value of benefits associated with the resulting change in outcomes B and C? How big an impact must an intervention program produce to be worthwhile? Is a cheaper-by-half, scaled-back version of a proven but very expensive parenting program likely to provide at least half the benefits of the proven program? If several interventions have proven benefits but a decision maker cannot fund all of them, how should she choose among the alternatives?

Cost-benefit frameworks (Gramlich, 1990; Levin, 1983) provide a way of addressing all of these issues. Key is a systematic assessment of the costs and benefits of an intervention program, based on a careful (ideally random-assignment) comparison of participants offered the program services and otherwise similar participants not offered program services. When both costs and benefits can be quantified, a cost-benefit accounting can produce an estimate of a program's *social rate of return*—the return on the investment of public dollars in the intervention (Karoly et al., 1998).

How should we go about estimating the benefits? In the case of long-run impacts, labor-market employment and earnings are obvious outcomes. In the short term, IQ and school achievement are commonly measured outcomes for intervention programs directed at young children. Presumably, IQ gains, if maintained, translate into academic success and increased productivity. However, abundant developmental evidence documents the importance of other developmental domains, in particular physical and emotional health, in promoting academic success and well-being in adulthood (Shonkoff & Phillips, 2000). We would certainly want to know how many of the children needed special education services during primary school. Suppose that 20 of the children in the experimental group needed a year of special education, but 30 of the comparison children did too. Because special education classes require specially trained teachers and often separate classrooms, the costs to taxpayers for providing only a year of special education to the additional 10 students could easily total about $80,000 (Chambers, Parrish, & Harr, 2004). If, as is often the case, special education classes are needed for two, three, or even more years, then the taxpayer savings could be several times this amount.

Suppose that we also collect the police records of the children as they move through their teen years and into adulthood. Many will not be involved in the criminal justice system at all, but if the academic skills or positive behavior learned through the intervention somehow help keep children out of trouble later on, then we might find differences in criminal activity. Economic studies conclude that the costs of crime, especially violent crime, are very large because they involve not only the police and court system, including expenses for arrests, trials, and incarceration, but also the victims' costs for medical treatment, earnings losses, and the like. Miller, Cohen, and Wiersema (1996) estimate that the costs associated with each violent crime amount to roughly $8,000 and for each property crime about $500. So even if the program children go on to commit only a select fewer crimes than children not attending the program, the savings to taxpayers and crime victims could be considerable.

On the more positive side, the program might prevent high school dropout and enhance employment opportunities. Suppose we track the earnings and unemployment experiences of the children into adulthood and find that the earnings of program children are $.50 per hour higher than comparison children, and that 10 more children participating in the program have avoided long spells of joblessness, relative to children in the comparison group. Even after accounting for the fact that these labor-market advantages are reaped two or more decades after money is spent on the program, these employment and earnings differences for the 200 children can easily exceed $100,000. And in this case the program's effects on earnings are enjoyed by both the individuals themselves (in the form of higher income) and taxpayers (because of the higher taxes paid by these individuals as well as lower welfare benefits paid to them).

These are the kinds of steps that need to be taken to arrive at a proper accounting of all of the benefits and costs of parent-based interventions and early-education programs. When completed, the accounting provides an answer to the question of whether government spending on these programs yields a "profit" to society. The purpose of this chapter is to review evidence from parent-based intervention and preschool program evaluations. We first provide an overview of several parent-based intervention programs and relate evidence from the small number of programs for which costs and benefits have been reliably determined. We then present the same information for early childhood education programs.

PARENT-BASED INTERVENTIONS

Two theoretical assertions are the foundation of most parenting interventions. First, parental behavior has a strong influence on children's healthy development. Second, positive parenting can be learned or, in the case of economic interventions, improved by increases in economic resources. Both of these assertions are controversial.

That parents influence children is beyond debate; the relative contribution of environmental, including parental, and genetic influences to development remains a point of contention. Developmentalists, such as Scarr (1992), argue that genetic forces leave little room for developmental consequences on the part of all but the most extreme family conditions.

Collins, Maccoby, Steinberg, Hetherington, and Bornstein (2000) agree that past studies may have overstated parental influence on children by failing to attend to the potential effects of genetics but argue that parenting may still be a profoundly important influence on children. They also point out that parenting behaviors appear to have differing, but systematic, influences on children with differing genetically determined characteristics. Therefore, although one type of parenting may not have an effect on all children, it may have substantial effects on particular types of children (Collins et al., 2000).

Even if children benefit from changes in parent–child interaction patterns or in the quality of their home learning environments, the success of parent-based interventions is premised on the ability of interventions to improve parents' behavior in cost-effective ways. The literature we review suggests that effecting change in parents through parenting programs is indeed possible, although more difficult than previously thought.

A long line of research (reviewed in McLoyd, 1990, 1998) has found that low-income parents, as compared with middle-class parents, are more likely to use an authoritarian and punitive parenting style and are less likely either to support their children or to provide them with stimulating learning experiences in the home. Low-income parents are more likely to use physical punishment and other forms of power-assertive discipline and are less likely to ask children about their wishes, reward children for positive behavior, or be responsive to children's expressed needs. In the extreme, these behaviors may lead to child abuse or neglect, both of which are more common among poor than among advantaged parents (Trickett, Aber, & Carlson, 1991). Depending on the particular domains considered and the extent to which research designs account for omitted variable biases, the associations between parenting and children's outcomes range from weak to moderate (McLoyd, 1998). Some evidence seems to suggest that the home learning environment is most closely linked to children's cognitive development and achievement, whereas parent–child warmth and discipline practices have the strongest associations with children's behavior (McGroder, 2000).

Parent Education Programs

Interventions have set out to teach parents how to be better parents and to connect parents with supportive services in their community. Parenting interventions may include home visits, group supports, and informational sessions. Some combine both parent-focused and child-focused strategies into a single program. Parenting interventions typically provide mothers with some form of social support, emotional and instrumental, as well as instructional information about child development. The expectation is that this combination of services will improve mothers' capacities to provide their children with sensitive caregiving as well as other experiences that promote healthy development (Gomby, Culross, & Behrman, 1999; Seitz & Provence, 1990).

Disappointingly, although programs focused solely on parents have demonstrated an ability to improve some of the aspects of parenting, they have not improved the cognitive development or social behavior of low socioeconomic status (SES) children (Brooks-Gunn, Berlin, & Fuligni, 2001; Yoshikawa, 1994). Brooks-Gunn and colleagues (2001) reviewed evaluations of 24 parent-focused home interventions for low SES children. Remarkably, 19 of these programs produced favorable effects on parenting outcomes, including more sensitive parenting and a higher-quality home environment. However, positive program impacts on parenting usually failed to translate into positive impacts on children's cognitive or behavioral outcomes.

A recent meta-analysis of home-visiting programs by Sweet and Appelbaum (2004) provides a more optimistic picture of the effectiveness of these programs. They report that home-visiting programs on average have a modest positive effect on children's cognitive development. However, their closer examination found that the effects of programs evaluated most rigorously (with random assignment) were about one-third the size of effects of programs evaluated with weaker designs (.13 compared with .38). It is unclear what accounts for this discrepancy in findings, but certainly the experimental studies offer the best estimate of causal effects. Consequently, this research points to positive, but small and perhaps selective, effects of home-visiting programs on children's cognitive outcomes.

An example is Parents as Teachers (PAT), a parent-education home-visiting program for parents of children from birth to three years of age. The program began in Missouri in the early 1980s and has since expanded to sites in 49 states. During monthly home visits, the parent educators follow a set curriculum designed to strengthen parenting skills and parents' knowledge of child development. The educators' home visits include periodic screenings of children's health and referrals for needed community services. In addition, voluntary group meetings are offered to parents. Results of an evaluation of PAT programs that served working- and middle-class families found that the program had a positive effect on children's home environments, but not on measures of children's development or well-being (Owen & Mulvihill, 1994). A subsequent evaluation with low-income families found that the program affected neither parenting practices nor child outcomes for most families, although it did show some favorable impacts on Spanish-speaking Latino mothers and children (Wagner & Clayton, 1999).

The successes of a few intensive parenting intervention programs are noteworthy. Most famously, the experimental evaluation of an intensive nurse home-visitation program by Olds et al. (1999) in Elmira, New York, found that the program had lasting effects on important indicators of disadvantaged children's well-being. In particular, a 15-year follow-up study found that unmarried mothers assigned to the program group had fewer verified reports of child abuse and neglect than mothers assigned to the control group. Furthermore, their children had fewer emergency health-related visits, reported arrests, and lifetime sex partners, and they reported less tobacco and alcohol use than did children in the control group (Olds et al., 1999). Olds and colleagues have undertaken replication studies in two sites: Memphis and Denver. Results from a three-year follow-up study of the Memphis program indicate positive but more limited impacts on parenting and child outcomes (Olds et al., 1999). Evidence from additional follow-up studies in Memphis and Denver will provide important information about the likelihood of replicating the success of the Elmira program.

Involving an average of nine visits during the pregnancy and 23 visits during the first two years of the child's life by registered nurses and costing approximately $6,000, Olds's program was clearly at the intensive end of parenting programs. As with early-education programs, it is crucial to ask whether the positive child impacts from intensive programs such as Olds's would carry over to more practical, less intensive programs. As suggested by the review by Gomby et al. (1999), the answer appears negative. Given the different program designs and populations served by parenting education programs, it is difficult to determine whether the lack of consistently positive impacts is due to flaws in implementation of the programs or weaknesses in the theoretical models underpinning them.

Parent Management Training Programs

In contrast to parent education programs, parent management training programs appear to be a more promising strategy, at least in the case of improving the behavior of children with severe behavior problems. These programs were developed in response to research showing that maladaptive parenting and parent–child interaction patterns are common in families of severely conduct-disordered children (Kazdin, 1997; Kazdin & Weisz, 1998; Taylor & Biglan, 1998). Often described as coercive, this type of parenting involves harsh but inconsistent punishment for children's problem behavior and a failure to attend to positive child behavior (Dumas, 1989; Patterson, DeBaryshe, & Ramsey, 1989). Parent management training programs teach parents to respond more appropriately to their children's behavior. Specifically, parents are taught to reward and attend to their children's positive behavior, but to ignore or punish their child's problem behavior appropriately and consistently. Parents are taught to identify and react to their children's behavior in new ways. Treatment sessions provide parents with the opportunity to observe appropriate parenting skills as well as practice and refine their own use of these skills.

A successful example of parenting management training is Webster-Stratton's group discussion videotape program, now known as the PARTNERS program (Webster-Stratton, Kolpacoff, & Hollinsworth, 1988). The evaluation of this program involved random assignment of parents to one of three variations of this treatment (individual videotape only, group discussion only, or videotape and group discussion) or to a control group that received no training. In the group discussion/videotape treatment, parents of children with severe behavior problems attended clinic-based training sessions for 10 to 12 weeks. During these sessions parents watched videotapes that contained two-minute vignettes that modeled parenting skills. Each vignette was followed by a focused discussion in which a trained therapist highlighted the important points and solicited parents' questions and reactions to the material. All three variations of the program treatment had positive effects on observational and parent-report measures of parent–child interactions as well as parent and teacher reports of children's behavior. However, program impacts were more consistent and pronounced among families in the group discussion/videotape treatment. A one-year follow-up indicated that the positive gains among the experimental groups were maintained (Webster-Stratton & Hammond, 1990).

More generally, reviews of evaluations of parent management training programs show that these programs can lead to meaningful reductions in children's problem behaviors. One review suggests that approximately two-thirds of the children exhibit clinically significant improvements in behavior at the completion of the program (Taylor & Biglan, 1998). Another review suggests that the average effect size was .87—a large effect (Durlak, Fuhrman, & Lampman, 1991).

The reviews also suggest that parent management training may be less effective with adolescents than with younger children. Differential effects, however, may be due to the severity of the problem behavior rather than the child's age (Ruma, Burke, & Thompson, 1996). Adolescents' behavior problems tend to be more severe than young children's, and for this reason, parent management training may be less successful at improving their behavior. Parents of adolescents are more likely to drop out of parenting training programs, and this may also explain why adolescents benefit less from parent-focused programs (Dishion & Patterson, 1992).

Although reviews of parent management training programs conclude that these programs can reduce children's problem behavior substantially, whether such conclusions hold up depends on the quality of the research reviewed. Not all of the included studies used random assignment to experimental and control groups, sample sizes were typically quite small, and attrition rates, if reported, were high. Perhaps most worrisome is that when families dropped out of treatment, they were not included in the follow-up study, suggesting that the evaluation findings reflect the effect of completing the program. Few studies have follow-up data beyond six months after program treatment, and, therefore, the long-term benefit of parenting programs is still questionable (Greenberg, Domitrovich, & Bumbarger, 2001). None of these studies provides an accounting of program costs and benefits.

Finally, it is important to keep in mind that most parents who participated in these studies were referred for treatment or were seeking help for their children's behavior. For example, to be admitted to Webster-Stratton's group videotape program, parents had to be referred to the clinic for children's "excessive non-compliance, aggression, and oppositional behavior for more than six months" (Webster-Stratton, 1990, p. 145). It is possible that one reason that parenting interventions have been more successful at reducing severe problem behavior than at promoting academic achievement is that parents of children with severe behavior problems may be more likely to be engaged in parenting programs than parents of children with less severe problems because they find themselves "under siege" (Webster-Stratton & Spitzer, 1996).

Family Resource Interventions

What about interventions that target family economic resources? In four income-maintenance experiments in the 1960s and 1970s, treatment families received an income supplement that varied with the family's income from work and other sources (Institute for Research on Poverty, 1976; Kershaw & Fair, 1976; Salkind & Haskins, 1982; U.S. Department of Health and Human Services, 1983). However, parenting and child outcomes were not measured very well. School performance and attendance were affected positively in some sites among elementary-school-age children, but not among high-school-age adolescents. In the two sites reporting program impacts on high school completion and advanced education, these outcomes were higher for the experimental group.

Child and family outcomes were more of a measurement priority in a number of welfare-to-work experiments begun in the 1990s. Some of these programs augmented family economic resources, whereas others did not (Morris, Huston, Duncan, Crosby, & Bos, 2001). In all cases, participants were randomly assigned to a treatment group that received the welfare-reform package or to a control group that continued to live under the old welfare rules.

Comparable analyses of these data by Morris et al. (2001) revealed that welfare reforms that both increased work and provided financial supports for working families generally promoted children's achievement and positive behavior, although children's achievement appeared to improve more than their behavior. In contrast, welfare reforms that mandated work but did not provide financial support had few impacts—positive or negative—on children.

Thus, it appeared that merely increasing maternal employment had no impact on children's achievement, but increasing both work and income did. Welfare-reform impacts on children depended crucially on the ages of the children studied. Elementary school children were helped by the reforms that increased family resources, and, for the most part, unsupportive ones did not harm them. For adolescents, more limited evidence suggested that even generous reforms that promoted maternal employment may have increased school problems and risky behavior (Gennetian et al., 2002). We speculate that the complicated developmental tasks of adolescence may reduce their ability to profit from two-generation programs aimed at enhancing the resources of their parents (Duncan & Magnuson, 2004).

Stepping back from the successful impacts on children's achievement, it is interesting to ask whether programs included in the Morris et al. (2001) synthesis affected parents. Almost all of them increased parental employment rates. Interestingly, there were virtually no significant impacts of any of the programs on either mothers' mental health or parenting. Thus, the hopes of welfare reformers that employment would transform family life for the better failed to materialize. Nor were the worst fears of reform critics, who argued that work would add unbearable levels of stress to families that were already struggling, confirmed. Despite this experimental evidence, whether family resources affect child development remains a controversial issue that has generated a large nonexperimental literature (Blau, 1999; Brooks-Gunn & Duncan, 1997; Haveman & Wolfe, 1995; Mayer, 1997). Duncan and Brooks-Gunn (1997) provide an overview of links between poverty and children's development by coordinating analyses of 12 groups of researchers working with 10 different nonexperimental developmental data sets. On the whole, the results suggest that family income may have substantial, but selective, associations with children's academic attainments. The selective nature of effects included the following: (a) family income had much larger associations with measures of children's ability and achievement than with measures of behavior, mental health, and physical health; (b) family economic conditions in early childhood appeared to be more important for shaping ability and achievement than did economic conditions during adolescence; and (c) the association between income and achievement appeared to be nonlinear, with the biggest impacts at the lowest levels of income. These conclusions were reinforced by Duncan, Brooks-Gunn, Yeung, and Smith (1998) analyses that found that children's completed schooling was more closely associated with household incomes in early childhood than in middle childhood.

Not all of the sophisticated studies in the literature support these conclusions. Using the Panel Study of Income Dynamics and the National Longitudinal Survey of Youth, Mayer (1997) provides a set of tests for omitted-variable bias and finds large reductions in the estimated impact of parental income on achievement and behavior problems, leading her to conclude that much of the estimated effect of parental income on children in the literature is spurious. Blau (1999) uses data from the National Longitudinal Survey of Youth to estimate a number of models relating income and other aspects of parental family background to children's ability, achievement test scores, and behavior problems. In general, he finds small and insignificant effects of current income and larger (though still modest) effects of long-run income.

Assume that redistribution policies successfully boost poor children's family incomes by, say, $5,000 per year for five years. What impact would we expect this to have on children's developmental outcomes? If estimates by Duncan and colleagues (1998) are accurate, a $5,000 increment to income averaged over each of the first five years of life for children in low-income families would produce nearly a half-year increase in completed schooling, and a 70 percent increase in the odds of finishing high school, but would have no significant impact on the risk of a nonmarital teen birth for females. A comparable income increment in middle childhood or adolescence would be associated with no significant increases in any of the measured schooling or fertility outcomes. Furthermore, the nonlinear nature of the family income/child outcome relation estimated in Duncan et al. (1998) suggests that the reduction in income of more affluent families needed to finance the $5,000 increments to low-income families would not significantly reduce schooling or increase teen fertility among these families.

The more general message of the welfare-reform experiments and the Duncan and Brooks-Gunn (1997) conference volume is that family resource increments are more likely to improve children's achievement than other aspects of their development. To the extent that it is both profitable and important to improve children's social behavior as well, it appears prudent to look beyond redistribution and toward direct intervention as a way of enhancing children's outcomes.

EARLY-CHILDHOOD PROGRAMS

The Perry Preschool Program

Launched in 1962, the Perry Preschool program provided one or two years of enriched early education for 58 low-income African American children. During the school year, the program provided two-and-a-half hours of class during weekdays. The educational model was geared to the children's ages and capabilities, emphasizing child-initiated learning activities, which were supported and observed by program staff. Children were encouraged to engage in play activities that would promote their problem-solving skills as well as their intellectual, social, and physical development. During the afternoons, the program staff visited each family once a week for an hour and a half. The four teachers served only 20 to 25 children each year, providing enough staff to accommodate the regular home visits and ensure a low child-to-teacher ratio (Schweinhart, Barnes, & Weikart, 1993).

The program's benefits were assessed by comparing the Perry children with similar children who did not attend any type of early-education program. Information was collected on children's cognitive development, academic achievement, and educational outcomes when the children were of school age and their educational outcomes, occupational success, and criminal activity when they were adults. Analyses demonstrated that attending Perry Preschool positively affected children's intellectual and cognitive abilities (e.g., IQ) through age seven. More important were the program's longer-lasting beneficial effects on other measures of school success and well-being in adulthood.

Schweinhart et al. (1993) provide the accounting of program costs and benefits shown in Table 2.1. Although the program was free to the participating families, the program's staff and facilities costs (in 2003 dollars) amounted to $16,186 per child. The social profitability question is whether the program's benefits exceeded these substantial costs.

During their primary and secondary schooling, children who attended the Perry Preschool program were less likely to be held back and require special educational services. For example, Perry children received special education services for an average of 1.1 years, whereas comparison children received these services for an average of 2.8 years. Expressed in dollar terms, these per-child expenses for K–12 schooling produced a $9,000 savings to taxpayers. Ironically, the higher school achievement of children in the program carried with it a cost of $1,137 to taxpayers, which appear as negative amounts in the benefit portion of Table 2.1. Because taxpayers support some of the costs of the public colleges, the fact that more program children attended college meant higher subsidies from taxpayers.

Table 2.1
Benefits and Costs of the Perry Preschool Program

	For Participants	For Public	Total
Total costs of the program	$ 0	$ 16,186	$ 16,186
Program benefits			
More efficient K–12 education, such as less grade retention and higher achievement	0	9,002	9,002
Increases in publicly funded higher education costs	0	–1,137	–1,137
Increase in participants' earnings and employee benefits		11,588	39,734
Decrease in welfare payments	–3,475	3,823	347
Decrease in crime	0	92,199	92,199
Other	967	371	1,338
Total benefits of the program	$ 25,637	$ 115,846	$ 141,483
"Profit" (benefits minus costs)	$ 25,637	$ 99,661	$ 125,296

All amounts are expressed in 2003 dollars.

Source: Schweinhart, Barnes, & Weikart, 1993.

As they moved into their adult years, children who attended Perry Preschool worked and earned more than the group of comparison children. In fact, over the course of their lives, the difference in earnings is estimated to be $39,734 per child. About one-third of this earnings differential went to the government in the form of higher tax payments, but the remaining two-thirds made its way into the pockets of the program participants in the form of take-home income. The higher earnings were coupled with about $3,500 less in welfare benefits—a plus for taxpayers but an offsetting minus for the participants themselves.

More important from an economic point of view were the large differences in rates of arrest, conviction, and incarceration between the children who attended Perry Preschool and children in the comparison group. Police and court information indicate that by the age of 28, the Perry children averaged 2.3 arrests. In comparison, children who did not attend preschool averaged 4.6 arrests. The disparity in arrests was even more pronounced among males, with close to 12 percent of the preschool boys having been arrested five or more times compared with 49 percent of the non-preschool boys. The economic value of these differences was huge—more than $90,000 per child.

These various benefits totaled $115,000 per child for taxpayers and $25,000 per child for the participants and their families. Summing these two figures produces the estimated total social benefit of more than $140,000 per child, more than eight times higher than the $16,000 program cost. Indeed, it is precisely these data that produce the often-quoted statement that investing $1 now in early education will provide $8 in benefits later on.

Just because a single, rather intensive program offered to several dozen children appears to provide eight times the volume of benefits relative to costs, there is little reason to expect that all efforts to boost child well-being through early interventions would be as profitable. For one thing, less intensive programs may not make enough of a difference in the children's lives to provide even a fraction of Perry Preschool's benefits. For another, it is very difficult to maintain quality when small programs are scaled up into real-world efforts offered to thousands of children.

The Carolina Abecedarian Program

The Carolina Abecedarian program was a center-based preschool program provided to children at risk of school failure. Between 6 and 12 weeks of age, 112 children were randomly assigned to the program group or a comparison group. The teacher/child ratios were quite low— 1:3 for infants and 1:6 for older children. The center was open five days a week, 10 hours a day, for 50 weeks a year. The curriculum emphasized language development as well as development in other domains. The program provided free transportation as well as medical and nutritional services. Children in the comparison group had access to the same medical and nutritional services (Campbell, Ramey, Pungello, Sparling, & Miller-Johnson, 2002).

The Abecedarian and comparison-group children have been followed through age 21. The evaluation found large and long-lasting differences in children's cognitive development and academic achievement. Masse and Barnett (2003) estimated the Abecedarian program costs and benefits, and we provide a summary of their work in Table 2.2.

This high-quality program had a correspondingly high price tag, with per-year per-child program cost estimates (in 2003 dollars) ranging from less than $11,000 to more than $16,000. Children in the comparison group also participated in center-based child care, although not for as long a time as

Table 2.2
Benefits and Costs of the Chicago Child-Parent Centers and the Abecedarian Program

	Carolina Abecedarian[b]	Chicago Child-Parent Center[a]
Total costs of the program	$ 36,581	$ 7,562
Program benefits		
Reductions in special education and grade retention	9,013	5,505
Increases in publicly funded higher education costs	−8,291	−629
Increases in participants' earnings and employee benefits	38,282	31,369
Increases in maternal earnings	75,080	—
Health Benefits (e.g., reductions in smoking)	18,137	—
Reductions in child abuse/neglect	—	870
Decreases in juvenile and adult crime	—	14,983
Other	200	1,872
Total benefits of the program	$ 138,257	$ 53,968
"Profit" (benefits minus costs)	$ 112,582	$ 46,406

All amounts are expressed in 2003 dollars.

[a] *Source:* Reynolds, Temple, Robertson, & Mann, 2002.

[b] *Source:* Masse & Barnett, 2003.

the Abecedarian children and at less expense. Consequently, the estimated expense of the Abecedarian program for birth through age five—$36,581— amounts to the difference in child care costs between the program and control groups.

Improvements in Abecedarian children's school success yielded savings in expenditures for special education and grade retention of $9,013 per child. However, because Abecedarian children were also more likely to attend postsecondary schooling than comparison children, additional costs of $8,291 per child were incurred in college tuition. Improvements in educational attainment translate into higher earnings in the labor market, and the Abecedarian program's lifetime earnings benefits are estimated at more than $37,000 per child. The provision of stable, high-quality child care also benefited program children's mothers by creating increased employment opportunities and higher earnings. The increases in mothers' earnings are even more substantial—close to $3,750 per year, yielding a total increase in maternal earnings of $75,080.

A survey conducted during adolescence found lower levels of smoking among Abecedarian children (39% vs. 55%). Estimating the economic value of likely decreases in mortality provides an estimate of the economic value for better health behaviors ($18,137). Unlike Perry Preschool, the Abecedarian program did not appear to reduce children's criminal behavior, and so the program does not provide any benefits in this area. Abecedarian's estimated benefits sum to $138,257, a figure quite close to Perry Preschool's total benefits. However, with a marginal cost of $36,581, nearly twice Perry's costs, the cost-benefit accounting suggests that each $1 invested in providing such an intensive and high quality program yielded almost $4 worth of benefits.

Chicago Child–Parent Centers

The Chicago Child–Parent Centers (CPC) program is noteworthy both for its evaluation and for the fact that it is a large-scale early-education program undertaken by the Chicago public schools with federal Title I funds. Twenty-four separate CPC programs were located in or near public schools in the poorest neighborhoods in Chicago. These programs provided educational and family-support services to children between the ages of three and nine (preschool through third grade). The preschool program ran for two-and-a-half hours a day, five days a week during the school year and for six weeks during the summer. The structured curriculum emphasized language and math skills and provided children with diverse learning experiences, including such activities as field trips. The preschools had low staff-to-child ratios (1:8) and well-trained teachers. The centers offered comprehensive services, including health care and food, as well as a strong parent and community outreach component designed to involve parents in their children's schooling, for example, by volunteering in their child's classroom and attending school events. The school-age services included reduced class sizes, a teacher's aide for each class, continued parent and community outreach, as well as extra instructional materials and academic enrichment activities for children.

An evaluation conducted by Reynolds, Temple, Robertson, and Mann (2001) followed a cohort of CPC children and a matched comparison group that entered kindergarten in 1985. The latest data were collected during early adulthood (age 21). The comparison children typically did not attend early-education programs, although a small proportion participated in Head Start. Although the programs provide services through third grade, the evaluation is able to differentiate between the costs and benefits of the preschool component and the follow-on program. Participation in the CPC preschool program had remarkable effects on children. Not only have they experienced better school and labor-market outcomes than the comparison children, but they were also less likely to be victims of child abuse or neglect or to engage in criminal activities.

Reynolds, Temple, Robertson, and Mann (2002) provide a detailed accounting of the program's costs and benefits, and we summarize their main findings in Table 2.2. At $5,505 per child, CPC's savings in the costs of grade retention and special education placement are more modest than for either Perry Preschool or Carolina Abecedarian. However, lower college tuition costs are incurred ($629). The estimated increases in participants' earnings are substantial ($31,369 per child). Reductions in crime were also more modest for CPC children (17% of CPC children vs. 25% of comparison children) than for Perry children, resulting in modest savings for criminal activity ($14,938). The evaluation undertaken by Reynolds and colleagues found that participation in CPC preschools reduced reports of abuse and neglect. CPC children had only half as many substantiated reports of abuse or neglect as comparison children (5% vs. 10%). By reducing administrative and protective custody costs, this difference led to savings of $870 per child.

Estimated at $53,968, the total benefits of the CPC centers are more modest than those of either Carolina Abecedarian or Perry Preschool. However, the program cost considerably less than the other programs, and so the payoff for the investment is nearly on par with Perry Preschool. Each $1 invested in CPC yielded $7 in return.

COMBINED PARENT AND CHILD APPROACHES

Does adding parenting education programs to child-based programs result in additional benefits for children? Unfortunately, the evidence is inconclusive. The fact that the most successful early childhood education programs have included some form of parenting program suggests that the parenting component may contribute to the program's effectiveness. For example, Perry Preschool included weekly home visits to mothers, and in several other programs parental involvement in the classroom was an explicit goal of the program (e.g., Abecedarian, CPC). However, it is difficult to evaluate the relative importance of these parenting components of early childhood education programs. The evaluation studies do not provide much information about parents' participation in the program or about program effects on parenting.

To date, no available studies compare a child education program to the same child education program combined with parenting education. This type of study would provide an important contribution to our knowledge base. What information we do have comes from nonexperimental studies of programs that have combined child and parent programs. Two studies have examined whether early-education programs improved aspects of parenting or parent well-being, and if so whether these program effects were related to the programs' impacts on children. Burchinal, Campbell, Bryant, Wasik, and Ramey (1997) set out to determine whether improvements in either children's home learning environments or parents' authoritarian parenting attitudes accounted for some of the positive impacts of early-education programs on children. Analyses revealed that these programs did not have a positive effect on children's home learning environments or authoritarian attitudes of parents. Consequently, these avenues could not have been responsible for the program's success.

Using data from the Infant Health and Development Program (IHDP), Klebanov, Brooks-Gunn, and McCormick (2001) tried to determine whether reductions in maternal distress and improvements in mothers coping strategies accounted, at least in part, for positive program impacts on children. IHDP included a home-visiting program for mothers during the child's first three years, in addition to an intensive early-education program. The home-visiting program utilized a problem-solving curriculum and emphasized the formation of an emotionally supportive relationship between mothers and the home visitor. Their results indicate that the program had some selective positive effects on mothers. It reduced maternal distress, although it did not improve mothers' coping strategies. Improvements in maternal well-being did not contribute to the program-induced improvements in children's academic achievement or behavior. Although research has not definitively proved that parenting programs do not contribute to the success of early-education programs with respect to children's academic achievement, the bulk of the evidence seems to indicate that it is unlikely that these programs have a positive effect.

In contrast, there is reason to believe that including parent management training in child-based programs for problem behavior yields better results. Parent- and child-based interventions target distinct domains of developmental models of problem behavior, and, for this reason, the treatment is complementary. Child-focused programs improve children's cognitive-behavioral repertoires, whereas parent-training programs ensure that children's prosocial behavior is supported. Two studies have compared the benefits of combined parent and child programs with the benefits of child-only and parent-only programs (Kazdin, Siegal, & Bass, 1992; Webster-Stratton & Hammond, 1997). Results from both studies indicate that although parent-only and child-only programs benefited children, the benefits of the combined approach exceeded that of the other approaches, although neither study formally tested whether program impacts were significantly different.

For example, Kazdin and colleagues' (1992) evaluation of these approaches with children ages 7 to13 found that parental reports of child behavior problems were within a normative range one year after treatment completion only among children whose family was assigned to the combined parent- and child-program. Ongoing evaluations of multicomponent programs, such as the Fast Track prevention program, will yield important information about the ability of these programs to effect long-term change in children's problem behavior (Conduct Problems Prevention Research Group, 2002).

CONCLUSIONS

The years in which children live with parents provide abundant opportunities for parent-focused interventions designed to enhance human potential. We have focused on the extent to which parent-based programs promote children's achievement and positive behavior and have sought to place such programs within the broader context of policy approaches to improving children's well-being.

The indirect nature of parent-focused programs suggests that these programs may yield few success stories. Although the typical parenting education program does appear to have modest effects on parenting practices, it has not demonstrated significant impacts on children's academic achievement. The typical parent management program for parents of children with severe problem behaviors appears to be a more promising avenue of intervention. Some of these programs reduce children's problem behavior, at least in the short term. These programs appear most effective for children rather than adolescents and for families with greater resources. Turning to economic interventions, evidence from recent welfare-to-work programs indicates that increasing the economic resources of low-income families promotes positive achievement and behavior for children, although the effect sizes are modest, and we do not know how long the positive impacts will be maintained.

Interventions targeting young children directly may be the most effective of all at promoting academic achievement and reducing problem behavior. Although a handful of careful studies of very intensive early-education programs support this view, the lamentably small amount of evidence on the payoffs for more practical, less expensive programs leaves us cautious about drawing definitive conclusions regarding the long-term benefits of these programs. Similarly, child-focused problem-behavior interventions, including problem-solving skills training, have resulted in short-term reductions in children's problem behavior. But these programs have not yet proved their long-term worth, and it may be that the combination of parent- and child-based programming is the most effective form of intervention.

There are lessons to be learned from the fact that parenting programs appear more successful in reducing problem behavior than in promoting academic achievement. In particular, screening children and directing services to those with a demonstrated need may be particularly important for producing cost-effective program benefits. However, in order to effectively develop programs, it is necessary to understand the developmental progression of school failure. Remarkably little research addresses the developmental processes that contribute to academic underachievement and more generally establish academic trajectories (Alexander & Entwisle, 1988). With a greater understanding of the processes that determine a child's academic course, intervention services may be better designed and targeted to promote children's academic achievement.

Our preoccupation with the economic aspects of interventions is rooted in a desire to inform policy makers about choices among competing real-world intervention programs as well as "interventions" that alter family resources with tax and transfer policies. Although much more needs to be learned, our tentative conclusion is that the bulk of intervention resources should be focused on child-based, especially preadolescent child-based, programs. It may also make sense to tilt transfer programs explicitly toward families with young children, as the French have done with single-parent benefits that end with the child's third birthday, or that countries could do with age-graded child allowances or tax credits.

Remarkably, a number of careful evaluations have established that intensive early-education programs *can* generate a handsome social profit. Although some of the programs are far too expensive to consider for widespread use, one of them—the Chicago Child–Parent Center program—has actually been implemented at a scale that could serve as a model. We eagerly await evidence on the short-term impacts of the nation's Head Start programs because it will provide a much more definitive look at scaled-up early-education programs.

Although intensive programs appear to have proved their worth, less intensive programs have yet to do so. Therefore it is a mistake to say that evidence from Perry Preschool programs proves that any money spent on early education will provide appreciable social dividends. On the basis of the available evidence, it appears that a more targeted approach, in which intensive programs are aimed directly at children most in need of them, makes the most economic sense. Table 2.3 presents a condensed synopsis of policy-relevant inferences and conclusions from our reviews of the published literature in this area (Duncan & Magnuson, in press).

Table 2.3
Synopsis of Major Inferences about Costs and Benefits of Programmatic Early Interventions from Reviews of Published Literature in Duncan & Magnuson (in press)

1. Expensive preschool interventions that focus on education provide a handsome social profit for disadvantaged children by increasing subsequent school success and reducing problem behavior.

2. School-aged interventions present a mixed picture, with some gains from reducing class size. To date, dropout prevention and job-training programs for adolescents are less successful, especially at enhancing employment or earnings for youth. Similarly, most sexual education or pregnancy-prevention programs have failed to reduce teen birth rates.

3. Intensive mentoring programs appear to be beneficial for adolescents, with some evidence that they improve a range of key outcomes.

4. Although most parenting interventions have failed to substantially improve children's academic outcomes, some of these programs appear to hold promise as an avenue to improve children's behavior problems.

5. Benefits of increases in family income are quite selective: (a) affecting ability and achievement more than behavior or mental or physical health, (b) benefiting younger children more than adolescents, and (c) having the largest impacts in the poorest families.

6. Welfare reforms that increase work and income for poor families promote young children's achievement and positive behavior, but reforms that mandate work *without* supplementing income have no impacts—either positive or negative—on children. Hence, increasing maternal employment does not improve children's achievement *unless* income also increases.

7. Ecologically realistic tests of program effectiveness are required before even the most promising experimental interventions should be widely disseminated.

8. IQ and school achievement are usually touted as primary benefits of intervening early, but "social rates of return" are greatest for health, social behavior, and crime.

9. There is a dearth of rigorous evaluations of Head Start, but recent nonexperimental analyses show long-term behavioral and academic benefits in improving high school graduation rates, increased college attendance, less crime among blacks, and positive "spillover" effects on younger siblings.

REFERENCES

Alexander, K. L., & Entwisle, D. R. (1988). Achievement in the first two years of school: Patterns and processes. *Monographs of the Society for the Research in Child Development, 53*(2, Serial 218).

Blau, D. M. (1999). The effect of income on child development. *Review of Economics and Statistics, 8,* 261–276.

Bradley, S. J., Jadaa, D. A., Brody, J., Landy, S., Tallett, S. E., Watson, W., et al. (2003). Brief psychoeducational parenting program: An evaluation and 1-year follow-up. *Journal of the American Academy of Child & Adolescent Psychiatry, 42*(10), 1171–1178.

Brooks-Gunn, J., Berlin, L. J., & Fuligni, A. (2001). Early childhood intervention programs: What about the family? In S. Meisels and J. Shonkoff (Eds.), *The handbook of early intervention* (2nd ed., pp. 549–588). New York: Cambridge University Press.

Brooks-Gunn, J., & Duncan, G. (1997). The effects of poverty on children and youth. *The Future of Children, 7,* 55–71.

Burchinal, M. R., Campbell, F. A., Bryant, D. M., Wasik, B. H., & Ramey, C. T. (1997). Early intervention and mediating processes in cognitive performance of children of low-income African American families. *Child Development, 68,* 935–954.

Campbell, F. A., Ramey, C. T., Pungello, E., Sparling, J., & Miller-Johnson, S. (2002). Early childhood education: Young adult outcomes from the Abecedarian Project. *Applied Developmental Science, 6*(1), 42–57.

Chambers, J. G., Parrish, T. B., & Harr, J. J. (2004). *What are we spending on special education services in the United States?* Center for Special Education Finance. Retrieved March 4, 2004, from http://csef.air.org/publications/seep/national/AdvRpt1.PDF

Collins, W. A., Maccoby, E. E., Steinberg, L., Hetherington, E. M., & Bornstein, M. H. (2000). Contemporary research on parenting: The case for nurture and nature. *American Psychologist, 55,* 218–232.

Conduct Problems Prevention Research Group. (2002). Evaluation of the first three years of the Fast Track Prevention Trial with children at high risk for adolescent conduct problems. *Journal of Abnormal Child Psychology, 30*(1), 19-35..

DeGarmo, D. S., Patterson, G. R., & Forgatch, M. S. (2004). How do outcomes in a specified parent training intervention maintain or wane over time? *Prevention Science, 5*(2), 73–89.

Dishion, T. J., & Patterson, G. R. (1992). Age effects in parent training outcome. *Behavior Therapy, 23,* 719–729.

Dumas, J. E. (1989). Treating anti-social behavior in children: Child and family approaches. *Clinical Psychology Review, 9,* 197–222.

Duncan, G., & Brooks-Gunn, J. (Eds.). (1997). *Consequences of growing up poor.* New York: Russell Sage.

Duncan, G., Brooks-Gunn, J., Yeung, J., & Smith, J. (1998). How much does childhood poverty affect the life chances of children? *American Sociological Review, 63,* 406–423.

Duncan, G., & Magnuson, K. (in press). Can society profit from investing in early education programs? In A. Tarlov (Ed.), *Nurturing the national treasure: Childhood education and development before kindergarten..* New York: Palgrave Macmillan.

Duncan, G., & Magnuson, K. (2004). Individual and parent-based intervention strategies for promoting human capital and positive behavior. In P. L. Chase-Lansdale, K. Kiernan, & R. Friedman (Eds.), *Human development across lives and generations: The potential for change* (pp. 209–235). Cambridge: Cambridge University Press.

Durlak, J.A., Fuhrman, T., & Lampman, C. (1991). Effectiveness of cognitive-behavioral therapy for maladapting children: A meta-analysis. *Psychological Bulletin, 2,* 204–214.

Gennetian, L., Duncan, G., Knox, V.W., Vargas, W., Clark-Kaufman, E., & London, A.S. (2002). *How welfare and work policies for parents affect adolescents.* New York: Manpower Demonstration Research Corporation.

Gomby, D.S., Culross, P.L., & Behrman, R.E. (1999). Home visiting: Recent program evaluations analysis and recommendations. *The Future of Children, 9*(1), 4–26.

Gramlich, E. (1990). *A guide to cost-benefit analysis.* Englewood Cliffs, NJ: Prentice-Hall.

Greenberg, M., Domitrovich, C., & Bumbarger, B. (2001).The prevention of mental disorders in school-aged children: Current state of the field. *Prevention & Treatment, 4,* Article 1..

Haveman, R., & Wolfe, B. (1995). The determinants of children's attainments: A review of methods and findings. *Journal of Economic Literature, 23,* 1829–1878.

Institute for Research on Poverty. (1976). *The rural income maintenance experiment.* Madison: University of Wisconsin, Author.

Karoly, L.A., Greenwood, P.W., Everingham, S.S., Houbé, J., Kilburn, M.R., Rydell, C., et al. (1998). *Investing in our children: What we know and don't know about the costs and benefits of early childhood interventions.* Santa Monica, CA: RAND.

Kazdin, A.E. (1997). Parent management training: Evidence, outcomes, and issues. *Journal of the American Academy of Child and Adolescent Psychiatry, 36,* 1349–1356.

Kazdin, A.E., Siegal, T.C., & Bass, D. (1992). Cognitive problem-solving skills training and parent management training in the treatment of anti-social behavior in children. *Journal of Consulting and Clinical Psychology, 60,* 733–747.

Kazdin, A., & Weisz, J.R. (1998). Identifying and developing empirically supported child and adolescent treatments. *Journal of Consulting and Clinical Psychology, 66,* 19–36.

Kershaw, D., & Fair, J. (1976). *The New Jersey Income Maintenance Experiment* (Vol. 1). New York: Academic Press.

Klebanov, P.K., Brooks-Gunn, J., & McCormick, M.C. (2001). Maternal coping strategies and emotional distress: Results of an early intervention program for low birth weight young children. *Developmental Psychology, 37,* 654–667.

Levin, H. (1983). *Cost effectiveness: A primer.* Beverly Hills, CA: Sage.

Masse, L.N., & Barnett, W.S. (2003). *A benefit cost analysis of the Abecedarian Early Childhood Intervention.* National Institute for Early Education Research, Rutgers University. Retrieved March 4, 2004, from http://nieer.org/resources/research/AbecedarianStudy.pdf

Mayer, S. (1997). *What money can't buy: The effect of parental income on children's outcomes.* Cambridge, MA: Harvard University Press.

McGroder, S. (2000). Parenting among low-income African American single mothers with preschool-age children: Patterns, predictors, and developmental correlates. *Child Development, 71,* 752–771.

McLoyd, V. (1990). The impact of economic hardship on black children and families: Psychological distress, parenting, and socio-emotional development. *Child Development, 61,* 311–346.

McLoyd, V. (1998). Socioeconomic disadvantage and child development. *American Psychologist, 53,* 185–204.

Miller, T., Cohen, M., & Wiersema, B. (1996). *Victim costs and consequences: A new look.* Washington, DC: U.S. Department of Justice, National Institute of Justice.

Morris, P.A., Huston, A.C., Duncan, G.J., Crosby, D.A., & Bos, J.M. (2001). *How welfare and work policies affect children: A synthesis of research.* New York: Manpower Demonstration Research Corporation.

Olds, D., Henderson, C.R., Kitzman, H.J., Eckenrode, J.J., Cole, R.E., & Tatelbaum, R.C. (1999). Prenatal and infancy home visitation by nurses: Recent findings. *The Future of Children, 9,* 44–65.

Owen, M.T., & Mulvihill, B.A. (1994). Benefits of a parent education and support program in the first three years. *Family Relations, 43,* 206–212.

Patterson, G.R., DeBaryshe, B.D., & Ramsey, E. (1989). A developmental perspective on anti-social behavior. *American Psychologist, 44,* 329–335.

Reynolds, A.J., Temple, J.A., Robertson, D.L., & Mann, E.A. (2001). Long term effects of an early childhood intervention on educational achievement and juvenile arrest: A 15 year follow-up of low income children in public schools. *Journal of the American Medical Association, 285,* 2339–2346.

Reynolds, A.J., Temple, J.A., Robertson, D.L., & Mann, E.A. (2002). *Age 21 cost-benefit analysis of the Title 1 Chicago Child–Parent Centers.* Discussion paper retrieved March 4, 2004, from University of Wisconsin-Madison, Institute for Research on Poverty (1245–02) Web site: http://www.ssc.wisc.edu/irp/pubs/dp124502.pdf

Ruma, P.R., Burke, R.V., & Thompson, R.W. (1996). Group parent training: Is it effective for parents of all ages? *Behavior Therapy, 27,* 159–169.

Salkind, N.J., & Haskins, R. (1982). Negative income tax: The impact on children from low-income families. *Journal of Family Issues, 3,* 165–180.

Scarr, S. (1992). Developmental theories for the 1990s: Development and individual differences. *Child Development, 63,* 1–19.

Schweinhart, L.J., Barnes, H.V., & Weikart, D.P. (1993). *Significant benefits: The High/Scope Perry Preschool Study through age 27.* Ypsilanti, MI: High/Scope Educational Research Foundation.

Seitz, V., & Provence, S. (1990). Caregiver-focused models of early intervention. In S.J. Meisels & J.P. Shonkoff (Eds.), *Handbook of early childhood intervention* (pp. 400–427. New York: Cambridge University Press.

Shadish, W.R., Cook, T., & Campbell, D.T. (2002). *Experimental and quasi-experimental designs for generalized causal inference.* New York: Houghton Mifflin.

Shonkoff, J.P., & Phillips, D.A. (Eds.). (2000). *From neurons to neighborhoods: The science of early childhood development.* Washington, DC: National Academy Press.

Stormshak, E.A., Kaminski, R.A., & Goodman, M.R. (2002). Enhancing the parenting skills of Head Start families during the transition to kindergarten. *Prevention Science, 3*(3), 223–234.

Sweet, M., & Appelbaum, M.I. (2004). Is home visiting an effective strategy? A meta-analytic review of home visiting programs for families with young children. *Child Development, 75,* 1435–1456.

Taylor, T.K., & Biglan, A. (1998). Behavioral family interventions for improving child-rearing: A review of the literature for clinicians and policy makers. *Clinical Child & Family Psychology Review, 1*(1), 41–60.

Trickett, P.K., Aber, L.J., & Carlson, V. (1991). Relationship of socioeconomic status to the etiology and developmental sequelae of physical child abuse. *Developmental Psychology, 37,* 148–158.

U.S. Department of Health and Human Services. (1983). *Overview of the Seattle-Denver Income Maintenance Experiment and final report.* Washington, DC: Author.

Wagner, M.M., & Clayton, S.L. (1999). The Parents as Teachers program: Results from two demonstrations. *The Future of Children, 9*(1), 91–115.

Webster-Stratton, C. (1990). Long-term follow-up with young conduct problem children: From preschool to grade school. *Journal of Clinical Child Psychology, 19,* 144–149.

Webster-Stratton, C., & Hammond, M. (1990). Predictors of treatment outcomes in parenting training with conduct problem children. *Behavior Therapy, 21,* 319–337.

Webster-Stratton, C., & Hammond, M. (1997). Treating children with early onset conduct problems: A comparison of child and parent training interventions. *Journal of Consulting and Clinical Psychology, 65,* 93–109.

Webster-Stratton, C., Kolpacoff, M., & Hollinsworth, T. (1988). Self-administered videotape therapy for families with conduct problem children: Comparison with two cost-effective treatments and a control group. *Journal of Consulting and Clinical Psychology, 56,* 558–566.

Webster-Stratton, C., & Spitzer, A. (1996). Parenting a young child with conduct problems: New insights using qualitative methods. In T.H. Ollendick & R.J. Prinz (Eds.), *Advances in clinical child psychology* (pp. 1–62). New York: Plenum Press.

Yoshikawa, H. (1994). Prevention as cumulative protection: Effects of early family support and education as chronic delinquency and its risk. *Psychological Bulletin, 115,* 28–54.

Chapter 3

HOUSING POLICY *IS* SCHOOL POLICY

David Rusk

Let us look at recent report cards for two schools in metro Buffalo, New York. In state English, math, and science exams, Harris Hill Elementary School in suburban Clarence Center remarkably ranked first in all three subjects among the region's 113 elementary schools. Buffalo Elementary School of Technology was ranked last. What was the difference? Was a lot more money spent per pupil in Harris Hill? No. As a matter of fact, per-pupil expenditures in Buffalo City District were 15 percent higher than in Clarence Central District. Were class sizes smaller at Harris Hill? No. Technology had a 25 percent lower pupil/teacher ratio than did Harris Hill. The big difference was that only 7 percent of Harris Hill pupils came from low-income families. By contrast, the proportion of low-income children at Technology was 81 percent. In short, Harris Hill's kids were overwhelmingly middle class (and upper middle class at that). Technology's kids were overwhelmingly poor. It made a world of difference.

SCHOOL SUCCESS AND FAMILY INCOME

The impact of the socioeconomic background of schoolchildren's families on academic outcomes was first documented by James Coleman in *Equality of Educational Opportunity* (1966), a massive study of U.S. schools. For almost 40 years there has been no more consistent finding of educational research: The most powerful predictors of educational success or failure are family income and parents' educational attainment. That certainly holds true for schoolchildren in Buffalo-Erie County's 113 elementary schools (divided between 28 different school districts). Each school's percentage of low-income children explained from 75 percent of the school-by-school variation in math scores to 87 percent of the variation in English scores. What was the explanatory influence statistically of expenditures per pupil (that vary within a 50% range)? Zero. And how much influence could be attributed statistically to variations in pupil-teacher ratios, ranging from 10.4 pupils per teacher (Buffalo's PS 72) to 20.8 (West Seneca's West Elementary)? Again, zero.

Spending more money and having smaller class sizes in school A than in school B would probably produce somewhat better results for school A when both pupil populations have almost identical socioeconomic backgrounds. But when there are significant socioeconomic disparities, the effects of poverty and low parental education just wipe out other factors.

Discovering this phenomenon is not rocket science, though some rocket scientists from the Rand Corporation have weighed in with a recent study. The Rand study found that "the most critical factors associated with the educational achievement of children ... appear to be socioeconomic ones. These factors include parental education levels, neighborhood poverty, parental occupation status, and family income" (Lara-Cinisomo et al., 2004).

In this era of the school accountability movement, however, we do not need the Rand Corporation with its PhD researchers and mainframe computer banks to do such a study. All the information we need is right on the Internet: annual school-by-school report cards that anyone can copy and plug into a spreadsheet with a standard regression analysis package that can be analyzed without employing the Rand Corporation. I am not trained as a professional educational researcher, but I have done such analyses many times to make a point for my audiences. To illustrate, a correlation of 1.00 means an absolute and unvarying rate of change between a dependent variable (e.g., test scores) and an independent variable (e.g., socioeconomic status). Computerized archives revealed that the correlation between a school's percentage of socioeconomically advantaged pupils and standardized test scores was:

- 0.77 for each school's percentage of students that achieved proficient and advanced levels on third, fourth, and fifth grade reading, writing, and math tests of the Colorado School Assessment Program (CSAP) for 2000, 2001, and 2002 in all 391 public elementary schools in metro Denver's 17 school districts.
- 0.74 for the fourth grade battery of Connecticut Mastery Tests (CMT) for all 518 elementary schools in 149 school districts in the state of Connecticut in 2000–2001; the correlation between CMT scores and five school-based independent variables (average class size, pupil-staff ratio, average years of teacher experience, percentage of teachers with master's degrees, and percentage of noncertified teachers) was 0.04.

- 0.87 for fourth grade test scores for 22 elementary schools in the Alachua County Public Schools (Gainesville, Florida) in 1994–1996; the correlation between test scores and three school-based independent variables (expenditures per pupil, average class size, and percentage of teachers with more than 10 years of experience) was 0.46, seemingly very explanatory as well until one realizes that spending more per pupil and smaller class sizes were *negatively* related to pupil performance. (Clearly, with federal aid targeted on low-income pupils, greater spending and smaller classes were simply proxies for the pupils' low socioeconomic status.)

- 0.65 for third grade test scores at 51 elementary schools in 1991 and 0.62 for third and fourth grade test scores at 61 elementary schools in 34 school districts in the three-county Peoria-Pekin, Illinois, area in 1996.

- 0.85 for the battery of ISTEP tests for all grades in 16 Lake County, Indiana (Gary-Hammond-East Chicago), school districts (plus statewide averages) in 1998–1999; 0.85 for percentage of students achieving math and English standards in 1998–1999; and 0.89 for SAT scores in 1998–1999. The correlations between two school-based inputs (expenditures per pupil and average teacher salary) and these three academic "outputs" were –0.09, –0.09, and –0.05 (all *negatively* related so they were proxies for socioeconomic status as well).

- 0.81 for three-year average composite results of second and fourth grade math and reading scores on the Comprehensive Test of Basic Skills in 373 elementary schools of the seven school districts of Baltimore, Maryland, in 2000–2002.

- 0.82 for three-year average composite results of second and fourth grade math and reading scores on the Comprehensive Test Basic Skills in 125 elementary schools of the Montgomery County, Maryland, Public Schools (the 13th wealthiest county in the United States) in 2000–2002.

- 0.50 for four-year average composite results of fourth and fifth grade reading, writing, math, and science exams of the Michigan Educational Assessment Program (MEAP) at 483 elementary schools in an 18-county area of southwestern Michigan from 1994 to 1998. That region of the state included many schools in farming communities where nominal family cash incomes were low (thereby qualifying more children for subsidized meals), but parental educational attainment was relatively high. (That same phenomenon was at work in farming communities of the three-county Peoria-Pekin, Illinois, area. Children from family-owned farms score higher than their family's income level would predict if they were from urban settings.)

- 0.75 for eight-year composite results for third graders and 0.78 for eight-year composite results for fifth graders on the Iowa Test of Basic Skills battery in 78 elementary schools of the Albuquerque, New Mexico, Public Schools from 1983–1984 to 1991–1992.

- 0.77 for three-year average pass rate of fourth graders on a five-test battery at 110 elementary schools in the three-county Toledo, Ohio, area from 1999 to 2001. The correlation between two school-based inputs (total expenditures per pupil and average teacher salary) and academic "output" was 0.41, which implies successful strategic deployment of scarce public resources; however, higher per-pupil expenditures were negatively associated with test scores, and greater proportions of low-income pupils were associated with lower teacher salaries.

- 0.67 for two-year averages in fifth grade math and reading scores for 43 elementary schools (in 16 school districts) of York County, Pennsylvania, in 2000–2002.

- 0.66 for three-year averages on the Texas Academic Achievement System (TAAS) tests for 189 school districts in the five largest metro areas of Texas (Austin, Dallas, Fort Worth, Houston, and San Antonio) in 1994–1997.

- 0.75 for three-year averages for achieving Advanced and Proficient (A&P) thresholds on the five-test battery for fourth graders in 60 elementary schools in Dane County (Madison) Wisconsin, in 1999–2001. At the level of the 16 school districts, the correlation between the district's percentage of low-income pupils and A&P-level performance was –0.67; the correlation between test performance and two school-based inputs (education cost per pupil and pupil-teacher ratio) was –0.18. The association of higher expenditures per pupil and smaller class sizes with lower test performance demonstrates again that more money and smaller class sizes flow toward lower-income pupils because of federal mandates for education aid.

- 0.80 for four-year averages in achieving Advanced and Proficient (A&P) thresholds in third and fourth grade reading at 43 elementary schools in eight school districts in Brown County (Green Bay), Wisconsin, in 2000–2004.

My 14 studies (amid scores of such analyses done by others) are cited to hammer home a point. All consistently document one of James Coleman's central findings: "The educational resources that a child's classmates bring to school are more important than the educational resources that the school board provides." So important are fellow students, the report found, that "the social composition of the student body is more highly related to achievement, independent of the student's own social background, than is any school factor" (Kahlenberg, 2001, p.26).

POOR CITIES/POOR SCHOOLS

I have been a speaker and consultant in more than 100 metro areas. In about half of them, the proportion of poor children in the central city school district is more than 60 percent. From Allentown to Youngstown, from smallish Muskegon to giant New York City, the stories I hear always seem the same: "The city schools are terrible.... The school board is always fighting.... Superintendents come and go constantly.... We must fix the city schools before the city can make a comeback."

After several dozen repetitions, one begins to suspect these complaints are just symptoms, not causes. The *primary* cause is the high concentration of poverty in city schools. The schools must grapple with the various problems and minimal home support that many poor children bring to school.

Does Money Solve the Problem?

Perhaps we just are not spending enough extra money, many school reformers argue. Even in New Jersey, where the state supreme court in *Abbott v. Burke* ordered state government to spend $7.3 billion to rebuild school facilities in 30 poverty-impacted, urban school districts, court-ordered annual per-pupil expenditures are only 35 percent higher in the *Abbott* districts than in New Jersey's 519 other districts. Reform advocates contend that much more must be spent to overcome the complex, negative environment of poverty-impacted schools.

Well, how about spending almost twice as much money? In 2000–2001, I served as an itinerant visiting professor of urban planning at the University of Amsterdam. In the context of carrying out a study for the Dutch government on sprawl and segregation, I learned a good deal about the Dutch educational system (Rusk, 2001). Since 1919, the Dutch national government provides 100 percent of the funding not only for all nonsectarian public schools, but also for all Catholic, Protestant, Jewish, Muslim, and other private schools. Moreover, all parents are constitutionally guaranteed total freedom of choice in where to send their children to school.

Recognizing the special problems that low-income children must often overcome, the national funding formula provides a 25 percent bonus per student for "low-income" ethnic Dutch students (so-called 1.25 students) and a 90 percent bonus per student for "low-income" ethnic minority students (so-called 1.90 students), whose parents have emigrated primarily from Turkey, Morocco, Suriname, and the Netherlands Antilles.

In the United States, conservative reformers now champion "school choice" to provide tax-supported vouchers for low-income children to attend both private nonsectarian and private religious schools. The controversies that wrack the U.S. political scene about tax-funded vouchers, freedom of choice, and tax support for religious educational institutions have been settled public policy in the Netherlands for almost a century.

School choice is hardly the cure-all that U.S. conservatives envision. When compared to their closest U.S. counterparts, neighborhoods in Dutch metropolitan areas are about as ethnically segregated as neighborhoods in similar U.S. metropolitan areas. However, Dutch neighborhoods are substantially less *economically* segregated than U.S. neighborhoods because of the widespread dispersion of "social housing." (Social housing accounts for about 40 percent of the Dutch housing supply, whereas less than 5 percent of the U.S. housing supply is dedicated to "public housing" and federal housing vouchers.)

After all parental "choices" about where their children attend school are sorted out, Dutch *schools* are substantially more segregated than the norm for Dutch *neighborhoods* and even more segregated—both ethnically and economically—than their U.S. counterparts. This has led to the emergence of so-called black schools (i.e., majority low-income immigrant schools) in several larger Dutch cities. Academic performance at black schools is particularly low and resistant to the influence of more funds. Most recent Dutch educational research confirms similar socioeconomic effects as in the United States. In effect, the benefits Dutch society gains from having more economically integrated neighborhoods are substantially nullified by having more economically segregated schools.

A recent report by the Dutch Court of Audit concluded that it is unclear whether or not an annual expenditure of 1.2 billion guilders in compensatory education for 1.25 and 1.90 students has had any positive impact. Educational goals are not clearly established, nor are adequate administrative controls in effect, the Court of Audit complained. After 35 different evaluation studies over the course of two decades, the court concluded, the results of substantial compensatory funding are unclear.

In the United States, "education reform is out there trying to make 'separate but equal' work." Progressives have embraced a variety of modest steps: reducing class size, adopting voluntary national standards, ending social promotion, ensuring better teacher training, promoting so-called charter schools, and equalizing state school funding. However, "increased spending on school inputs has not been shown to be an effective way to improve student achievement in most instances" (Burtless, 1996, p.40).

What Can Be Done?

What can be done is to pay serious attention to the second major finding of James Coleman's monumental study four decades ago: Poor children learn best when surrounded by middle-class classmates. My own studies of several metro areas have shown that:

- in an Albuquerque study of 1,108 individual pupils, the average pupil from a public-housing household increased Iowa Test of Basic Skills scores by 0.22 percentile point for every 1 percent increase in middle-class classmates (Rusk & Mosley, 1994); the difference between a public-housing child's attending Cochiti Elementary (80 percent low-income classmates) and that child's attending John Baker Elementary (80 percent middle-class classmates) would be, on average, a 13 percentile improvement in the child's ITBS ranking;

- in a study of 373 elementary schools in metropolitan Baltimore, for every 1 percent increase in middle-class classmates, a low-income pupil's scores improved, on average, 0.18 percentile point on the Comprehensive Test of Basic Skills (Rusk, 2003); the difference between a low-income pupil's attending Mosher Elementary in Baltimore City (80 percent low-income classmates) and that child's attending Rivera Beach Elementary in Anne Arundel County (80 percent middle-class classmates) would be, on average, an 11 percentile improvement in the child's CTBS ranking;

- in a study of 186 school districts in the five largest metro areas of Texas, for every 1 percent increase in middle class pupils, low-income pupils increase their chances of achieving a passing rate on the Texas state exams (Texas Assessment of Academic Skills, or TAAS) by 0.27 percentile point (Rusk, 1998); the difference between a low-income child's attending a typical elementary school in the Southside Independent School District (80 percent low-income classmates) and a typical elementary school in suburban Alamo Heights Independent School District (80 percent middle-class classmates), on average, would be a 16 percentage point improvement in their chances of achieving a passing rate in TAAS; and

- in a study of 60 elementary schools in Madison-Dane County, for every 1 percent increase in middle-class classmates, the average low-income fourth grade pupil's likelihood of achieving Advanced or Proficient levels on the state WINSS tests improved 0.64 percentage point in reading; 0.50 percentile point in language; 0.72 percentage point in math; 0.80 percentage point in science; and 0.74 percentage point in social studies (Rusk, 2002). In other words, the difference between a low-income pupil's attending a school with only 45 percent middle-class classmates (e.g., Lincoln or Mendota) and that pupil's attending a school with 85 percent middle-class classmates (e.g., Crestwood or Northside) would typically be a 20 to 32 percentage point improvement in that low-income pupil's probability of achieving A&P thresholds.

In September 2002 the Century Foundation issued *Divided We Fail,* the report of its Task Force on the Common School (Kahlenberg, 2002). Chaired by former U.S. Senator and Connecticut Governor Lowell P. Weicker, Jr., the

Task Force was composed of two dozen distinguished educators, researchers, civil rights attorneys, and former public officials. I served as a member of the task force and wrote one of the studies, "Trends in School Segregation," that it commissioned. The task force report was drafted by Richard D. Kahlenberg, its staff director, and author of *All Together Now: Creating Middle-Class Schools through Public School Choice* (2001). The task force's report deserved far more public attention than it received. I cannot do better by the issue than to quote extensively the report's introductory words:

> Nearly forty years ago, Alabama Governor George Wallace declared in his inaugural address, "Segregation today, segregation tomorrow, segregation forever." Today, almost no American would embrace what was once the reigning ethos, but the everyday reality lived by millions of schoolchildren is not too far from Wallace's vision. No longer segregated by law, our nation's schools are increasingly segregated in fact—both by race and ethnicity and, increasingly, by economic class. Our nation made great strides to eradicate segregated schooling from the early 1970s to the mid-1980s, but since then we have seen increasing racial and economic segregation, and almost no one—from either political party—has articulated a clear plan for addressing this disastrous trend.
>
> The past twenty years have seen an explosion of education policy debates, over issues ranging from raising academic standards to lowering class size, from improving teacher training to promoting after-school programs. But current discussions largely ignore the central source of school inequality: segregation by race and class. All of history suggests that separate schools, particularly for poor and middle-class children, are inherently unequal. A child growing up in a poor family has reduced life chances, but attending a school with large numbers of low-income classmates poses a second, independent strike against him or her. While some look at the link between poverty and achievement and conclude that failure is inevitable, the members of the Task Force believe that poor children, given the right environment in school, can achieve at very high levels.
>
> There exists today a solid consensus among researchers that school segregation perpetuates failure, and an equally durable consensus among politicians that nothing much can be done about it. Education reformers take as a given that schools will reflect residential segregation by class and race and therefore any solutions are narrowly conceived to make separate schools more equal. We believe that this approach is seriously flawed. (Kahlenberg, 2002, p.11)

Written for a national audience, this introduction, it seems to me, aptly characterizes our self-created national educational failure. In 1954, the U.S. Supreme Court (the Warren Court) unanimously (9–0) declared that racial school segregation was unconstitutional in its epochal *Brown v. Board of Education.* Just 20 years later, in 1974, a bitterly divided U.S.

Supreme Court (the Burger Court), by 5–4 vote in *Milliken v. Bradley,* declared that suburban school districts had no obligation to cooperate with central city districts in areawide racial desegregation plans unless each suburban district could be proven to have intentionally segregated. Twenty-one years after that, in 1995, the U.S. Supreme Court (the Rehnquist Court) by 5–4 vote in *Missouri v. Jenkins* rejected state responsibility for segregation in schools and neighborhoods; the court placed the blame for the deterioration and segregation of city schools on "normal pattern[s] of human migration." The majority opinion never discussed the history of housing discrimination, lending bias, public-housing construction, federal home loan mortgage practices, exclusionary zoning, or other governmental causes of racial and economic segregation. But as legal scholar John A. Powell has written, "The efforts of the federal courts to treat housing and school segregation as independent are counterfactual. State courts and policy makers, however, are not bound by the federal approach to segregated schools and housing. Policy makers have it within their power to address the interrelationship of housing and education" (Powell, Kearney, & Kay, 2001, p.19).

Housing policy *is* school policy. Over the last 30 years, whereas housing barriers based on race have been slowly coming down, housing barriers based on income have been steadily going up. In most U.S. housing markets, Jim Crow by income is replacing Jim Crow by race. As a result, schools are more economically segregated than ever before.

The next section will explore what local school boards, as state-authorized policy makers, can achieve to create greater economic integration—the heart of the matter. It will explore briefly what three communities (La Crosse, Wisconsin; Wake County, North Carolina; and Cambridge, Massachusetts) have done. Then I will model the degree of economic integration that could be achieved if local school boards within two major metropolitan areas (Denver and Baltimore) would pursue socioeconomic (SES) integration policies within each school district.

THREE EXAMPLES OF ECONOMIC SCHOOL INTEGRATION

Each of these case studies is developed in greater detail in *Divided We Fail* (Kahlenberg, 2002). I have edited them substantially to reduce their length yet retain what I believe is the core of the story. However, whenever I felt that any paraphrasing of mine would not improve upon the original authors' words, I have included such sections without quotation marks, reserving those for important statements of local officials, educators, and parents.

La Crosse, Wisconsin (Mial, 2002)

La Crosse is a city of 52,000, surrounded by a suburban area of about 37,000. Hemmed in by the Mississippi River on the west (forming the Wisconsin state line) and suburban townships along the bluffs to the east, the city has annexed land modestly; since about 1970, the city's population has been stagnant, and new subdivisions, shopping malls, and office complexes rose exclusively in its suburbs.

The region had few minorities until a large immigration of Hmong refugees from Vietnam occurred in the 1980s. The Hmongs were better known as the Montagnards, the hill peoples of Laos who were staunch U.S. allies during the Vietnam War. By 2000, the La Crosse area was still 94 percent Anglo, but two-thirds of all minorities and almost 70 percent of Asians lived within the city of La Crosse. The records of the La Crosse Hmong Mutual Assistance Association showed 3,491 Hmong residents of La Crosse County rather than the 2,282 reported by the 2000 Census. Suburbanization of more affluent families and concentration of low-income minorities in the city brought city per capita income down to 76 percent of suburban levels by 1999.

In the La Crosse public schools, however, minorities were proportionally greater; in October 2000, there were 1,070 Asian students (13.9 percent), 255 black students (3.3 percent), 85 Native Americans (1.1 percent), and 73 Hispanic students (0.95 percent). Anglo students made up 80 percent of the total 7,605 students in the district.

By the late 1980s, school leaders were worried about concentrations of low-income students (often minority) that were developing. Districtwide, 30 percent of students qualified for free lunches. However, in 1991–1992, Jefferson Elementary had 69 percent and Hamilton Elementary had 63 percent qualifying for free lunches. By contrast, State Road School in an affluent neighborhood had only 4.8 percent.

Faced with the need to redistrict because of the construction of two new elementary schools to meet the rising, immigration-driven enrollment, Superintendent Richard Swantz and his staff saw an opportunity to correct the big poverty imbalances in La Crosse's elementary schools. In May 1991, school board members approved 10 guidelines for redistricting, including "redistricting shall attempt to establish a socio-economic percentage of poverty students in each school that represents the district's average; ...when re-assigning students to achieve a socio-economic balance, an attempt shall be made to place them in the closest school."

Realizing that achieving a 30 percent target in each school would be impossible, school officials set a goal of a range from 15 percent to

45 percent low-income students in each school. Under the proposed plan, 45 percent of the district's 3,700 elementary school students would have to be bused to another school for the 1992–1993 school year.

After months of deliberations and three public hearings, on January 7, 1992, the La Crosse School Board voted 8–1 to approve the plan to achieve socioeconomic (SES) balance in its 11 elementary schools through boundary changes and busing. On January 22, a group named the Recall Alliance announced that it would soon begin collecting signatures for the recall of board members that supported the plan and that a new board would fire Superintendent Swantz. A countergroup, the Coalition for Children, was formed the next day. At the regular election already scheduled for April, two pro-plan incumbents were defeated and a third did not stand for reelection. All were replaced by busing opponents.

With the recall campaign heating up, *The New York Times, Washington Post, Boston Globe,* news magazines, and TV networks descended on La Crosse. They broadcasted far and wide the news that, on July 14, three incumbents were defeated and replaced by busing opponents. Then the national news media disappeared and failed to report (to borrow radio commentator Paul Harvey's phrase) "the rest of the story."

First, the new board could not fire Superintendent Swantz, whose contract had been extended for three years by the old board with a $250,000 buy-out provision. Second, with school about to begin, the board found that rolling back the busing plan would be too disruptive. They contented themselves with adding a choice provision to the plan. Any parent who did not want to send a child to a different school for SES balance could opt out. Fewer than 200 (of the 1,700 chosen for reassignment) refused the new assignment under the parental choice option during the first year. All but two schools met the SES targets that first year. Third, most remarkably, just nine months after the recall election, in April 1993, three anti-busing board members were defeated and were replaced by two members of Coalition for Children and a Hmong candidate (who supported the SES balance plan)—the first Hmong elected to public office in La Crosse.

Fourth, the busing plan progressed. Most parents and children adjusted to their new schools. As one board member said, "People got to experience it, that it wasn't awful. Moving to different schools wasn't awful. Leaving your neighborhood school wasn't awful. The kids benefited from it. People backed off. The staff at all the different schools made sure that it worked." Fifth, public support for the SES balance plan has grown. In 1994, just two years after the recall election, 60 percent of district residents surveyed said they favored "the idea of attempting SES balance in the schools" and 29 percent said they opposed it. In a follow-up survey in April 2001, 64 percent favored SES balance; only 21 percent were opposed.

Finally, SES balance has been an academic success. La Crosse has a fairly high poverty rate with only Milwaukee County and two Native American reservations higher in Wisconsin. Yet, according to former Superintendent Swantz, the district's test scores are at 83 percent of the national average.

In 1992, La Crosse was in the forefront of a movement to look at the impact of SES balance in the schools and to create schools in which the majority of students were middle class with middle-class education values. However, parents were allowed to use school choice to opt out of the program, making SES balance potentially more difficult to achieve. Demographic changes over the years allowed some schools to slip back to high percentages of low-income students, and Hamilton School's small and dense attendance made that school's income makeup particularly difficult to change. The impact of La Crosse's socioeconomic balance plan was immediately evident in metropolitan segregation indexes (that cover seven school districts) in the mid-1990s as well as the slow erosion since then because of parents opting out and continuing neighborhood changes. Table 3.1 lists annual averages for three time periods and a transition year. An economic segregation index of 4 for 1992–1993 (the first year of the plan) is so low that it raises the possibility of missing data. The impact of the La Crosse district's changing enrollment policies is reflected in declining metropolitan segregation trends both economically and socially.

La Crosse's new superintendent, Thomas C. Downs, sums up La Crosse's continuing challenge, "We've got to do what we need to do to support socioeconomic balance. It raises the achievement of the lower-income kids and doesn't in any way hurt the achievement of the more advantaged kids. I believe that it's a higher value for me now."

Wake County, North Carolina (Silberman, 2002)

With 105,000 students, Wake County Public Schools is one of the nation's premier "big box" school systems. It has also been one of the nation's most racially integrated systems since local officials merged the county school system with the separate Raleigh city system in 1974 and instituted a countywide policy of busing and magnet schools to achieve racial balance. By 1999, however, Wake County school officials could see the handwriting on the wall regarding their explicit student assignment policies to promote racial balance. The federal Fourth Circuit Court of Appeals (which includes the Raleigh area) was moving to strike the racially based assignment policies in Arlington County, Virginia, and Montgomery County, Maryland. In the adjacent circuit court district, the federal judge was dismantling Charlotte-Mecklenburg's racial balance

Table 3.1
Average Segregation Indexes for La Crosse, Wisconsin, over Time

	Segregation Index	
Period	Low-Income	Asian
1988–92	33	61
1992–93	4	35
1993–95	21	40
1995–99	27	41

plan that had been implemented since the historic *Swann v. Charlotte-Mecklenburg School District* case in which the U.S. Supreme Court first authorized districtwide busing to achieve racial balance.

Reflecting on a tense meeting seeking a workable alternative, one school official recalls: "What I remember most intensely was that a number of people would say, 'It makes us sick to our stomachs because we are walking away from 20 years of doing something that had been good for the school system and good for the community.'" A legal analysis summarized the evolving new federal judicial policy:

> In essence, the new decisions forbid all school boards (unless they are operating under federal desegregation decrees) from considering race or ethnicity as they assign children to public schools. The prohibition holds even if it leads to desegregated schools, even if most parents desire their children to attend racially diverse schools, and even if school boards are acting in good faith to ensure that students receive the educational benefits that may come from a diverse school environment.

School leaders had reviewed extensive local and national research regarding the linkage between socioeconomic status and educational achievement. They decided to replace the system of student assignment to achieve racial balance with a system of student assignment to achieve socioeconomic balance. For the 1999–2000 school year, the school board adopted new student assignment criteria designed to assure that no school would have more than 40 percent low-income pupils or more than 25 percent of students with low academic performance levels.

Before examining how housing patterns may increasingly frustrate progressive school policies, we should pause to compare the Denver, Baltimore, and Raleigh areas. Denver is a five-county metro area with a single central city and 17 school districts (three countywide: Denver, Jefferson, and Douglas counties). Baltimore is a seven-county metro area with one other minor central city (Annapolis) but seven countywide school ("big box") districts. The six-county Raleigh-Durham-Chapel Hill area, as the name conveys, has three central cities. However, all its school districts are unified, countywide "big box" districts, generally with deliberate school integration policies in effect. Table 3.2 compares both metro areas and the systems serving the principal central cities. Unlike Denver Public Schools and Baltimore City Public Schools, the Wake County Public School system embraces Raleigh, its suburbs, and substantial rural areas.

Demographically, Denver, Baltimore, and Raleigh-Durham-Chapel Hill were somewhat comparable. All three areas had comparable percentages of Anglo (non-Hispanic white) pupils: 61 percent, 56 percent, and 58 percent, respectively. Metro Denver's primary minority group were Hispanics (26%), whereas blacks were the principal minority group in metro Baltimore (37%) and metro Raleigh (34%). Metro Baltimore had a somewhat higher rate of low-income, or FARM, pupils (31%) than did metro Denver (24%) or metro Raleigh (28%). (FARM is an acronym that stands for Free and Reduced Meals, a federal program for school lunch subsidies for children from families with incomes up to 185 percent of the federal poverty index.)

However, in terms of racial and economic integration, the Research Triangle region bested the Denver and Baltimore regions by substantial

Table 3.2

Racial and Economic School Segregation in Denver, Baltimore, and Raleigh Area Elementary Schools in 1999–2000

Pupil Group	Metro Denver	Metro Baltimore	Metro Raleigh	Wake County
Elementary pupils	197,165	229,195	136,442	55,844
Anglo	61%	56%	58%	63%
Black	9%	37%	34%	28%
Hispanic	26%	2%	5%	4%
FARM	24%	31%	28%	22%
Segregation indices (SI)				
Black SI	67	73	32	21
Hispanic SI	56	44	40	32
FARM SI	56	56	35	30
Average pupils and classmates				
Non-FARM	80%	78%	70%	77%
FARM	56%	60%	50%	36%

Note: The figures cited for Metro Raleigh include Wake County.

margins in every category. As a region, the black school segregation index of metro Raleigh-Durham was less than half (32) the Denver region's index (67) or the Baltimore region's index (73). Economic segregation was one-third lower in the Carolina region (35) than the Colorado region (56) and Maryland region (56). (And that was in the year *before* Wake County Public Schools implemented its economic integration plan).

Nevertheless, the Wake County Public School system has a tough challenge to attain its goals in the face of a regional housing market that promotes more and more economic segregation. Though Raleigh itself has expanded its boundaries rapidly (from 11 square miles in 1950 to 115 square miles in 2000), it continues to be home to 60 percent of Wake County's African Americans. Meanwhile, the white population is exploding in four towns in western Wake County—most importantly, Cary, the bedroom community for Research Triangle Park. Their schools are geographically distant from minority neighborhoods in south Raleigh.

The early academic returns from Wake County's new pupil assignment policy are encouraging. In 2001, 64 percent of Wake County students eligible for free and reduced-price meals performed at or above grade level, a rate that outpaces most low-income students in urban districts. As Wake County Superintendent of Schools Bill McNeal explains, "The reason that you want to create middle class schools is expectations as much as anything. How do you know what excellence is without seeing it. You've got to be able to touch it and feel it."

Cambridge, Massachusetts (Fiske, 2002)

In December 2001, the Cambridge School Committee adopted a policy of controlled school choice to achieve SES balance in the district's 14 elementary schools. With 48 percent of elementary school pupils qualifying for subsidized meals, starting with kindergarten, the school board set a goal of having each school fall within 15 percentage points of the districtwide average (that is, between 33% and 63% FARM) for 2002–2003. The permissible range would be narrowed to 10 percentage points for 2003–2004 and to 5 percentage points for 2004–2005.

The new policy builds on 20 years of experience in implementing a controlled choice policy to achieve *racial* balance in the city's schools. (Cambridge's elementary schools cover K–8, and the district has a single high school). No school had a majority of any one racial group except Fletcher/Maynard Academy, which was 52 percent black in 2000–2001. (One-quarter of the academy's black enrollment was not African American but Haitians, West Indians, and African immigrants.) Overall, the district's elementary schools were 40 percent Anglo (non-Hispanic whites), 34 percent black, 14 percent Hispanic, 11 percent Asian, and 1 percent Native American. Table 3.3 calculates the familiar segregation indexes for 2000. The following four facts stand out:

- First, though the residential segregation of blacks (ages 5–17) was the highest (46) of any group, the controlled school choice program brought school segregation of black pupils down to an astonishingly low index of 13. Many black parents clearly sought out "better" schools beyond the boundaries of the moderately segregated neighborhoods in which they lived.
- Second, Hispanic and Asian enrollments mirrored neighborhood patterns.
- Third, Anglo pupils were grouped in certain schools rather than in neighborhoods—again, a function of more aggressive parents utilizing the controlled choice system to their advantage. However, one-third of Anglo school-age children were not attending Cambridge Public Schools. (More than 90 percent of school-age children from all other groups attended the public schools.)
- Fourth, economic segregation was not diminished by the racially based controlled choice policy. Schools were as economically segregated (35) as neighborhoods (36). The schools' economic imbalance ranged from a low of 19 percent low-income pupils (Cambridgeport) to a high of 79 percent (King).

It is important to note that the comparison between school and neighborhood is somewhat of an apples-to-oranges comparison. The two age groups are not identical as the schools' K–8 range is compared with the 2000 census's 5–11 age grouping (roughly K–6). Of potentially more consequence, the residential calculation is based on children below the poverty line, whereas FARM eligibility for partial subsidies cuts off at 185 percent

Table 3.3
School and Neighborhood (Ages 17 and Younger) Segregation Indexes for Cambridge, Massachusetts (2000) (0 to 100; 100 = total apartheid)

Group	School	Neighborhood
Anglo	15	10
Black	13	46
Hispanic	36	36
Asian	28	30
Native American	29	41
Low-income	35	36*

* This index is calculated for ages 5–11 (in effect, grades K–6).

of the poverty line. Nonetheless, it was this last disparity plus concern about the uncertain legal status of a race-based controlled choice plan and the growing understanding of the linkage between SES status and academic outcomes that caused the district to shift to controlled choice for SES balance in December 2001.

Since that time, the minority population within Cambridge elementary schools has increased as the proportion of Anglo pupils has declined slightly (from 40% in 2000–2001 to 37% in 2004–2005)—a nationwide trend. However, the proportion of low-income pupils has dropped more markedly (from 48% in 2000–2001 to 40% in 2004–2005). Though they have missed the board's ideal targets, the range between "regular" elementary schools has narrowed from Peabody and Tobin (27% low-income pupils) to King (59% low-income pupils). Ironically, the most poverty-impacted schools are two charter schools, special academies set up at parents' behest: Amigos (68% Hispanic; 61% low income) and Fletcher-Maynard (58% black and 23% Hispanic; 73% low income). By a substantial margin, these two academies have the lowest test scores in the system (a reminder of the old adage: "Be careful what you wish for; you may get it.").

The impact of the district's policies on economic integration can be clearly seen in Table 3.4, which compares segregation indexes between 2000–2001 and between 2004–2005 (the latter listing separately all elementary schools and then only "regular" elementary schools, excluding the two special academies). The comparison shows that Cambridge schools continue to be very balanced in terms of racial diversity and that the district's SES policies significantly improved economic integration (shown in the bottom row). Considering all elementary schools, the economic segregation index was cut from 35 to 23—a 35 percent improvement. Setting aside the two academies where many black and Hispanic parents were electing to enroll their children without regard to the school district's SES policy, the economic segregation index among "regular" elementary schools was halved from 35 to 17. In the process, average test scores improved modestly. Third graders that achieved advanced and proficient levels on the Stanford 9 reading test increased from 44 percent in 2000–2001 to 51 percent in 2003–2004.

Cambridge Public Schools and La Crosse Public Schools are relatively small school districts in "little boxes" regions. The La Crosse, Wisconsin–Minnesota, metro area (126,838 residents in 2000) has seven school districts, whereas the Boston, Massachusetts–New Hampshire, metro area (3,406,829 residents) has 105 school districts. Absent constitutional compulsion, achieving greater integration among multiple "little boxes" school districts through school board action is an impossible task. The next section will examine, however, the potential for local school board

Table 3.4
School Segregation Indexes Pre- and Post-SES Integration Plan in Cambridge, Massachusetts (0 to 100; 100 = Total Apartheid)

Group	All 2000–01	All 2004–05	Excluding Academies 2004–05
Anglo	15	20	16
Black	13	19	16
Hispanic	36	38	18
Asian	28	24	23
Native American	29	23	21
Low-income	35	23	17

action in the Denver and Baltimore areas that, like Raleigh-Durham-Chapel Hill, are "big box" regions. What are the limits of what could be achieved if local school boards in the Baltimore and Denver areas adopted SES balancing plans within each district?

SES INTEGRATION IN BALTIMORE AND DENVER

The Baltimore region has fewer school districts (seven) than any comparably sized, multicounty region in the country. In 2002, the economic segregation index for metro Baltimore's elementary schools, I have calculated, was 61.7. What would the result be if each school board adopted a common policy to achieve maximum economic integration *within* each of the seven districts? The goal would be to have FARM enrollment in every school equal to their districtwide average (plus or minus 15 percentage points).

I have simulated the effects of such a policy for the Baltimore metro area. Table 3.5 lists the current and simulated distribution of pupils by SES status. For all schools I maintained their 2002 enrollment levels. However, within each district, I replaced FARM pupils with non-FARM pupils in high-poverty schools until I had brought each school to within 15 percentage points of the districtwide FARM percentage. Then I shifted enough FARM pupils into low-poverty schools until all transfers within the district balanced out. (The floor for the lowest FARM schools may be closer to the districtwide FARM average than 15 percentage points.)

Substantial realignment occurs within Anne Arundel County, Baltimore County, and Harford County. A modest realignment occurs within Howard County. Little realignment occurs within Carroll County, and none within Queen Anne's County. With only one elementary school

Table 3.5
Simulated SES Integration of FARM Pupils in Baltimore Area Elementary Schools by School Board Action within Each District in 2002

School District	Percentage FARM	Current Percentage Range	Projected Percentage Range	Percentage of Pupils Reassigned
Baltimore City	84	99–29	90–69	4.0
Anne Arundel County	19	78–0	34–12	11.4
Baltimore County	33	79–1	48–21	15.8
Carroll County	9	28–2	24–4	1.2
Harford County	19	72–3	34–11	12.4
Howard County	—	45–0	25–4	3.8
Queen Anne's County	—	31–8	31–8	0.0

below 50 percent FARM, such an SES policy would not be worth implementing in Baltimore City, but I carried out the mathematical exercise anyway.

The net effect of having school boards maximize socioeconomic integration within each district in this way would be to lower the economic school segregation index from 61.7 percent to 53.5 percent—about a 13 percent improvement.

Table 3.6 applies the same strategy to the Denver region's 17 school districts. Within each district, school officials would reassign elementary school pupils so that no school's proportion of FARM pupils would be 15 percentage points greater or 15 percentage points less than the districtwide percentage of FARM pupils. That 30-point range would be altered only when insufficient seats in low-poverty schools (e.g., Northglenn-Thornton, Cherry Creek, Littleton, Adams-Arapahoe, and Jefferson) would be available to accommodate transfers from higher poverty schools; then the targeted adjustment would have to be reduced somewhat.

The economic segregation index for the region's 391 elementary schools for 2001–2002 was a high 58.9. Implementing a policy of SES balance as outlined previously within the 17 school districts would lower the economic school segregation rate to 48.4—about a 20 percent improvement. These policies are well worth pursuing. However, the greatest economic segregation occurs not within each district but among districts because of disparities created by economically segregated housing patterns.

Table 3.6
Projected Impact of Socioeconomic Integration Policy within 17 Denver School Districts in 2002

School District	Percentage FARM	Current Percentage Range	Projected Percentage Range	Percentage of Pupils Reassigned
Denver City	68	96–6	78–48	10.1
Adams County				
Mapleton 1	46	64–32	61–31	1.6
Northglenn-Thornton	25	80–1	40–17	8.5
Adams County 14	74	83–66	89–59	0.0
Brighton 27J	35	68–13	50–20	5.3
Bennett 29J	16	na	na	na
Strasburg 31J	14	na	na	na
Westminster 50	42	64–3	57–27	1
Arapahoe County				
Englewood 1	41	52–31	56–26	0.0
Sheridan 2	68	74–61	83–53	0.0
Cherry Creek 5	13	49–0	28–7	3.6
Littleton 6	14	56–1	29–9	6.1
Deer Trail 26J	16	na	na	na
Adams-Arapahoe 28J	40	80–1	55–31	7.5
Byers 32J	31	na	na	na
Douglas County RE-1	2.5	10–0	15–0	0.0
Jefferson County R-1	18	76–0	33–12	7.0

INCLUSIONARY ZONING: MIXING UP THE NEIGHBORHOOD

To achieve much greater racial and economic integration, we must act on a metropolitan-wide basis through changes in the housing market. More racially and economically integrated neighborhoods will produce more racially and economically integrated neighborhood schools. But producing more economically integrated neighborhoods (with their concomitant greater racial integration) requires changing local governments' traditional practices in shaping their housing markets.

Where and what kinds of housing are built are not the result of the workings of some unfettered "free market." Such a "free market" is a myth. "Public policy dictates where development occurs," the National Association of Homebuilders (NAHB) has acknowledged. Local governments' zoning decisions regulate the allowable uses of land: what can be built and at what density of development. Building and engineering codes set standards that private developers must follow. Public taxes (sometimes without developer cost-sharing) install the utility systems, create the street network, and provide the parks, schools, fire stations, and other public facilities that are essential for most urban development.

Many suburban governments carry out these policies and programs in ways that seek to exclude low-income households from their communities: large minimum lot sizes for new homes, severe restrictions (even outright bans) on townhouse and apartment development, deep building setbacks mandated from lot lines and excessive off-street parking requirements. All of these contribute to a pattern of what is typically termed *exclusionary zoning*. More than 135 local communities, however, have adopted "inclusionary zoning" policies that deliberately seek to create economically diversified new housing. These communities seek to assure that housing for modest proportions of moderate and low-income families will be provided in any new, market-rate housing developments.

For almost 30 years, Montgomery County, Maryland, has had the most comprehensive inclusionary zoning policy in the United States. Complying with the near-countywide policy adopted in 1973, private, for-profit home builders have delivered more than 11,000 moderately priced dwelling units (MPDUs) as integral parts of new subdivisions and apartment complexes. Carrying out another provision of the county law, the county's public housing authority, the Housing Opportunities Commission, has purchased 1,700 highly scattered MPDUs and rents another 1,500 for very-low-income families. The basic provisions of the MPDU are

- any new housing development of 35 or more units must include at least 12.5 percent MPDUs that are affordable for households at no more than 65 percent of the county's median household income (the lowest one-third of the income scale);
- as a cost offset for providing up to 15 percent MPDUs, the county offers density bonuses of up to 22 percent (in effect, removing all land costs for both MPDUs and for bonus market rate units);
- resale prices and rents of MPDUs are controlled for 30 years; and
- the county's public housing authority is directed to buy or rent one-third of the MPDUs in order that the program will assist very-low-income households. (Nonprofit agencies can acquire another 6.66 percent.)

The MPDU policy is the most innovative centerpiece of Montgomery County's 40,000 mixed-income housing units. Its progressive policies have facilitated a remarkable social and economic transformation. In 1970, Montgomery County had the look of a classic suburb: wealthy and white (92%). By 2000, Montgomery County had a "rainbow look": 16 percent black, 12 percent Hispanic, 12 percent Asian. It still was the

13th wealthiest county in the United States as it became one of the more racially and economically integrated communities in the nation. Over three decades, its residential economic segregation index hardly changed from 27.2 in 1970 to 27.9 in 2000—low and stable.

By providing housing for all occupational levels, the county helped promote a diversified local economy centered on its I-270 Technology Corridor. In a generation, Montgomery County has become the global center of biomedical and genetic research. Adopting a Montgomery County–type inclusionary zoning law would be the most important single step that any metro area—including greater Baltimore and greater Denver—could take to reverse trends toward greater economic segregation.

INCLUSIONARY ZONING FOR THE BALTIMORE AND DENVER AREAS

I have simulated what might have been the results of adopting Montgomery County's type of inclusionary zoning laws by all local governments (primarily the seven county governments) in metro Baltimore for the last 20 years. Some 316,000 new housing units were built from 1980 to 2000 (about 30% of the total housing stock). A regionwide MPDU policy would have produced 15,800 units of workforce housing for modest-income workers (young teachers, police recruits, sales clerks, etc.) and another 7,900 units of "welfare-to-workforce housing" (for very-low-income households). Less than 10 percent of the MPDUs (1,650 units) would have been located in Baltimore City. Most MPDUs would have been integrated into new, middle-class subdivisions and new, market-rate apartment complexes in newly developing communities.

The Urban Institute has calculated that 95,225 poor persons would have had to move from high-poverty to low-poverty census tracts to have totally eliminated economic segregation in the Baltimore region in 2000 (that is, to reach a segregation index of 0). The 18,375 poor persons that could have been moved through a regional MPDU policy would have achieved 20 percent of that ideal goal. Hypothetically, metro Baltimore's residential economic segregation index for 2000 would have been reduced from 43.3 to 34.6—15 percent below the economic segregation index of 40.1 recorded three decades earlier.

The previous calculations focus only on the relocation of families eligible for public housing ("welfare-to-workforce housing"). However, setting the MPDU eligibility ceiling at 65 percent of median household income approximates the ceiling for FARM eligibility. In other words, all 23,700 MPDU units built during our 20-year period would have come into play.

I have simulated what would have been the impact on school economic integration if the school boards' SES policy had been reinforced by an MPDU policy implemented by county and municipal governments. I have assumed that 75 percent of the MPDUs built would have been available to low-income families with children and that such families would have had one child enrolled in public elementary school. Furthermore, the number of low-income pupils transferring (that is, moving into new attendance zones) would have been limited so that no suburban district would have been lifted above the regional average of FARM pupils (35.8 percent in 2002). Effectively, this would have limited the number of newcomers to Baltimore County (33.1% FARM) that was already close to the regional FARM average by 2002.

The effects would be dramatic. Progressive enrollment policies like those in Cambridge and Wake County, if adopted by area school boards, would hypothetically reduce economic school segregation by 15 percent from 61.7 to 53.5; adding a regionwide MPDU policy like the one in Montgomery County for 20 years would further reduce economic school segregation to 25.8—a 60 percent reduction!

The consequences for Baltimore City would be impressive. From a system with 84 percent FARM pupils, the district average would be reduced to 53 percent. Meanwhile, no suburban district would exceed the regional FARM average (35%). No suburban elementary schools would have majority FARM enrollments. Although the schools attended by the "designer clothes" set would no longer be the former preserves of near-exclusive privilege, they would typically have about 25 percent FARM pupils—many of them the children of the public employees, retail, and service workers whom the "designer clothes" class sees and relies upon within their communities every day.

Let us apply the same methodology and assumptions to the Denver area. A total of 320,296 units were built during the 20-year period (more than one-third of all of the Denver area's housing stock). Assuming that half of the housing built were individual "spec" homes or in small developments, an MPDU policy like that in Montgomery county would result in 16,015 "workforce" MPDUs and 8,007 "welfare-to-workforce" MPDUs, or 24,022 MPDUs altogether. Some 7,738 would be created in higher-than-average FARM school districts (Denver Public Schools et al.) that would serve to promote more economic balance within those districts. But another 16,284 MPDUs would be built primarily in newer, low-poverty subdivisions in the Cherry Creek, Jefferson, and Douglas school districts. Under a regionwide eligibility list, these MPDUs would be available for low- and very-low-income families who would choose to move into them. These families would otherwise be limited to seeking older, low-cost housing in high-poverty neighborhoods, thus sending their children to poverty-impacted neighborhood schools in primarily the Denver and Adams-Arapahoe districts.

By our assumptions, the families of more than 12,000 FARM pupils would move into MPDUs in the Northglenn-Thornton, Cherry Creek, Littleton, Douglas County, and Jefferson County school districts. One beneficial effect would be to reduce substantially the high concentration of FARM pupils in sending districts, particularly in Adams County 14 (73.9% to 44.3%), Denver Public Schools (67.9% to 44.1%), and Adams-Arapahoe (39.8% to 31.2%). There would, of course, be an increase in FARM pupils in the receiving districts, for example, in the case of Douglas County, a more than six-fold increase (2.5% to 16.9%). By our assumptions, many of those new pupils would be eligible for fully subsidized meals. That is, their family incomes would have been less than $23,490 for a family of four in 2000. Undoubtedly, some would be from very poor families receiving public assistance, but most would have parents who work full-time in low-paying jobs. Many other new pupils whose parents earn up to $32,190 (for a family of four) would be eligible for only partially subsidized meals. Their parents would be working in jobs paying up to $15.50 an hour—a wide range of jobs in the retail trades, service industries, and local government.

However, reinforcing what school boards have the authority to do (instituting SES-balancing pupil assignment policies) with an MPDU policy that city and county governments have the authority to do would reduce the school economic segregation index to 13.9—a three-quarters reduction in economic school segregation! That would make metro Denver's schools the third most economically integrated in the nation. (Flagstaff, Arizona [8.5], and Eau Claire, Wisconsin [10.6], ranked first and second in 1999–2000.) By achieving just half that level (27.8), which is readily within the range of realistic implementation, greater Denver would have the second most economically integrated schools of any major metropolitan area. Among the 100 largest metro areas, Scranton-Wilkes Barre, Pennsylvania (27.5), which has no minority population to speak of, ranked first; Greenville-Spartanburg, South Carolina (28.7), was second; and Charlotte, North Carolina–South Carolina (33.8), was third.

All this could flow from a change in public zoning policies whose net effect would require just 2.5 percent of all new housing built to be acquired by a regional public housing authority for very-low-income families and just 5.0 percent of all new housing to be affordable to persons in what used to be described as the "working class." Indeed, this analysis illustrates not just the hypothetical effect of *inclusionary* zoning but how relentlessly and thoroughly local governments in Douglas County (as the most extreme example) have actually practiced *exclusionary* zoning.

SUMMING UP

Some may view the preceding analysis as simply an exercise in "fantasy math," based on uniform policies across all jurisdictions and flawless implementation (which is rarely achieved). Montgomery County's MPDU program, however, has come very close to hitting its policy targets. The 11,210 MPDUs built by private, for-profit home builders represent 7.4 percent of 152,000 units built. The Housing Opportunities Commission has bought or rents 29 percent of the MPDUs (close to its one-third target allocation). Nonetheless, this analysis frames the outer limits of what could be achieved by such policies.

Critics usually argue, however, changing housing patterns as you recommend would take too long. Should not all efforts be concentrated on providing low-income children with the best possible quality education in their current neighborhood schools? I agree that we have a responsibility to do the best that we can to educate low-income children wherever they are right now. I would not advocate simply abandoning such efforts. But, at the federal level, we have been following a conscious remediation strategy for almost 40 years, principally through $7.2 billion a year in Chapter I support for poverty-impacted schools. The most comprehensive, federally sponsored evaluation of Chapter I, tracking the progress of 40,000 students over four years, found that Chapter I intervention failed to narrow the learning gap between the low-income students it served and non-low-income students (Hoff, 1997). [See also the blistering evaluations by the economists and interventionists in the present volume!—Editor]

"High-poverty schools put disadvantaged students in double jeopardy," the researchers concluded. "School poverty depresses the scores of all students in schools where at least half of the students are eligible for [federally] subsidized lunch, and seriously depresses the scores when over 75 percent of students live in low-income households." To the response that some high-poverty schools do succeed, "the authors warned that the sample of successful schools was too small to be scientifically reliable."

A recent book, *No Excuses,* published by the Heritage Foundation of Washington, DC, focused on case studies of 21 high-poverty schools around the country that were succeeding in raising low-income children's academic achievement (Thernstrom & Thernstrom, 2003). "Quite true," the Century Foundation's Richard Kahlenberg commented to me. "They usually reflect special circumstances where an inspired principal, given a largely free hand, has recruited a corps of talented, highly motivated teachers, corralled additional resources, and successfully engaged parents in school activities. But if that magic could be bottled and spread throughout whole school districts," he concluded, "there wouldn't be a need for books like *No Excuses.*"

That conclusion was confirmed several years ago when *Education Week* dispatched a reporter on a nationwide tour to find an "urban" school district with more than 60 percent low-income pupils (such as the Denver Public School District) *that is successful.* The reporter's conclusion: "Unfortunately, there are none."

The most effective educational reform is to mainstream poor children in middle-class schools—not just as classmates six hours a day, 185 days a year (which school board policies on social class can achieve) but also as playmates 365 days a year through creating mixed-income neighborhoods. Inclusionary zoning is a key tool to achieve the goal of an inclusionary society. A little bit of everything built goes a long way. In the 100 largest metro areas in the United States, 30 million new houses and apartments were built in the past 20 years. Metrowide inclusionary zoning laws would have produced 3.6 million affordable housing units. That is almost three times as much subsidized housing as is now owned by the 3,300 public housing authorities in the United States. That is producing affordable housing at twice the annual rate supported by federal Low-Income Housing Tax Credits. Unlike most public housing and tax credit projects, inclusionary zoning reverses economic segregation because affordable units are integrated into market-rate developments. Economically integrating neighborhoods would economically integrate neighborhood schools.

The Coleman Report's findings have been both consistently reconfirmed and even more consistently—I would say, deliberately—ignored by most politicians and many educators, who will not challenge the racial and class structure of U.S. society. That challenge is now being taken up by grassroots groups in many communities, spearheaded by faith-based coalitions affiliated with the Gamaliel Foundation. Baltimore's BRIDGE, Empower Hampton Roads, New Jersey Regional Coalition, and others are championing inclusionary zoning ("opportunity-based" housing) before city councils, county commissions, and state legislatures.

Their rallying cry: "Anyone good enough to work here is good enough to live here." And their children are good enough to go to our schools.

REFERENCES

Burtless, G. (Ed.). (1996). *Does money matter? The effect of school resources on student achievement and adult success.* Washington, DC: Brookings Institution Press.

Coleman, J. (1966). *Equality of educational opportunity* (Vol. 2). Washington, DC: National Center for Educational Statistics, Government Printing Office.

Fiske, E. B. (2002). Controlled choice in Cambridge, Massachusetts. In R. D. Kahlenberg (Ed.), *Divided we fail, coming together through public school choice: The report of the Century Foundation Task Force on the Common School* (pp. 167–208). New York: Century Foundation Press.

Hoff, D. J. (1997). Chapter I study documents impact of poverty. *Education Week, "Chapter I Aid Failed to Close Learning Gap."* Retrieved September 14, 2005 from http://www.edweek.org/ew/articles/1997/04/16/29title.h16. html?querystring=Chapter%201%20Study%20Documents

Kahlenberg, R. D. (2001). *All together now: Creating middle-class schools through public school choice.* Washington, DC: Brookings Institution Press.

Kahlenberg, R. D. (Ed.). (2002). *Divided we fail, coming together through public school choice: The report of the Century Foundation Task Force on the Common School.* New York: Century Foundation Press.

Lara-Cinisomo, S., Pebley, A. R., Vaiana, M. E., Maggio, E., Berends, M., & Lucas, S. R. (2004). A matter of class: Educational achievement reflects family background more than ethnicity or immigration. *RAND Review, 28*(3), 10–15.

Mial, R. (2002). La Crosse: One school district's drive to create socioeconomic balance. In R. D. Kahlenberg (Ed.), *Divided we fail, Coming together through public school choice: The report of the Century Foundation Task Force on the Common School* (pp. 115–140). New York: Century Foundation Press.

Powell, J. A., Kearney, G., & Kay, V. (Eds.). (2001). *In pursuit of a dream deferred: Linking housing and education policy.* New York: Peter Land.

Rusk, D. (1998). Texas: Classmates count in Texas schools. *The Abell Report, 11*(2), 5–7.

Rusk, D. (2001). *Inside game/outside game: Segregation and Spatial Planning in Metropolitan Areas.* Retrieved June 17, 2005 from http://www.gamaliel. org/strategic/StrategicpartnersRuskNIROVdoc.htm

Rusk, D. (2002). *Classmates count: A study of the interrelationship between socioeconomic background and standardized test scores of 4th grade pupils in the Madison-Dane County public schools.* Retrieved June 17, 2005 from http://www.gamaliel.org/DavidRusk/Unified%20final%20report.pdf

Rusk, D. (2003). *Housing policy is school policy: An analysis of the interaction of housing patterns, school enrollment, and academic achievement in the Baltimore Area Schools.* Retrieved June 17, 2005 from http://www.gama-liel.org/DavidRusk/Abell%202%20school%20final%20report.pdf

Rusk, D., & Mosley, J. (1994). *The academic performance of public housing children: Does living in middle class neighborhoods and attending middle class schools make a difference?* Washington, DC: The Urban Institute. Retrieved June 17, 2005 from http://www.gamaliel.org/Strategic/Strategi cpartnersRuskCarnege.htm.

Silberman, T. (2002). Wake County schools: A question of balance. In
    R. D. Kahlenberg (Ed.), *Divided we fail, coming together through public
    school choice: The report of the century foundation task force on the
    common school* (pp. 141–166). New York: Century Foundation Press.
Thernstrom, S., & Thernstrom, A. (2003). *No excuses: Closing the racial gap in
    learning.* New York: Simon & Schuster.

THE ROLE OF
THE HOME AND FAMILY

Chapter 4

PROMOTING EARLY LANGUAGE DEVELOPMENT

Todd R. Risley and Betty Hart

Like many other professionals inspired by John F. Kennedy and Martin Luther King, Jr., we devoted our early careers to programs to give poor children a head start on learning. We all thought we could break the "cycle of poverty" in one generation through preschool education. We all learned instead that providing 20 to 30 hours a week of enriched experience and practice when they were four and five did not bring poor children up to the level of the average American child in later school and life success. Our own response to this was to consider the family lives of the children before they entered preschool. Because children are awake (and able to learn) about 100 to 110 hours a week, they would already have accumulated more than 20,000 hours of learning-opportunity time by the time they entered preschool at age four. We wanted to know how full or empty of learning experience were those hours of opportunity and to compare the early lives of children from poor families with the lives of children from working-class and professional families.

Our book, *Meaningful Differences in the Everyday Experience of Young American Children* (Hart & Risley, 1995) was the first report of the voyage of exploration that we began in 1982 when we set out to find out what parents and babies actually do, all day long, in real life, in U.S. homes. From birth announcements in Kansas City newspapers we recruited 42 new babies from a wide variety of families—some parents were doctors and lawyers, some were business owners, some had white-collar jobs, some had blue-collar jobs, some were working poor, and some were on welfare. When the babies were 7 months old we began to visit their homes each month at different times when they were awake on days, evenings and weekends, until they were 36 months old. During each visit we recorded (with audiotape and notes) everything said to the baby, everything the baby overheard, and everything the baby did or said during an hour of daily life. Each of the resulting 1,200 hours of recordings took 16 more hours of work: 8 hours to transcribe; another hour to independently transcribe a sample to assess interobserver agreement; and 7 more hours to code each utterance for context and grammar and to enter it into the computer. We had asked the simple, natural history question, "What actually goes on between American parents and babies in everyday family life while babies are learning to talk?" After 22,000 person-hours—or 11 person-years—of work, we had collected enough reliable data on enough families to give a first approximate answer to that question.

We had our own notions of what we might find—hypotheses, we called them—but the most important things we found surprised us. Because the findings seem to have also surprised most people who read that book, we think of them as discoveries. There were seven surprising discoveries that we reported in *Meaningful Differences in the Everyday Experience of Young American Children* (Hart & Risley, 1995), and in our book, *The Social World of Children Learning to Talk* (Hart & Risley, 1999). This chapter reviews those discoveries.

1. A lot of talk goes on between average parents and typical infants and toddlers in everyday home life. We found that during each hour they were awake at home average American babies heard an average of 340 utterances and 1,440 words per hour addressed to them. They were personally responded to 150 times and received 17 affirmations per hour from their parents. If this is the average amount of language experience that typical one- and two-year-old American children get at home, how do infant and toddler out-of-home daycare programs compare? How do the home lives of special needs babies, or older children, or children of other cultures compare? And most important to remember, this is the language experience received—hour after hour, month after month—by those "average" children against whom all other children are measured.

2. There are large and consistent differences between families in the amount of time, encouragement, and talk given to their infants and toddlers. We found that, in an hour together, some parents spent more than 40 minutes of their time interacting with their babies, and some spent less than 15 minutes. Some parents took more than 500 turns of interaction in their "social dance" with their babies, and some took fewer than 150 turns an hour. Some parents expressed approval and encouragement of their babies' actions more than 40 times in an hour of family life, and some fewer than 4 times. And some parents said more than 3,000 words, and some said fewer than 200 words in an average hour to their babies.

For each family, the amount that parents talked to their babies was consistent across time, so the differences mounted up. When we extrapolate the talk that we recorded for parents across the waking hours of their infants' and toddlers' lives, we estimate that, by the time children were four years old and starting preschool, some children would have already heard more than 50 million words said to them by their parents, whereas others would have heard only 10 million; and some would have already heard more than 800,000 affirmative statements about their actions from their parents, whereas others would have heard fewer than 80,000.

This was our most surprising discovery: The size of the differences between families in the amount of talk to babies is enormous, and those differences add up to massive advantages or disadvantages for children in language experience long before they start preschool.

3. *"Extra" talk is more complex and positive—automatically!* We found that both talkative and taciturn parents used similar numbers of initiations, imperatives, and prohibitions per hour to govern their children. This is the "business" talk that all parents of young children must do: "stop that"; "come here"; "what you got there"; "hold still", "put that down." The most taciturn parents usually said little else beyond this necessary business talk, but whenever parents talked more than was necessary for just business, the "extra" talk was *not* more business talk. Instead it was "conversational talk" about other things. It was chitchat and gossip and running commentary that was automatically rich in the varied vocabulary, complex ideas, subtle guidance, and positive reinforcement that are thought to be important to intellectual development—the "good stuff" of developmental psychology.

This discovery is vitally important to any effort at parent training. Many parent training programs set out to change parenting style, where *style* is defined as a ratio of good stuff to total stuff. Good stuff is a part of conversational talk and not-good stuff is the essence of business talk. If a parent only talks a little, the language used is almost always only the necessary minimum of business topics—the not-good stuff—and their ratio of good stuff to not-good stuff (i.e., their style) is poor. When a parent talks more, or can be induced to talk more, most of the extra talk *must* be descriptive and conversational. As commentary and conversation increase, business talk will stay constant, and the parent's ratio or "good" parenting style will automatically improve. Focusing on parenting style misdirects our efforts. We do not have to (try to) get parents to learn *how* to talk differently to their children. We just have to help them practice talking *more*. (Even the most taciturn mothers in our study had moments of ebullience when they were sociable with their children—and at those moments their talk to their babies was the complex and positive good stuff.)

4. Toddlers' talkativeness stops growing when it matches the level of their parents' talkativeness. We found that parents talk to their infants and toddlers at the frequency per hour that is typical between all members of their family: amount of talking is a characteristic of the microculture of a family. In a taciturn family, talk among the members is mostly only to get something done, only about necessary business, whereas in a talkative family everyone has conversations and engages in commentary and "thinking aloud" in addition to the necessary business talk. As toddlers begin talking, their utterances, containing recognizable words, increase in frequency until their utterances match their parent's frequency of talking. At this point growth in talking levels off, and a toddler's frequency of talking stabilizes at whatever level is typical within her or his family—because they are talking about the same kinds of things: business only or business *and* commentary and conversation.

5. Expressive language practice is linked to receptive language experience. We found that at age three children of average families express themselves in language about 400 times per hour, children of the most talkative families express themselves more than 600 times per hour, whereas children of the most taciturn families express themselves less than 200 times per hour. We assume that children's fluency in using language is a function of amount of practice. If we extrapolate across the waking hours of toddlers' lives, we estimate that by the time they are four years old average American children will have accumulated 15 million words of expressive language practice, and children of the most talkative families will have accumulated more than 22 million words, whereas children of the most taciturn families will have accumulated less than 7 million words—less than half the expressive language practice of the average children when they enter preschool.

6. The amount of family talk is a characteristic of low and high social class. We found that welfare parents were taciturn. Working-class parents (with either blue-collar or white-collar occupations) varied greatly from the most talkative to the most taciturn. Parents with advanced, professional degrees were uniformly talkative.

We were shocked by this discovery—and amused at our shock. We, like our friends and colleagues in our college environs, unconsciously assumed that almost everyone was more-or-less like us, except, of course, for those people who were in trouble. Virtually all the people *we* knew talked a lot to their children—and to everyone else. It was a shock to realize that we, and all our super-educated friends, were as deviant from average Americans in one direction as welfare recipients were in the other. We now listen "with the third ear" to the talk of our colleagues for the casual assumption that most people think and act like we with graduate degrees do. We hear it often, and smile. Conversely, in our experience with taciturn families, we find that they are bemused by people who "talk all the time" to babies and often think it an odd, even silly, thing for adults to be doing.

More important was to find such great diversity among American working-class families. Some working-poor families talked to their babies as much as professionals, and some affluent business families talked as little as did those on welfare. Their amount of talk—not their social class or income or race—predicted their children's intellectual accomplishments.

*7. Amount of family talk accounts for children's vocabulary growth and related intellectual outcomes.*We found that the large differences in the amount of parent talk that infants and toddlers received, particularly the amount of nonbusiness conversation and commentary, was powerfully related to large differences in the size of the toddlers' vocabulary growth and to standardized test measures of their intellectual achievement at ages three ($r = .78$) and at nine ($r = .77$). Parent talkativeness to babies accounted for *all* the correlation that existed between socioeconomic status (SES)—and/or race—and the verbal intellectual accomplishments of these American children.

SES and race were moderately correlated with measures of intellectual achievement. Most scholars assume that SES and race are only marker variables and that the "real" things contributing to intellectual achievement are simply associated with SES or race. From our findings, parent talkativeness or, more broadly, parent "sociability" seems to be that real variable because it accounted for all the variance (other than measurement error) in those children's intellectual achievement.

Most scholars also assume that both experience and biology are always involved in human behavior and that both culture and genetic makeup interact and contribute to children becoming similar to their parents. Parents may be taciturn or talkative due to both their biological temperament and their own childhood experiences. Of course, they pass along their biological temperament to their children through their genes. It is through their family microculture that they pass on to their children—while their children are still babies—the habits of talking a lot or a little, of what things to talk about, and of talking for pleasure or only for business. It is through this family experience that parents pass along their family culture to the next generation—a culture of family life full of words and social dance or empty of those important things.

There are massive differences in the vocabulary growth and subsequent intellectual achievement between American children. We have known this since the War on Poverty initiative in 1965. This is why hundreds of pre-school intervention programs were created at that time. Our longitudinal research measured vocabulary growth more thoroughly and carefully than ever before so that these differences were seen directly, with little obscuring measurement error, very early in children's lives. That there are equally massive differences in the amount of language *experience* accumulated by American babies we did not know but discovered through our longitudinal research. Babies' receptive and expressive language experience was also measured so thoroughly and carefully that differences could be seen clearly with low measurement error. This thorough and careful measurement of both language outcomes and language experience permitted the surprising discovery that the large differences in the amount of language experience that had accumulated before the children were three years old accounted for most of the equally large differences in vocabulary growth and verbal intellectual outcomes by age three—and for years to come. By age three, some children were so hopelessly behind in total language experience and resultant vocabulary growth that no later preschool or school intervention could catch them up.

Many parents are raised in a family culture of sociability. They give to their babies the benefits of that culture in the activities and conversation they share and the vocabulary growth it engenders. And they pass on to their babies the culture of sociability (and conversation) itself, a pattern that is repeated for generations to come. These are advantaged families and advantaged children. In many of the family subcultures of poverty, infant-toddler awake time is mostly empty of adult-provided structure and symbolic accompaniment. To change these family cultures we must focus on teaching parents, and potential parents, how to fill up all the waking time of babies with activities and conversation so that they are accumulating as much coherent and symbolic experience and social dance practice as their average American age-mates—hour after hour, day after day, month after month, from the very beginning.

REFERENCES

Hart, B., & Risley, T. R. (1995). *Meaningful differences in the everyday experience of young American children.* Baltimore: Paul H. Brookes.

Hart, B., & Risley, T. R. (1999). *The social world of children learning to talk.* Baltimore: Paul H. Brookes.

Chapter 5

THE HOME ENVIRONMENT

Robert H. Bradley

Every retrospective of the year 2004 is likely to begin with a recounting of the devastating tsunami that hit Indonesia, Sri Lanka, India, and parts of Africa. During the weeks that followed, the media was filled with pictures and accounts of lives torn apart, property rendered useless—none more heart wrenching than those of family members describing the loss of their children. In the disaster, 150,000 died, property in the tens of billions was destroyed, and life for millions was severely disrupted. Against such a backdrop, four elemental truths about home life consistently emerged: (1) the essential functions enacted by parents on behalf of children, (2) the deep attachment most parents have for their children, (3) the central role of place in organizing family life, and (4) the power of context in shaping daily activity. This chapter will focus on these four truths, beginning with an extended treatment of the key functions carried out by parents on behalf of their children.

THE PRIMARY TASKS OF PARENTING

What adults do in their roles as parents has changed over the centuries as a function of technological, social, and economic adjustments. That said, the goal of parenting has remained essentially the same: to enable children to become competent, caring adults who are ready to function well within society (Maccoby, 1992). Attaining this goal requires a plethora of specific parenting actions (carried out over a lengthy period of time) that are fitted to a particular child's needs and are executed within the boundaries of the resources and constraints present.

About a decade ago, we constructed a system for organizing the tasks of parenting (Bradley & Caldwell, 1995). Central to our framework is the notion that *optimal parenting* (a facilitative home environment) is best conceived of as a set of regulatory acts and conditions aimed at successful adaptation and at successful exploitation of opportunity structures for children (Saegert & Winkel, 1990). Such a conception seems in keeping with ecological developmental theories that portray human beings as phylogenetically advanced, self-constructing organisms and the environment as a regulator (actually, coregulator) of complex developmental processes (Ford & Lerner, 1992). This framework is also consonant with the idea that children are conscious agents who are active in adapting to their environments (Lewis, 1997). Finally, it is consistent with recent notions about the value of building positive personal assets (Scales & Leffert, 1999). Starting from this basic notion, we identified six basic regulatory tasks (or functions) performed by parents: (1) *s*ustenance/safety, (2) *s*timulation, (3) *s*upport, (4) *s*tructure, (5) *s*urveillance, and (6) *s*ocial integration—the six *S*s of parenting.

The first three parenting tasks are derived from what is known about human needs and arousal systems. Specifically, Maslow (1954) contended that human beings need environments that promote survival, provide information (including enlistment of attention), and affirm worth. For complex living systems such as human beings, the task of maintaining internal unity is quite complicated due to the large number of component subsystems involved and the elaborateness of their organization (Ford & Lerner, 1992). To deal with the child's individuality and complexity, parents must perform other functions that assure that the direct inputs designed to sustain, stimulate, and emotionally support the child are maximally fitted to the child's current needs, proclivities, and competencies as well as the demands and constraints in the communities where they live; hence, structure and surveillance. To increase the likelihood that the child will maximally benefit from societal resources and be protected from adversity by societal institutions and social networks, parents must also act in such ways as to promote the child's integration into social networks and organizations (Weisner, 2002).

SUSTENANCE/SAFETY

From time immemorial, promoting the physical well-being of children has been considered the sine qua non of parental responsibility. Recent depictions of life during and immediately following the 2004 tsunami provide ample testimony as to the importance accorded this function by both individual parents and society at large. Nothing so graphically illustrates the depth and urgency of feeling attached to this function as the tearful accounts of parents (and other family members) when describing children ripped from their arms as both were being swept away by surging tides.

We have organized those acts and conditions designed to promote physical health under the joint class, sustenance/safety. Parents must provide adequate nutrients, shelter, and health care to ensure both survival and the level of biological integrity needed for physical and psychological development (Pollitt, 1988). Several of The United Nations Children's Fund's (UNICEF) major goals include the provision of adequate nutrition, sanitation and health care, protection from environmental toxins, and the assurance of basic safety. Although their focus is predominantly on children living in so-called Third World countries, the issues are the same for children everywhere—especially poor children. In the United States, threats to well-being such as malnutrition are relatively rare, although not as uncommon as is popularly believed. However, many U.S. children suffer from poor nutrition and poor eating habits, resulting in compromises to their health (e.g., many children suffer vitamin and mineral deficiencies and obesity) and increasing the likelihood of poor immune response and abnormal brain growth (Lozoff, Jiminez, & Wolf, 1991; Ogden, 1998). Dealing effectively with these nutritional problems requires different types of investments, such as being vigilant in watching what children eat, establishing good eating routines, and helping children monitor their own eating patterns. In the United States, access to health care is reasonably good but inconsistent across socioeconomic groups (Bradley & Corwyn, 2002). Making sure children have routine well-child visits and immunizations is also associated with good health (Committee on Health and Behavior, 2001).

The need to protect children from threats to their safety is obvious. The leading cause of morbidity and mortality in children beyond age one is accidents, many of which are preventable (Garbarino, 1988; U.S. Department of Health and Human Services, 1991). For example, there is evidence that the use of car restraints results in fewer injuries (Christerphersen, 1989). Likewise, there is evidence that parents can protect children from pathogenic conditions such as pollutants, passive cigarette smoke, and exposure to heavy metals (Evans, Kliewer, & Martin, 1991; Jacobson, Jacobson, Padgett, Brummitt, & Billings, 1992; Tong & McMichael, 1992). However, there is additional evidence (mostly anecdotal or from case studies) that parents vary widely in how much time and energy they invest in protecting children from physical hazards, including toxic substances and sharp objects (Peterson & Gable, 1998). Analysis of data from the National Longitudinal Survey of Youth (NLSY), aggregated over five biennial assessments (1986–1994), shows that the safety of a child's home varies by poverty status (Bradley, Corwyn, Burchinal, McAdoo, & Garcia Coll, 2001). Only 10 percent of children younger than age three and living in poverty had a safe home play area (no potentially hazardous health or structural obstacles), compared with 90 percent of children generally. Homes become more hazardous as children age. For children ages six to nine,

75.9 percent of nonpoor white children and 68.9 percent of poor white children resided in a home with no potentially dangerous structural or health hazards within reach. These figures were approximately 5 percent lower for African American children (71% nonpoor and 63.8% poor, respectively). For some children, the threats to physical well-being extend beyond the immediate boundaries of home (i.e., dangerous neighborhoods, even farms).

STIMULATION

To ensure competence and continued effort toward life-enhancing goals, the environment must provide sensory data that engage attention and provide information (i.e., stimulation). According to Kagan (1984), the main catalyst for environmentally mediated change is stimulation. Indeed, there is an abundance of both psychological theory and empirical data to buttress the significance of stimulation for cognitive, psychomotor, and social development (Bradley et al., 1994; Horowitz, 1987; Shonkoff & Phillips, 2000). Illustrative evidence of the value of stimulation comes from studies of parent talk. The research of Hart & Risley (1995) and Hoff (2003) provide compelling documentation of the value of providing children with more labels for objects, responding contingently to children's speech, making efforts to elicit conversation from children, sustaining conversations with children, and just talking to them more often.

Stimulation is important because it shapes the course of development, including neural development. Neuronal organization is determined in part by asymmetries of stimulation. In general, the more stimulation a particular behavioral system receives, the more the neuronal structures serving it will gain ascendancy (Rosenweig, Krech, Bennett, & Diamond, 1962). In their penetrating analysis of how children learn, the Committee on Developments in the Science of Learning showed that people learn by actively encountering objects, actions, events, and concepts in their environments (Bransford, Brown, & Cocking, 2000). To move from novice learner to expert in any particular area of knowledge or skill requires substantial experience (usually guided experience) in that area (meaning much stimulation).

According to the committee, "Along with children's natural curiosity and their persistence as self-motivated learners, what they learn during their first 4 or 5 years is not learned in isolation. Infants' activities are complemented by adult-child relationships that encourage the gradual involvement of children in the skilled and valued activities of the society in which they live. Research has shown that learning is strongly influenced by these social interactions" (pp. 102–103). A good example of socially mediated stimulation is reading. Reading has long been considered a hallmark of the quality of stimulation, with research indicating that it is strongly associated with academic performance (Bradley, 1994). Sixty-seven percent of white, nonpoor mothers reported reading to their children (birth to age three) at least three times per week (Bradley, Corwyn, McAdoo, & Garcia Coll, 2001). This compares with only 45 percent of poor white mothers. Percentages were lower for African American mothers (44% nonpoor, 32% poor) and Hispanic mothers (42% nonpoor, 25% poor). For all three groups, the percentages increased for children aged three to six. For example, 49 percent of nonpoor Hispanic mothers reported reading to their children at least three times a week, and 30 percent of poor Hispanic mothers did.

The number of books in a household is another important indicator of stimulation. More than 60 percent of infants from nonpoor white homes have at least 10 developmentally appropriate books available for reading. This compares to only about 40 percent of poor white children. The figures for African American and Hispanic children are far lower (e.g., only 16% of poor Hispanics). The figures for preschool children (ages three to six) are higher across the board, ranging from a low of 38 percent among poor Hispanics to 93 percent for nonpoor whites. The numbers of developmentally appropriate books available remains fairly constant until adolescence, at which point numbers decline significantly, nearly to levels reported during infancy. Young children from all ethnic and social class groups also tend to have a significant number of toys available. More than 50 percent of children in all groups had at least seven cuddly or role-playing toys during infancy, with fewer than 5 percent in any group having none. The majority of preschool children have access to some type of electronic device to play music, story tapes, and records.

Beyond reading to the child, most parents also report teaching their children specific skills and concepts. The vast majority of parents from all income and ethnic groups (75% to 97%) report teaching such basic concepts as colors, shapes, the alphabet, and numbers to preschool children. Data from the 1996 National Household Education Survey showed that almost 40 percent of all families help children with homework at least three times per week. About one-third help children once or twice a week, and only about one-fourth rarely or never help their children (National Center for Education Statistics, 2002). These social interactions are most critical in early childhood, not only for cognitive and psychomotor growth but also for normal development of many biological subsystems (e.g., vision; Cohen, DeLoache, & Strauss, 1979).

Parental efforts to stimulate children take many forms, such as talking to them, reading to them, teaching them specific skills, and involving children in household activities and family projects. Although research does not exist on every particular type of stimulation, there is ample evidence showing that with more exposure to a variety of stimulation, the child has a greater likelihood of achieving academic and even social success (Bradley, 1994; Bradley & Corwyn, 2003; Kagan, 1984). As children enter school, parents rely more and more on out-of-home experiences as a way of helping their children develop new competencies. That said, fewer than half of all children either receive special lessons or belong to organizations or clubs designed to promote their competence. In comparison, more that 60 percent of mothers reported taking their children to cultural experiences such as museums and art galleries during the past year, albeit only about 10 percent report doing so once a month or more. Although there are socioeconomic (SES) differences within each ethnic group studied, there are fewer ethnic group differences in this area of stimulation than in directly providing lessons and club memberships.

Theory provides no precise guidance on how to best organize the diverse array of objects, actions, events, and conditions that produce stimulation for children. However, the literature on the subject can be usefully organized into four major categories: (1) the availability of toys, books, learning materials, and other common objects children can use for learning and pleasure; (2) the language and literacy environment; (3) efforts to teach specific skills and otherwise encourage development; and (4) child involvement in enriching out-of-home experiences orchestrated by the family. Opportunities in these four areas promote competence in every area of development.

Although the literature on stimulation is rich with findings that buttress the idea that stimulation facilitates cognitive and academic functioning, it is a bit myopic. It suffers from a restricted view of how stimulation functions in children's lives: in effect, too much focus on children as passive recipients of information rather than as active agents in their own development (Ford & Lerner, 1992). Stimulation is not just information that can be stored and processed, but it has the potential to directly engage intrinsic motives such as curiosity/exploration and mastery as well as a variety of extrinsic motives. As such, it connects to capacities for self-regulation and self-management. A case in point: We recently looked at the relationship between having opportunities for *productive activity* (our umbrella term for access to the four types of stimulation described previously) and behavior problems in children (Bradley & Corwyn, 2005). We argued that self-regulation emerges as a by-product of engaging in intrinsically motivated activities (Ryan & Deci, 2000). According to self-determination theory, intrinsic motives such as curiosity, affiliation, and mastery energize and direct the pursuit of goals beginning in infancy. These motives can be more frequently enacted when a child is exposed to a rich array of objects, people, and events. Frequent exposure to a variety of objects, people, and situations, particularly under the guidance of adults or more accomplished peers, not only helps satisfy the motives for curiosity and mastery but gradually promotes attention focusing, volitional control, and strategic planning. A sense of autonomy emerges that increases the child's comfort and well-being. A by-product of the experience is a gradual integration of both discovered and prompted regulation to the self (Ryan & Deci, 2000).

In a stimulus-rich environment, there is a much greater likelihood that a child's activity will become goal-directed and productive (i.e., directed toward satisfying some instrumental or hedonic goal—there is something to be gained from the effort). There is also a much greater likelihood that a child will develop self-regulatory capacities in that self-regulation emerges when "feedback from prior performance is used to make adjustments during current efforts" (Zimmerman, 2000, p. 14). The social cognitive perspective on self-regulation stipulates that self-regulatory skills emerge as part of the acquisition of a wide range of task competencies, from personal care and psychomotor performance to academic learning (Schunk & Zimmerman, 1997). In the process, self-regulatory competence may begin to emerge as a child observes and then emulates those who are more competent. However, advanced levels of self-regulation come with deliberate practice and opportunities to make adjustments based on outcomes, the latter leading to a sense of agency (Bandura, 1997). Stimulus-poor environments can lead to dysfunctions in self-regulation as a result of the apathy or disinterest. In effect, there is no need for a child to anticipate, plan, or direct efforts because there are few opportunities that afford the child a chance to direct efforts toward desired outcomes. There is a higher probability that children in such circumstances will use reactive rather than proactive methods to manage personal outcomes, thus never developing a sense of agency or self-control. Additionally, stimulus-poor environments tend to give rise to depression and mood disorders, which tend to work against the development of effective self-regulatory strategies (Zimmerman, 2000).

Kuhl (2000) argues that "whenever a sufficient number of opportunities are encountered for associating activation of the self with the elicitation of positive or the down regulation of negative affects, the self acquires the capacity to control positive and negative affects, respectively" (p. 142). Central to his Personality Systems Interaction Theory (PSIT) is the notion of extension memory. Extension memory concerns self-representations; that is, ideas and vignettes about personal preferences, needs, emotional states, and options for action in particular situations and past experiences involving the self. Activation of extension memory (i.e., those memories most focused on ideas and scripts associated with the self) connects to the neurobiological mechanisms (i.e., hippocampal functions) involved in self-relaxation. According to Kuhl (2000), "Any activity that capitalizes on the extended semantic networks provided by extension memory and the feeling system supported by it can help downregulate negative affect" (p. 138). PSI theory stipulates that, to the extent that a situation activates appropriate self-representations (e.g., values associated with the activity), it tends to generate anticipatory and ongoing positive affect. Positive affect, in turn, tends to support self-regulation and self-enhancing (adaptive) behavior. In effect, the more potentially useful and meaningful objects, events, and activities to which a child has access (within limits), the more likely the child will experience positive, self-sustaining affect and the less likely the child will engage in maladaptive behavior.

Using these theoretical arguments as a framework, we examined relations between having opportunities for productive activity (access to stimulation of various types) from birth through age four-and-a-half and behavior problems during first grade, controlling for family demographics, maternal sensitivity (see "Support" following), use of harsh punishment, and time spent in child care (Bradley & Corwyn, 2005). The greater a child's access to productive activity, the lower were both mother-reported and teacher-reported behavior problems. The connection was mediated by child self-control.

SUPPORT

As valuable as stimulation is for self-regulation and good emotional health, optimal social-emotional development depends on having an environment that responds to human social and emotional needs directly as well (Bretherton & Waters, 1985). This is an extraordinary challenge in that it means helping children cope with basic anxieties, fears, and feelings of emotional insecurity. It also means inculcating a sense of belonging and worth, facilitating a sense of happiness and fulfillment, and promoting a sense of responsibility and concern for others.

One of the most important investments parents make in their children is assisting them with emotion regulation (Thompson, 1994). The emotion arousal system is rather easily triggered in conditions that pose threat or conditions that offer opportunities for exploration. Emotions also provide a primitive regulatory process that operates before a person constructs evaluative thoughts and constructs values, preferences, and personal goals. To ensure optimal fit with environmental affordances and demands, children need parents who invest their time and energy enlisting and modulating the motivational properties of emotions (Eisenberg, Cumberland, & Spinrad, 1998). Sometimes this means that parents must take action in advance of expressed needs (e.g., assuring a child that the babysitter will be there to take care of the child while they are away or assuring the child that things will be okay at that first day of school). Other times it means taking action after the needs are expressed (e.g., comforting a child awakened by a nightmare or frightened by a bully). Parents may help the child with emotion regulation by comforting, distracting, or redirecting attention to safer and more enjoyable pursuits. Studies indicate that responsive, social interactions on the part of mothers assist infants in regulating arousal (Fogel, Diamond, Langhorst, & Demos, 1982) and may contribute to a general capacity to regulate arousal (Gable & Isabella, 1992). As children get older, socioemotional support from parents may take the form of assisting them to realistically appraise situations so that stress is minimized, effective coping strategies can be employed, and goals leading to a sense of fulfillment can be pursued (Lazarus, 1993). It may even take the form of "emotion coaching" (Johnson & Lieberman, 1999).

According to Erikson, responsive care builds a sense of trust in others and the environment more generally. Predictable, responsive care also contributes to a secure attachment (Ainsworth, 1973; Bowlby, 1969). Children who are securely attached to their parents are in an advantaged position to develop a balanced sense of self (Cassidy, 1988), positive social relationships (Park & Waters, 1989), and an increased capacity to modulate stress reactions (Caldji et al., 1998). Importantly, a secure attachment moves a child toward an orientation of mutuality in which there is greater receptivity for other parental actions, such as socialization on getting along with others and investing in learning activities (Kochanska, 1997).

Socioemotional support entails more than just responding to expressed needs and helping children regulate their emotions. Children thrive when they feel wanted. Feeling wanted motivates children to pursue life-enhancing goals. Rohner (1986) compiled evidence from several large cross-cultural studies showing that warm, supportive relationships help promote good adjustment, a sense of well-being, good health, and a wealth of other positive developmental outcomes. There is also evidence that children benefit from positive affirmation of worth (Ausubel, 1968; Roberts, 1983). That is, to be supportive, parents must be reinforcing (in a proactive sense) as well as responsive (in a reactive sense). How worth is affirmed varies substantially from culture to culture. In some societies, worth is closely tied to individual accomplishments or status; in others, it is more strongly tied to collective commitments and involvement.

The extent to which parents show affection to their child has been examined in the Panel Study of Income Dynamics (PSID) and the National Longitudinal Survey of Youth (NLSY) data sets. Both of these large data sets involve nationally representative cohorts of families in the United States.

Ninety-one percent of mothers and 77.2 percent of fathers in the PSID indicated that they hugged or showed physical affection to their child in the past month (Yeung, 1999). A smaller percentage of mothers and fathers said "I love you" to the child (86.5% and 66.9%, respectively), and even fewer said words of appreciation to the child (35.1% and 38.8%, respectively).

Using NLSY data, Bradley, Corwyn, McAdoo, et al. (2001) found ethnic group and poverty status differences in the responsiveness of parents. Eighty-seven percent of nonpoor white and 73.4 percent of poor white parents showed physical affection to their infant or toddler during the one-hour, in-home interview. Hispanic parents showed similar levels of affection, and African American parents showed lower levels of physical affection. Eighty percent of nonpoor African American families and 64.3 percent of poor African American families showed physical affection to the child. Parents were less likely to show physical affection as the child aged. Only 63.2 percent of nonpoor white, 48.7 percent of poor white, 46.2 percent of nonpoor African American, and 31.7 percent of poor African American parents were observed kissing or hugging their three- to five-year-old child.

A supportive environment is also one in which there is encouragement and guidance for adequate functioning outside the family environment (Pettit, Dodge, & Brown, 1988). Part of this takes the form of reinforcing behaviors that lead to competence and engagement in activities that promote success outside the home. Part takes the form of expressions of expectations for involvement and success (Steinberg, 1986). Finally, part may take the form of modeling of adaptive behaviors (Putallaz, 1987). A good example of the latter is maintaining calm during periods of threat or stress. Such behavior has been shown to reduce the negative impact of events (e.g., storms) and conditions (e.g., war) that often produce traumatic reactions in children (Klingman, 2002). At its base, support is an investment that provides motivation to comfortably and productively engage the broader environment.

To function well within social groups (and society at large), children not only must learn how to regulate their emotions but to control their behavior (Bronson, 2000). Accordingly, parents must provide the kind of productive discipline that facilitates behavioral control. Although issues surrounding the use of corporal punishment remain controversial, there is ample evidence that harsh and inconsistent punishment has negative consequences. By contrast, discipline styles that include more use of reasoning, problem solving, and consistent limit setting are associated with more optimal outcomes (Hart, DeWolf, Wozniak, & Burts, 1992; Larzelere, 2000). That said, there is evidence that there are sociocultural differences in the use and consequences of more restrictive and controlling forms of discipline (McLoyd, Cauce, Takeuchi, & Wilson, 2000; Whaley, 2000). There is suggestive evidence that, because respect for authority is more normative in African American and Latino families, strictness short of harsh punishment may have fewer negative consequences in such families.

Ordinary life presents most parents sufficient challenge when it comes to providing adequate social and emotional support for children. However, the giant tsunami that arose in the Indian Ocean in 2004 reminds us that real human life is pockmarked with disturbances and conditions that can markedly change the flow and effect of ordinary daily routines and parenting practices (from exposure to war and family conflict, to encounters with bullies and predators, to living with family members who abuse drugs or are mentally ill, to the experience of parental death or family disruption, and so forth). For some of these highly destabilizing circumstances (e.g., natural disasters, divorce), the negative impacts on child social and emotional functioning are reasonably well documented, and for some there is a wealth of professional advice on how to handle the aftermath (Brohl, 1996; La Greca & Prinstein, 2002; Monahon, 1993). For other situations, much less is known. The fact is, children (especially young children) have limited capacities to regulate powerful emotional responses. Therefore, highly distressing events and conditions may trigger a bifurcation in the cognitive/emotional attractors around which adaptive functioning is organized (Lewis & Junyk, 1997). The experience of serious trauma or loss can result in: (1) increased fear and anxiety; (2) a severe undermining of basic trust or social support; (3) a strong sense of instability, unmanageability, or confusion; or (4) damage to the capacity to form personal assets. In effect, serious trauma and loss have the potential to affect long-lasting detrimental change in the organization of personality, particularly through disruptions to emotional security and undermining of coping capacities. It remains unclear whether the ordinary types of parental supports for social and emotional well-being (being sensitive and responsive, being warm and affirming, providing models and expectations for appropriate social behavior, using positive approaches to discipline) will be enough for children challenged by serious trauma and loss or whether something more and different may be needed (van der Kolk, 1996). The limited research available suggests that parents are likely to need to "up the ante" in most of these areas, at least in the short term, and that more careful monitoring (see "Surveillance") and structuring (see "Structuring") may be required as well. Hence, the need for more targeted and integrated research on the problem of parental responses to traumatic events and major adverse conditions in children's lives.

Another area badly in need of additional research is differential responsiveness of children to parental efforts to provide socioemotional support. Belsky (2005) makes an argument, based on evolutionary psychology, that there is differential susceptibility to the force of parental actions. Nowhere is this perhaps more apparent than children's responses to parental warmth and sensitivity. For example, Crockenberg (1981) found that parental sensitivity was much more strongly linked to attachment security for children who were initially difficult to soothe than for children who were more easily soothed. Another way to look at Belsky's argument is that perhaps some children *need* parental support more than others, notably children who have greater difficulty self-regulating. Following this notion, we looked at the relation of maternal sensitivity and behavior problems. In our analyses we controlled for family demographics, mother-child conflict, amount of time in child care, parental use of harsh punishment, and access to stimulating materials and experiences. With these controls we found no evidence that level of maternal sensitivity was related to mother-reported behavior problems in first grade (parental harshness and exposure to stimulation did matter). For teacher-reported behavior problems, maternal sensitivity mattered, but only for temperamentally difficult children.

STRUCTURE

Although children need sustenance, stimulation, and support for optimal growth and development, there also is evidence that the relation between these inputs and either growth or development is not constant. Receiving equal amounts of these inputs does not seem to result in equal amounts of "good" growth and development. The arrangement of inputs may be as crucial to development as amount. In sum, optimal parenting consists of not only ensuring that sufficient amounts of stimulation, sustenance, and support reach a child but also configuring or structuring a child's encounters with those direct inputs so that "fit" is achieved (Wachs, 2000). For example, preterm infants, infants exposed to drugs prenatally, and some children with autism can be overwhelmed by levels of stimulation that are quite comfortable for normal children (Als, 1986; Friedman & Sigman, 1992). Likewise, Kagan (2003) discusses the difficulty so-called shy children have with social stimulation. Such children quickly become fearful in unfamiliar surroundings. For each temperamental style there is a distinct neurochemistry that affects excitability, with more excitable children requiring greater structure and support from their environments. Consider even the mundane task of feeding a child. It is not enough that the parent provides sufficient nourishment. Research shows that poor timing and pacing of feeding may contribute to failure to thrive (Drotar, 1985). Parental efforts to control food can also affect the likelihood that children will become obese (Birch & Davison, 2001).

Parents tend to invest considerable energy structuring the physical surroundings of children. Environmental psychologists have long been interested in how physical structures influence behavior and facilitate adaptive functioning (e.g., how physical arrangements within a home help to ensure privacy; Altman, 1977). In effect, the design of the physical space enables and encourages people to do certain things and constrains them from doing others (Rapoport, 1985). Among the most revealing studies of the influence of physical structure are those by Moore (1988) on the spatial organization of daycare centers. He found that, in contrast to children in both fully open-plan and fully closed-plan spatial organization, children in modified open-plan environments were more visually and actively engaged in developmentally oriented tasks. Group size was smaller, age mixing was greater, and there was almost twice as much social interaction. In open-plan centers, there was more random nontask behavior. In closed-plan centers, there was more withdrawn behavior and more teacher-directed behavior. Orderly environments enable children to learn the meaning and function of things more readily. Having distinctive, well-situated landmarks makes it easier for children to orient themselves and to get around in their surroundings (Evans et al., 1991).

Children have limitations in their ability to effectively deal with their environments. For instance, the number of objects that a person can manage effectively at any one point in time increases with age (Kuhn, 1992). Young children in particular also have less developed cognitive strategies for selecting, remembering, and dealing with information and are, therefore, more dependent on instructional or other environmental aids to assist them in problem solving (Bjorlund, 1990). Children also are limited in their ability to deal with stress and complexity, to obtain needed materials for use or consumption, to exercise control over their own bodies, and to manage social situations (Ford & Lerner, 1992). Accordingly, parents must structure a child's encounters with the environment to benefit the child.

The Committee on Developments in the Science of Learning concluded that, "Parents and others who care for children arrange their activities and facilitate learning by regulating the difficulty of the tasks and by modeling mature performance during joint participation in activities" (Bransford et al., 2000, p. 103). Likewise, studies of language development show that parental scaffolding of children's early language experiences (i.e., providing a predictable referential and social context for communication) contributes significantly to language acquisition (Bruner, 1983). The research on dialogic reading tells the same story. Specifically, children's language scores and early competence in reading were superior when adults helped the children tell the story in a book rather than just reading the story to them (Whitehurst, Arnold, Epstein, & Angell, 1994). The fact is, parents invest their time in structuring productive learning activities in a myriad of ways, from placing an object to be manipulated in the hands of an infant, to setting up routine times for homework, to providing increasingly challenging lessons on driving to the adolescent. Learning is also easier in the absence of distracting stimuli (Wohlwill & Heft, 1977). In general, the evidence shows that children's cognitive development is influenced by how parents organize the physical and temporal features of a child's environment (Bradley & Caldwell, 1976). Gutman and McLoyd (2000) found that careful management of a child's education within the home was especially important for low-income African American children living in urban settings, including careful monitoring of homework (see "Surveillance").

For children, meaning also comes from having order in the social environment. This often takes the form of routines and family rituals. There is evidence attesting to the general value of establishing family routines, as they provide a kind of overarching structure to the child's daily life, thus making life more predictable and manageable (Melamed, 2002). Family rituals not only provide a sense of order but serve as a means of socialization (Fiese, Hooker, Kotary, & Schwagler, 1993). One routine that is assessed in national surveys is how often families eat meals together. Analysis of NLSY data show that eating family meals together varies by poverty status, ethnicity, and the child's age (Bradley, Corwyn, McAdoo, et al., 2001). Among children younger than age three, the percentage who ate at least one meal a day with both parents was 74.1 percent for nonpoor white children, 65.3 percent for poor white children, 59.9 percent for nonpoor African American children, and 36.7 percent for poor African American children. The percentages for Hispanic children were very similar to those of white children. The percentages for children older than age 12 were: nonpoor whites, 64.2 percent; poor whites, 51 percent; nonpoor African Americans, 37.4 percent; and poor African Americans, 25.7 percent. Parents also assist their children in developing friendships. Ladd and Goltner (1988) found that children whose parents initiated peer contacts had more playmates and more consistent play companions in their preschool peer networks.

As stated in the previous section "Support," additional structure may be particularly important for children faced with threats, chaos, and uncertainty. Perhaps the most obvious situations for which the role of organizer of a child's experiences is important are events like war and natural catastrophes because they often produce disruptions in daily routines. One of the most common reactions to loss and trauma is the perception of lack of control over the situation (Tennen & Affleck, 1990). The sense of powerlessness produces a high degree of distress and may lead to very ineffective coping strategies. Absent some assistance, a child may get stuck in a pattern of ineffective coping (Falsetti & Resnick, 1995). For example, it is common to show some behavioral regression after experiencing trauma (Monahon, 1993). Likewise, they may function in a near constant state of wariness out of fear the trauma will return. Accordingly, they may withdraw or be far less spontaneous as regards activities and interactions with others (for some, the responses are just the reverse). Killan and Agathangelou (2001) found that children fare better when parents were able to foster a continuing sense of family cohesion and a general sense that there is still coherence and manageability in life, a finding consistent with research showing that routines generally promote good mental health (Fiese et al., 1993). Silverman and La Greca (2002) reported that reactions to natural disasters tend to be more severe and long lasting when accompanied by other disruptions to daily life (e.g., displacement from home, school closings). Thus, the recommendation for maintaining as much routine and "normalcy" as possible. That said, the kind of structuring needed to help children with many traumatic events and high-stress conditions is not always obvious. For children living in high-risk communities, use of restrictive management strategies resulted in more expressed anger and poor school performance, whereas use of promotive management strategies resulted in better academic performance (Gutman, Friedel, & Hitt, 2003).

Events such as divorce or incarceration of a parent often initiate a prolonged period of instability (Kazura, 2001). Children move from a time when there was an established set of family rituals and roles through a time when a new set is being established, from a time when there was a set of places and connections associated with family life through a time disassembling then reassembling those associations, from a time when they had two parents to turn to for comfort, advice, and just a good time to a time when there was only one. In effect, just when the protective function of established places, roles, and rituals is most needed, routines are crumbling along with the family itself (Lewis, 1983). How parents deal with this process of disassembling and reassembling is largely unknown, except by anecdote. What is reasonably well established is that parents tend to do less monitoring and exercise less control in the immediate aftermath of divorce (Hetherington, Stanley-Hagan, & Anderson, 1989). However, Strength (1991) found that consistent enforcement of limits was actually beneficial in that it made the child feel cared for. Less is known about incarceration (Kazura, 2001). According to Nichols (1984), the postdivorce period (a period that often lasts many months) is a time for parents to focus on reorganizing the family system and reconnecting family members to social and institutional support structures. It is also a time for parents to resume their customary pursuits as well as encourage their children to do the same (Wallerstein, 1983). Research by Bradley and colleagues (1994) suggests that parental efforts to provide greater structure in family life is likely to be helpful in most situations in which there is increased family instability. However, there is little to suggest precisely what additional types of routines and structures might be needed as regards particular types of traumatic and highly destabilizing events and conditions.

In overview, there are a number of potentially useful strategies parents might use to help provide additional structure in the aftermath of trauma or periods of destabilization. They include various techniques for structuring the physical environment, structuring social encounters, scaffolding learning experiences, and maintaining routines. Likewise, there are a number of strategies that parents can employ for ongoing circumstances in which there is substantial threat or uncertainty (e.g., living with a mentally ill or abusive parent, living in a dangerous neighborhood). Unfortunately, in situations in which children are faced with chaos, danger, and uncertainty, parents are themselves likely to be faced with chaos, danger, and uncertainty, therefore they are less able to provide the needed additional structure for their children. The same double whammy also pertains to adverse situations generally. Lower SES parents are less likely to provide consistent daily routines (Britto, Fuligni, & Brooks-Gunn, 2002). Although little is known about most strategies aimed at providing productive structure for children, success will depend on the broader context in which it occurs. For example, the effectiveness of parental efforts to help manage children's behavior in dangerous surroundings is likely to depend on the level of social cohesion and value consensus in the community or neighborhood (Steinberg, Darling, Fletcher, Brown, & Dornbusch, 1995).

SURVEILLANCE

To be effective in managing children's lives, parents must keep track of their whereabouts and activities. Most commonly, surveillance has been thought of as keeping track of the child and of environmental conditions to which the child is exposed so as to protect the child from harm (Darling & Steinberg, 1993; Lozoff, 1989; Patterson, DeBaryshe, & Ramsey, 1989; U.S. Department of Health and Human Services, 1991). A significant proportion of accidental or unintentional injury occurs because of parental failure to adequately monitor and supervise children (Garbarino, 1988; Peterson & Gable, 1998). The level of child monitoring and the parent's overall supervisory style (i.e., the parent's degree of active attention to removing or attending to potentially dangerous objects and conditions) directly contribute to the likelihood of injury, and both are connected to parental perceptions about the level of risk present and the controllability of the hazards (Greaves, Glik, Kronenfeld, & Jackson, 1994). There are concerns about sexual predators and exposure to violence on TV (Dorr, Rabin, & Ireland, 2002). For such circumstances, the research on surveillance is limited, but it seems clear that the amount and type of surveillance needed changes with age (Peterson, Ewigman, & Kivlahan, 1993).

What and how often parents must monitor in order to assure children's safety and well-being depends on their social and physical surroundings, the *setting* in the classic sense used by environmental psychologists. Each setting, because of the particular persons, objects, and activities it contains, imposes different pressures on parents in terms of maintaining visual or physical contact with a child. These pressures vary in accordance with a child's competence and proclivities. Closer proximity is generally required in malls and near busy streets than on a neighborhood playground. Baby-proofing the household is a common response when children are infants and toddlers. In crowded, chaotic, resource-poor settings such as exist in Brazilian shantytowns, adequate monitoring can be very difficult. Parents frequently impose on older siblings part of the responsibility for such tasks. By contrast, in stable neighborhoods where there is a high degree of social integration and relatively few physical dangers, monitoring is often distributed across members of the community. Steinberg et al. (1995) found, however, that social integration only has benefits for children when most of the parents in the neighborhood practice good parenting, including close monitoring of child activities.

There is considerable evidence that surveillance is important to adaptive behavior. For example, Steinberg (1986) found that latchkey children who report home after school, whose parents know their whereabouts and who have been reared authoritatively, are less susceptible to peer pressure than those who hang out with peers after school and whose parents provide little supervision. Crouter, MacDonald, McHale, and Perry-Jenkins (1990) examined relations between parental monitoring and children's school performance and conduct. They found that less-monitored boys received lower grades than did other children, and less-monitored boys from dual-earner families had poorer conduct. Studies have shown that parental monitoring is related to substance abuse, juvenile delinquency, and school achievement for children in middle childhood and adolescence (Brown, Mounts, Lamborn, & Steinberg, 1993; Dornbusch, Ritter, Leiderman, Roberts, & Fraleigh, 1987; Loeber & Dishion, 1983). Patterson et al. (1989) concluded from their review of antisocial behavior that poor monitoring and supervision of children's activities often contribute to the development of antisocial behavior. Unmonitored children are more likely to respond to peer pressure and to engage in risky behavior. In their report, the Committee on Community-Level Programs for Youth of the National Research Council and Institute of Medicine concluded that, "Across settings, there is more positive development and fewer problem behaviors with consistent monitoring by parents" (Eccles & Gootman, 2002, p. 92). That said, monitoring of children, adolescents in particular, is not always so easy to effect, as recent studies have shown (Stattin & Kerr, 2000). Effective monitoring may require developing good parent–child relationships as well (see "Support").

Very little is known about how much parents keep tabs on young children. Based on NLSY data on whether the parent kept the focal child in view during a one-hour home visit, nonpoor families were more likely to keep track of infants and toddlers than poor families (Bradley, Corwyn, McAdoo, et al., 2001). Approximately 90 percent of nonpoor white and 81 percent of poor whites kept the child in view during the interview. Fewer nonpoor and poor African American (85.3% and 78.2%, respectively) and nonpoor and poor Hispanics (84.7% and 82.9%, respectively) kept the child in view. The bulk of research on parental monitoring has focused on adolescence. The National Survey of American Attitudes on Substance Abuse asks teens about 12 surveillance actions they attribute to their parents: monitoring television, monitoring the Internet, restricting music they buy, knowing their whereabouts after school, expecting to be told the truth about where the teen is going, very aware of academic performance, imposing a curfew, making clear they do not approve of marijuana use, eating dinner with teen six or seven times a week, turning off television during dinner, assigning teen regular chores, and being present when teen returns from school. Only 27 percent of teens indicated that their parents consistently took 10 or more of these actions (National Center for Addiction and Substance Abuse, 2001). Nearly one-fifth (18%) of teens reported that their parents took five or fewer of these actions.

There is a tendency among those who write about the importance of monitoring to restrict the conversation to issues around monitoring children so that they are protected from harm and do not engage in bad behavior. However, to effectively carry out such tasks as stimulation, structure, and support means that parents also have to be on the lookout for circumstances that afford ways for their children to be productively engaged with the environment. At present there is almost no information on this aspect of parental surveillance.

SOCIAL INTEGRATION

For anthropologists, it is accepted as axiomatic that a major goal of parenting is to effectively connect children to the social fabric of society

(Weisner, 2002), for it is in connecting to important social networks and groups that children are most likely to thrive. To a large degree, Coleman's (1988) argument in behalf of the importance of social capital (resources achieved through social connections) makes much the same point. Scott-Jones (1995) discusses the value of parental efforts to help children to become effectively engaged in school as an avenue for high achievement. She mentions that parental expectations are often a means of increasing such engagement. Nickerson (1992) presents evidence that one way parents help children forge productive connections with learning institutions is through modeling and sharing stories about their own involvement in education. Indeed, there is reason to believe that parents may help children forge productive connections to a variety of social networks and organizations through their own involvement in such networks. Pianta and Walsh (1996) use systems theory as a framework for elucidating how families forge productive partnerships with schools. They mention taking children to school for visits, family involvement in school activities, and assisting children with homework as examples. As well, they include deliberate encounters with teachers and other school personnel. There is emerging evidence that parental involvement in schools increases school engagement and that school engagement increases student achievement (Brody, Flor, & Gibson, 1999).

Although there is more literature dealing with connections to school than any other social institution, there is at least some evidence pointing to the value of connections with other institutions as well. Most notable, perhaps, is involvement in religious organizations. Brody and Flor (1998) found that affiliation with church contributed to effective parenting and child competence in poor, single-parent African American families. Involvement in religious activities was associated with stronger social networks for urban youth and gave them greater access to social resources (King & Furrow, 2004). There is also evidence that social integration within the neighborhood and community more generally can have benefits. For example, in tight-knit communities, monitoring of children tends to be distributed across adults in the surrounding area. As a result there tends to be fewer injuries (Rivara & Mueller, 1987).

The specific processes used by parents to help children connect better to social networks and institutions have not been documented in detail. However, it almost certainly begins by having regular encounters and involvements with kith and kin. It is also likely to include having the child involved with various social groups and institutions (be they churches, social organizations, informal social networks, schools, or the like). The parents own involvement (independent of the child) in social networks and institutions is also likely to help a child with social integration, via modeling and occasional contacts. Further, there are cultural considerations that will impact the degree and types of institutions that families interact with. For example, recent immigrants may lack a deep understanding of the institutions that are dominated by the new (unfamiliar) culture, generating conflict and confusion between teachers and parents (Greenfield, Quiroz, & Raeff, 2000).

Does careful attention to these six parenting tasks promote positive adaptation in children? The most straightforward answer is: The research is incomplete. However, there is suggestive evidence. For example, we conducted a study of 243 premature, low-birth-weight children living in chronic poverty. The purpose was to determine whether the availability of protective factors in the home environment at age one and at age three increased the probability of resiliency. Resiliency was operationalized as being in good to excellent health, being within the normal range for growth, not being below clinically designated cutoffs for maladaptive behavior on the Child Behavior Checklist, and having an IQ of 85 or greater. Six home environment factors were considered potentially protective: (1) low household density, (2) the availability of a safe play area, (3) parental acceptance and lack of punitiveness, (4) parental responsivity, (5) the availability of learning materials, and (6) variety of experiences. The first two would be classified under the category sustenance, the second two under the category support, and the final two under the category stimulation. Fifteen percent of the children with three or more protective factors present in the home at age one were classified as resilient. By contrast, only 2 percent of children with two or fewer protective factors were classified as resilient. Similarly, 20 percent of children with three or more protective factors present in the home at age three were classified as resilient, whereas only 6 percent of children with two or fewer protective factors were resilient (Bradley et al., 1994).

Context + Consciousness = Complexity

Although research findings indicate that parents can be instrumental in moving children along a positive developmental course, even the best parenting is no guarantee. The evidence does not show that parenting is highly deterministic of children's long-term well-being but rather that it combines with other influences in quite complex ways (Collins, Maccoby, Steinberg, Hetherington, & Bornstein, 2000). In his tantalizing book *Altering Fate,* Lewis (1997) made much of the fact that it is extraordinarily difficult to predict the course of individual lives. It is not just that the measures of parenting and the measures of children's characteristics are imperfectly reliable. It is not just that developmental theory is imprecise. It is not even just that there are myriad biological and contextual factors that impinge on development. Lewis (1997) argued that predicting the course of individual development is difficult because accidental occurrences pervade our real lives. He also argued that predicting the course of development for any given person is difficult because humans are conscious beings; thus, part of our fate is in our own hands. We make meaning of what we experience, and we make choices that affect our lives.

Developmental theory stipulates that the meaning a child makes of any particular action on the part of parents is conditioned by the full tableaux of experiences within the family and in those other microcontexts in which the child spends time (e.g., child care, school, peer group; Bronfenbrenner, 1995; Ford & Lerner, 1992). Family life is complexly organized, and its influence on the lives of children involves a myriad of interwoven processes. At the moment when it is encountered, a specific parenting action operates at the foreground of a child's conscious awareness. That action is set against a background of other actions, objects, events, and conditions occurring both in and through time. It is this background, together with the foreground, that determines the meaning a child makes of the specific action. Unfortunately, the vast majority of studies on parenting do not consider the impact of each child's background of experience when examining particular types of parenting actions, opting instead to treat all other experiences as if they somehow do not matter or balance out. Such an approach is inconsistent with both theory and research.

Although we know very little about how often parents engage in most actions included as part of the six Ss, what we know is that they vary greatly and that the variability is linked to the context of parenting and to characteristics of the child. Over the years, any number of models have emerged that have depicted the relation among family processes, child development, and the context in which both occur. Urie Bronfenbrenner's (1995) bioecological systems process-person-context-time model is one of the most well regarded of these models. The essence of his model is captured in two propositions.

Proposition 1. Human development takes place through processes of progressively more complex reciprocal interaction between an active, evolving organism and the persons, objects, and symbols in its immediate environment. To be effective, the interaction must occur on a fairly regular basis over extended periods of time. Such enduring forms of interaction are referred to as *proximal processes.*

Proposition 2. The form, power, content, and direction of the proximal processes affecting development vary systematically as a joint function of the characteristics of the developing person, of the environment, both immediate and more remote, in which the processes are taking place, and the nature of the developmental outcomes under consideration.

Although culture and social class (and, to a lesser extent, community) are almost always mentioned when discussing contextual influences on parenting practice, Bronfenbrenner's (1995) model is far more inclusive. Parents are also influenced by governmental regulations and policies (Temporary Assistance for Needy Families regulations have had mixed impacts on the time spent with children), laws (e.g., seat-belt laws), public health campaigns (sudden infant death syndrome deaths have declined), and educational programs. What parents do is often influenced by social institutions. Bronfenbrenner referred to this set of influences as *meso system relations.* The activities, practices, and expectations present at school, work, and church often help shape how parents act toward their children.

One reason it is hard to estimate just how much yield will accrue to particular types of parenting behavior is that actions of a particular kind do not occur in isolation from the larger portfolio of parental activities, nor do they function in isolation from those other activities. The same parent who provides a rich array of stimulating experiences for a child also tends to structure those experiences such that they have the effect of promoting competence and enjoyment. Likewise, the parent who provides a child with expressions of affection and affirmation is likely to carefully monitor the child's whereabouts. There is ample evidence that parents who score high in one area of positive action also tend to score high in other areas of positive action (Bradley, 1994). Accordingly, it is difficult to tease apart the value of particular types of investments.

Unfortunately, the literature on parenting and child development is not very helpful in that the vast majority of studies focus on only one type of parenting behavior at a time, too often attributing any "effect" observed to that type and ignoring its covariation with other types of investments. An interesting exception is in studies of malnutrition. For several decades, researchers who want to understand the impact of poor nutrition on cognitive competencies have understood the importance of controlling for the level of stimulation available to the child.

We recently conducted a series of analyses on data from the National Longitudinal Survey of Youth (NLSY) that attest to the value of simultaneously considering several aspects of the home environment (Bradley & Corwyn, 2003). We examined the relation of learning stimulation and maternal responsiveness to a diversity of outcomes in three different ethnic groups over three developmental periods. In each analysis, we included both types of family process measures. We often found that each aspect of parenting contributed to the prediction of child developmental outcomes when controlling for the other aspects but that predictions were lower than the simple bivariate correlation between each specific process and each particular outcome.

Another reason it is difficult to estimate the yield for a particular parenting process is that the impact of these processes depends not only on when they occur (i.e., the timing) but on how long they continue (i.e., the duration or constancy). A good example of research on timing is a study by Duncan, Brooks-Gunn, and Klebanov (1994) that showed that poverty early in childhood has a greater negative impact on intelligence than poverty later in childhood. As regards duration, there is evidence that persistent poverty has deeper and more long-lasting effects than transient poverty (Bradley & Corwyn, 2002). Bradley, Caldwell, and Rock (1988) found that some types of parental behavior seem to have greater impact on particular child outcomes if the behavior occurs early in a child's life, other types of behavior seem to have greater impact if they occur closer in time to when the outcome is measured, yet others seem to have a cumulative impact through time. Recently, based on seven waves of data from the NLSY, maternal responsiveness during early adolescence was found to be related to Peabody Picture Vocabulary Test scores even when controlling for maternal responsiveness during middle childhood. By contrast, learning stimulation measured when children were in early adolescence was correlated with Peabody Individual Achievement Test Reading scores, but the effect became nonsignificant when controlling for the learning stimulation during prior developmental periods (Bradley & Corwyn, 2003).

"No man is an island" said John Dunne in his famous poem of the same title. Nowhere does this admonition seem to fit so well as in the case of siblings. What a child makes of a particular parental action also reflects how the parent treats other household members in similar situations, as research on differential treatment of siblings has shown (Plomin & Daniels, 1987). That is, the child will compare his or her treatment to the treatment given others. Suppose, for example, that Eddie's father generally manifests a low level of communicative responsiveness to Eddie. Although that will generally have a negative effect on Eddie's socioemotional well-being, Eddie's reaction to Dad's failure to fully respond to his bid for attention will depend on Eddie's belief about how responsive Dad is to siblings or whoever else lives in the house. Moreover, as Feinberg, McHale, Crouter, and Cumsille (2003) have shown, perceived inequitable treatment affects how siblings respond to one another.

A child's reaction to a particular parent action is also a function of the overall ambiance or style (e.g., the overall amount of conflict present, the degree of optimism or cohesion in the family, a general style of interaction among family members, an overall level of organization or harmony) present in the home. As a rule, these pervading conditions are more distal than behaviors aimed directly at the child by other household members present; albeit, there are exceptions such as background noise. Ambient conditions indirectly affect children, and they moderate the effect of direct exchanges between children and those persons and objects in the home environment (e.g., a high level of background noise reduces the effectiveness of parental attempts to teach the child, a high degree of parental conflict may reduce the effectiveness of parental attempts to nurture the child). Darling and Steinberg (1993) proposed, for example, that parenting style is best viewed as a context that modifies the influence of specific parenting practices. Cummings, Zahn-Waxler, and Radke-Yarrow (1981) observed that toddlers exposed to frequent marital conflict reacted more intensively to later episodes of parental conflict than children who experienced less frequent conflict.

The message from these studies seems to be that life is not just a collection of isolated events or experiences but a composite of many experiences in and through time. The impact of any one type of parenting process investment depends on its consistency across time and the array of other environmental inputs present, both from the family and from outside (e.g., school). Accordingly, to better understand the yield on any particular parenting process requires examining that investment in light of other processes using more finely tuned measures, with attention paid to particular processes through time.

CONCLUSION

If the past only dimly foreshadows what is to come, then one may wonder what the future of parenting science holds. The realities of child rearing in the twenty-first century present extraordinary obstacles to definitive research, with complexity and diversity in arrangements compounding the ordinary problems of linking particular parenting practices to the trajectory of development in highly evolved, phylogenetically advanced organisms living in rich, multilayered contexts. As the future intrudes into daily life with ever-increasing speed and persistence, the job of parenting will rely less on prescriptions and more on flexible problem-solving strategies aimed at finding the best fit between long-term goals for a child, the child's current needs and capabilities, and what the environment affords by way of demands and opportunities. Parenting science must move quickly to develop new theories and methodologies just to keep up.

REFERENCES

Ainsworth, M. (1973). The development of infant-mother attachment. In B. Caldwell & H. Riccuiti (Eds.), *Review of child development research* (Vol. 3, pp. 2–94). Chicago: University of Chicago Press.

Als, H. (1986). A synactive model of neonatal behavioral organization: Framework for the assessment of neurobehavioral development in the premature infant and for support of infants and parents in the neonatal intensive care environment. *Physical & Occupational Therapy in Pediatrics, 6,* 3–55.

Altman, I. (1977). Privacy regulation: Culturally universal or culturally specific? *Journal of Social Issues, 33,* 66–84.

Ausubel, D. (1968). *Educational psychology: A cognitive view.* New York: Holt, Rinehart and Winston.

Bandura, A. (1997). *Self-efficacy: The exercise of control.* New York: Freeman.

Belsky, J. (2005). Differential susceptibility to rearing influence: An evolutionary hypothesis and some evidence. In B. Ellis & D. Bjorklund (Eds.), *Origins of the social mind: Evolutionary psychology and child development* (pp. 139–163). New York: Guilford.

Birch, L., & Davison, K. (2001). Family environmental factors influencing the developing behavioral controls of food intake and child overweight. *Pediatric Clinics of North America, 48,* 893–907.

Bjorlund, D. (Ed.). (1990). *Children's strategies: Contemporary views of cognitive development.* Hillsdale, NJ: Lawrence Erlbaum.

Bowlby, J. (1969). *Attachment and loss: Attachment* (Vol. 1). New York: Basic Books.

Bradley, R. H. (1994). The HOME Inventory: Review and reflections. In H. Reese (Ed.), *Advances in child development and behavior* (pp. 241–288). San Diego, CA: Academic Press.

Bradley, R. H., & Caldwell, B. M. (1976). The relation of infants' home environments to mental test performance at fifty-four months: A follow-up study. *Child Development, 47,* 1172–1176.

Bradley, R. H., & Caldwell, B. M. (1995). Care giving and the regulation of child growth and development: Describing proximal aspects of care giving systems. *Developmental Review, 15,* 38–85.

Bradley, R. H., Caldwell, B. M., & Rock, S. L. (1988). Home environment and school performance: A ten-year follow-up and examination of three models of environmental action. *Child Development, 59,* 852–867.

Bradley, R. H., & Corwyn, R. F. (2002). SES and child development. *Annual Review of Psychology, 53,* 371–399.

Bradley, R. H., & Corwyn, R. F. (2003). Age and ethnic variations in family process mediators of SES. In M. H. Bronstein & R. H. Bradley (Eds.), *Socioeconomic status, parenting, and child development* (pp. 161–188). Mahwah, NJ: Erlbaum.

Bradley, R. H., & Corwyn, R. F. (2005). Productive activity and the prevention of behavior problems. *Developmental Psychology, 41,* 89–98.

Bradley, R. H., Corwyn, R. F., Burchinal, M., McAdoo, H. P., & Garcia Coll, C. (2001). The home environments of children in the United States. Part 2: Relations with behavioral development through age 13. *Child Development, 72,* 1868–1886.

Bradley, R.H., Corwyn, R.F., McAdoo, H.P., & Garcia Coll, C. (2001). The home environments of children in the United States. Part 1: Variations by age, ethnicity, and poverty status. *Child Development, 72,* 1844–1867.

Bradley, R.H., Whiteside, L., Mundfrom, D.J., Casey, P.H., Kelleher, K.J., & Pope, S.K. (1994). Early indications of resilience and their relation to experiences in the home environments of low birthweight, premature children living in poverty. *Child Development, 65,* 246–260.

Bransford, J.D., Brown, A.L., & Cocking, R.R. (Eds.). (2000). *How people learn: Brain, mind, experience, and school.* Washington, DC: National Academy Press.

Bretherton, I., & Waters, E. (1985). Growing points of attachment theory . *Monographs of the Society for Research in Child Development, 50* (209).

Britto, P., Fuligni, A.S., & Brooks-Gunn, J. (2002). Reading, rhymes,, and routines: American parents and their young children. In N. Halfvon & K.T. McLearn (Eds.), *Child rearing in America: Challenges facing parents with young children* (pp. 117–145). New York: Cambridge University Press.

Brody, G.H., & Flor, D.L. (1998). Maternal resources, parenting practices, and child competence in rural, single-parent African American families. *Child Development, 69,* 803–816.

Brody, G.H., Flor, D., & Gibson, N.M. (1999). Linking maternal efficacy beliefs, developmental goals, parenting practices, and child competence in rural single-parent African American families. *Child Development, 70,* 1197–1208.

Brohl, K. (1996). *Working with traumatized children.* Washington, DC: CWLA Press.

Bronfenbrenner, U. (1995). The bioecological model from a life course perspective: Reflections of a participant observer. In P. Moen, G.H. Elder, & K. Luscher (Eds.), *Examining lives in context* (pp. 619–647). Washington, DC: American Psychological Association.

Bronson, M.B. (2000). *Self-regulation in early childhood.* New York: Guilford.

Brown, B., Mounts, N., Lamborn, S., & Steinberg, L. (1993). Parenting practices and peer group affiliation in adolescence. *Child Development, 64,* 467–482.

Bruner, J. (1983). *Child talk: Learning to use language.* Oxford: Oxford University Press.

Caldji, C., Tannenbaum, B., Sharma, D., Francis, D., Plotsky, P.M., & Meaney, M.J. (1998). Maternal care during infancy regulates the development of neural systems mediating the expression of fearfulness in the rat. *Proceedings of the National Academy of Sciences of the United States of America, 95*(9), 5335–5340.

Cassidy, J. (1988). Child-mother attachment and the self in six-year-olds. *Child Development, 59*(1), 121–134.

Christerphersen, E.R. (1989). Injury control. *American Psychologist, 44,* 237–241.

Cohen, L.B., DeLoache, J.S., & Strauss, M.S. (1979). Infant visual perception. In J.D. Osofsky (Ed.), *Handbook of infant development* (pp. 393–438). New York: Wiley.

Coleman, J. S. (1988). Social capital in the creation of human capital. *American Journal of Sociology, 94*(Suppl.), S95–S120.

Collins, W. A., Maccoby, E. E., Steinberg, L., Hetherington, E. M., & Bornstein, M. H. (2000).Contemporary research on parenting: The case of nature and nurture. *American Psychologist, 55*(2), 218–232.

Committee on Health and Behavior, Institute of Medicine. (2001). *Health and behavior: The interplay of biological, behavioral, and societal influences.* Washington, DC: National Academy Press.

Crockenberg, S. (1981). Infant irritability, mother responsiveness, and social support influences on the security of infant-mother attachment. *Child Development, 52,* 857–865.

Crouter, A., MacDonald, S., McHale, S., & Perry-Jenkins, M. (1990). Parental monitoring and perceptions of children's school performance and conduct in dual- and single-earner families. *Developmental Psychology, 26*(4), 649–657.

Cummings, E. M., Zahn-Waxler, C., & Radke-Yarrow, M. (1981). Young children's responses to expressions of anger and affection by others in the family. *Child Development, 52,* 1274–1282.

Darling, N., & Steinberg, L. (1993). Parenting style as context. *Psychological Bulletin, 113*(3), 487–496.

Dornbusch, S. M., Ritter, P. L., Leiderman, P. H., Roberts, D. F., & Fraleigh, M. J. (1987). The relation of parenting style to adolescent school performance. *Child Development, 58,* 1244–1257.

Dorr, A., Rabin, B. E., & Ireland, S. (2002). Parenting in a multimedia society. In M. H. Bornstein (Ed.), *Handbook of parenting* (2nd ed., Vol. 5, pp. 349–374). Mahwah, NJ: Erlbaum.

Drotar, D. (1985). *New directions in failure-to-thrive: Research and clinical practice.* New York: Plenum.

Duncan, G. J., Brooks-Gunn, J., & Klebanov, P. (1994). Economic deprivation and early-childhood development. *Child Development, 62,* 296–318.

Eccles, J., & Gootman, J. A. (Eds.). (2002). *Community programs to promote youth development.* Washington, DC: National Academy Press.

Eisenberg, N., Cumberland, A., & Spinrad, T. L. (1998). Parental socialization of emotion. *Psychological Inquiry, 9,* 241–273.

Evans, G. W., Kliewer, W., & Martin, J. (1991). The role of the physical environment in the health and well-being of children. In H. E. Schroeder (Ed.), *New directions in health psychology assessment* (pp. 127–157). New York: Hemisphere.

Falsetti, S. A., & Resnick, H. S. (1995). Helping the victims of violent crime. In J. R. Freedy & S. E. Hobfol (Eds.), *Traumatic stress—from theory to practice* (pp. 263–285). New York: Plenum.

Feinberg, M. E., McHale, S. M., Crouter, A. C., & Cumsille, P. (2003). Sibling differentiation: Sibling and parent relationship trajectories in adolescence. *Child Development, 74,* 1261–1274.

Fiese, B. H., Hooker, K. A., Kotary, L., & Schwagler, J. (1993). Family rituals in the early stages of parenthood. *Journal of Marriage & Family, 55,* 663–642.

Fogel, A., Diamond, G. R., Langhorst, B. H., & Demos, V. (1982). Affective and cognitive aspects of the 2-month-old's participation in face-to-face interaction with the mother. In E. Z. Tronick (Ed.), *Social interchange in infancy: Affect, cognition, and communication* (pp. 37–58). Baltimore: University Park Press.

Ford, D. H., & Lerner, R. M. (1992). *Developmental systems theory: An integrative approach.* Newbury Park, CA: Sage.

Friedman, S. L., & Sigman, M. D. (Eds.). (1992). *The psychological development of low birthweight children.* Norwood, NJ: Ablex.

Gable, S., & Isabella, R. (1992). Maternal contributions to infant regulation of arousal. *Infant Behavior and Development, 15,* 95–107.

Garbarino, J. (1988). Preventing childhood injury: Developmental and mental health issues. *American Journal of Orthopsychiatry, 58,* 25–45.

Greaves, P., Glik, D. C., Kronenfeld, J. J., & Jackson, K. (1994). Determinants of controllable in-home child safety hazards. *Health Education Research, 9,* 307–315.

Greenfield, P. M., Quiroz, B., & Raeff, C. (2000). Cross-cultural conflict and harmony in the social construction of the child. In S. Harkness, C. Raeff, et al. (Eds.), *Variability in the social construction of the child: New directions for child and adolescent development* (pp. 93–108). College Park, MD: University of Maryland.

Gutman, L. M., Friedel, J. N., & Hitt, R. (2003). Keeping adolescents safe from harm: Management strategies of African-American families in a high-risk community. *Journal of School Psychology, 41,* 167–184.

Gutman, L. M., & McLoyd, V. C. (2000). Parents' management of their children's education within the home, at school, and in the community: An examination of African-American families living in poverty. *Urban Review, 32*(1), 1–24.

Hart, B., & Risley, T. (1995). *Meaningful differences in the everyday experience of young American children.* Baltimore: Brookes.

Hart, C. H., DeWolf, D. M., Wozniak, P., & Burts, D. C. (1992). Maternal and paternal disciplinary styles: Relations with preschoolers' playground behavioral orientations and peer status. *Child Development, 63,* 879–892.

Hetherington, E. M., Stanley-Hagan, M., & Anderson, E. R. (1989). Marital transitions: A child's perspective. *American Psychologist, 44*(2), 303–312.

Hoff, E. (2003). Causes and consequences of SES-related differences in parent-to-child speech. In M. H. Bronstein & R. H. Bradley (Eds.), *Socioeconomic status, parenting, and child development* (pp. 145–160). Mahwah, NJ: Erlbaum.

Horowitz. F. D. (1987). *Exploring developmental theories: Toward a structural/behavioral model of development.* Hillsdale, NJ: Erlbaum.

Jacobson, J.L., Jacobson, S.W., Padgett, R.J., Brummitt, G.A., & Billings, R.L. (1992). Effects of prenatal PCB exposure on cognitive processing efficiency and sustained attention. *Developmental Psychology, 28,* 297–306.

Johnson, K.L., & Lieberman, A.F. (1999, April). *Protecting 3–5-year-old children from the effects of witnessing domestic violence: The roles of mothers as "emotion coaches."* Paper presented at the biennial meeting of the Society for Research in Child Development, Albuquerque, NM.

Kagan, J. (1984). *The nature of the child.* New York: Basic Books.

Kagan, J. (2003). Biology, context, and developmental inquiry. *Annual Review of Psychology, 54,* 1–23.

Kazura, K. (2001). Family programming for incarcerated parents: A needs assessment among inmates. *Journal of Offender Rehabilitation, 32,* 67–83.

Killan, K.D, & Agathangelou, A.M. (2001). Catastrophe: Refugee families' adaptation to war trauma. *Family Focus, 10,* F15–F17.

King, P.E., & Furrow, J.L. (2004). Religion as a resource for positive youth development: Religion, social capital, and moral outcomes. *Developmental Psychology, 40,* 703–713.

Klingman, A. (2002). Children under stress of war. In A.M. La Greca & W.K. Silverman (Eds.), *Helping children cope with disasters and terrorism* (pp. 359–380). Washington, DC: American Psychological Association.

Kochanska, G. (1997). Multiple pathways to conscience for children with different temperaments: From toddlerhood to age 5. *Developmental Psychology, 33,* 228–240.

Kuhl, J. (2000). A functional-design approach to motivation and self-regulation: The dynamics of personality systems and interactions. In M. Boekaerts, P.R. Pintrich, & M. Zeidner (Eds.), *Handbook of self-regulation* (pp. 111–170). San Diego, CA: Academic Press.

Kuhn, D. (1992). Cognitive development. In M.H. Bornstein & M.E. Lamb (Eds.), *Developmental psychology: An advanced textbook* (3rd ed., pp. 211–272). Hillsdale, NJ: Erlbaum.

Ladd, G.W., & Goltner, B. (1988). Parents' management of preschoolers' peer relations: Is it related to children's social competence? *Developmental Psychology, 24,* 109–117.

La Greca, A.M., & Prinstein, M.J. (2002). Hurricanes and earthquakes. In A.M. Le Greca, W.K. Silverman, E.M. Vernberg, & M.C. Roberts (Eds.), *Helping children cope with disasters and terrorism* (pp. 107–138). Washington, DC: American Psychological Association.

Larzelere, R.E. (2000). Child outcomes of nonabusive and customary physical punishment by parents: An updated literature review. *Clinical Child & Family Psychology Review, 3,* 199–221.

Lazarus, R.S. (1993). From psychological stress to emotions: A history of changing outlooks. *Annual Review of Psychology, 44,* 1–21.

Lewis, M. (1997). *Altering fate.* New York: Guilford.

118   THE CRISIS IN YOUTH MENTAL HEALTH

Lewis, M.D., & Junyk, N. (1997). The self-organization of psychological defenses. In F. Masterpasqua & P.A. Perna (Eds.), *The psychological meaning of chaos* (pp. 41–74). Washington, DC: American Psychological Association.

Lewis, P. (1983). Innovative divorce rituals: Their psycho-social functions. *Journal of Divorce, 6,* 71–81.

Loeber, R., & Dishion, T.J. (1983). Early predictors of male adolescent delinquency: A review. *Psychological Bulletin, 94,* 68–99.

Lozoff, B. (1989). Nutrition and behavior. *American Psychologist, 44,* 231–236.

Lozoff, B., Jiminez, E., & Wolf, A.W. (1991). Long-term developmental outcome of infants with iron deficiency. *New England Journal of Medicine, 325,* 687–694.

Maccoby, E.E. (1992). The role of parents in the socialization of children: An historical perspective. *Developmental Psychology, 28,* 1006–1017.

Maslow, A.H. (1954). *Motivation and personality.* New York: Harper and Row.

McLoyd, V.C., Cauce, A.M., Takeuchi, D., & Wilson, L. (2000). Marital processes and parental socialization in families of color: A decade review of research. *Journal of Marriage & Family, 62,* 1070–1093.

Melamed, B.G. (2002). Parenting the ill child. In M.H. Bornstein (Ed.), *Handbook of parenting* (2nd ed., Vol. 5, pp. 329–347). Mahwah, NJ: Erlbaum.

Monahon, C. (1993). *Children and trauma.* San Francisco: Jossey-Bass.

Moore, G.T. (1988). *Interactions between the spatial organization of the sociophysical environment and cognitive and social behavior.* Unpublished manuscript, University of Wisconsin-Milwaukee.

National Center for Addiction and Substance Abuse. (2001). *National survey of American attitudes on substance VI: Teens.* New York: Columbia University.

National Center for Education Statistics. (2002). *Digest of education statistics 2001* (NCES publication no. 2002–130). Washington, DC: Author.

Nichols, W.C. (1984). Therapeutic needs of children in family system reorganization. *Journal of Divorce, 7*(4), 23–44.

Nickerson, R.S. (1992). On the intergenerational transfer of high-order skills. In T. Stricht, B. McDonald, & M. Beeler (Eds.), *The intergenerational transfer of cognitive skills* (Vol. 2, pp. 159–171). Norwood, NJ: Ablex.

Ogden, C. (1998). *Third national health and nutrition examination survey.* Unpublished analyses, Atlanta, GA, Centers for Disease Control.

Park, K.A., & Waters, E. (1989). Security of attachment and preschool friendships. *Child Development, 60,* 1076–1081.

Patterson, G.R., DeBaryshe, B.D., & Ramsey, E. (1989). A developmental perspective on antisocial behavior. *American Psychologist, 44,* 329–335.

Peterson, L., Ewigman, B., & Kivlahan, C. (1993). Judgments regarding appropriate child supervision to prevent injury: The role of environmental risk and child age. *Child Development, 64,* 934–950.

Peterson, L., & Gable, S. (1998). Holistic injury prevention. In J.R. Lutzker (Ed.), *Handbook of child abuse research and treatment* (pp. 291–318). New York: Plenum.

Pettit, G. S., Dodge, K. A., & Brown, M. M. (1988). Early family experience, social problem solving patterns, and children's social competence. *Child Development, 59,* 107–120.

Pianta, R. C., & Walsh, D. J. (1996). *High-risk children in schools.* New York: Routledge.

Plomin, R., & Daniels, D. (1987). Why are children in the same family so different from one another? *Behavior & Brain Sciences, 14,* 373–427.

Pollitt, E. (1988). A critical review of three decades of research on the effect of chronic energy malnutrition on behavioral development. In B. Schureh & M. Scrimshaw (Eds.), *Chronic energy depletion: Consequences and related issues.* Luzanne, Switzerland: IDEC–Nestlé Foundation.

Putallaz, M. (1987). Maternal behavior and children's sociometric status. *Child Development, 58,* 324–340.

Rapoport, A. (1985). Thinking about home environment, A conceptual framework. In I. Altman & C. M. Werner (Eds.), *Home environments* (pp. 255–286). New York: Plenum.

Rivara, F., & Mueller, B. (1987). The epidemiology of childhood injuries. *Journal of Social Issues, 43,* 13–31.

Roberts, K. (1983). *Youth and leisure.* London: George Allen and Unwin.

Rohner, R. (1986). *The warmth dimension.* Beverly Hills, CA: Sage.

Rosenweig, M. R., Krech, D., Bennett, E. L., & Diamond, M. C. (1962). Effects of environmental complexity and training on brain chemistry and anatomy: A replication and extensions. *Journal of Comparative & Physiological Psychology, 55,* 429–437.

Ryan, R. M., & Deci, E. L. (2000). Self-determination theory and the facilitation of intrinsic motivation, social development, and well-being. *American Psychologist, 55,* 68–78.

Saegert, S., & Winkel, G. H. (1990). Environmental psychology. *Annual Review of Psychology, 41,* 441–477.

Scales, P., & Leffert, N. (1999). *Developmental assets.* Minneapolis, MN: Search Institute.

Schunk, D. H., & Zimmerman, B. J. (1997). Social origins of self-regulatory competence. *Educational Psychologist, 32,* 195–208.

Scott-Jones, D. (1995). Parent–child interactions and school achievement. In B. Ryan, G. Adams, T. Gulloltta, R. Weissberg, & R. Hampton (Eds.), *The family-school connection* (pp. 75–107). Thousand Oaks, CA: Sage.

Shonkoff, J. P., & Phillips, D. A. (Eds.). (2000). *From neurons to neighborhoods.* Washington, DC: National Academy Press.

Silverman, W. K., & La Greca, A. M. (2002). Children experiencing disasters: Definitions, reactions, and predictions of outcomes. In A. M. Le Greca, W. K. Silverman, E. M Vernberg, & M. C. Roberts (Eds.), *Helping children cope with disasters and terrorism* (pp. 11–34). Washington, DC: American Psychological Association.

Stattin, H., & Kerr, M. (2000). Parental monitoring: A reinterpretation. *Child Development, 71,* 1072–1085.

Steinberg, L. (1986). Latchkey children and susceptibility to peer pressure: An ecological analysis. *Developmental Psychology, 22,* 433–439.

Steinberg, L., Darling, N., Fletcher, A., Brown, B., & Dornbusch, S. (1995). Authoritative parenting and adolescent adjustment: An ecological journey. In P. Moen, G. Elder, & K. Luscher (Eds.), *Examining lives in context* (pp. 423–466). Washington, DC: American Psychological Association.

Strength, J. M. (1991). Factors influencing the mother-child relationship following the death of the father. *Dissertation Abstracts International, 52,* 3310B.

Tennen, H., & Affleck, G. (1990). Blaming others for threatening events. *Psychological Bulletin, 108,* 209–232.

Thompson, R. A. (1994). Emotion regulation: A theme in search of a definition. In N. A. Fox (Ed.), *The development of emotional regulation: Biological and behavioral considerations. Monographs of the Society for Research in Child Development, 59*(Serial No. 240), 25–52.

Tong, S., & McMichael, A. J. (1992). Maternal smoking and neuropsychological development in childhood: A review of the evidence. *Developmental Medicine & Child Neurology, 34,* 191–197.

U.S. Department of Health and Human Services. (1991). *Healthy people 2000.* Washington, DC: U.S. Government Printing Office (DHHS Pub. No. PHS 91–50212).

van der Kolk, B. A. (1996). The complexity of adaptation to trauma self-regulation, stimulus discrimination, and characterological development. In B. A. van der Kolk, A. C. McFarlane, & L. Weisaeth (Eds.), *Traumatic stress* (pp. 183–213). New York: Guilford.

Wachs, T. D. (2000). *Necessary but not sufficient.* Washington, DC: American Psychological Association.

Wallerstein, J. S. (1983). Children of divorce: The psychological tasks of the child. *American Journal of Orthopsychiatry, 53,* 230–243.

Weisner, T. S. (2002). Ecocultural understandings of children's developmental pathways. *Human Development, 45,* 275–281.

Whaley, A. L. (2000). Sociocultural differences in the developmental consequences of the use of physical discipline during childhood for African Americans. *Cultural Diversity & Ethnic Minority Psychology, 6,* 5–12.

Whitehurst, G. J., Arnold, D. S., Epstein, J. N., & Angell, A. L. (1994). A picture book reading intervention in day care and home for children from low-income families. *Developmental Psychology, 30,* 679–689.

Wohlwill, J. F. & Heft, H. (1977). Environments fit for the developing child. In H. McGurk (Ed.), *Ecological factors in human development* (pp. 1–22). Amsterdam: North Holland Publishing.

Yeung, W. J. (1999, April). *How multiple domains of paternal involvement affect children's well-being.* Paper presented at the Biennial Meeting of the Society for Research in Child Development, Albuquerque, NM.

Zimmerman, B. J. (2000). Attaining self-regulation, A social cognitive perspective. In M. Boekaerts, P. R. Pintrich, & M. Zeidner (Eds.), *Handbook of self-regulation* (pp. 13–41). San Diego, CA: Academic Press.

Chapter 6

ADAPTIVE AND MALADAPTIVE PARENTING: INFLUENCE ON CHILD DEVELOPMENT

Catherine C. Ayoub

Rock a bye baby on the tree top,
When the wind blows the cradle will rock,
When the bough breaks the cradle will fall,
And down will come baby, cradle and all.

—Nursery Rhyme

OVERVIEW

This familiar nursery rhyme is attributed to a young Pilgrim boy—a passenger on the *Mayflower*—written as he watched Native American mothers suspend birch-bark cradles from the branches of trees so that the wind could rock their children to sleep. The rhyme holds both great comfort and warning on the choice of bough and the fortuitous gentleness or fierceness of the wind. A parent must judge not only the baby's wakefulness or need for sleep but also the character of the elements, the strength of the branches, and the safety of the natural surroundings. This rhyme colorfully reflects the dynamics of parenting challenges. Parenting interactions are influenced by a host of protective and risk factors and are tempered across time by the different personalities, family systems, and cultural practices as well as by both genetic and constitutional characteristics of the players. Adaptive and maladaptive parenting practices evolve in a transactional manner over time—starting in childhood—reflecting a blend of those diverse influences, and often are incorporated into the parenting practices of that child in adulthood.

Parents and children develop over time within four overlapping spheres of environmental influence: the ontogenic sphere, the microsystem, the exosystem, and the macrosystem (Bronfenbrenner, 1979). The ontogenic sphere is closest to the child and the parent and includes adaptive factors inherent in each individual's character and temperament. The next level up is the microsystem, composed of the physical and social aspects of the parenting and family environment. The exosystem consists of neighborhood and community settings in which the family lives. Finally, in the macrosystem, most removed from the parent and child, are societal-level cultural beliefs and values. A child's developmental path and the adult's approach and execution in parenting functions are shaped by factors at each of these levels. As examples of the reciprocal influence of parenting and child behaviors, this chapter will focus on three aspects of family ecology, all of which carry some potential to yield adverse outcomes: the household's economic resources, family behavior (conflict, violence, and child maltreatment), and parental attributes (depression and substance abuse).

PARENTING PROCESSES

In a transactional model, parenting processes can be viewed on a continuum from risk to protection (Sameroff & Seifer, 1987). The level, proximity, and duration of risk and protective factors are important predictors of parenting behavior and attitudes over time. These factors interact with each other at various points in the developmental process to shape the child's (and the parent's) present behavior and to construct a perpetually refined framework for living together. The balance between the number of factors in a child's environment that create risk or protection, immediately or later, enduring or transient, determines whether a child is likely to display developmental competence or incompetence (Lynch & Cicchetti, 1998).

Evidence shows that children living in adversity who experience one risk factor are likely to go on to experience a series of risks (Sameroff & Fiese, 2005). Furthering the notion of cumulative risk, Rutter (1979) argued that it was not any particular risk but the *accumulation* of risk factors in a child's history that leads to psychiatric disorder. Sameroff and Fiese (2005) agree, concluding that adverse child outcomes are determined by the clustering of multiple risks in the absence of protective factors. This transactional systems perspective (Sameroff & Chandler, 1975) proposes that parenting practices are influenced by a number of major stressors, including poverty, mental illness, substance abuse, family conflict, violence, or maltreatment. A parallel pyramid of cumulating protective factors could also be assumed to have a favorable impact on child development, as well.

Along with the sheer number of risk and protective factors, the type and duration of those factors influence a parent's caretaking capacities, or the transactions defined as *parenting*. Maslow (1954) described a hierarchy of human need fulfillment some years ago. Sandler (2001) refers to the downslope of that hierarchy, which he calls the *ecology of adversity,* as the place, time, and social context in which basic human needs are threatened. A parent's own basic needs must be met in order to enable her to give positively to another. The more basic and prolonged the need deprivation, the less able individual parents will be to reach out to others, most specifically to their children. Individual strengths and weaknesses of parents and their family systems can be evaluated in terms of met and unmet needs, attitudes and skills, and relationship models. These patterns help define what have been called *parenting practices*. Several authors suggest theoretical frameworks and dimensions for evaluating parenting practices and capacity. Thomas Grisso (1986) published one of the first papers offering such constructs from both developmental and legal perspectives. He described seven areas of focus: (1) nurturing and physical care; (2) training and channeling of psychological needs (e.g., those required in toilet training, weaning, provision of solid foods); (3) teaching and skill training to facilitate care and ensure safety (in areas such as language, perceptual skills, physical skills, self-care); (4) orienting the child to the immediate world of kin, neighborhood, community, and society; (5) transmitting cultural and subcultural goals and values and motivating the child to accept them for his own; (6) promoting interpersonal skills, motives, and modes of feeling and behaving in relation to others; and (7) guiding, correcting, and helping the child to formulate his own goals and plan his own activities.

Building on Grisso's model, Richard Barnum (2001) divides parenting capacities into two major categories: protection and care. Protection encompasses the parent's attention to safety as well as his or her role as advocate for the child. In the context of protection, parents are expected to make reasonable efforts to keep their children safe from foreseeable harm and to model positive and caring roles; issues of discipline and conflict resolution also fall under this heading. Although models of both correction and support may vary culturally, the child should be protected from hurt or harm, including both physical and emotional injury as well as educational and social mistreatment. From the strength perspective, the parent serves as a safe base from which the child can explore and learn but also as an active and supportive spokesperson for the child's interests in the world.

In order to fulfill Barnum's criteria of protection, parents must understand their children's individual needs and habits and make reasonable and consistent efforts to provide for those needs. For example, if a child has a mental or physical handicap or disability, the parent is expected to recognize the difficulty and to provide assistance to the child directly and through support from others in the community. Patterns of care as well as critical incidents might illustrate inadequate parenting in the context of this interplay between the child's needs and the parent's anticipatory assessment and response.

Care, the second domain of parenting capacity described by Barnum, comprises the complex processes of socialization. These processes are essential to the nurturing and teaching functions of parents, aimed at promoting the child's growth and development. Included in this category are three crucial domains: cognitive development and skill building, supervision and discipline, and emotional support, nurturance, and direction. Cognitive development and skill building involve exchanges between parent and child that include teaching, modeling, supporting independent learning, and reinforcing the learning process. At the core of the skill-building relationship is the parent–child interaction that allows for the balance between age-appropriate autonomy and support. The accurate assessment of the child's individual needs and capacities and the so-called fit between parent and child are critical, as is the parent's ability to find or take advantage of existing opportunities for the child to learn in the areas of language, self-care skills, and scholastic and vocational functioning. Problem-solving skills across domains are enhanced through assistance and an understanding of the child's ongoing learning processes. Overinvolvement or underinvolvement can be problematic.

Supervision and discipline serve not only to protect but also to teach. Parents have a responsibility to promote good habits and ways of living by teaching, modeling, and shaping the child's environment through their supervision and selection of others to supervise when they are unavailable. The first component of supervision and discipline skills is parental awareness of the child's behavior and emotions, capabilities, and routines. Consistent and appropriate responses to this awareness build the foundation for supervision and limit-setting that systematically reinforce positive behavior and deliver negative sanctions for unwanted behavior.

Third in Barnum's model, emotional support, nurturance, and direction is the most important cluster of parenting skills. The parents' own emotional and social coping, as well as the ability to meet their own needs, will have a considerable impact on their ability to provide for their children. Parental mood, frustration tolerance, and anxiety also play an important role in shaping the parent–child relationship. If parental coping is dominated by anger and conflict or by serious sadness and lethargy, this can negatively affect even the very youngest child (Shonkoff & Phillips, 2000). Overly critical or rejecting parents, as well as those who are disinterested and emotionally distant, fail to establish and maintain the critically important attachment relationships with their children that will serve as working models for the child's future relationships. Positive emotional interchanges between parent and child represent the most constructive interactions and promote secure attachment in the child that serves as a foundation for positive identity development, as illustrated in this volume by Risley and Hart.

Finally, Bradley (this volume) defines optimal parenting as the six Ss of parenting: sustenance/safety, stimulation, support, structure, surveillance, and social interaction. He envisions parenting as an active process that builds positive assets in children and parents and is supported within each ecological sphere (Scales & Leffert, 1999) where the fit between parent, child, and family is simultaneously ever changing and grounded in past models of interaction, influenced by biological and learned differences and affected by circumstance.

PARENTING PRACTICES AND CHILD DEVELOPMENT

So what do we know about the influence of parenting practices on early child development? How do we begin to understand the adaptive or maladaptive aspects of the parenting process so that we can effectively design interventions and craft policy? To answer these questions, we need to address the nature of the developmental process in context. The defining feature of development is the emergence of new forms; *development* inherently denotes change, and change is nowhere more rapid than in early childhood. One approach to understanding similarities and differences in development has been called *integrative pathways*. This approach considers the behavior of young children in context as adaptive and complex rather than as simply delayed or dysfunctional. From our perspective, simplistic mischaracterizations of delay in groups of so-called different children stem from the persistent and erroneous view that development in a domain occurs in a general and unidirectional way, regardless of context. In contrast, we consider it more accurate to view parenting practices in the framework of the child's context, assuming enormous variation in developmental patterns across children; this places the child in a unique developmental web in which adaptation to the environment takes account of biological strengths and weaknesses in the service of survival (Fischer et al., 1998; Schlichtmann & Ayoub, 2004).

It is popular to divide attachment working models into three organized categories—secure, ambivalent, or avoidant—as well as a fourth (disorganized) category as a starting point for understanding parent–child relationship patterns over time. Developing relationships in young children are likely to be much more complex and differentiated than these four categories suggest, but considerable progress has been made in describing the diverging pathways commonly observed in children's coping with varying early parenting experiences. Progressive strides in understanding those relationships include attention to context and culture as well as to security in the development of working models of relationships (LeVine & Miller, 1990). These contextual aspects of the working models of attachment offer improvements in describing the influence of parents on alternative developmental pathways in children.

Skills in emotional regulation, a set of core competencies of early childhood, are deeply embedded in early parenting or caregiving relationships. Arousal is regulated through parent attachment relationships as well as temperamental characteristics (Van der Kolk, 1996). Over time, cognition and emotion flow together into the development of patterns of mutually regulated interaction. The acquisition of behavioral, emotional, and ultimately cognitive self-control has been proposed as the fundamental building block of competent functioning (Bronson, 2000; Kopp, 2000).

As children mature cognitively through a series of transformations in acting, thinking, and feeling, their initial working models of relationships become more complex but grounded in their specific experiences in close parenting relationships. This grounding specifies the particular worldview of each child for self and others in caregiving role relationships, which establishes a broad evaluative posture toward life as primarily positive and nurturing or as primarily negative and threatening. From these parenting relationships a child incorporates a framework for human interactions that forms the foundation for later close relationships that, according to attachment theory, are sustained throughout the life span (Adam, Gunnar, & Tanaka, 2004).

Some children experience significant and repeated trauma, conflict, or loss in early childhood (e.g., confronting the dilemma of interacting with a depressed parent or enduring the pain of losing a primary parenting figure); that is likely to alter their social-emotional perspective of relationships in fundamental ways (Ayoub, Fischer, & O'Connor, 2003). These alternations also have impact on the child's cognitive focus, motivation, and attention skills, which in turn may change the way they respond to parenting. If such negative experiences are severe, cumulative, or prolonged, they can fundamentally alter the young child's developmental trajectory across domains in ways that may mutually reinforce each other.

As children grow, their physical states become less reliable indicators of their emotions, and feelings hinge on interpretations of context and causal understandings based on previous relationships with their caregivers. Both individual and cultural meanings transmitted from parent to child affect how children construe and react to their environments (Miller, Fung, & Mintz, 1996). Throughout early childhood, the frontal neocortex matures and becomes organized to serve more accurate appraisal and self-regulation of emotions. As the infant soon differentiates a cry—one for pain, one for discomfort, and one for hunger—the toddler quickly refines those responses into differentiated feelings of anger, fear, guilt, joy, and love that continue to be elaborated throughout the preschool years.

In the process of coordinated, adaptive parenting, the adult caregivers move with the child through developmental milestones, learning to attend to, correctly interpret, and respond to the child's cues in caring, timely, and appropriate ways. When this happens, young children develop a positive bias about themselves and those around them, which continues into adulthood (Shaver, Schwartz, Kirson, & O'Connor, 1987). In good part, this foundation of trust and positive expectations of self and others forms the basis for future emotional and cognitive learning.

Children, from birth, begin to make sense of the world in many ways, including spatial reasoning, physical causality, problem solving, categorization, and counting and quantification. Learning over the first six years of life in these areas provides the foundation for complex reasoning. Infants become attuned to causal parental relationships and can distinguish causal sequences as well as the effects of their own behaviors on others (Mangeldorf, 1992). For example, toddlers can recognize that their parents have different tastes or preferences, and by age four young children can recognize everyday categories for sorting objects in the world. By age five children can predict another person's intentions and recognize deception. Although they may universally be able to understand causality, adopt another's perspective, and sort objects by categories, kindergarten children differ tremendously in their ability to learn, sequence, organize, and self-regulate their emotions; these differences often account for the most common problems described by their kindergarten teachers (Lyon, & Kisiel, 1996).

Acquisition of these readiness skills is influenced by parent–child interactions. For example, children who have better relationships with their mothers score higher on tests of cognitive skill development (Londerville & Main, 1981). Children whose parents provide them with higher levels of cognitive and language stimulation, through both their interactions and learning materials in the home, also perform better on tests of cognitive skill (National Institute of Child Health and Human Development [NICHD], 2000). In contrast, high levels of negative emotionality in early childhood, characterized by an inability to regulate one's negative emotions, increase the risk of problem behaviors as well as diminished cognitive performance during the school-age years (Buckner, Mezzacappa, & Beardslee, 2003).

For the young child, language serves primarily social goals, such as negotiating intimacy with the parent, defining a self separate from the parent, communicating needs and desires, and representing one's own point of view, but increasingly over the preschool years language is used as the mechanism for gaining access to information about the physical and social world. The vocabulary spurt that typically occurs late in the second year of life presages an increasing focus on acquiring new words that in turn index access to new domains of knowledge, ranging from the biological (e.g., animal names, bodily functions), to the social (e.g., kinship terms, games), to the psychological (e.g., inner-state words, relationships). Beginning around age two, substantial individual and social-class differences in rate of vocabulary acquisition begin to emerge, yielding striking differences in total vocabulary size even before children enter preschool. Such language differences are in part related to parental interactions around literacy (Risley & Hart, this volume).

In spite of the powerful biological and supportive environmental influences that promote adaptive parenting, there are risks, just like there are risks for the mother in hanging the baby's cradle on the bough. These risks may be balanced by protective factors and also by the child's resilience resources. The following section of this chapter will consider several of the major risks to positive developmental outcomes, emphasizing early childhood mental and social health to illustrate the interplay between adaptive and maladaptive parenting and child developmental pathways. The major risk factors addressed include poverty, family conflict (including separation, family violence, and child maltreatment), and parental mental illness and substance abuse. Although far from a comprehensive list, these are featured in the current literature as having primary impact on the quality of parenting and subsequent child well-being (Osofsky & Thompson, 2000).

MAJOR RISKS TO POSITIVE DEVELOPMENTAL OUTCOMES

Poverty

Childhood poverty is widespread in the United States, with rates highest for children younger than six years of age. The last United States census reported that 16.7 percent of U.S. children live in families with incomes below the poverty line (U.S. Bureau of the Census, 2005). The negative effects of poverty on child development are far-reaching, impacting social, health, behavioral, and cognitive domains. Research demonstrates that although poor children perform near expected national norms on standardized tests of cognitive skill in infancy, as a group their scores are significantly lower than national norms by the preschool years (Black, Hess, & Berenson-Howard, 2000). This negative association between poverty and cognitive performance exists across cultures and persists throughout the school years (Bradley & Corwyn, 2002).

Research examining the effects of poverty on social and cognitive skill performance has focused on comparing the abilities of poor and nonpoor children, resulting in the characterization of poverty as a one-dimensional risk factor that negatively impacts children's performance (Evans, 2004). Certain clusters of demographic risks tend to be more prevalent in families living in poverty; these include marital status, education, and employment status (Aber, Jones, & Cohen, 2000). Poor children are more likely to live in single-family households with mothers who have not finished high school and who are not working full time. Researchers have found that poor mothers tend to have more hostile, intrusive, and less sensitive interactions with their young children than do their more economically advantaged counterparts (Shaw & Vondra, 1995). Insecure attachment styles, increased risk for maltreatment, and higher rates of behavior problems are documented more often in poor children as well (Cicchetti & Toth, 1995). Poor parents also share higher rates of depression and alcohol and substance abuse, which increase the likelihood of maladaptive parenting and subsequent child difficulties (McLeod & Shanahan, 1993).

In spite of considerable evidence of the significant impact of poverty on parenting and child development, treating poverty as one-dimensional has serious limitations. In fact, there is considerable variation among poor children on tests of cognitive and social skill over the course of development (Bradley & Corwyn, 2002). Some poor children exhibit average or above-average levels of performance on tests of social and cognitive ability. These children's success in the face of poverty indicates the presence of protective factors that offset the effects of risk (Bradley & Corwyn, 2002). With this in mind, we will examine three of the most common groups of environmental risks that, together with poverty, place children in adverse or maladaptive parenting situations.

Family Conflict, Violence, and Child Maltreatment

Early exposure to serious family conflict, child maltreatment, or family violence has serious and long-lasting effects on children's social development (Margolin & Gordis, 2000). Effects of child maltreatment include aggressive behavior, withdrawal (Keiley, Howe, & Dodge, 2001), depression, negative sense of self, poor social competence (Toth & Cicchetti, 1996), and poor behavioral regulation (Shields, Cicchetti, & Ryan, 1994).

Exposure to parental conflict and marital violence has been associated with internalizing and externalizing problems (Margolin, 1998), lower social competence, and poor peer functioning (Wolfe, Jaffe, Wilson, & Zak, 1985). Other effects of family violence and maltreatment include psychobiological changes, increased incidence of post-traumatic stress disorder (Teicher, 2000), and low-quality teacher-child relationships (Pianta, Hamre, & Stuhlman, 2003).

Theorists and researchers alike have called attention to the critical need to examine multiple forms of family violence and maladaptive parenting jointly. In addition to child maltreatment (abuse, neglect, sexual abuse), witnessing domestic violence and family conflict takes a significant toll on parent–child relationships and ultimately on child well-being. In examining the association between family conflict and violence, Wallerstein and Kelly (1980) noted that approximately 30 percent of divorcing couples with children engage in serious interparental conflict for three to five years following divorce. Interparental conflict has been consistently identified as a significant predictor of adjustment difficulties in children following divorce.

Amato and Keith (1991) conducted a meta-analysis involving 92 studies and 13,000 children, comparing children from divorced and intact families to assess the differences in well-being between these two groups. They found that family conflict in both intact and divorced families is associated with poorer children's functioning. Research has shown that as the level of interparental conflict increases, the number of emotional and behavioral difficulties children exhibit increases (Sales, Manber, & Rohman, 1992). This finding extends to interparental conflict occurring before the marital disruption as well as conflict during and after the divorce (Jekielek, 1998). The duration of conflict is also associated with children's emotional and behavioral reactions. For example, Johnston, Campbell, and Mayes (1985) found that as the length of time parents are in conflict increases, so does the risk of behavioral and psychological difficulties for their children. Furthermore, there is consistent evidence indicating that interparental conflict is more strongly associated with problems in children than is the divorce itself (Stewart, Copeland, Chester, Malley, & Barenbaum, 1997).

Children who live in homes characterized by parental violence are at increased risk of being physically abused themselves (Gelles & Straus, 1988). Findings in the literature of this "double whammy" range from 6 percent to 100 percent of children who witness violence between their parents (Appel & Holden, 1998). In a review of the literature on the co-occurrence of spousal abuse and physical child abuse, Appel & Holden (1998) concluded from 31 studies that when a conservative definition of child abuse is used, a co-occurrence rate of 40 percent is found.

Although experiencing marital conflict alone is a powerful predictor of emotional distress in children, the contribution of witnessing domestic violence within the context of a highly conflicted parental relationship should not be underestimated (Ayoub, Deutsch, & Maraganore, 1999). In our 1999 study of conflicted custody we found that more than 50 percent (52.4%) of the 100 children in our sample witnessed domestic violence as well as experienced some form of child maltreatment. As a result, they experienced an exponential increase in emotional distress when compared to children in divorcing families without histories of family violence. These findings emphasize the pervasiveness of violent encounters between parents who are engaged in acrimonious disputes and its association with significant emotional distress in their children. Although we could not predict causality to the association, we did describe the simultaneous occurrence of both factors. Our study supported earlier research that indicates that the experience of witnessing domestic violence is as powerful as the actual experience of abuse for children, and the cumulative emotional impact is much more than additive (Wolfe et al., 1985).

Children incorporate the templates for coping skills developed in primary parental or family relationships into their own socioemotional structures and transform them at each level in cognitive-emotional development through adulthood. Thus, it is not surprising that children who experience significant and repeated trauma in early childhood (e.g., physical or sexual abuse or witnessing violence between parents in disrupted or dysfunctional families) typically develop worldviews of relationships that are fundamentally different from children who have not experienced violence. For maltreated children, the massive disruptions that occur in relationships during early development combine with trauma-influenced worldviews to produce a number of coherent, distinctive pathways to psychopathology and violence. These pathways subsume both continuities of coping mechanisms in violent, controlling relationships and maturational transformations to increasingly complex relational models that connect multiple roles (Ayoub et al., 2003).

The development of these interaction models is constructed from both experiences in specific close relationships and the emotions tied to those relationships (Fischer, Shaver, & Carnochan, 1990; Lazarus, 1991). Forming emotions toward relationship models is a coping effort as well as an internal experience. Such models may assist children in attaining closeness with an abusive, yet important, adult. However, these models may also inhibit children from forming effective relationships with other adults or peers. For example, maltreated children may learn to act timidly with maltreating parents to allay their anger. Such timidity may shield children from some abuse but can also cause other adults to ignore them, thereby cutting them off from potentially beneficial relationships.

Internal models are thus grounded in specific activities and experiences with parents, who in Gibson's (1979) term *afford* (make possible and contribute to) the quality and types of relational interactions. Working within their internal models, people evaluate how a situation relates to their relational goals, expectations, and concerns and then react emotionally based on that evaluation. It has been suggested that children who experience violent trauma related to maladaptive parenting may be unable to adequately update their working models beyond early childhood even when they are later exposed to more positive relational models. Specifically, Bowlby (1980) theorized that individuals may engage in defensive exclusion through which they ward off perceptions, feelings, and thoughts they expect to inflict anxiety and suffering. If this defensive exclusion precludes the incorporation of new, pertinent, positive information into negative working models, the attachment system may be misregulated or deactivated. Bowlby further hypothesized that due to defensive exclusion, children may develop two irreconcilable working models of self and attachment figures. One set may be consciously available but based on incorrect information, whereas another set may be consciously unavailable yet reflect the child's actual experiences (Bretherton & Mulholland, 1999).

More recently, researchers have theorized that maltreated children typically evidence disorganized and apathetic attachment (Crittenden, 1985, 1988). These children have been described as demonstrating moderate-to-high avoidance coupled with moderate-to-high resistance, which has been most commonly seen as crankiness or aggression that seemed out of context. Crittenden studied disorganized attachment among infants and reported that they demonstrated stereotypic or maladaptive behaviors such as cocking the head or huddling on the floor when reunited with their mothers after brief separations from them. Such behaviors have been described as both disorganized and disoriented.

Main and Solomon (1990) described children with disorganized attachments as not having any consistent strategy for dealing with the stress of separation in the *Strange Situation*. These inconsistent strategies are theorized to be associated with parenting behaviors that are frightened and/or frightening. Parents of disorganized children often engage in a range of frightening behaviors from sudden looming movements to abuse. These behaviors place the child in an irresolvable paradox because the attachment figure is also the source of fear. The consequence of this paradox, according to many researchers, is a disintegration of the child's attachment strategies (Lyons-Ruth & Jacobvitz, 1999). Furthermore, *disorganized attachment* behaviors may be neither disorganized nor disoriented but instead represent a coherent trauma dance composed of adaptive fight-flight coping mechanisms that evolve in response to trauma and physical threat and eventually produce distinctively complex, biologically supported tactics that are highly sophisticated for adapting to traumatic environments (Ayoub et al., 2003).

Parental Depression and Substance Abuse

A full 20 percent of Americans will suffer a major depression sometime during their lifetimes. Ironically, depression is the most treatable of the major mental illnesses, yet only about 30 percent of those who need treatment receive it. Numerous studies have reported elevated rates of psychiatric disorders in children from homes of affectively ill parents; such children are two to four times more likely to develop an affective disorder than are children with non-ill parents (Beardslee, Versage, & Gladstone, 1998). These children are also at increased risk for language and cognitive problems, insecure attachments, emotional deregulation, social incompetence, and behavioral problems (Gladstone & Beardslee, 2002).

Recent studies (Administration for Children and Families, 2002) document the prevalence of depression among families with children in Early Head Start and Head Start programs. In the Administration for Children and Families (ACF) research, 48 percent of Early Head Start mothers at enrollment reported enough symptoms to be considered depressed; one-third of mothers of one-year-olds and one-third of mothers of three-year-olds were depressed as well. Depression was chronic among 12 percent of the mothers—that is, they were depressed when their children were both one and three years old. Depression was also a major factor for Early Head Start fathers, with 18 percent presenting symptoms when their child was two years of age and 16 percent for fathers with three-year-old children. Studies of inner-city mothers of young children report depression rates of 12 percent to 47 percent in pediatric practice settings (Heneghan, Silver, Bauman, Westbrook, & Stein, 1998) and note that having either several young children or a child with a chronic illness in the household exacerbate these rates.

Depression has been associated with problems in parenting, including parental unresponsiveness, unpredictability, and increased hostility. The link between responsive relationships and the emotional and cognitive development of very young children has been well established in the literature (Shonkoff & Phillips, 2000), highlighting the risk these children face when primary caregivers are impaired by mental illness. Depression profoundly affects parenting functions for extended periods of time, placing children in these families at risk for longstanding impairment without intervention (Beardslee et al., 1998). Work with depressed parents demonstrates the importance of parental recognition of the effect of their depression upon their developing child as a first step toward their reaching out for treatment. Parental recognition and understanding of depression is one essential goal of prevention strategies.

Most of the findings related to children of depressed parents focus on those who are clinically depressed; yet experts estimate that up to 24 percent of the general population has experienced some form of moderate depression. The effects of moderate depression on young children are unclear; however, Early Head Start research has found that the program has its strongest positive impact upon children whose mothers are moderately depressed.

Children who experience harsh parenting and depressed caregiving are at higher risk for repeating kindergarten and first grade; poor parenting practices and verbal/physical aggression against children are predictive of lower achievement test scores for children (Kinard, 1999). During the first five years of life, two major areas of socioemotional development that predict the child's future emotional adjustment and school readiness are the regulation and expression of emotion and the development of a positive sense of self and view of the world (Shaver et al., 1987). Both of these developments are rooted in early parent–child relationships and interaction, and each has implications for children's later social competence with adults and peers. These findings emphasize the need to support positive and active relationships between young children and the adults in their lives, which are often negatively impacted by parental depression.

There is growing evidence that preschool children who have been exposed to significant and persistent negative experiences, including parental depression, are less adept at behavioral and affective regulation (Shields et al., 1994) and may develop rigid and controlling ways of interacting with others (Fischer et al., 1998). In contrast, parents who talk about feelings and conflicts tend to have children who develop a better understanding of emotion; those who encourage appropriate expression of negative emotions have children who tend to be more sympathetic and socially competent. Enhancing parents' and teachers' abilities to understand and appropriately relay and describe emotions to young children is a protective mechanism that enhances positive relationship building and holds the potential to counter parental depression.

Children whose parents practice harsh or neglectful parenting as the result of depression, in combination with other stressors, are also likely to develop negative views of self and the world. Dean, Malik, Richards, and Stringer (1986) found that school-age children from these backgrounds tend to justify adult harsh behavior or unkind acts based on their own perceived "badness." Similarly, Fischer and colleagues (1998) describe preschoolers exposed to recurrent negative life experiences—including those children with a depressed parent—as seeing the world and themselves as "bad" and threatening. These children often show heightened levels of physical and verbal aggression in their interactions with adults and peers (Haskett & Kistner, 1991). In contrast, children who have a positive sense of self and the world tend to be respected by peers (Denham & Holt, 1993), are able to develop friendships, and are viewed by teachers as competent in kindergarten readiness skills (Kurdek & Sinclair, 2000). They also display confidence, curiosity, initiative, and adaptive reactions to change or stress (Verschueren, Marcoen, & Schoefs, 1996).

Parental emotional distress and depression can in many cases be mitigated by consistent, high quality services targeted at families with young children. Beardslee's work (2002) using psychoeducational approaches to treat families with parental depression has been quite successful in targeting mechanisms that increase children's resilience, and there is a considerable empirical knowledge base to support its value. This model takes a public health, family-based prevention approach operationalizing key principles for preventing depression and working with adults on their roles as parents to motivate them to engage with hope in the face of adversity. Beardslee's intervention system, for example, is built on forging alliances; assisting with development of more flexible and intense services; reconceptualizing depression for families, children, and staff; emphasizing parenting in an effort to reduce isolation and support positive parent–child engagement; focusing on resilience with both families and caregivers; and enhancing understanding and communication between adults and children. Child-based strategies are also embraced, focusing on the child's needs as a way of connecting with depressed parents, confronting issues of loss and violence in a safe setting, and balancing risks with an emphasis on parental strengths. Outcomes with older children include lowered scores on self-report measures of depressive symptomatology after intervention (Beardslee, Gladstone, Wright, & Cooper, in press).

Substance abuse has long been identified as potentially affecting parents' ability to care for their children (Brown, 1987) and is often correlated with marital violence and child abuse as well as mental illness (Fitzgerald, Zucker, Mun, Puttler, & Wong, 2002). Although variables related to the parent–child and parent-parent relationship have been examined in cases involving substance abuse, the extent to which a substance-abusing parent may affect the emotional or behavioral adjustment of a child warrants further analysis. Although it is not possible to disentangle the contributions of genetic, biological, psychological, and relational risks, multiple factors do appear to be densely intertwined, leading to an elevated risk of future drug and alcohol use for children with substance-abusing parents (Fitzgerald et. al., 2002). For example, family environments high in negative emotional expressiveness and spousal violence contribute to externalizing problem behaviors (Wong, Zucker, Puttler, & Fitzgerald, 1999), which in turn are part of a vulnerability index for substance abuse that Fitzgerald and his colleagues (2002) call the *systemic risk structure*.

PROTECTIVE FACTORS AND RESILIENCE IN PARENTING RELATIONSHIPS

Protective resources are those enduring characteristics of parents and families that prevent, counteract, or ameliorate the effects of adverse conditions. Protective resources, like risk factors, are found in multiple ecological spheres. Key protective factors in parenting include warm and supportive relationships between parent and child (Wolchik, Wilcox, Tein, & Sandler, 2000), appropriate use of discipline (Forgatch, Patterson, & Ray, 1996), and synchronous shared values and beliefs. Cultural values such as family loyalty and cultural identity mitigate low self-esteem and problem behaviors in some cultural groups (Gil, Vega, & Dimas, 1994). Osofsky and Thompson (2000) describe the importance of reciprocity—the shared or complementary affect and experience—as a key condition of adaptive parenting. Building mutually satisfying relationships between parent and child involves *affect attunement* and a second kind of reciprocity that they call *emotional availability*. The parent's accessibility and capacity to read and appropriately respond to the emotional cues of the child is critical to positive development. Furthermore, there is evidence that a well-functioning primary parent may protect against children's poor adjustment in a family with a significant level of interparental conflict or adversity (Kline, Johnston, & Tschann, 1991).

CONCLUSION

To provide support for parents, social-network building and sensitive treatment for mental illness, substance abuse, and trauma are imperative. Programs should be directed, goal oriented, and well grounded. Both classroom and home-based programs show promise in the work of supporting families in their parenting. Most programs include outreach, engagement, and "partnerships in change" through combinations of family support and child-developmental program modules. The most effective interventions for addressing parenting practices appear to be those that start early and are comprehensive, systems-oriented, and flexible. A number of such programs, particularly those that are two-generational in design, have demonstrated efficacy in actively promoting adequate parenting and reducing maladaptive parenting; a number of these intervention systems are described in this volume.

As interventionists, researchers, and policy makers, it is important to consider the supports and obstacles to adaptive parenting as well as the significant needs of those families for whom risk factors make such parenting difficult. Over the next decade we should strive to articulate and implement program models that illustrate what we call the full circle of *innovative prevention practice* (Figure 6.1). These models would demonstrate the process of conceptualizing, developing, implementing, and evaluating innovative multidisciplinary practices that target the individual/group and institutional/systemic spheres that impact parenting practices. Our aim is to create innovative models for twenty-first-century prevention and to train intervention specialists in order to help invigorate practice and support the well-being of young children in the full spectrum of life circumstances. Development and replication of a number of the interventions described in this volume have the potential to reduce the risks to children and families and to enhance our potential as individuals and as a nation. If our intent truly is to leave no child behind, then we must accompany our most general reform initiatives with equally effective specialized approaches for our neediest parents and their children.

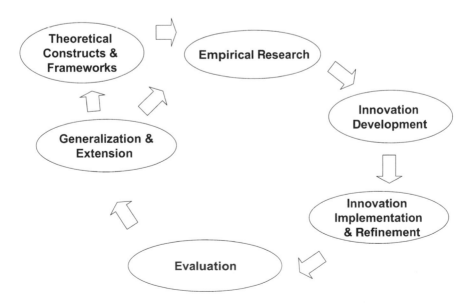

Figure 6.1 Cycle of innovation

REFERENCES

Aber, L., Jones, S., & Cohen, J. (2000). The impact of poverty on mental health and development of very young children. In C. Zeanah, Jr. (Ed.), *Handbook for infant mental health* (2nd ed., pp. 113–129). New York: Guildford.

Adam, E. K., Gunnar, M. R., & Tanaka, A. (2004). Adult attachment, parent emotion, and observed parenting behavior: Mediator and moderator models. *Child Development, 75*(1), 110–122.

Administration for Children and Families. (2002). *Making a difference in the lives of infants and toddlers and their families: The impacts of early Head Start.* Washington, DC: U.S. Department of Health and Human Services.

Amato, P. R., & Keith, B. (1991). Parental divorce and the well-being of children: A meta-analysis. *Psychological Bulletin, 110,* 26–46.

Appel, A. E., & Holden, G. W. (1998). The co-occurrence of spouse and physical child abuse: A review and appraisal. *Journal of Family Psychology, 12*(4), 578–599.

Ayoub, C., Deutsch, R., & Maraganore, N. (1999). Children who experience conflicted divorce: The impact of domestic violence on emotional adjustment, *Family Conciliation Courts Review, 37*(3), 297–314.

Ayoub, C., Fischer, K., & O'Connor, E. (2003). Analyzing development of working models for disrupted attachments: The case of family violence. *Attachment & Human Development, 5*(2), 97–120.

Barnum, R. (2001). Parenting assessment in cases of neglect and abuse. In D. Shetky & E. Benedek (Eds.), *Comprehensive textbook of child and adolescent forensic psychiatry.* Washington, DC: American Psychiatric Association Press.

Beardslee, W. R. (2002). *Out of the darkened room: When a parent is depressed. Protecting the children and strengthening the family.* Boston: Little, Brown.

Beardslee, W. R., Gladstone, T., Wright, E., & Cooper, A. (in press). A family based approach to the intervention of depressive symptoms in children at-risk: Evidence of parental and child change. *Pediatrics.*

Beardslee, W., Versage, E., & Gladstone, T. (1998). Children of affectively ill parents: A review of the past 10 years. *Journal of the American Academy of Child and Adolescent Psychiatry, 37*(11), 1134–1141.

Black, M. M., Hess, C. R., & Berenson-Howard, J. (2000). Toddlers from low-income families have below normal mental, motor, and behavior scores on the revised Bayley scales. *Journal of Applied Developmental Psychology, 21*(6), 655–666.

Bowlby, J. (1980). *Attachment and loss.* New York: Basic Books.

Bradley, R. H., & Corwyn, R. F. (2002). Socioeconomic status and child development. *Annual Reviews Psychology, 53,* 371–399.

Bretherton, I., & Mulholland, K. A. (1999). Internal working models in attachment relationships. In J. Cassidy & P. R. Shaver (Eds.), *Handbook of attachment: Theory, research, and clinical applications* (pp. 3–40). New York: Guilford.

Bronfenbrenner, U. (1979). Contexts of child rearing: Problems and prospects. *American Psychologist, 34*(10), 844–850.

Bronson, M. B. (2000). *Self-regulation in early childhood: Nature and nurture.* New York: Guilford.

Brown, S. (1987). *Treating children of alcoholics: A developmental perspective.* New York: Wiley.

Buckner, J. C., Mezzacappa, E., & Beardslee, W. R. (2003). Characteristics of resilient youths living in poverty: The role of self-regulatory processes. *Development and Psychology, 15,* 139–162.

Cicchetti, D., & Toth, S. (1995). Developmental psychopathology and disorders of affect. In D. Cicchetti & D. Cohen (Eds.), *Developmental psychopathology* (Vol. 2, pp. 369–420). New York: Wiley.

Crittenden, P. M. (1985). Social networks, quality of parenting, and child development. *Child Development, 56,* 1299–1313.

Crittenden, P. M. (1988). Relationships at risk. In J. Belsky & T, Nexworski (Eds.), *Clinical implications of attachment theory.* Hillsdale, NJ: Erlbaum.

Dean, A. L., Malik, M. M., Richards, W., & Stringer, S. A. (1986). Effects of parental maltreatment on children's conceptions of interpersonal relationships. *Developmental Psychology, 22*(5), 617–626.

Denham, S. A., & Holt, R. W. (1993). Preschoolers' likeability as cause or consequence of their social behavior. *Developmental Psychology, 29*(2), 271–275.

Evans, G. W. (2004). The environment of childhood poverty. *American Psychologist, 59*(2), 77–92.

Fischer, K., Ayoub, C., Singh, I., Noam, G., Maraganore, A., & Raya, P. (1998). Psychopathology as adaptive development along distinctive pathways. *Development and Psychopathology, 9,* 749–779.

Fisher, K. W., Shaver, P. R., & Carnochan, P. (1990). How emotions develop and how they organize development. *Cognition and Emotion, 4*(2), 81-127.

Fitzgerald, H., Zucker, R., Mun, E., Puttler, L., & Wong, M. (2002). Origin of addictive behavior. In H. Fitzgerald, K. Karraker, & T. Luster (Eds.), *Infant development ecological perspectives.* New York: Routledge Falmer.

Forgatch, M. S., Patterson, G. R., & Ray, J. A. (1996). Divorce and boys' adjustment problems: Two paths with a single model. In M. E. Hetherington & E. A. Blechman (Eds.), *Stress, coping, and resiliency in children and families* (p. 245). Hillsdale, NJ: Erlbaum.

Gelles, R. J., & Straus, M. A. (1988). *Intimate violence.* New York: Simon & Schuster.

Gibson, J. J. (1979). *The ecological approach to visual perception.* Boston: Houghton-Mifflin.

Gil, A. G., Vega, W. A., & Dimas, J. M. (1994). Acculturative stress and personal adjustment among Hispanic adolescent boys. *Journal of Community Psychology, 22*(1), 43–54.

Gladstone, T. R. G., & Beardslee, W. R. (2002). Treatment, intervention, and prevention with children of depressed parents: A developmental perspective. In S. H. Goodman & I. H. Gotlib (Eds.), *Children of depressed parents: Mechanisms of risk and implications for treatment* (pp. 277–305). Washington, DC: American Psychological Association.

Grisso, T. (1986). *Evaluating competencies.* New York: Plenum.

Haskett, M. E., & Kistner, J. A. (1991). Social interactions and peer perceptions of young physically abused children. *Child Development, 62*(5), 979–990.

Heneghan, A., Silver, E., Bauman, L., Westbrook, L., & Stein, R. (1998). Depressive symptoms in inner-city mothers of young children: Who is at risk? *American Academy of Pediatrics, 102*(6), 1394–1400.

Jekielek, S. M. (1998). Parental conflict, marital disruption and children's emotional well-being. *Social Forces, 76*(3), 905–935.

Johnston, J. R., Campbell, L.E.G., & Mayes, S. S. (1985). Latency children in postseparation and divorce disputes. *Journal of the American Academy of Child Psychiatry, 24,* 563–574.

Keiley, M. K., Howe, T. R., & Dodge, K. A. (2001). The timing of child physical maltreatment: A cross-domain growth analysis of impact on adolescent externalizing and internalizing problems. *Development & Psychopathology, 13*(4), 891–912.

Kinard, E. M. (1999). Psychosocial resources and academic performance in abused children. *Children & Youth Services Review, 21*(5), 351–376.

Kline, M., Johnston, J. R., & Tschann, J. M. (1991). The long shadow of marital conflict: A model of children's postdivorce adjustment. *Journal of Marriage & the Family, 53*(2), 297–309.

Kopp, C. B. (2000). Self-regulation in children. In J. J. Smelser & P. B. Baltes (Eds.), *International encyclopedia of the social and behavioral sciences.* Oxford, UK: Elsevier.

Kurdek, L. A., & Sinclair, R. J. (2000). Psychological, family, and peer predictors of academic outcomes in first- through fifth-grade children. *Journal of Educational Psychology, 92*(3), 449–457.

Lazarus, R. S. (1991). *Emotion and adaptation.* New York: Oxford University Press.

LeVine, R. A., & Miller, P. M. (1990). Commentary. *Human Development, 33,* 73–80.

Londerville, S., & Main, M. (1981). Security of attachment, compliance and maternal training methods in the second year of life. *Developmental Psychology, 17,* 289–299.

Lynch, M., & Cicchetti, D. (1998). An ecological-transactional analysis of children and contexts: The longitudinal interplay among child maltreatment, community violence, and children's symptomatology. *Developmental & Psychopathology, 10,* 235–257.

Lyon, J. S., & Kisiel, C. (1996). Domestic violence and social policy: Integrating theory and practice in the prevention of spousal and child abuse. In C. E. Stout (Ed.), *Integration of psychological principles in policy development* (p. 286). Westport, CT: Praeger/Greenwood.

Lyons-Ruth, K., & Jacobvitz, D. (1999). Attachment disorganization: Unresolved loss, relational violence, and lapses in behavioral and attentional strategies.

In J. Cassidy and P. R. Shaver (Eds.), *Handbook of attachment: Theory, research, and clinical applications* (pp. 520–555). New York: Guilford.

Main, M., & Solomon, J. (1990). Procedures for identifying infants as disorganized/disoriented during the Ainsworth strange situation. In M. T. Greenberg, D. Cicchetti, & E. M. Cummings (Eds.), *Attachment in the preschool years* (pp. 121–160). Chicago: University of Chicago Press.

Mangeldorf, S. C. (1992). Development changes in infant stranger interactions. *Infant Behavior and Development, 15*(2), 191–208.

Margolin, G. (1998). Effects of domestic violence on children. In P. K. Trickett (Ed.), *Violence against children in the family and the community* (pp. 57–101). Washington, DC: American Psychological Association.

Margolin, G., & Gordis, E. B. (2000). The effects of family and community violence on children. *Annual Review of Psychology, 51,* 445–479.

Maslow, A. H. (1954). *Motivation and personality.* New York: Harper.

McLeod, J. D., & Shanahan, M. J. (1993). Poverty, parenting, and children's mental health. *American Sociological Review, 58*(3), 351–366.

Miller, P. J., Fung, H., & Mintz, J. (1996). Self-construction through narrative practices: A Chinese and American comparison of early socialization. *Ethos, 24*: 1-44.

National Institute of Child Health and Human Development (NICHD) Early Child Care Research Network (ECCRN). (2000). The relation of child care to cognitive and language development. *Child Development, 71,* 823–839.

Osofsky, J., & Thompson, M. D. (2000). Adaptive and maladaptive parenting. In J. Shonkoff & S. Meisels (Eds.), *Handbook of early childhood intervention* (2nd ed., pp. 54–75). Cambridge: Cambridge University Press.

Pianta, R. C., Hamre, B., & Stuhlman, M. (2003). Relationships between teachers and children. In W. M. Reynolds & G. E. Miller (Eds.), *Handbook of psychology: Educational psychology* (Vol. 7, pp. 199–234). New York: Wiley.

Rutter, M. (1979). Protective factors in children's responses to stress and disadvantage. In M. W. Kent & J. E. Rolf (Eds.), *Primary prevention of psychopathology: Vol. 3. Social competence in children* (pp. 49–74). Hanover, NH: University Press of New England.

Sales, B., Manber, R., & Rohman, L. (1992). Social science research and child-custody decision making. *Applied and Preventive Psychology, 1,* 23–40.

Sameroff, A. J., & Chandler, M. (1975). Reproductive risk and the continuum of caretaking causality. In F. D. Horowitz (Ed.), *Review of child development research,* (Vol. 4, pp. 187–244), Chicago: University of Chicago Press.

Sameroff, A. J., & Fiese, B. (2005). Models of development and developmental risk. In C. Zeanah, Jr. (Ed.), *Handbook of infant mental health* (2nd ed., pp. 3–19). New York: Guildford.

Sameroff, A. J., & Seifer, R. (1987). Multiple determinants of risk and invulnerability. In E. J. Anthony (Ed.), *The invulnerable child* (pp. 51–69). New York: Guilford.

Sandler, I. (2001). Quality and ecology of adversity as common mechanisms of risk and resilience. *American Journal of Community Psychology, 29*(1), 19–60.

Scales, P., & Leffert, N. (1999). *Developmental assets: A synthesis of the scientific research on adolescent development.* Minneapolis, MN: Search Institute.

Schlichtmann, G. R., & Ayoub, C. (2004, October). *Adaptive and complex developmental pathways: The example of maltreated children.* Paper presented at Building Usable Knowledge in Mind, Brain, and Education Conference, Cambridge, MA.

Shaver, P., Schwartz, J., Kirson, D., & O'Connor, C. (1987). Emotion knowledge: Further exploration of a prototype approach. *Journal of Personality & Social Psychology, 52*(6), 1061–1086.

Shaw, D. S., & Vondra, J. I. (1995). Infant attachment security and maternal predictors of early behavior problems: A longitudinal study of low-income families. *Journal of Abnormal Child Psychology, 23*(3), 335–357.

Shields, A., Cicchetti, D., & Ryan, R. (1994). The development of emotional and behavioral self-regulation and social competence among maltreated school-age children, *Development and Psychopathology, 6,* 57–75.

Shonkoff, J., & Phillips, D. (Eds.). (2000). *From neurons to neighborhoods: The science of early child development/Committee on integrating the science of early childhood development.* Washington, DC: National Academy Press.

Stewart, A. J., Copeland, A. P., Chester, N. L., Malley, J. E., & Barenbaum, N. B. (1997). *Separating together,* New York: Guilford.

Teicher, M. (2000). Wounds that time won't heal: The neurobiology of child abuse. *Cerebrum: The Dana Forum on Brain Science, 2*(4), 50–67.

Toth, S. L., & Cicchetti, D. (1996). Patterns of relatedness, depressive symptomatology, and perceived competence in maltreated children. *Journal of Consulting & Clinical Psychology, 64*(1), 32–41.

U.S. Bureau of the Census. (2005). *Statistical abstract of the United States: 2004–2005.* Washington, DC: U.S. Government Printing Office.

Van der Kolk, B. A. (1996). The body keeps score: Approaches to the psychobiology of posttraumatic stress disorder. In B. A. Van der Kolk, A. C. McFarlane, & L. Weisaeth (Eds.), *Traumatic stress: The effects of overwhelming experience on mind, body and society.* New York: Guilford.

Verschueren, K., Marcoen, A., & Schoefs, V. (1996). The internal working model of the self, attachment, and competence in five-year-olds. *Child Development, 67*(5), 2493–2511.

Wallerstein, J., & Kelly, J. (1980). *Surviving the breakup: How children and parents cope with divorce.* New York: Basic Books.

Wolchik, S. A., Wilcox, K. L., Tein, J. Y., & Sandler, I. N. (2000). Maternal acceptance and consistency of discipline as buffers of divorce stressors on children's psychological adjustment problems. *Journal of Abnormal Child Psychology, 28*(1), 87–102.

Wolfe, D.A., Jaffe, P., Wilson, S.K., & Zak, L. (1985). Children of battered women: The relation of child behavior to family violence and maternal stress. *Journal of Consulting and Clinical Psychology, 53,* 657–665.

Wong, M., Zucker, R., Puttler, L., & Fitzgerald, H. (1999). Heterogeneity of risk aggregation for alcohol problems between early and middle childhood: Nesting structure variations. *Development and Psychopathology, 11,* 727–744.

CHILD CARE AND PRESCHOOL INTERVENTION

Chapter 7

THE NURSE-FAMILY PARTNERSHIP

David L. Olds

INTRODUCTION

Since 1977, my colleagues and I have developed, tested, and refined a program of prenatal and infancy home visiting by nurses known as the Nurse-Family Partnership. This program has been grounded in theory, epidemiology, and the clinical insight and wisdom of numerous talented colleagues. As an undergraduate I had the privilege to take courses with Mary Ainsworth and to work with her as a research assistant coding data from her Baltimore study of infant attachment. Mary played a pivotal role in shaping my intellectual interest in early development and providing me with a framework to think about the emotional needs of young children.

After finishing undergraduate school in 1970, I worked in an inner-city day-care center for low-income children, where I taught a classroom of

The work reported here was made possible by support from many different sources. These include the Administration for Children and Families (90PD0215/01 and 90PJ0003), Biomedical Research Support (PHS S7RR05403-25), Bureau of Community Health Services, Maternal and Child Health Research Grants Division (MCR-360403-07-0), Carnegie Corporation (B-5492), Colorado Trust (93059), Commonwealth Fund (10443), David and Lucile Packard Foundation (95-1842), Ford Foundation (840-0545, 845-0031, and 875-0559), Maternal and Child Health, Department of Health and Human Services (MCJ-363378-01-0), National Center for Nursing Research (NR01-01691-05), National Institute of Mental Health (1-K05-MH01382-01 and 1-R01-MH49381-01A1), Pew Charitable Trusts (88-0211-000), Robert Wood Johnson Foundation (179-34, 5263, 6729, 9677, and 35369), U.S. Department of Justice (95-DD-BX-0181), and the W.T. Grant Foundation (80072380, 84072380, 86108086, and 88124688).

four-year olds and arranged parent groups that met at nap time to address their concerns about their children's needs. I approached this work with the hope that if I provided a more nurturing and cognitively stimulating classroom environment for the children and helped their parents support one another with parenting issues, their children would have better prospects in life. It soon became clear to me, however, that for many children, a supportive preschool environment was simply too little and too late.

One little boy in my classroom was the victim of child abuse and was withdrawn and fearful. His mother would beat him if he wet himself during nap time, which he did frequently when he slept. So, during nap time he would lie awake, afraid to sleep. His mother never attended the parent-group sessions. Another boy had profound language delays and communicated by gesturing. He was cared for by a heroic grandmother who faithfully attended the parent-group meetings. This boy's biological mother had abused drugs and alcohol during pregnancy and had abandoned him before his grandmother gained custody. We suspected that his profound language problems were the result of his prenatal exposure to drugs and alcohol during pregnancy.

Obviously, a program that begins when children reach preschool could not prevent these damaging earlier experiences. Moreover, the children were growing up in neighborhoods devastated by drugs, crime, and limited employment opportunities; they and their parents had almost no personal experiences or models within the community to give them hope for a better life. I realized that I knew too little about the multiplicity of influences on children's development and that I had no power to influence those factors that appeared to shape their lives, so I went to graduate school and studied with Urie Bronfenbrenner, who was just beginning to formulate his theory of human ecology (Bronfenbrenner, 1979).

These firsthand experiences with children and families living in poverty and my studying with Mary Ainsworth and Urie Bronfenbrenner have had profound influences on the work that I describe in this chapter. I have come to realize that any single theory, either attachment or human ecology, is insufficient by itself to develop an effective preventive

I thank John Shannon for his support of the program and data gathering through Comprehensive Interdisciplinary Developmental Services, Elmira, New York; Robert Chamberlin for his contributions to the early phases of this research; Jackie Roberts, Liz Chilson, Lyn Scazafabo, Georgie McGrady, and Diane Farr for their home-visitation work with the Elmira families; Geraldine Smith, for her supervision of the nurses in Memphis; Jann Belton and Carol Ballard for integrating the program into the Memphis/Shelby County Health Department; Kim Sidora and Jane Powers for their fine work on the Elmira and Memphis trials; the many other home-visiting nurses in Memphis and Denver; and the participating families who have made this program of research possible.

intervention for children and parents living in poverty, in which the set of influences shaping children's development extend far beyond parents' own child-rearing histories and their ability to respond competently to their children's communicative signals. Interventions would gain strength, I reasoned, if they were able to reduce biological risks for children's compromised neurological development during pregnancy and if they reduced critical contextual risks for child and family functioning. Moreover, I realized that neither human ecology theory nor attachment theory provided a solid theoretical basis for guiding adaptive behavioral change. They were essentially theories of development but with no firm basis for how one might reliably bring about changes in women's prenatal health, parenting, or family circumstances. We needed a theory of motivation and behavioral change, and for this our team turned to Bandura's self-efficacy theory (Bandura, 1977).

Throughout the history of this program, I have been deeply concerned that the program make sense to parents—that it resonate with their views of the world and their beliefs about what was needed to ensure their children's healthy development, that the content and approach embodied in the program be assimilable. Moreover, parents would have to find the program sufficiently compelling to find the investment of their time worth the effort, a concern addressed most cogently with the Health-Belief Model, which I describe below. With this set of concerns in mind, I drafted the first version of the Nurse-Family Partnership, a program of prenatal and infancy home visiting by nurses for low-income families, which we tested first in Elmira, New York, through a nonprofit organization known as Comprehensive Interdisciplinary Developmental Services. Nurses would be in a unique position to observe factors in the home, parents' care of their children, and women's health that might influence children's health and development.

What, exactly, however, are those important influences? Although having good theory is an important ingredient for effective preventive intervention, having a solid grasp of important risks and protective factors for compromised health and development would help focus the intervention on those factors that theory and evidence indicate are likely to leverage the greatest positive change in the life-course trajectories of the children and families we wished to help. The approach eventually developed by our Elmira team (Bob Tatelbaum, an obstetrician, and Bob Chamberlin, a pediatrician, and a talented team of nurses—Jackie Roberts, Lyn Scazafabo, Diane Farr, Georgie McGrady, and Liz Chilson) was later expanded when we conducted a replication of the Elmira trial in Memphis, Tennessee, to include Harriet Kitzman, a nurse investigator, Bob Cole, a social psychologist with an interest in mental health and development, and Charles Phelps, a health economist. The team was further expanded when we conducted a subsequent trial in Denver and included Ruth O'Brien, another nurse investigator, JoAnn Robinson, a developmental psychologist, and Susan Hiatt, also a developmental psychologist. The program and research our team developed over the years is consistent with Shep Kellam's developmental epidemiology (Kellam & Werthamer-Larsson, 1986).

Evidence on the effectiveness of early center-based interventions for preschoolers (Darlington, 1980) was just beginning to emerge when we began this work in 1976, but there was virtually no convincing evidence on the effectiveness of home-visiting programs or any other type of program devoted to helping parents improve the care of their children. If we were really going to make a difference in the lives of children and families, we would need to know whether or not the intervention really worked, and the only way to answer this question reliably was to test its effectiveness in the form of a randomized controlled trial.

Today, the program has been tested in three separate randomized trials and has been replicated outside of research contexts in more than 250 counties throughout the United States. The growth of the program as a credible preventive intervention rests entirely with its having replicated evidence of effectiveness on socially and clinically important outcomes derived from separate randomized controlled trials, with different populations, living in different contexts, and at different points in our country's history.

This chapter describes the empirical and theoretical foundations upon which this program of research was founded; the design of the program itself; and the research designs, methods, and findings from the three. The findings summarized below have already been published in earlier reports. The final section provides an examination of the policy implications of the findings and describes our current initiative to replicate the program model outside of research contexts while maintaining fidelity to the model tested in the trials.

A RESEARCH-BASED AND THEORY-DRIVEN MODEL

The program tested in this series of randomized trials has been firmly grounded in epidemiology and theories of child development and behavioral change (Kellam & Werthamer-Larsson, 1986; Olds, Kitzman, Cole, & Robinson, 1997).

Research-Based

Developmental and epidemiologic research has guided decisions about the families to be served and the content of the program. All of the studies have examined program impact with women who have had no previous live births, and each has focused recruitment on women who were low income, unmarried, and adolescents. The primary difference among the studies is that in the Elmira trial any woman bearing a first child was allowed to register, although those who were poor, unmarried, and teens were actively recruited. Women with these characteristics were recruited because the problems the program was designed to address (e.g., poor birth outcomes, child abuse and neglect, and diminished economic self-sufficiency of parents) are concentrated in those populations (Elster & McAnarney, 1980; Furstenberg, Brooks-Gunn, & Morgan, 1987; Overpeck, Brenner, Trumble, Trifiletti, & Berendes, 1998). In addition, program effects in Elmira were greater for the higher-risk families, so the subsequent Memphis and Denver trials focused recruitment more exclusively on those with overlapping risks (i.e., being both unmarried and from a low-income family).

All three of the trials focused on women who had no previous live births because it was hypothesized that such women would be more receptive to home-visitation services concerning pregnancy and child rearing than would women who had already given birth. Moreover, as parents learn parenting and other skills through the program, they should be better able to care for subsequent children, and the program should have an even greater positive effect by focusing on women during their first pregnancies. Finally, if the program helped parents plan subsequent births, then it would be easier for parents to finish their education and find work because of fewer problems with child care (Furstenberg et al., 1987), and the children would benefit from more focused parental nurture and guidance (Tygart, 1991). In the United States, 40 percent of all births are to women bearing first children.

The content of the program is also research-based. The program seeks to modify specific risks that are associated with the negative outcomes: poor birth outcomes, child abuse and neglect, injuries, and compromised parental life course.

Figure 7.1 summarizes how these influences are thought to reinforce one another over time. On the far left side of this figure we note the three broad domains of proximal risks and protective factors that the program was designed to affect: prenatal health-related behaviors; sensitive, competent care of the child; and early parental life course (pregnancy planning, parents' completion of their education, finding work, and father involvement in the lives of their children). The middle set of outcomes reflects corresponding child and parental outcomes that the program was designed originally to influence: birth outcomes (obstetric complications, preterm delivery, and low birth weight); child abuse, neglect, and unintentional injuries; child neurodevelopmental impairment (perturbations

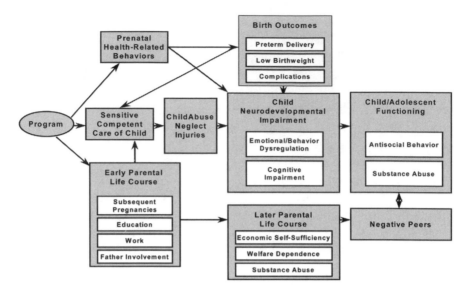

Figure 7.1   Conceptual model of program influences on maternal and child health and development

in emotional, behavioral, and cognitive development); and later parental life course (family economic self-sufficiency, welfare dependence, maternal substance abuse). On the far right, we show child and adolescent outcomes that the program might affect years after completion of the program at child-age two, including school failure, antisocial behavior, and substance abuse. Part of the program effect on adolescent functioning was thought to be affected by reducing children's exposure and susceptibility to negative peer influences. When our team began this program of research in 1977, we did not allow ourselves to imagine that the changes the nurses attempted to make during pregnancy and the first two years of the child's life might really have an impact on adolescent outcomes. Nevertheless, results of the Elmira trial summarized below indicate that the program indeed affected adolescent behavior. Each of these sets of influences is discussed in greater depth below.

Prenatal Health Behaviors: Modifiable Risks for Poor Birth Outcomes and Child Neurodevelopmental Impairment

Prenatal exposure to tobacco, alcohol, and illegal drugs are established risks for poor fetal growth (Kramer, 1987) and, to a lesser extent, preterm birth (Kramer, 1987) and neurodevelopmental impairment (e.g., attention deficit disorder or poor cognitive and language development; Fried, Watkinson, & Dillon, 1987; Mayes, 1994; Milberger, Biederman, Faraone,

Chen, & Jones, 1996; Olds, 1997; Olds, Henderson, & Tatelbaum, 1994a, 1994b; Streissguth, Sampson, Barr, Bookstein, & Olson, 1994). In all three trials (Elmira, Memphis, and Denver) the home visitors therefore sought to reduce mothers' use of these substances. The prenatal protocols also address other behavioral factors that increase the risk for low birth weight, preterm delivery, and poor child development: inadequate weight gain (Institute of Medicine, 1990), inadequate diet (Institute of Medicine, 1990), inadequate use of office-based prenatal care (Klein & Goldenberg, 1990), and early identification and treatment of obstetric complications, such as genitourinary tract infections and hypertensive disorders (high blood pressure; Klein & Goldenberg, 1990).

Sensitive, Competent Care of the Child: Modifiable Risks for Child Abuse and Neglect and Injuries to Children

Parents who empathize with their infants and sensitively read and respond to their babies' communicative signals are less likely to abuse or neglect their children and are more likely to read their children's developmental competencies accurately, leading to fewer unintentional injuries (Peterson & Gable, 1998). Although it makes sense to target these proximal behaviors, it is helpful to understand and address the general sets of influences that affect parents' abilities to care for their children. We have hypothesized that these influences on parenting skills can be moderated with targeted intervention strategies.

Parents' caregiving skills are affected by their own child rearing histories and their current levels of stress and support. Parents who grew up in households with punitive, rejecting, abusive, or neglectful caregiving are more likely to abuse or neglect their own children (Egeland, Jacobvitz, & Sroufe, 1988; Quinton & Rutter, 1984; Rutter, 1989). Parents' psychological immaturity and mental health problems can reduce their ability to care for their infants (Newberger & White, 1990; Sameroff, 1983). Although it is impossible to change parents' personal histories and is very difficult to reduce personal immaturity and mental illness, as indicated in the following section, the program has sought to mitigate the effect of these influences on parents' caregiving. In addition, unemployment (Gil, 1970), poor housing and household conditions (Gil, 1970), marital discord (Belsky, 1981), and isolation from supportive family members and friends (Garbarino, 1981) are all associated with higher rates of abuse and neglect, perhaps because they create stressful conditions in the household that interfere with parents' ability to care for their children (Bakan, 1971; Kempe, 1973). As noted in the following section, the program is designed to improve parents' economic self-sufficiency, help parents find safe housing, improve partner communication and commitment, and reduce social isolation.

Moreover, recent evidence suggests that children's characteristics may affect the degree to which their parents care for them competently. Children born with subtle neurological perturbations resulting from prenatal exposure to substances such as tobacco and alcohol and maternal stress and anxiety during pregnancy are more likely to be irritable and inconsolable and to have difficulty habituating to auditory stimuli in the first few weeks of life (Clark, Soto, Bergholz, Schneider, 1996; Saxon, 1978; Streissguth et al., 1994), making it more difficult for parents to find enjoyment in their care. Children with attention deficit/hyperactivity disorder are at increased risk for becoming seriously injured (DiScala, Lescohier, Barthel, & Li, 1998), a link that may be explained in part by the difficulties parents may have with regulating and guiding their children's behavior. Thus these child characteristics (which are affected to some degree by the quality of the uterine environment) may contribute to parents' abilities to become competent parents. Parents who are mature, married to supportive spouses, who have adequate incomes, and few external stressors are more likely to manage the care of difficult newborns better than those parents without these resources. Unfortunately, children with subtle neurological vulnerabilities are more likely to be born into households where these salutary conditions are not present, multiplying the likelihood that caregiving will be compromised.

Early Parental Life Course (Subsequent Pregnancies, Education, Work, and Father Involvement): Modifiable Risks for Compromised Maternal Life-Course Development

One of the major risks for compromised maternal educational achievement and workforce participation is rapid, successive pregnancy, particularly among unmarried women (Furstenberg et al., 1987). Such pregnancies often occur when women have limited vision for their future in the areas of education and work (Musick, 1993) as well as a limited belief in their control over their life circumstances and over their contraceptive practices in particular (Brafford & Beck, 1991; Heinrich, 1993; Levinson, 1986).

One of the more significant questions that young mothers must address is the role that the child's father will play in their lives. As indicted in the following section, the program actively promotes fathers' involvement with their partners and children. In most cases, fathers are eager to be supportive partners and providers for their children. In some cases, they are ambivalent, unprepared, abusive, and involved in criminal activities. Couples who are married are more likely to achieve economic self-sufficiency, and their children are at lower risk for a host of problems (McLanahan & Carlson, 2002). It would be a mistake, however, to conclude from this that simply promoting marriage for unmarried pregnant women is the right approach, without considering the quality of the possible relationship and the risk for domestic violence. These decisions are complex and require careful consideration of whether or not the father (or other prospective partner) can be a good spouse and positive caregiver.

To the extent that families improve their economic conditions over time, they are less likely to live in unsafe, crime-ridden neighborhoods where children are exposed to negative peer influences. And even if children are exposed to negative peers, nurse-visited children are less likely to be susceptible to those negative influences because they will have stronger relationships with their parents, which will have helped them develop a stronger moral core (Emde & Buchsbaum, 1990).

The young women consult with nurses as they make these significant life-shaping decisions. This counseling takes many forms: helping women to envision a future consistent with their deepest values and aspirations; evaluating different contraceptive methods, child-care options, and career choices; and developing concrete plans for achieving their goals.

Modifiable Risks for Early-Onset Antisocial Behavior

Many of the factors listed previously are risk factors for early-onset antisocial behavior (Olds, 1997; Olds, Kitzman, et al., 1997; Olds, Henderson, Cole, et al., 1998), a type of disruptive behavior that frequently characterizes children who grow up to become violent adolescents and, sometimes, chronic offenders (Moffitt, 1993; Raine, Brennan, & Mednick, 1994). For example, children who develop early-onset disorder are more likely to have subtle neurodevelopmental deficits (sometimes due to poor prenatal health; Milberger et al., 1996; Olds, 1997; Streissguth et al., 1994; Wakschlag et al., 1997) combined with abusive and rejecting care early in life (Moffitt, 1993; Raine et al., 1994). Recent evidence indicates that prenatal tobacco exposure is a unique risk for conduct disorder and youth crime (Wakschlag et al., 1997; Brennan, Grekin, & Mednick, 1999). Adverse prenatal influences on fetal neurological development are sometimes exacerbated by adverse postnatal experiences. Children who have been abused are more likely to develop negative attribution biases that make them more likely to interpret neutral behaviors on the part of others as threatening (Dodge, Bates, & Pettittt, 1990) and to have internal representations of interpersonal relationships characterized by dysregulated aggression and violence (Buchsbaum, Toth, Clyman, Cicchetti, & Emde, 1992), both of which probably reflect an adaptive neurological response to a threatening world (Teicher, 2000). They are more likely to come from large families, with closely spaced children (Tygart, 1991), where parents themselves are involved in substance abuse and criminal behavior (Moffitt, 1993).

Theory-Driven

As noted in the introduction to this chapter, the NFP is grounded in theories of human ecology (Bronfenbrenner, 1979, 1995), self-efficacy (Bandura, 1977), and human attachment (Bowlby, 1969). Together, these theories emphasize the importance of families' social context and individuals' beliefs, motivations, emotions, and internal representations of their experience in explaining the development of behavior. The integration of these theories has influenced the design of this program.

Human ecology theory, for example, emphasizes that children's development is influenced by how their parents care for them, and that, in turn, is influenced by characteristics of their families, social networks, neighborhoods, communities, and the interrelations between them (Bronfenbrenner, 1979). Drawing from this theory, nurses attempt to enhance the material and social environment of the family by involving other family members, especially fathers, in the home visits and by linking families with needed health and human services.

Parents help select and shape the settings in which they find themselves, however (Plomin, 1986). Self-efficacy theory provides a useful framework for understanding how women make decisions about their health-related behaviors during pregnancy, their care of their children, and their own personal development. This theory suggests that individuals choose those behaviors that they believe (1) will lead to a given outcome, and (2) they themselves can successfully carry out (Bandura, 1977). In other words, individuals' perceptions of self-efficacy influence their choices and how much effort they will put forth when they are faced with challenges.

The curriculum therefore is designed first to help women understand what is known about the influence of particular behaviors on their own health and on the health and development of their babies. The program guidelines are periodically updated to reflect the most recent evidence regarding influence on family and child health. Second, the home visitors help parents establish realistic goals and small achievable objectives that, once accomplished, increase parents' reservoir of successful experiences. In turn, these successes increase their confidence in taking on larger challenges.

Finally, the program is based on attachment theory, which posits that infants are biologically predisposed to seek proximity to specific caregivers in times of stress, illness, or fatigue in order to promote survival (Bowlby, 1969). Attachment theory hypothesizes that children's trust in the world and their later capacity for empathy and responsiveness to their own children once they become parents are influenced by the degree to which they formed a secure attachment with a caring, responsive, and sensitive adult when they were growing up. That, in turn, affects their internal representations of themselves and their relationships with others (Main, Kaplan, & Cassidy, 1985).

The program, therefore, explicitly promotes sensitive, responsive, and engaged caregiving in the early years of the child's life (Barnard, 1990; Dolezol & Butterfield, 1994). In addition, home visitors try to help mothers and other caregivers review their own child-rearing histories and make decisions about how they wish to care for their children in light of the way they were cared for as children. Finally, the visitors seek to develop an empathic and trusting relationship with the mother and other family members because experience in such a relationship is expected to help women eventually trust others and to promote more sensitive, empathic care of their children.

PROGRAM DESIGN

The same basic program design has been used in Elmira, Memphis, and Denver.

Frequency of Visitation

The recommended frequency of home visits changed with the stages of pregnancy and was adapted to the parents' needs. When parents were experiencing crises, the nurses were allowed to visit more frequently. Mothers were enrolled through the end of the second trimester of pregnancy. In Elmira and Memphis, the nurses completed an average of 9 (range 0–16) and 7 (range 0–18) visits during pregnancy, respectively; and 23 (range 0–59) and 26 (range 0–71) visits from birth to the child's second birthday, respectively. Each visit lasted approximately 75 to 90 minutes. Analyses of factors associated with frequency of visitation have revealed that the nurses completed substantially more visits with women who had few coping resources (limited belief in their control over their life circumstances in Elmira and limited psychological resources—limited intellectual functioning, high levels of mental health symptoms, and limited control beliefs—in Memphis) than they did with women who had greater coping resources. This is probably because the nurses recognized these women's greater need for help (Olds & Korfmacher, 1997).

Nurses as Home Visitors

Nurses were selected to be the home visitors because of their formal training in women's and children's health and their competence in managing the complex clinical situations often presented by at-risk families. Nurses' abilities to competently address mothers' and family members' concerns about the complications of pregnancy, labor, and delivery, and the physical health of the infant are thought to provide nurses with increased credibility and persuasive power in the eyes of family members. Nurses probably have additional persuasive power because the public views them as having the highest standards of ethics and honesty of all professionals (Gallup Organization, 2000). In addition, through their ability to teach mothers and family members to identify emerging health problems and to use the health-care system, nurses enhance their clinical effect through the early detection and treatment of disorders.

Program Content

During the home visits, the nurses carried out three major activities: (1) they promoted improvements in women's (and other family members') behavior thought to affect pregnancy outcomes, the health and development of the child, and parents' life course; (2) they helped women build supportive relationships with family members and friends; and (3) they linked women and their family members with other needed health and human services.

The nurses followed detailed visit-by-visit guidelines whose content reflects the challenges parents are likely to confront during specific stages of pregnancy and the first two years of the child's life. Specific assessments were made of maternal, child, and family functioning that correspond to those stages, and specific activities were recommended to address problems and strengths identified through the assessments.

During pregnancy, the nurses helped women complete 24-hour diet histories on a regular basis and plot weight gains at every visit; they assessed the women's cigarette smoking and use of alcohol and illegal drugs and facilitated a reduction in the use of these substances through behavioral change strategies. They taught women to identify the signs and symptoms of pregnancy complications, encouraged women to inform the office-based staff about those conditions, and facilitated compliance with treatment. They gave particular attention to urinary tract infections, sexually transmitted diseases, and hypertensive disorders of pregnancy (conditions associated with poor birth outcomes). They coordinated care with physicians and nurses in the office and measured blood pressure when needed.

After delivery, the nurses helped mothers and other caregivers improve the physical and emotional care of their children. They taught parents to observe the signs of illness, to take temperatures, and to communicate with office staff about their children's illnesses before seeking care. Curricula were employed to promote parent–child interaction by facilitating parent's understanding of their infants' and toddlers' communicative signals, enhancing parents' interest in playing with their children in ways that promote emotional and cognitive development, and creating households that are safer for children.

The nurses also helped women clarify their goals and solve problems that may interfere with their education, finding work, and planning future pregnancies.

OVERVIEW OF RESEARCH DESIGNS, METHODS, AND FINDINGS

In each of the three studies, women were randomized to receive either home-visitation services during pregnancy and the first two years of their children's lives or comparison services. Although the nature of the home-visitation services was essentially the same in each of the trials as described previously, the comparison services were slightly different, consisting of developmental screening and free transportation for regular prenatal and well-child care in Elmira, screening and transportation for prenatal care in Memphis, and screening for sensory and developmental problems and referral for further evaluation and treatment in Denver. All three studies employed a variety of data sources. The Elmira sample (N = 400) was primarily white. The Memphis sample (N = 1,138 for pregnancy and 743 for the infancy phase) was primarily black. The Denver trial (N = 735) consisted of a large sample of Hispanics (46%) and systematically examined the impact of the program when delivered by paraprofessionals (individuals who shared many of the social characteristics of the families they served) and by nurses. We looked for consistency in program effect across those sources before assigning much importance to any one finding. Findings corroborated by data from different sources have increased validity. All findings summarized below are statistically significant at the $p < .05$ level unless otherwise noted.

Elmira Results

Prenatal Health Behaviors

During pregnancy, compared to their counterparts in the control group, nurse-visited women improved the quality of their diets to a greater extent, and those identified as smokers smoked 25 percent fewer cigarettes by the 34th week of pregnancy. Analyses of serum cotinine (the major nicotine metabolite) on a subsample of 100 women showed that by the end of pregnancy nurse-visited women were more accurate in reporting the number of cigarettes they smoked than were women in the control group (Olds,

Henderson, Tatelbaum, & Chamberlin, 1986). By the end of pregnancy, nurse-visited women experienced greater informal social support and made better use of formal community services.

Pregnancy and Birth Outcomes

By the end of pregnancy, nurse-visited women had fewer kidney infections, and among women who smoked, those who were nurse-visited had 75 percent fewer preterm deliveries, and among very young adolescents (aged 14–16), those who were nurse-visited had babies who were 395 grams heavier than their counterparts assigned to the comparison group (Olds, Henderson, Tatelbaum, et al., 1986).

Sensitive, Competent Care of Child

At 10 and 22 months of the child's life, nurse-visited poor, unmarried teens, in contrast to their counterparts in the control group, exhibited less punishment and restriction of their infants and provided more appropriate play materials than did their counterparts in the control group (Olds, Henderson, Chamberlin, & Tatelbaum, 1986). At 34 and 46 months of life, nurse-visited mothers provided home environments that were more conducive to their children's emotional and cognitive development as rated by the HOME inventory and that were safer, based upon observations of safety hazards (Olds, Henderson, & Kitzman, 1994). Overall, nurse-visited mothers were observed to punish their 46-month-old children more frequently. Greater punishment among nurse-visited parents was associated with fewer injuries noted in the medical record, but among comparison families, an increase in punishment was associated with a greater number of injuries, suggesting that the functional meaning of punishment varied by treatment (Olds et al, 1994a).

Child Abuse, Neglect, and Injuries

During the first two years of the child's life, nurse-visited children born to low-income, unmarried teens had 80 percent fewer verified cases of child abuse and neglect than did their counterparts in the control group (one case or 4% of the nurse-visited teens, vs. eight cases or 19% of the control group, $p = .07$). During the second year of life, nurse-visited children were seen in the emergency department 32 percent fewer times, a difference that was explained in part by a 56 percent reduction in visits for injuries and ingestions.

As can be seen in Figures 7.2 and 7.3, the effect of the program on child abuse and neglect in the first two years of life and on emergency department

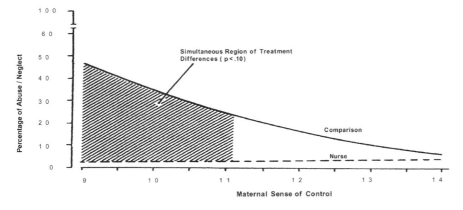

Figure 7.2 Concentration of program effects on child abuse and neglect in low-income, unmarried teens with little sense of mastery. Reprinted from *Pediatrics* (1986) *78*, 65–78.

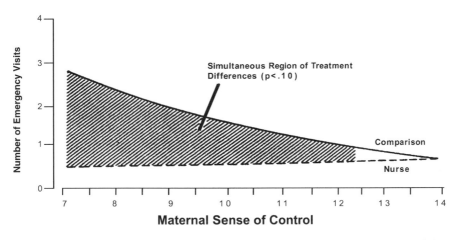

Figure 7.3 Concentration of program effects on emergency department visits for injuries among children born to women with few psychological resources. Reprinted from *Pediatrics* (1986) *78*, 65–78.

encounters in the second year of life was greatest among children whose mothers had little belief in their control over their lives when they first registered for the program (Olds, Henderson, Chamberlin, et al., 1986).

During the two years after the program ended, its impact on health-care encounters for injuries endured: Irrespective of risk, children of nurse-visited women were 35 percent less likely than their control-group counterparts to receive emergency room treatment (a per-child average of 1.00

versus 1.53 visits, $p = .001$) and 40 percent less likely to visit a physician for injuries and ingestions (Olds et al., 1994). The impact of the program on state-verified cases of child abuse and neglect, on the other hand, disappeared during that two-year period (Olds et al., 1994), probably because of increased detection of child abuse and neglect in nurse-visited families and the nurses' linkage of families with needed services (including child protective services) at the end of the program at the child's second birthday (Olds, Henderson, Kitzman, & Cole, 1995). When child abuse or neglect was identified in the first four years of the child's life, the nurse-visited cases were found to be less serious, again probably because of the early identification of less serious forms of maltreatment in the nurse-visited (Group 4) families (Olds et al., 1995).

Results from a 15-year follow-up of the Elmira sample (Olds, Eckenrode, et al., 1997) indicate that the Group 4-comparison differences in rates of state-verified reports of child abuse and neglect grew between the children's 4th and 15th birthdays. Overall, during the 15-year period after delivery of their first child, in contrast to women in the comparison group, those visited by nurses during pregnancy and infancy were 46 percent less likely to be identified as perpetrators of child abuse and neglect. This difference for the entire time period overrode the disappearance of program effects during the two-year period immediately following the end of the program and was greater for women who were poor and unmarried at registration (Olds, Eckenrode, et al., 1997).

Although this reduction in child abuse and neglect was quite promising, the program did not eliminate maltreatment. We therefore turned our attention to an analysis of why the program was not successful in preventing child abuse and neglect for certain families and hypothesized that the presence of domestic violence in the home would attenuate the preventive effects of the program. The program had no impact on the incidence of domestic violence, but domestic violence did moderate the impact of the program on child abuse and neglect. The program effect on child abuse and neglect was reduced in those households in which domestic violence was higher during the 15-year period following the birth of the first child. As a result of this analysis, we have intensified our efforts to help women cope with domestic violence and to promote effective communication between partners, including strategies to reduce the likelihood that miscommunication will escalate. It is important to note that the domestic violence did not moderate program effects on any other reported program effect on maternal or child functioning at the 15-year follow-up. The moderation was specific to child abuse and neglect (Eckenrode et al., 2000).

This analysis illustrates a more general strategy that we have begun to employ in assessing program impact on a variety of outcomes, such as program effects on the prevention of subsequent pregnancy. The systematic evaluation of those cases that failed to respond to the intervention as expected can be used to give us insight into why the program may have been less effective in these cases and can be used to strengthen the program over time.

Child Neurodevelopmental Impairment

At six months of age, nurse-visited poor, unmarried teens reported that their infants were less irritable and fussy than did their counterparts in the comparison group (Olds, Henderson, Chamberlin, et al., 1986). Subsequent analyses of these data indicated that these differences were really concentrated among infants born to nurse-visited women who smoked 10 or more cigarettes per day during pregnancy in contrast to babies born to women who smoked 10 or more cigarettes per day in the comparison group (Olds, Henderson, Kitzman, et al., 1998). Over the first four years of the child's life, children born to comparison-group women who smoked 10 or more cigarettes per day during pregnancy experienced a four- to five-point decline in intellectual functioning in contrast to comparison-group children whose mother smoked zero to nine cigarettes per day during pregnancy (Olds et al., 1994a). In the nurse-visited condition, children whose mothers smoked zero to nine cigarettes per day at registration did not experience this decline in intellectual functioning, so that at ages three and four their IQ scores on the Stanford Binet test were about four to five points higher than their counterparts in the comparison group whose mothers smoked 10 or more cigarettes per day at registration (Olds et al., 1994b).

Early Parental Life Course

By the time the first child was four year of age, nurse-visited low-income, unmarried women, in contrast to their counterparts in the control group, had 43 percent fewer subsequent pregnancies, intervals between the birth of the first and second child that were 12 months greater, and 82 percent greater participation in the workforce than their counterparts in the comparison group (Olds, Pettitt, et al., 1998).

Later Parental Life Course

At the 15-year follow-up, no differences were reported for the full sample on measures of maternal life course such as subsequent pregnancies or subsequent births, the number of months between first and second births, receipt of welfare, or months of employment. Poor unmarried women, however, showed a number of enduring benefits. In contrast to their counterparts in the comparison condition, those visited by nurses during both pregnancy and infancy averaged 32 percent fewer subsequent pregnancies, 31 percent fewer subsequent births, intervals between the birth of their first and second children that were 25 months longer, 30 fewer months on welfare, 37 fewer months receiving food stamps, 44 percent fewer behavioral problems due to substance abuse, and 69 percent fewer arrests (Olds, Eckenrode, et al., 1997).

Child/Adolescent Functioning

The follow-up study also assessed children of the original participants when the children were 15 years of age (Olds, Henderson, Cole, et al., 1998). There were no differences between nurse-visited and comparison-group adolescents for the whole sample, but there were differences between the children of poor, unmarried women. In contrast to adolescents born to poor, unmarried women in the comparison group, those visited by nurses during pregnancy and infancy reported 60 percent fewer instances of running away, 56 percent fewer arrests, 81 percent fewer convictions/violations of probation, 63 percent fewer lifetime sex partners, and 56 percent fewer days of having consumed alcohol in the six-month period preceding the interview. Parents of nurse-visited children reported that their children had 56 percent fewer behavioral problems related to use of drugs and alcohol (Olds, Henderson, Cole, et al., 1998). There were no program effects on other behavioral problems, such as teachers' reports of adolescents' acting out in school; suspensions; initiation of sexual intercourse; and parents' or children's reports of major acts of delinquency, minor antisocial acts, or other behavioral problems (Olds, Henderson, Cole, et al., 1998).

Cost Analysis

The Rand Corporation has conducted an economic evaluation of the program that extrapolates the results of the 15-year follow-up study to estimate cost savings generated by the program (Karoly et al., 1998). Although there were no net savings to government or society for serving families in which mothers were married and of higher social class, the savings to government and society for serving families in which the mother was low-income and unmarried at registration exceeded the cost of the program by a factor of four over the life of the child. The return on the investment was realized well before the child's fourth birthday, and the primary cost savings were found in reduced welfare and criminal-justice expenditures and increases in tax revenues.

Conclusion

In general, the beneficial effects of the program were greater for families at greater risk (e.g., for low-income or unmarried women and those who smoked during pregnancy). Moreover, the beneficial effects of the program during the first two years of life on child abuse and neglect and on childhood injuries were greater for mothers with little belief in their control over their life circumstances. This led us to give even greater attention to training the nurses in promoting parents' self-efficacy in the Memphis trial.

Memphis Results

Prenatal Health Behaviors

There were no program effects on women's use of standard prenatal care or obstetrical emergency services after registration in the study. By the 36th week of pregnancy, nurse-visited women were more likely to use other community services than were women in the control group. There were no program effects on women's cigarette smoking, probably because the rate of cigarette use was only 7 percent in this sample.

Pregnancy and Birth Outcomes

In contrast to women in the comparison group, nurse-visited women had 26 percent fewer yeast infections after randomization and 35 percent fewer instances of pregnancy-induced hypertension. Among women with pregnancy-induced hypertension, those who received a nurse home visitor had lower mean arterial blood pressures during labor than those in the comparison group, an indication of less severe cases (Kitzman et al., 1997).

Despite these differences, there were no program effects on birth outcomes such as average birth weight, percent low birth weight, length of gestation, spontaneous preterm delivery, indicated preterm delivery, or Apgar scores.

Sensitive, Competent Care of Child

Nurse-visited mothers reported that they attempted breast-feeding more frequently than women in the comparison group, although there were no differences in duration of breast-feeding. By the 24th month of the child's life, in contrast to their comparison-group counterparts, nurse-visited women held fewer beliefs about child rearing associated with child abuse and neglect. Moreover, the homes of nurse-visited women were rated on the HOME scale as more conducive to children's development (Kitzman et al., 1997).

Although there was no program effect on observed maternal teaching behavior, children born to nurse-visited mothers with low levels of psychological resources were observed to be more communicative and responsive toward their mothers than were their comparison-group counterparts.

Child Abuse, Neglect, and Injuries

The rate of substantiated child abuse and neglect in the population of two-year-old, low-income children in Memphis was too low (3%–4%) to serve as a valid indicator of child maltreatment in this study. We therefore hypothesized that we would see a pattern of program effects on childhood injuries that would be similar to the pattern observed in Elmira, reflecting a reduction in dysfunctional care of children.

During their first two years, nurse-visited children, overall, had 23 percent fewer health-care encounters in which injuries and ingestions were detected than did children in the comparison group, an effect that was accounted for primarily by a reduction in outpatient clinic encounters. Nurse-visited

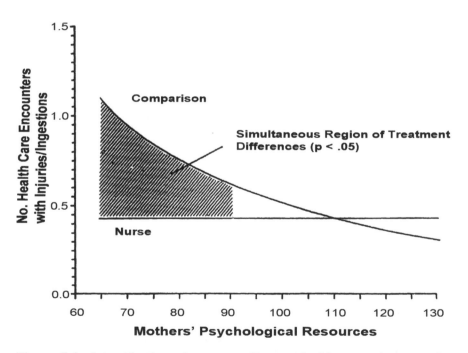

Figure 7.4 Intensification of program effect on health care encounters for injuries and ingestions concentrated among children born to mothers with few psychological resources. From C. Rovee-Collier, L. P. Lipsitt, & H. Hayne (Eds.), *Advances in Infancy Research* (Vol. 12). Copyright © 1998 by Ablex Publishing Corporation. Reproduced with permission of Greenwood Publishing Group, Inc., Westport, CT.

children also were hospitalized for 79 percent fewer days with injuries and/ or ingestions than were children in the comparison group.

As can be seen in Figures 7.4 and 7.5, the effect of the program on both total health-care encounters and number of days children were hospitalized with injuries and ingestions was greater for children born to women with few psychological resources, an effect similar to the one observed in Elmira for child abuse and neglect and emergency department encounters. In order to assist with its interpretation, the psychological resources scale has been standardized to a mean of 100 for this sample, with a standard deviation of 10.

An examination of the children's hospital records provides insight into reasons why nurse-visited children were hospitalized for fewer days than children in the comparison group. As can be seen in Table 7.1, nurse-visited children tended to be older when hospitalized and to have less-severe conditions. The 3 nurse-visited children who were hospitalized with injuries and ingestions were admitted when they were 12 months of age or older, whereas 6 of the 14 comparison children were hospitalized when they were younger than 6 months of age. Eight of the 14 comparison-group hospitalizations involved either fractures and/or head trauma,

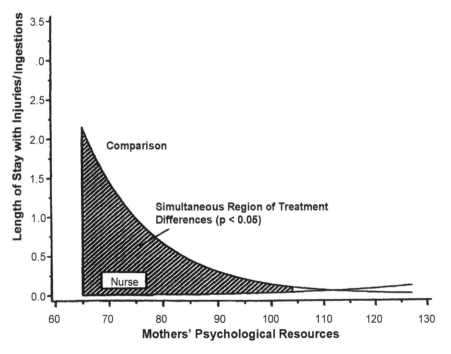

Figure 7.5 Intensification of program effect on days hospitalized for injuries and ingestions concentrated on children born to women with few psychological resources. From C. Rovee-Collier, L.P. Lipsitt, & H. Hayne (Eds.), *Advances in Infancy Research* (Vol. 12). Copyright © 1998 by Ablex Publishing Corporation. Reproduced with permission of Greenwood Publishing Group, Inc., Westport, CT.

Table 7.1
Results from the Memphis Study: Diagnoses for Hospitalizations in Which Injuries and Ingestions Were Detected—by Treatment Condition

Diagnosis	Age (Months)	Sex	Length of Hospital Stay (Days)
	Nurse-Visited (Group 4) N = 216		
First and second degree burns to face	12.0	M	2
Coin ingestion	12.1	M	1
Ingestion of iron medication	20.4	F	4
	Comparison Group (Group 2) N = 481		
Head trauma	2.4	M	1
Fractured fibula/congenital syphilis	2.4	M	12
Strangulated hernia with delay in seeking care/first degree burn to lips	3.5	M	12
Bilateral subdural hematoma[a]	4.9	F	19
Fractured skull	5.2	F	5
Bilateral subdural hematoma (unresolved)/ aseptic meningitis—second hospitalization[a]	5.3	F	4
Fractured skull	7.8	F	3
Coin ingestion	10.9	M	2
Child abuse/neglect suspected	14.6	M	2
Fractured tibia	14.8	M	2
Second degree burns to face/ neck	15.1	M	5
Second and third degree burns to leg[b]	19.6	M	4
Gastroenteritis/head trauma	20.0	F	3
Burns—second hospitalization[b]	20.1	M	6
Finger injury/osteomyelitis	23.0	M	6

[a] One child was hospitalized twice with a single bilateral subdural hematoma.
[b] One child was hospitalized twice for burns resulting from a single incident.

Source: Reprinted with permission from H. Kitzman, D. Olds, C. R. Henderson, Jr., C. Hanks, R. Cole, R. Tatelbaum, et al. (1997). Effect of prenatal and infancy home visitation by nurses on pregnancy outcomes, childhood injuries, and repeated childbearing. A randomized controlled trial. *Journal of the American Medical Association, 278*(8), 644–652.

whereas none of the nurse-visited hospitalizations did. In interpreting the number of hospitalizations, it is important to note that the comparison group (N = 465) had a larger number of cases than the nurse-visited group (N = 206). These profiles suggest that many of these hospitalized comparison-group children suffered from more seriously deficient care than children visited by nurses.

Child Neurodevelopmental Impairment

After two years in the program, children in nurse-visited and comparison groups did not differ in their mental development or reported behavioral problems, either for the full sample or for mothers with lower psychological resources. By child-age six, however, children visited by nurses had higher intellectual functioning and receptive vocabulary scores (92.34 vs. 90.24 and 84.32 vs. 82.13, respectively) and fewer behavior problems in the borderline or clinical range (1.8% vs. 5.4%). Nurse-visited children born to mothers with low psychological resources had higher arithmetic achievement test scores (88.61 vs. 85.42) and expressed less aggression (98.58 vs. 101.10) and incoherence (20.90 vs. 29.84) in response to story stems. At age six, children visited by nurses had higher intellectual functioning and receptive vocabulary scores (92.34 vs. 90.24, and 84.32 vs. 82.13, respectively) and fewer behavior problems in the borderline or clinical range (1.8% vs. 5.4%). Nurse-visited children born to mothers with low psychological resources had higher arithmetic achievement test scores (88.61 vs. 85.42) and expressed less aggression (98.58 vs. 101.10) and incoherence (20.90 vs. 29.84) in response to story stems.

Early Parental Life Course

At the 24th month of the first child's life, nurse-visited women reported 23 percent fewer second pregnancies and 29 percent fewer subsequent live births than did women in the comparison group. Nurse-visited women and their first-born children relied upon welfare for slightly fewer months during the second year of the child's life than did comparison-group women and their children, although there were no differences during the child's first year of life. There were no program effects on mothers' reported educational achievement or length of employment for either the whole sample or for those with few psychological resources (Kitzman et al., 1997).

Later Parental Life Course

During the four-and-a-half-year period following the birth of the first child, in contrast to counterparts assigned to the comparison condition, women visited by nurses had 14 percent fewer subsequent pregnancies, 50 percent fewer subsequent therapeutic abortions ($p = .08$), and durations between the birth of the first and second child that were four months longer; six fewer months that the mother and child used welfare (Aid to Families with Dependent Children [AFDC]) and food stamps; higher rates of living with a partner (43% vs. 32%), marriage (15% vs. 10%, $p = .10$), and living with the biological father of the child (19% vs. 12%); and partners who had been employed for longer durations (35.2 months vs. 26.5 months). There were no statistically significant effects on maternal educational achievement, employment, or use of Medicaid. By child-age six, in contrast to counterparts assigned to the comparison group, women visited by nurses had fewer subsequent pregnancies and births (1.16 vs. 1.38, $p = .01$ and 1.08 vs. 1.28, $p = .01$, respectively); longer intervals between births of first and second children (34.38 vs. 30.23 months, $p = .01$); longer relationships with current partners (54.36 vs. 45.00 months, $p = .02$); and since last follow-up at four-and-a-half years, fewer months of using welfare (7.21 vs. 8.96, $p = .01$) and food stamps (9.67 vs. 11.50, $p = .004$). Nurse-visited children were more likely to have been enrolled in formal out-of-home care between age two and four-and-a-half years (82.0% vs. 74.9%, $p = .05$).

Denver Results

In the Denver trial, we were unable to use the women's or children's medical records to assess their health because the health-care delivery system was too complex to enable us to abstract reliably all of their health-care encounters as we had done in Elmira and Memphis. This limited the number of health outcomes we could examine in this trial. Moreover, as in Memphis, the rate of state-verified reports of child abuse and neglect was too low in this population (3%–4% for low-income children from birth to two years of age) to allow us to use Child Protective Service records to assess the impact of the program on child maltreatment. We therefore focused more of our measurement resources on the early emotional development of the infants and toddlers.

Denver Results for Paraprofessionals

There were no paraprofessional effects on women's prenatal health behavior (use of tobacco), maternal life course, or child development, although at 24-months, paraprofessional-visited mother-child pairs in which the mother had low psychological resources interacted more responsively than did control-group counterparts. Moreover, although paraprofessional-visited women did not have statistically significant reductions in the rates of subsequent pregnancy, the reductions observed were clinically significant.

Two years after the program ended, women visited by paraprofessionals, compared to controls, were less likely to be married (32.2% vs. 44.0%) and to live with the biological father of the child (32.7% vs. 43.1%), but worked more (15.13 months vs. 13.38 months) and reported greater sense of mastery and better mental health. Mothers and children visited by paraprofessionals, compared to controls, displayed greater sensitivity and responsiveness toward one another and, in those cases in which the mothers had low psychological resources at registration, had home environments that were more supportive of children's early learning.

Denver Results for Nurses

The nurses produced effects consistent with those achieved in earlier trials of the program.

Prenatal Health Behaviors

In contrast to their control-group counterparts, nurse-visited smokers had greater reductions in urine cotinine (the major nicotine metabolite) from intake to the end of pregnancy. Use of other substances (e.g., cocaine, marijuana) was too low (by urinalysis) to serve as valid outcomes.

Sensitive, Competent Care of Child

During the first 24 months of the child's life, nurse visited mother-infant dyads interacted more responsively than did control pairs, an effect concentrated in the low-resource group.

At the four-year follow-up, nurse-visited mothers with low psychological resources at registration, compared to control-group counterparts, provided home environments that were more supportive of children's learning.

Child Neurodevelopmental Impairment

At six months of age, nurse-visited infants, in contrast to control-group counterparts, were less likely to exhibit emotional vulnerability in response to fear stimuli, and those born to women with low psychological resources were less likely to display low emotional vitality in response to joy and anger stimuli (24% vs. 40% and 13% vs. 32%, respectively). At 21 months, nurse-visited children were less likely to exhibit language delays than were children in the control group (6% vs. 12%), an effect concentrated among children born to mothers with low psychological resources (7% vs. 18%). Nurse-visited children born to women with low psychological resources also had superior language and mental development in contrast to control-group counterparts (101.52 vs. 96.85 and 90.18 vs. 86.20, respectively).

At four years of age, nurse-visited children whose mothers had low psychological resources at registration, compared to control-group counterparts, had more advanced language (91.39 vs. 86.73), superior executive functioning (100.16 vs. 95.48) and better behavioral adaptation during testing (95.95 vs. 92.35 standard score points).

Early Maternal Life Course

By 24 months after delivery, nurse-visited women, compared to controls, were less likely to have had a subsequent pregnancy (29% vs. 41%) and birth (12% vs. 19%) and had longer intervals until the next conception. Women visited by nurses were employed longer during the second year following the birth of their first child than were controls (6.87 months vs. 5.73 months).

At the follow-up conducted at child-age four, nurse-visited women reported greater intervals between the birth of their first and second children (24.51 vs. 20.39 months), less domestic violence (6.9% vs. 13.6%), and enrolling their children less frequently in either preschool, Head Start, or licensed day care than did controls.

Estimates of Nurse versus Paraprofessional Effects

While the program was in operation, for most outcomes on which there was an effect for either program, paraprofessionals produced effects that were approximately half the size of those produced by nurses. Aside from significantly superior language development for nurse- vs. paraprofessional-visited children born to mothers with low psychological resources at 21 months, none of the other differences was statistically significant.

Paraprofessional-visited mothers began to experience benefits from the program two years after the program ended at child-age two, but their children were not statistically distinguishable from their control-group counterparts on most outcomes. Nurse-visited mothers and children continued to benefit from the program two years after it ended, although the nurse-visited children were not statistically superior to the children visited by paraprofessionals. The impact of the nurse-delivered program on children was concentrated on those born to mothers with low psychological resources.

SUMMARY OF RESULTS, POLICY IMPLICATIONS, AND PROGRAM REPLICATION

Many of the beneficial effects of the program found in the Elmira trial that were concentrated in higher-risk groups were reproduced in the Memphis and Denver replications. Overall, the Elmira and Memphis trials demonstrate that the nurse home-visitation program achieved two of its most important goals—the reduction in dysfunctional care of children and the improvement of maternal life course. The impact on pregnancy outcomes, however, was equivocal.

Policy Implications

One of the clearest messages that have emerged from this program of research is that the functional and economic benefits of the Nurse-Family Partnership are greatest for families at greater risk. In the Elmira study, it was evident that most-married women and those from higher socio-economic households managed the care of their children without serious problems and that they were able to avoid lives of welfare dependence, substance abuse, and crime without the assistance of the nurse home visitors. Similarly, their children on average avoided encounters with the criminal justice system, the use of cigarettes and alcohol, and promiscuous sexual activity. Low-income, unmarried women and their children in the comparison group, on the other hand, were at much greater risk for these problems, and the program was able to avert many of these untoward outcomes for this at-risk population. Cost analyses suggested that the program's cost savings for government are solely attributable to benefits accruing to this higher-risk group. Among families at lower risk, the financial investment in the program was a loss.

This pattern of results challenges the position that these kinds of intensive programs for targeted at-risk groups ought to be made available on a universal basis. Not only is it likely to be wasteful from an economic standpoint, but it may lead to a dilution of services for those families who need them the most because of insufficient resources to serve everyone well.

During the past five years, new studies have been reported that have led us to doubt the effectiveness of home-visitation programs that do not adhere to the elements of the model studied in these trials (Gomby, Culross, & Behrman, 1999; Olds, Hill, Robinson, Song, & Little, 2000), including, especially, the hiring of nurses and the use of carefully constructed program protocols designed to promote adaptive behavior (Olds et al., in press). Most home-visiting programs for low-income families studied in randomized controlled trials have failed to alter clinically important maternal, child, and family outcomes (Gomby et al., 1999). These results should give policy makers and practitioners pause as they consider investments in home-visitation programs without careful consideration of program structure, content, methods, and likelihood of success.

Indeed, the Washington State Institute for Public Policy has recently conducted an extensive economic evaluation of hundreds of preventive interventions from prenatal to the adolescent period that have been evaluated in the form of studies that have employed control groups. Using sophisticated economic modeling, they have found that the range of economic returns on investments in early childhood programs varies tremendously, with some programs, such as the Nurse-Family Partnership, showing strong returns on the investment, whereas others show functional and economic impacts so small as to produce losses on investment, sometimes very large losses. These analyses show that neither investing in early intervention nor spending a lot guarantees success. I suspect that success depends, at least in part, upon effective targeting of the intervention, crafting the intervention to address important risk factors for adverse outcomes, and using intervention strategies that are grounded in well-tested theories of behavioral change.

Replication and Scale-Up of the Nurse-Family Partnership

Even when communities choose to develop programs based on models with good scientific evidence, such programs run the risk of being watered down in the process of being scaled up. Therefore, it is with some apprehension that our team has been working to make the program available for public investment in new communities (Olds, Hill, O'Brien, Racine, & Moritz, 2003). Under grants from the United States Department of Justice, the Administration for Children and Families (DHHS), David and Lucile Packard, Robert Wood Johnson Foundations, Doris Duke Charitable Trust, and the Edna McConnell Clark Foundation, a nonprofit organization known as the National Nurse-Family Partnership (NFP) national office has been created to help new communities develop the program outside of traditional research contexts. The NFP national office is organized around the creation in state and local organizations of the fundamental capacities necessary for the success of the program. Communities and states pay for part of the training and evaluation services provided by the NFP national office. These payments, however, cover only part of the cost incurred to provide replication services.

The focus of this effort is to help create sufficient capacity to carry out the program with fidelity and sustain it over time. Studies are being conducted to determine what influences the quality and performance of the program in community settings and to refine the resources and services the NFP offers to support program development.

State and local governments are securing financial support for the Nurse-Family Partnership (about $8,200 per family for two-and-a-half years of services, in 2005 dollars) out of existing sources of funds, such as Temporary Assistance to Needy Families, Medicaid, the Maternal and Child Health Block-Grant, and child-abuse and crime-prevention dollars. Sharing the costs between several government agencies reduces the strain on any one agency's budget and is an approach the National Nurse Family Partnership is encouraging states and communities to consider given the breadth of the outcomes the Nurse-Family Partnership is able to produce.

Each site choosing to implement the Nurse-Family Partnership needs certain capacities to operate and sustain the program with high quality, ideally expanding it gradually to reach a significant portion of the target population. These capacities include having (1) an organization and community that are fully knowledgeable and supportive of the program, (2) a staff that is well trained and supported in the conduct of the program model, and (3) real-time information on implementation of the program and its achievement of benchmarks to guide efforts in continuous quality improvement. Staff members at the NFP national office are organized around these major functions.

CONCLUSIONS

The Nurse-Family Partnership is grounded in epidemiology and theories of development and behavior change, is specified in detailed visit-by-visit guidelines, and has produced enduring and replicated effects with different populations, in different contexts, and at different points in time in a series of randomized controlled trials. Trials of the program show considerable promise for reducing some of the most damaging and widespread problems faced by low-income children and families in our society. Since publication of the results from the trials, the demand for the program in local communities and states has been strong, perhaps in part because dissemination began in the middle of the long U.S. economic boom of the 1990s. The NFP's efforts in disseminating this evidence-based preventive intervention for vulnerable women, children, and families, although fraught with challenges, have met with reasonable success so far. If the Nurse-Family Partnership will continue to be sustained and grow as economic conditions fluctuate is not yet known. Ironically, it is during periods of economic stagnation and high unemployment that this program is needed most.

In 1964, President Lyndon B. Johnson signed the Economic Opportunity Act, which embodied the federal government's commitment to conduct a war on poverty, that "most ancient of mankind's enemies." Although the evidence on the success of this effort is mixed, it is time to reinvigorate a public commitment to addressing the ravages of poverty—especially as they relate to the development of young children, as such investments hold considerable promise for improving long-term human functioning and improving the economic productivity of our society. Not all programs work, however, so it is not just a matter of political will, money, or theory, although all of these are needed. This time, such an effort needs to be guided more completely by the results of randomized controlled trials, as interventions guided by the results of other types of research are likely to send us in the wrong direction (Snell, 2003). The children and families we seek to help deserve programs that really work, and we taxpayers deserve to have scarce public resources allocated in ways that will improve the good of all of us.

REFERENCES

Bakan, D. (1971). *Slaughter of the innocents: A study of the battered child phenomenon.* San Francisco: Jossey-Bass.

Bandura, A. (1977). Self-efficacy: Toward a unifying theory of behavioral change. *Psychological Review, 84,* 191–215.

Barnard, K.E. (1990). *Keys to caregiving.* Seattle: University of Washington Press.

Belsky, J. (1981). Early human experience: A family perspective. *Developmental Psychology, 17,* 3–23.

Bowlby, J. (1969). *Attachment and loss: Vol. 1. Attachment.* New York: Basic Books.

Brafford, L.J., & Beck, K.H. (1991). Development and validation of a condom self-efficacy scale for college students. *Journal of American College of Health, 39,* 219–225.

Brennan, P.A., Grekin, E.R., & Mednick, S.A. (1999). Maternal smoking during pregnancy and adult male criminal outcomes. Retrieved February 18, 2002, from http://www.ama-assn.org/special/womh/library/scan/vol_5/no_9/yoa8114a.htm

Bronfenbrenner, U. (1979). *The ecology of human development: Experiments by nature and design.* Cambridge, MA: Harvard University Press.

Bronfenbrenner, U. (1995). Developmental ecology through space and time: A future perspective. In P. Moen, G.H. Elder, Jr., & K. Luscher (Eds.), *Examining lives in context* (pp. 619–647). Washington, DC: American Psychological Association.

Buchsbaum, H.K., Toth, S.L., Clyman, R.B., Cicchetti, D., & Emde, R.N. (1992). The use of a narrative story stem technique with maltreated children: Implications for theory and practice. *Development and Psychopathology, 4,* 603–625.

Clark, A. S., Soto, S., Bergholz, T., & Schneider, M. (1996). Maternal gestational stress alters adaptive and social behavior in adolescent rhesus monkey offspring. *Infant Behavioral Development, 19*,453–463.

Darlington, R. (1980). Preschool programs and later school competence of children from low-income families. *Science, 208,* 202–208.

DiScala, C., Lescohier, I., Barthel, M., & Li, G. (1998). Injuries to children with attention deficit hyperactivity disorder. *Pediatrics, 102*(6), 1415–1421.

Dodge, K. A., Bates, J. E., & Pettitt, G. S. (1990). Mechanisms in the cycle of violence. *Science, 250,* 1678–1683.

Dolezol, S., & Butterfield, P. M. (1994). *Partners in parenting education.* Denver, CO: How to Read Your Baby.

Eckenrode, J., Ganzel, B., Henderson, C. R., Jr., Smith, E., Olds, D., & Powers, J. (2000). Preventing child abuse and neglect with a program of nurse home visitation: The limiting effects of domestic violence. *Journal of the American Medical Association, 284,* 1385–1391.

Egeland, B., Jacobvitz, D., & Sroufe, L. A. (1988). Breaking the cycle of abuse. *Child Development, 59,* 1080–1088.

Elster, A., & McAnarney, E. (1980). Medical and psychosocial risks of pregnancy and childbearing during adolescence. *Pediatric Annals, 9,* 13.

Emde, R. N., & Buchsbaum, H. K. (1990). "Didn't you hear my": Autonomy with connectedness in moral self-emergence. In D. Chicchetti & M. Beeghly (Eds.), *The self in transition* (pp. 35–60). Chicago: University of Chicago Press.

Fried, P. A., Watkinson, B. W., & Dillon, R. F. (1987). Neonatal neurological status in a low-risk population after prenatal exposure to cigarettes, marijuana, and alcohol. *Developmental & Behavioral Pediatrics, 8,* 318–326.

Furstenberg, F. F., Brooks-Gunn, J., & Morgan, S. P. (1987). *Adolescent mothers in later life.* Cambridge: Cambridge University Press.

Gallup Organization. (2000). Nurses remain at top of honesty and ethics poll. Honesty/Ethics in Professions Poll, 2000.

Garbarino, J. (1981). An ecological perspective on child maltreatment. In L. Pelson (Ed.), *The social context of child abuse and neglect.* New York: Human Sciences Press.

Gil, D. (1970). Violence against children: Physical child abuse in the United States. Cambridge, MA: Harvard University Press.

Gomby, D. S., Culross, P. L., & Behrman, R. E. (1999). Home-visiting: Recent program evaluations—analysis and recommendations. *The Future of Children: Home Visiting: Recent Program Evaluations, 9,* 4–26.

Heinrich, L. (1993). Contraceptive self-efficacy in college women. *Journal of Adolescent Health, 14,* 269–276.

Institute of Medicine. (1990). *Nutrition during pregnancy.* Washington, DC: National Academy Press.

Karoly, L. A., Greenwood, P. W., Everingham, S. S., Hoube, J., Kilburn, M. R., Rydell, C. P., et al. (1998). *Investing in our children: What we know and don't know about the costs and benefits of early childhood interventions.* Santa Monica, CA: RAND Corporation.

Kellam, S.G., & Werthamer-Larsson, L. (1986). Developmental epidemiology: A basis for prevention. In M. Kessler & S.E. Goldston (Eds.), *A decade of progress in primary prevention* (pp. 154–180). Hanover, NH: University Press of New England.

Kempe, C. (1973). A practical approach to the protection of the abused child and rehabilitation of the abusing parent. *Pediatrics, 51,* 804.

Kitzman, H., Olds, D.L., Henderson, C.R., Jr., Hanks, C., Cole, R., Tatelbaum, R., et al. (1997). Effect of prenatal and infancy home visitation by nurses on pregnancy outcomes, childhood injuries, and repeated childbearing: A randomized controlled trial. *Journal of the American Medical Association, 278,* 644–652.

Klein, L., & Goldenberg, R.L. (1990). Prenatal care and its effect on preterm birth and low birthweight. In I.R. Merkatz & J.E. Thompson (Eds.), *New perspectives on prenatal care.* New York: Elsevier.

Kramer, M.S. (1987). Intrauterine growth and gestational duration determinants. *Pediatrics, 80,* 502–511.

Levinson, R.A. (1986). Contraceptive self-efficacy: A perspective on teenage girls' contraceptive behavior. *Journal of Sex Research, 22,* 347–369.

Main, M., Kaplan, N., & Cassidy, J. (1985). Security in infancy, childhood, and adulthood: A move to the level of representation. In I. Bretherton & E. Waters (Eds.), *Growing points of attachment theory and research. Monographs of the Society for Research in Child Development, 50*(1–2, Serial No. 209), 66–104.

Mayes, L.C. (1994). Neurobiology of prenatal cocaine exposure: Effect on developing monoamine systems. *Infant Mental Health Journal, 15,* 121–133.

McLanahan, S., & Carlson, M. (2002, Winter/Spring). Welfare reform, fertility, and father involvement. *The Future of Children, 12,* 147–166.

Milberger, S., Biederman, J., Faraone, S., Chen, L., & Jones, J. (1996). Is maternal smoking during pregnancy a risk factor for attention deficit hyperactivity disorder in children? *American Journal of Psychiatry, 153,* 1138–1142.

Moffitt, T.E. (1993). Adolescence-limited and life-course-persistent antisocial behavior: A developmental taxonomy. *Psychological Review, 100,* 674–701.

Musick, J.S. (1993). *Young, poor and pregnant.* New Haven, CT: Yale University Press.

Newberger, C.M., & White, K.M. (1990). Cognitive foundations for parental care. In D. Cicchetti & V. Carlson (Eds.), *Child maltreatment: Theory and research on the causes and consequences of child abuse and neglect* (pp. 302–316). Cambridge: Cambridge University Press.

Olds, D.L. (1997). Tobacco exposure and impaired development: A review of the evidence. *Mental Retardation and Developmental Disabilities Research Reviews, 3,* 1–13.

Olds, D.L., Eckenrode, J., Henderson, C.R., Jr., Kitzman, H., Powers, J., Cole, R., et al. (1997). Long-term effects of home visitation on maternal life course and child abuse and neglect: 15-year follow-up of a randomized trial. *Journal of the American Medical Association, 278,* 637–643.

Olds, D.L., Henderson, C.R., Jr., Chamberlin, R., & Tatelbaum, R. (1986). Preventing child abuse and neglect: A randomized trial of nurse home visitation. *Pediatrics, 78,* 65–78.

Olds, D., Henderson, C.R., Jr., Cole, R., Eckenrode, J., Kitzman, H., Luckey, D., et al. (1998). Long-term effects of nurse home visitation on children's criminal and antisocial behavior: 15-year follow-up of a randomized trial. *Journal of the American Medical Association, 280,* 1238–1244.

Olds, D.L., Henderson, C.R., Jr., & Kitzman, H. (1994). Does prenatal and infancy nurse home visitation have enduring effects on qualities of parental caregiving and child health at 25 to 50 months of life? *Pediatrics, 98,* 89–98.

Olds, D.L., Henderson, C.R., Jr., Kitzman, H., & Cole, R. (1995). Effects of prenatal and infancy nurse home visitation on surveillance of child maltreatment. *Pediatrics, 95,* 365–372.

Olds, D.L., Henderson, C.R., Jr., Kitzman, H., Eckenrode, J., Cole, R., Tatelbaum, R., et al. (1998). Prenatal and infancy home visitation by nurses: A program of research. In C. Rovee-Collier, L.P. Lipsitt, & H. Hayne (Eds.), *Advances in infancy research* (Vol. 12). Stamford, CT: Ablex.

Olds, D.L., Henderson, C.R., Jr., & Tatelbaum, R. (1994a). Intellectual impairment in children of women who smoke cigarettes during pregnancy. *Pediatrics, 93,* 221–227.

Olds, D.L., Henderson, C.R., Jr., & Tatelbaum, R. (1994b). Prevention of intellectual impairment in children of women who smoke cigarettes during pregnancy. *Pediatrics, 93,* 228–233.

Olds, D.L., Henderson, C.R., Jr., Tatelbaum, R., & Chamberlin, R. (1986). Improving the delivery of prenatal care and outcomes of pregnancy: A randomized trial of nurse home visitation. *Pediatrics, 77,* 16–28.

Olds, D.L., Hill, P.L., O'Brien, R., Racine, D., & Moritz, P. (2003). Taking preventive intervention to scale: The nurse-family partnership. *Cognitive and Behavioral Practice, 10*(4), 278–290.

Olds, D.L., Hill, P., Robinson, J., Song, N., & Little, C. (2000). Update on home visiting for pregnant women and parents of young children. *Current Problems in Pediatrics, 30*(4), 105–148.

Olds, D.L., Kitzman, H., Cole, R., & Robinson, J. (1997). Theoretical foundations of a program of home visitation for pregnant women and parents of young children. *Journal of Community Psychology, 25,* 9–25.

Olds, D.L., & Korfmacher, J. (1997). Maternal psychological characteristics as influences on home visitation contact. *Journal of Community Psychology, 26,* 23–36.

Olds, D.L., Pettittt, L.M., Robinson, J., Henderson, C., Jr., Eckenrode, J., Kitzman, H., et al. (1998). Reducing risks for antisocial behavior with a program of prenatal and early childhood home visitation. *Journal of Community Psychology, 26,* 65–83.

Olds, D.L., Robinson, J., O'Brien, R., Luckey, D.W., Pettittt, L.M., Henderson, C.R., Jr., et al. (in press). Home visiting by nurses and by paraprofessionals: A randomized controlled trial. *Pediatrics.*

Overpeck, M. D., Brenner, M. D., Trumble, A. C., Trifiletti, L. B., & Berendes, H. W. (1998). Risk factors for infant homicide in the United States. *New England Journal of Medicine, 339*(17), 1121–1216.

Peterson, L., & Gable, S. (1998). Holistic injury prevention. In J. R. Lutzker (Ed.), *Handbook of child abuse research and treatment* (pp. 291–318). New York: Plenum Press.

Plomin, R. (1986). *Development, genetics, and psychology.* Hillsdale, NJ: Erlbaum.

Quinton, D., & Rutter, M. (1984). Parents with children in care: II. Intergenerational continuities. *Journal of Child Psychology and Psychiatry, 25,* 231–250.

Raine, A., Brennan, P., & Mednick, S. A. (1994). Birth complications combined with early maternal rejection at age 1 year predispose to violent crime at age 18 years. *Archives of General Psychiatry, 51,* 984–988.

Rutter, M. (1989). Intergenerational continuities and discontinuities in serious parenting difficulties. In. D. Cicchetti & V. Carlson (Eds.), *Child maltreatment: Theory and research on the causes and consequences of child abuse and neglect* (pp. 315–348). Cambridge: Cambridge University Press.

Sameroff, A. J. (1983). Parental views of child development. In R. A. Hoekelman (Ed.), *Minimizing high-risk parenting* (pp. 31–45). Media, PA: Harwal.

Saxon, D. W. (1978). The behavior of infants whose mothers smoke in pregnancy. *Early Human Development, 2,* 363–369.

Snell, M. E. (2003). Applying research to practice: The more pervasive problem? *Research & Practice for Persons with Severe Disabilities, 28*(3), 143–147.

Streissguth, A. P., Sampson, P. D., Barr, H. M., Bookstein, F. L., & Olson, H. C. (1994). The effects of prenatal exposure to alcohol and tobacco: Contributions from the Seattle longitudinal prospective study and implications for public policy. In H. L. Needleman & D. Bellinger (Eds.), *Prenatal exposure to toxicants* (pp. 148–183). Baltimore: Johns Hopkins University Press.

Teicher, M. H. (2000). Wounds that time won't heal: The neurobiology of child abuse. *Cerebrum, 2*(4), 50–67.

Tygart, C. E. (1991). Juvenile delinquency and number of children in a family: Some empirical and theoretical updates. *Youth & Society, 22,* 525–536.

Wakschlag, L. S., Lahey, B. B., Loeber, R., Green, S. M., Gordon, R. A., & Al, B. L. (1997). Maternal smoking during pregnancy and the risk of conduct disorder in boys. *Archives of General Psychiatry, 54,* 670–680

Chapter 8

EARLY HEAD START: A BOLD NEW PROGRAM FOR LOW-INCOME INFANTS AND TODDLERS

Helen H. Raikes[1] and Robert N. Emde

Early Head Start is a new federal, two-generation, child-development program for very-low-income children under the age of three and their families. This comprehensive intervention program, which began in the mid-1990s, has sometimes been referred to as the boldest initiative within the Head Start family of programs (Mann, Bogle, & Parlakian, 2004). In this report we will illustrate features of the program, provide findings about its effectiveness from a randomized control trial, and describe how the unique relation between research and program has led to innovation in research, program services, and new knowledge about the development of low-income infants and toddlers. Early Head Start (EHS) has been referred to as bold because it implemented alternative service models that are tailored locally to meet family needs, was embedded from the outset in a rigorous national evaluation, and embraced collaborations within communities that benefit children and families beyond those directly served by Early Head Start.

CHARACTERISTICS OF EARLY HEAD START PROGRAMS

Early Head Start originated in 1994 when the U.S. Congress passed legislation reauthorizing Head Start and mandated that 3 percent of the Head Start budget for 1995 be used to establish a new program of comprehensive services for families with infants and toddlers below preschool age. That same year, then-Secretary of Health and Human Services Donna Shalala convened a committee of experts in the field of early education and infant development to lay out the principles and operating features for the new program, published in the Advisory Committee Report on Services to Families with Infants and Toddlers (U.S. Department of Health and Human Services [DHHS], 1994). The first 68 programs were funded in 1995, and most years thereafter additional programs have been funded so that, as of 2005, Early Head Start has served more than 63,000 children and families in more than 700 American communities. Expansion of the program accelerated with the Coats Human Services Amendments of 1998 that increased the Early Head Start appropriations incrementally by year to 10 percent of the total Head Start budget (the current level). Despite this rapid expansion, Early Head Start today only serves about 3 percent of the infants and toddlers who are eligible for services (Gish, 2004; Mann et al., 2004).

Early Head Start belongs to the Head Start family of programs that provides preschool services for children aged three to five, including migrant families and Native Americans. As is true for all of these programs, quality in Early Head Start is ensured by adherence to the Head Start Performance Standards (Administration for Children and Families [ACF], 1996), which are followed by all Head Start programs and formally monitored every three years. Early Head Start offers discrete service models that may be home based (weekly home visits with bimonthly group meetings for parents and children), center based (high-quality center care combined with regular parenting education meetings), or a mixture of these services. Early Head Start also provides family support and referrals to community agencies that address special needs of families. Local programs have been encouraged to find ways to adapt their services to family needs, leading to rapid expansion of more complicated "mixed approaches" to serving families. For example, some families may receive home-based services, some center-based services, and, more commonly, many may receive the benefits of both program models (a feature that has yielded the greatest gains by age three for children and families).

Families served by Early Head Start are typically those with greatest needs in their community. Most of the families served have incomes at the poverty level or below, but other criteria may also be employed to target underserved families locally (e.g., teen parents and non-English speaking families). At least 10 percent of the enrollments must be offered to children with disabilities, and up to 10 percent of children may be from families with incomes above the poverty line, especially to meet the disability quota. In the Program Information Report (PIR) data for 2003–2004 (ACF, 2005d), about 22 percent of families enrolled in Early Head Start do not speak English as their primary language. The majority of the non-English-speaking families speak Spanish (86%), and the most common other languages spoken are East Asian, Central or South American languages other than Spanish, European and Slavic languages, and African languages (with fewer than 3% in each of those groups). About one-third of the enrollees in Early Head Start are white (33%), 26 percent are African American, 27 percent are of Hispanic origin, 4 percent are Native Americans or Alaskan natives, with the remaining from other racial or mixed-racial groups.

STATE AND PRIVATE EFFORTS TO BUILD ON EARLY HEAD START

There have been efforts within and across states to extend the core Early Head Start program. These efforts have extended the program into the private sector and built on the quantity and the quality of the national program in several states. This expansion has been made possible through additional resources provided with state and private funding. The state of Kansas has supported Early Head Start partnerships as have the states of Missouri and Nebraska, and the EDUCARE effort has added resources to Early Head Start programs in several localities. These are encouraging examples of dissemination of the Early Head Start model that may be emulated elsewhere.

Since early in this century, the state of Kansas has appropriated from $5 million to $7.2 million annually of Temporary Assistance for Needy Families (TANF) funds for Early Head Start expansion. These funds have enabled Kansas to serve additional children through expanded Early Head Start services in the state. In 2004, and similarly in several previous years, Nebraska appropriated $147,000 of earmarked Infant/Toddler Funds for seven Early Head Start programs to provide professional development opportunities for home- and center-based providers, enhancing the quality of environments for more than 600 infants and toddlers beyond those served directly by Early Head Start. Missouri has appropriated state gaming funds to expand Early Head Start services statewide. In that state in 2002, these funds enabled comprehensive EHS services for an additional 2,008 low-income pregnant women, infants, and toddlers and provided Infant/Toddler training for 80 early-childhood professionals from across the state.

Another innovative way of expanding Early Head Start has been initiated through EDUCARE, in partnerships with local Early Head Start programs. These programs are coordinated through the Bounce Learning Network, under the shared leadership of the Ounce of Prevention Fund (Chicago, Illinois) and the Buffett Early Childhood Fund (Omaha, Nebraska). Supported by the Buffetts and other private philanthropists, this new effort strategically adds resources to Early Head Start programs for bachelor-level teachers with early-childhood credentials in all classrooms, favorable student-teacher ratios, center-based services in architecturally outstanding facilities proximal to elementary schools, strong programming in the arts, and research that augments continuous program improvement and use of evidence-based practices. In each of the network communities, local philanthropists partner with providers to cover the capital costs of new centers and to help leverage additional operating funds from all three levels of government (federal, state, and school district). EDUCARE Early Head Start programs are located in Chicago (Ounce of Prevention), Kansas City (Project Eagle), Milwaukee (Next Door Foundation), Omaha (EDUCARE of Omaha), and Tulsa (EDUCARE of Tulsa).

RESEARCH AND EVALUATION OF PROGRAM EFFECTIVENESS

Research and evaluation have played an important role in the development of the new Early Head Start program. Evaluation was mandated by the original congressional legislation, and impact reports were further mandated in subsequent authorizing legislation. The 1998 authorization specified that expansion of the program would be contingent on demonstration of benefits from the evaluation reports. Irrespective of congressional mandates, the Advisory Committee for Services to Families with Infants and Toddlers also recommended rigorous and multifaceted research to provide information about "what works, for whom and under what circumstances." Thus, there was little question that Early Head Start was to have a strong research component, and, as a result, the Early Head Start Research and Evaluation Project was launched at the same time the programs began. Information about the Early Head Start research, its contribution to evaluation methodology, and its contribution to the field of early-child development will be summarized in subsequent sections of this chapter. Government reports are also available at: http://www.acf.hhs. gov/programs/opre/ehs/ehs_resrch/index.html.

The research employed an experimental design in which 3,001 families were randomly assigned to program and control groups at 17 sites located in 15 states. These research sites were typical of the first two waves of programs funded in terms of location (rural/urban) and race/ethnicity status. Programs recruited families using typical procedures, and families assigned randomly to the control group were invited to use all of the services available in their communities, *except for Early Head Start*. The programs that participated in the research were located throughout the United States in Washington State (2), California, Utah, Colorado (2), Kansas, Missouri, Iowa, Arkansas, Tennessee, Michigan, Pennsylvania, New York, Vermont, South Carolina, and Virginia. Analyses of descriptive characteristics of the research samples documented that they were representative of program families served by all Early Head Start programs funded in 1996 and 1997 (ACF, 2002a, 2003a). We shall describe first the scientific design of this ambitious experiment before discussing the methods and results obtained thus far.

A Randomized Control Trial Design

The strong recommendations of the national advisory committee for the design and evaluation methods of the Early Head Start experiment were taken seriously by federal funders and by the investigators chosen to implement the research. Policy makers had been advised that a randomized control trial (RCT) was a gold standard for such evaluations. Thus, despite its many controversial aspects in implementation, the RCT became the central framework for evaluating the new Early Head Start program. Fortunately, the considerable logistical and scientific challenges of implementing this design were met successfully, and they led to innovations that are worth underscoring as potential contributions to the larger field of research and evaluation methodology.

Challenges of the Design

What were the formidable challenges of the randomized control design? An RCT is a research design that compares an experimental group that receives a specified intervention against a control or comparison group that does not receive the intervention. Its key feature is the recruitment into the study with random assignment into groups *after* recruitment in order to ensure that the subjects in the two groups are truly comparable *before* the experimental group is influenced by the intervention. The integrity of the design requires assessment over time by evaluation teams who do not know the group assignments and, ideally, who are unaware of the scientific hypotheses being tested. These two considerations ensure the objectivity of the evaluators. An RCT is designed to minimize selection bias and thus maximize the basis for causal inference as to the efficacy of the intervention (Cook & Campbell, 1976; Shonkoff & Phillips, 2000). Typically, an RCT design is applied to an intervention that has had considerable pilot application and demonstrated promise, such that it can be standardized across sites with relatively focused components, can be constant over time, and can be monitored for its uniformity (McCall & Green, 2004). An RCT is not usually recommended for new programs with unspecified interventions, in various phases of start-up, or serving communities with diverse needs. These studies, however, are sometimes conducted during pilot or demonstration phases or with new programs. The latter was the case for the 17 different sites of the Early Head Start evaluation project. Early Head Start began as a national initiative when individual programs were selected from diverse communities across the United States and when the Early Head Start standards were being developed.

These challenges were met by adding elements of a so-called hybrid design to the RCT framework. Although the local EHS programs were just beginning and were varied, the national evaluator, Mathematica Policy Research, set up an implementation study whereby independent national teams periodically visited local EHS program sites to provide intensive evaluations of the extent to which each program was implementing the general guidelines outlined initially by the advisory committee and later refined by the more specific guidelines detailed in the Head Start Performance Standards. Moreover, the new programs were encouraged to consult with their local university research partners with regard to goal setting and clarifying their *theories of change* (i.e., what strategies they expected to be effective within their interventions) as they responded to diverse community needs of varying cultural groups. Efforts were also made to provide for adequate description not only of what interventions actually took place (both during home visits and center-based activities) but also for descriptions of child and family variations in resources, needs, and services used. In addition, Mathematica discussed programs' theories of change during site visits and presented analyses of how expected outcomes differed by program approach (Administration on Children, Youth, and Families [ACYF], 1999a, 2000). In other words, the RCT design was embedded in a study of context that went well beyond the comparisons in standard intervention research. Consistent with the recommendations of the advisory committee, it sought to understand program variations—what works for whom and under what circumstances—and thereby was responsive to a Head Start blueprint committee that recommended most useful directions for Head Start research (U.S. DHHS, 1990). Additionally, it added elements of a formative evaluation: learning how new programs addressed particular problems, successfully or not (ACF, 2003b; ACYF, 1999a, 1999b, 2000).

Another feature of the design, which is often not appreciated in an RCT, but deserves mention, is that the nonintervention group did get child-related services, some of which were undoubtedly motivated by participation in the study. The control-group parents, on occasion, expressed their satisfaction at the repeated interest and attention shown toward their child's development as well as their appreciation for the knowledge they acquired regarding their child's development. Thus the Hawthorne effects, from being observed and participating in research, were possibly a positive benefit for the nonintervention families. Additionally, the Early Head Start design allowed for the sharing of developmental screening information, under some circumstances. This benefited both nonintervention and EHS families alike. For example, if researchers had reason to suspect a significant developmental delay, they were authorized to mention this to parents and advise a more extensive evaluation that could result in services because they were also given a referral list of available community resources.

Challenges of the Process

Carrying out a national multisite RCT with its need for standard assessments and at the same time evaluating heterogeneous new programs responding to diverse local community needs presented challenges of a different sort. These were met by establishing a dynamic process that involved networking of multiple partnerships, both local and national. At the local level, the hybrid design model included university-based investigators who participated in ongoing ways with community-based Early Head Start service providers. The hybrid design allowed for close collaboration between research investigators and their program partners, including mutual goal setting, continuous improvement, personnel consultation and recruitment, and, on occasion, some community-based activities, such as parent nights and presentations to groups about the importance of research and evaluation, which was seen in a number of the Early Head Start program sites. Sometimes ideas about child development and program interventions were shared, even as commitment to the integrity of the RCT design was maintained.

At the national level, the network of partnerships was dramatic, not only in terms of the numbers of investigators involved but also in terms of the collaborative, highly committed, and generative working arrangements among those from multiple disciplines and settings. As noted previously, the national collaborative RCT was designed, directed, and managed by Mathematica Policy Research (MPR) in conjunction with the National Center for Children and Families at Columbia University and child development experts from the Administration for Children and Families (ACF). Prior to finalizing the design, advice was obtained from leading academic researchers and methodologists, and, after the local university investigators were convened, fine-tuning took place with input from this group as well. Multiple-day research consortium meetings took place two or more times a year, which were conducted jointly by MPR and ACF program officers and staff and included 60 to 75 university investigators, 4 to 7 participants from MPR, 3 or 4 participants from ACF, and 1 or 2 researchers from Columbia University. Additionally, EHS program directors joined the consortium meetings for some discussions.

National consortium meetings were devoted to vigorous planning and problem solving with regard to recruitment and retention of participants, choices for additional local measures, documentation of what works for families, and strategies for data analysis and planning for longitudinal follow-up.

Methodology

We turn next to a more specific description of the Early Head Start Research and Evaluation methodology. As noted earlier, the national research was coordinated by Mathematica Policy Research based out of Princeton, New Jersey, in conjunction with the National Center for Children and Families at Columbia University. Cross-site data collection was completed by the research universities located near the 17 service programs, following a common protocol that included child and parent measures collected when children were 14, 24, and 36 months of age and service interviews that took place at 7, 16, and 28 months after random assignment. It was important to measure service use in the control group as well as the program group because most control-group families participated in some community services. Child assessments included measures of cognitive development (Bayley Scales of Infant Development; Bayley, 1993), language development (MacArthur Communicative Development Inventory at 14 and 24 months; Fenson et al., 1994, and the Peabody Picture Vocabulary Test at 36 months; Dunn & Dunn, 1997), social emotional development (videotape assessments of child engagement, attention, and negativity using a variation of the 3-Box Test utilized in the National Institute of Child Health and Human Development [NICHD] study of early child care [1999]), and parent ratings of aggression (Achenbach Child Behavior Checklist; Achenbach, 2000). Parent assessments included Home Observation for Measurement of the Environment (HOME) resulting in full and factor subscores (Caldwell & Bradley, 1984); measures of parent supportiveness, detachment, intrusiveness, warmth, and negativity from the 3-Bag Test mentioned previously; self-ratings of time with child; and parent stressors, including the Parenting Stress Index Distress Scale (Abidin, 1995), the Parent–Child Dysfunctional Interaction Scale (Abidin, 1995), the Center for Epidemiological Studies-Depression scale (Radloff, 1977), and others.

Impacts

There have been multiple reports of the overall program impacts when children were 24 and 36 months of age (ACF, 2002b; Love et al., in press; Raikes, Love, Chazan-Cohen, & Brooks-Gunn, 2004) on services, children, parenting, and parent self-sufficiency. Impacts have also been reported by subgroups, consistent with one aim of the evaluation to understand for whom and under what conditions the programs achieved effects. In this section, we will summarize findings without providing details of statistical significance, although we will occasionally mention effect sizes (which reflect the magnitude of the intervention influences). Relevant statistical information and details are available elsewhere (ACF, 2002b).

Impacts on Services

Analyses when children were 24 and 36 months of age demonstrated that program families received significantly more services than control-group families, a pattern particularly true for home visits and parent education, and less pronounced, although still detectable, in regard to child care.

Impacts on Children

Early Head Start had impacts on children's development when children were both 24 and 36 months of age. Early Head Start children had significantly higher scores in cognitive, language and social emotional development (including fewer reported aggressive behaviors and better attention and engagement of adults) than control-group children at both ages. Differences occurred both in higher mean scores and in lower proportions of children scoring in low ranges of functioning. Although the differences overall were modest (with effect sizes from .10 to .20), they were considerably larger for some subgroups, as we discuss later in this chapter. Early Head Start also had some modest impacts on some children's health outcomes; notably, Early Head Start children had lower rates of hospitalization for accidents and injuries and significantly higher rates of immunizations (although both program and control groups had relatively high rates of preventative health services). Early Head Start children were breast-fed longer than control-group children during infancy. Finally, children in Early Head Start were more likely to receive early and timely referrals to Part C services for children with disabilities than were control-group children.

Impacts on Parenting

Because Early Head Start has a two-generation emphasis, the programs also aimed to influence parenting behaviors, self-sufficiency, and healthy family functioning. Home-based programs, particularly, but all programs to some extent, ascribed to a theory of change by which support for parenting was intended to lead to long-term effects for children (Raikes et al., currently in review). At both the 24- and 36-month assessments, Early Head Start parents had more stimulating and supportive home environments; were observed to be more supportive, less detached, and less negative in interaction with children; played and read with their children more; and were less punitive than the control-group parents. At 24 months, parents in the program reported less parenting stress and family conflict than did the control group. As we found for child impacts, there were many favorable impacts on parents across many domains, usually of modest magnitude but with considerably larger impacts for some subgroups, as we will report later.

Many of the programs aimed to help parents attain greater self-sufficiency. A fairly large proportion of parents had not graduated from high school when the program began. Additionally, the program was launched at the time that welfare reform was implemented through the Temporary Assistance for Needy Families (TANF) legislation. Early Head Start families were significantly more likely to be in school or training than control-group parents at multiple measurement intervals and were more likely to be employed when the program ended. There was no impact on cash assistance; both program and control-group families appreciably reduced reliance on cash assistance.

Subgroups: Impacts by Program Models and Implementation

Program Models

As we have stated, Early Head Start programs do not follow identical models. Rather, each program conducts a community assessment (officially, every three years) and selects which of several program options to make available to families. Again, these can be home-based, center-based, a combination of the two, or, as in a few cases, family child care models under special dispensation by the Head Start Bureau. The Head Start Performance Standards are applied to all the options. In the research sites, programs were classified as home-based (seven), center-based (four) or mixed (six) during three rounds of site visits that were conducted in the context of the Early Head Start implementation study (ACF, 2003b; ACYF, 1999a, 1999b, 2000).

When children were 24 and 36 months of age, there were favorable impacts in all program models, but patterns of impacts varied. At 24 months, home-based programs had multiple impacts on parenting behavior, and at 36 months, Early Head Start had some positive impacts on child social-emotional development and parent supportiveness and reduced parenting stress, relative to the control group. Center-based programs focused on enhancing children's cognitive and social-emotional development. These programs had some impacts on aspects of children's development and parenting but few on parents' self-sufficiency. Mixed-approach programs demonstrated the strongest pattern of impacts at both 24- and 36-month assessment intervals. The mixed-approach programs consistently enhanced children's language and aspects of social-emotional development, and these programs also enhanced a wide range of parenting behaviors and participation in self-sufficiency activities.

Program Implementation

An implementation study assessed the extent to which programs were implemented as designed, in effect, reflecting the extent to which the programs followed the Head Start Performance Standards. Programs were rated for adherence to 24 (25 in the second round of site visits) key aspects of the Head Start Performance Standards, relying on consensus ratings using standardized responses to extensive site-visit reports by a panel of experts. Six of the programs were rated as fully implemented following the first round of site visits and were known as *early implementers.* Following the second round of site visits, another six of the sites were rated as fully implemented, and these sites became known as *late implementers.* The remaining five sites implemented many features of the Head Start Performance Standards, but not all, and were labeled *incomplete implementers.* Early Head Start programs that implemented the standards early or later demonstrated a broader pattern of significant impacts than was true for the several programs that were never fully implemented. This finding underscores the importance of the Head Start Performance Standards for producing a breadth of impacts (across child, parenting, and self-sufficiency measures) and illustrates the hybrid nature of the RCT design, referred to previously, in which contextual information contributed to the experimental findings.

Finally, by comparing the impacts of three mixed-approach programs that were early implementers to those of three mixed-approach programs that were late or incomplete implementers, it was possible to examine the combined effects of implementation and program design. Children and parents in mixed-approach, fully implemented programs demonstrated some of the largest impacts seen in the study. Effect sizes larger than .20 (and ranging to .60) of a standard deviation were seen in these programs on children's cognitive, language and social-emotional development, parenting (observed supportiveness, avoidance of severe discipline strategies, daily reading, parent activities with children), and for self-sufficiency activities (e.g., education and employment).

Serving a Diverse U.S. Population: Impacts in Population Subgroups

Early Head Start serves very diverse low-income families. Therefore, unlike typical demonstration intervention studies that target a very specific single population group, the sample studied in the Early Head Start evaluation was heterogeneous. The evaluation sample included overlapping subgroups varying by race/ethnicity/culture (African American, Hispanic, white), English-speaking versus non-English-speaking, teen versus older mothers, child birth status (firstborn vs. later born), child gender, residency (father in residence, other adults in the household vs. single-parent home), years of education (no high school, high school, or more than high school), and occupation (whether attending school, employed, or neither). Finally, because the effects of cumulative demographic risks tend to increase exponentially (Sameroff & Fiese, 2000), five key demographic risks were summed to form an index of high risk. These risk factors include no high school graduation, unmarried, neither in school nor working, receiving Aid to Families with Dependent Children (AFDC)/TANF, and a teenager at the time of the child's birth. By combining these key demographic risk variables, we created a new high-risk subpopulation.

In all subgroups except one, program-group children and families performed better than their counterparts in the control group. Several population groups demonstrated notably large impacts, with effect sizes from .20 to .50 of a standard deviation in a number of measures. These notably strong patterns of impacts were seen for African Americans, in families with a moderate number of demographic risks, and for children whose mothers enrolled in the program during pregnancy (the latter reported in the next section).

African American Families

African American children in the program group demonstrated numerous impacts in language development and social-emotional development (e.g., they were better able to engage their parents during observed teaching tasks and play, had longer sustained attention and greater persistence during play, and their parents reported fewer aggressive behaviors). African American program parents were observed to be more supportive and less negative and intrusive during play and to be more supportive and less intrusive during an additional observed teaching task. These parents also provided more support for learning in the home environment, more often established a regular bedtime for their children, and reported less parenting stress and dysfunctional interaction. Program parents were more often employed or in training and received fewer welfare benefits of all types, including TANF, than control-group parents.

Families with a Moderate Number of Risk Factors

Families with a moderate number of risks had larger impacts. Among the families studied, about 45 percent had two or fewer demographic risks, about 30 percent had three demographic risk factors, and about 25 percent had extreme numbers (four or five) of risk factors. Although there were positive impacts on the group with two or fewer demographic risks, largest impacts were found in the group with three demographic risks. For the moderate-risk group, positive effect sizes in the .20 to .40 of a standard deviation range were found on child cognitive and social-emotional development (engagement of parents during play). Parents in this group were observed to have greater parent supportiveness during play and a teaching task, greater quality of assistance during the teaching task, and reduced detachment during play. These parents reported playing and reading more with their children and had less parenting stress when compared to control-group parents. They also accumulated more hours enrolled in education and training during the evaluation period and received less cash assistance than control-group families. In an exception to the pattern of positive impacts across subgroups, there were generally not positive impacts in the highest-risk group.

ENROLLING EARLY AND FOLLOWING UP: CONTINUITY OF SERVICES

The Advisory Committee on Services to Families with Infants and Toddlers (U.S. DHHS, 1994) recommended that Early Head Start services begin early, during pregnancy if possible, and that children be transitioned to high-quality early-childhood education programs following Early Head Start that ends at age three, thus providing continuity of services from before birth through the preschool years.

In the evaluation sample, approximately a quarter of enrollees were pregnant (ACF, 2002b). During 2003–2004, 18 percent of all enrollees in Early Head Start were pregnant, and the rest of enrollees were fairly equally divided between infants under age one, one-year-olds, and two-year-olds. About 10 percent of Early Head Start children are older than three years of age (ACF, 2005c; U.S. DHHS, 1994). The evaluation compared effects for pregnant enrollees with their control-group counterparts, similarly for those who enrolled either early or later in the first year of life. Although there were positive impacts for the latter groups, results were strongest for those who enrolled during pregnancy. Specifically, effect sizes from .20 to .60 were found in this latter group for children's social-emotional development (e.g., more engagement of parent, sustained attention and less negativity during play, more engagement and persistence during a teaching task) and cognitive development. Program parents were observed to be more supportive during play and a teaching task and to be less detached during the teaching task. Program parents also spanked less than control-group parents. In terms of self-sufficiency, program parents were more often employed or in training during the evaluation period and less often received welfare late in the evaluation period than did control-group parents.

At the end of the program, service providers are charged with ensuring that children receive transition support, which includes finding Head Start or quality early-childhood programs in their communities, or home-based services. The 2004 Head Start Program Information Report (ACF, 2005c) stated that, nationally, between one-quarter and half of two-year-old children in Early Head Start enroll in Head Start the next year as three-year-olds. A smaller percentage enroll in other early-childhood programs, often drawing on partnerships already established with community child care providers. Research conducted with evaluation sample children prior to children's kindergarten entry in our evaluation sample will enable more detailed descriptions of the early-childhood experiences of former Early Head Start and control-group children during the preschool years.

EARLY HEAD START IN COMMUNITY CONTEXT

Initiatives Featuring Service Integration

A number of initiatives have emerged since the inception of the Early Head Start program that are notable for demonstrating how the reach of the program has extended to building collaborations within communities and, in some cases, enhancing community infrastructure in ways that improve services for children beyond those exclusively served by Early Head Start. These initiatives typically address areas of specific need, and in several cases these areas were identified through the Early Head Start Research and Evaluation project. Special initiatives have focused on services for mental health, child care, child welfare, fatherhood, and children with disabilities. In many cases, new research will continue to investigate the interventions. A notable feature of these initiatives is that they typically involve liaisons between Early Head Start and other community partners. The Advisory Committee for Services for Families with Infants and Toddlers emphasized that Early Head Start "not be a silo" but rather use the new resources to help coordinate, blend, and extend services within communities so that families' experiences in working with service sectors can be simple and direct ("one-stop shopping"). This bold vision further suggested that many children (beyond those in Early Head Start) could benefit from the resources, focus, and collaboration that Early Head Start could bring to communities. We next illustrate how this blend of vision, research, need, initiative, and collaboration has resulted in innovation in a variety of areas.

Serving Children with Disabilities

Services to Early Head Start children under age three with disabilities require coordination of at least two systems: Early Head Start and Part C. From an Early Head Start perspective, programs must reserve up to 10 percent of their enrollment for children with disabilities; so many children with disabilities are served by Early Head Start. Some children in Early Head Start have identified disabilities when they enroll in the program, but many children's disabilities are identified during the infant/toddler years after their enrollment into Early Head Start. The process of identification includes a referral to a local Part C service provider (the Individuals with Disabilities Education Act [IDEA]), an assessment, and if the child qualifies, development of an individualized family service plan (IFSP), as defined by Part C.

Early Head Start programs have engaged in community collaborations to identify children with disabilities and to ensure that children receive the needed services. To aid with the Early Head Start and Part C collaboration, the Hilton Foundation and the Head Start Bureau developed the SpecialQuest initiative to train and strengthen community teams to provide seamless referral, identification, and services for children with disabilities. SpecialQuest is administered by Sonoma State College (Sonoma State University, 2005) and now has provided intensive training to several hundred community teams for enhanced coordination of Early Head Start and Part C services, building both systems for earliest identification and service provision of children with disabilities.

Successes for children with disabilities and their families have been documented in the Early Head Start Research and Evaluation Study. As already noted, significantly more children had been identified as eligible for Part C services in the Early Head Start program group than in the control group (ACF, 2002b). Moreover, within the program group, Early Head Start families who had a child with an identified disability were more often rated as *highly involved* in the program by staff (50% of families of a child with a disability were rated highly involved compared to 35% of other families), and these families stayed in the program longer on average than other families (27 months vs. 22 months). There was also some evidence that Early Head Start may have contributed to prevention of the need for disability services because significantly fewer Early Head Start children were in the lowest functioning cognitive and language groups as compared to the control group (ACF, 2002b). However, as has been found in other studies of Part C usage (Hebbeler, Spiker, Mallik, Scarborough, & Simeonsson, 2003), a lower proportion of children of color, of children with less-educated parents, and of children with higher levels of demographic risk, were enrolled in Part C than was true for other groups, even though other data suggested that children in these groups might have had greater need for Part C services (ACF, 2002b).

Initiatives to Meet the Mental Health Needs of Families

Families in Early Head Start have substantial mental health needs, requiring Early Head Start programs to draw upon mental health services within their communities. The evaluation study found that approximately half of mothers reported symptoms of depression at the time of program enrollment, as determined from data from eight sites that completed a measure of depressive symptoms at baseline. Moreover, detailed analysis in two sites found that maternal depression and problematic relationship attitudes, assessed at baseline, were significant moderators of Early Head Start impacts (Robinson & Emde, 2004). About one-third of mothers of one- and three-year-olds in all evaluation sites reported significant depressive symptoms (ACF, 2002b).

As a comprehensive child development program, Head Start has long been concerned with supporting the social and emotional well-being of children and families and with assessing and/or providing services for those families with mental health needs. The Head Start Performance Standards require each program to obtain a mental health consultant as well as timely and responsive services and family-centered mental health services and education. The evaluation demonstrated that the program did not increase mental health service use or reduce overall depressive symptoms, although there was a trend-level effect on reduced symptoms at 36 months in the eight-site subgroup of mothers who had been depressed at baseline. However, it is noteworthy that the program did help parents in their relationships with their children and in reducing harsh discipline practices, and this was true also for parents reporting initial depressive symptoms. As a result of recognized mental health needs in Early Head Start, the Head Start Bureau subsequently launched two new mental health initiatives, one focused on programs and one on research. The Early Head Start Mental Health Initiative highlighted problem areas, the existing knowledge base, and best practices in Early Head Start programs (ACF, 2005d), and five research-program partnerships were funded to implement specific interventions in the area of mental health (ACF, 2005a).

Partnerships with Community Child Care Providers to Address Child Care Quality

A large proportion of Early Head Start children use child care. At 14 months of age, half of the Early Head Start children in the research sample received 30 hours (full time) or more of child care; by 36 months, two-thirds of the children were in care full time; some of these were in Early Head Start center-based settings, others in community settings that partner with Early Head Start programs, and still others in settings of a family's choosing that were not affiliated with Early Head Start programs. About one-third of Early Head Start children received care during nonstandard hours (evenings or weekends), and about 15 percent were cared for in multiple arrangements.

We have referred to the partnerships formed with community child care providers by Early Head Start mixed-approach programs and to some extent by home-based programs (i.e., not offering direct center-based services). The Advisory Committee on Services to Families with Infants and Toddlers (U.S. DHHS, 1994) predicted that many Early Head Start children would have extensive child care needs, so program providers were charged with the responsibility of ensuring that children's child care environments were of high quality, meaning that they meet the high-quality standards established by the Head Start Performance Standards.

Early Head Start programs have taken the following steps to ensure children's child care environments are of good quality: measuring program quality, providing ongoing training and technical assistance to teaching staff both within Early Head Start and community centers, renovating classrooms to meet the Head Start Performance Standards, applying for National Association for the Education of Young Children accreditation, providing additional staff and materials in classrooms, visiting Early Head Start children in classrooms, forming new community-wide collaborations, and working to maximize resources from multiple funding sources, including government child care subsidies. The practice of forming partnerships gained popularity as programs increased the number of formal contractual agreements with community providers over time (ACF, 2003a). This framework for contracting for services and providing resources to community child care providers led to expanded programs that some states adopted even more widely, as described earlier.

The Early Head Start evaluation assessed the quality of children's child care settings (ACF, 2003b). Quality in Early Head Start centers was good at three assessment points when children were 14, 24, and 36 months (higher than 5.0 on the Infant-Toddler Environment Rating Scale [ITERS]). Quality in community centers that Early Head Start children attended increased over time, from lower than 4.0 on the ITERS at 14 months to nearly 5.0 at 36 months. A small proportion of children were in family child care settings. These child care facilities were rated in the 3.0 to 4.0 range on the Family Day Care Rating Scale (FDCRS). When Early Head Start children were compared to children within the control group, they were three times more likely to be in a good-quality center-based program when they were 14 and 24 months old and one-and-a-half times more likely to be in good-quality center care at 36 months. As a result of the rising numbers of partnerships between Early Head Start and community child care providers and because of their goal to meet the need of quality child care for Early Head Start children, the Head Start Bureau developed the Child Care Initiative that trained teams of Early Head Start, community child care providers, and State Child Care Administrators to meet the provisions of the charge.

Consistent with other studies (Burchinal, Roberts, Nabors, & Bryant, 1996; Cost, Quality and Child Outcomes Study Team, 1995), higher-quality child care in the evaluation sample was related to higher levels of children's cognitive development at 24 months and language development at 36 months (ACF, 2003b). Additionally, more time in center care was associated with higher levels of cognitive development at 24 months and cognitive and language development at 36 months. Unlike other research, the EHS study did not find time in center care to be associated with increases in aggressive behavior problems. It is reasonable to expect time in Early Head Start center care to be associated with better outcomes when the quality of care is good (Love et al., 2003).

Other Early Head Start Initiatives

Early Head Start has also sponsored initiatives in other areas that research or program staff have indicated needed support and information.

These initiatives include child welfare, fatherhood, and continuous improvement.

Child Welfare Initiative

A three-way partnership between Early Head Start, the Children's Bureau, and the Child Welfare System (CWS) was created to build an enhanced service system for CWS children and families that are two-generational, community-based, comprehensive, and sustained intensively over time. Through this joint venture, children and parents will be able to access more physical and mental health care, nutritional services, child-development services, and parent-education services that empower parents. Twenty-four Early Head Start program grants were awarded in 2002 to develop local Early Head Start and child welfare agency partnerships with these purposes in mind: (1) to promote and expand the partnerships between local Early Head Start programs and local CWS agencies, (2) to enhance and expand services for children and their families who are part of the CWS and to provide additional and more intensive services in local communities for this population, (3) to evaluate the initiative to determine best practice in services for a disadvantaged population, and (4) to disseminate initiative results.

Fatherhood Initiative

Father involvement has been a particular emphasis in Early Head Start and is also a focus of the Office of Child Support Enforcement. As a result, the Fatherhood Initiative was launched (ACF, 2005b), designed to build local partnerships between Early Head Start programs and local child-support enforcement offices and to build father involvement in programs and children's lives. In fiscal year 2002, ACF awarded grants to 21 Early Head Start projects in 17 states to develop new approaches to sustaining fathers' involvement in their children's lives. These grants, totaling $7.5 million over three years, were designed to provide strategies that other Early Head Start projects could use to involve fathers in their family-centered, community-based programs. These initiatives built on findings about fathers from the Early Head Start research studies. From the multiple studies conducted on father involvement in Early Head Start, it has become apparent that Early Head Start programs are able to increase father involvement in program services (Raikes & Bellotti, in press) and to increase fathers' positive influence in children's lives (ACF, 2002b). A number of features have been identified as well that have helped increase the program's level of father involvement and have helped to promote collaboration within communities (ACF, 2002b; Raikes & Bellotti, in press; Raikes, Roggman, & Summers, 2005).

Features such as having an explicit father-involvement component, a father-involvement coordinator, and providing training in father involvement are related to fathers becoming involved in an Early Head Start program.

Continuous Program Improvement

Urie Bronfenbrenner, as a member of the Advisory Committee on Services to Families with Infants and Toddlers, challenged the program, research, and his fellow committee members to use action research as the model for Early Head Start research. He envisioned research that would provide timely feedback to local programs about whether they were implementing the services as intended and as to whether they were achieving the aims they sought. Such an action-research model, he believed, should be instituted in every local Early Head Start program. At one level, this concept has been incorporated into the Head Start Performance Standards for program self-assessment. Programs determine if they are meeting their goals and make course corrections if not. This process has been expanded within the EDUCARE Bounce Learning Network and among some Early Head Start programs that have employed a local university or other research partner and/or have developed internal procedures for tracking information to determine the extent to which goals are being met. A number of illustrations of research informing local program improvement have appeared in the peer-reviewed literature and point the way to a more nuanced role for action research within Early Head Start programs (Gill, Greenberg, & Vazquez, 2002; Korfmacher & Spicer, 2002; Robinson et al., 2002; Spicer, Korfmacher, Hudgens, & Emde, 2002). It is possible that this innovative feature of research and program partnership will be expanded in the future as the fruits of such partnerships become better known.

A related positive feature of initiating Early Head Start research and evaluation early in the program's development is that continual feedback about where to make program improvements could be directed at programs. The Head Start Bureau has been notably responsive to this type of feedback. The research has informed many initiatives, as already noted, but it has also informed program practices directed at highest-risk children and families, health services for Hispanic families, and other areas. Research to Practice reports have been designed specifically for programs on specific topics (e.g., health, depression, children with disabilities, child care, home visiting, language and literacy, highest-risk families). These reports identify program strengths and make recommendations for program improvement. The Research to Practice reports are Web accessible and are frequently used in training and technical assistance by program staff at local, regional, and national levels.

Expanding the Knowledge Base: Low-Income Infants/Toddlers and Early Intervention

The Early Head Start Research and Evaluation project has produced a database that has enabled investigators to explore a large variety of questions pertaining to early-childhood development and the role that services play in the lives of low-income children and families. It has also enabled researchers to build on knowledge gained from studies with children age zero to three by conducting follow-up studies of sample children's school readiness prior to kindergarten entry and, potentially, beyond.

The Early Head Start data, containing measures of physical health, behavioral, cognitive, and social-emotional development at multiple intervals throughout the first three years of life for more than 2,000 children, have stimulated a wide array of analyses and new understandings of the development of low-income children. Articles by Early Head Start Research Consortium members working in cross-university teams are now in print, in press, and in progress (e.g., Ispa et al., 2004; Pan, Rowe, Spier, & Tamis-LeMonda, in press; Tamis-LeMonda, Shannon, Cabrera, & Lamb, 2004; Whiteside-Mansell et al., 2004). Construct data from the 0–3 phase of the project is currently available for public use from the Interuniversity Consortium for Political and Social Science Research at the University of Michigan (ICPSR) in a special topics archive on child care and early education. Data will also be available for restricted use that will include on-site access to the original videotapes from the Henry A. Murray Research Center of the Radcliffe Institute for Advanced Study at Harvard University.

Recently, another data point, collected during the spring before children's kindergarten entry, has been added to this rich database, and data will again be analyzed by consortium members and then will be made available for public use. Archived videotapes will include the prekindergarten phase. Researchers in many of the original 17 sites have obtained local funding to follow children's progress in lower elementary grades, and efforts are being extended to fund a later elementary follow-up study. The data set is a promising one for continued study and offers an opportunity to learn more about the development of low-income families from three racial/ethnic backgrounds in the context of an intervention program.

SUMMARY

Early Head Start is a relatively new program, now 10 years old, but much has been learned during its brief history, in part because of the bold step to implement a randomized control study. In its pure and hybrid forms, that design not only provided early information about program effects but also information pertaining to "for whom and under what conditions" the program was effective. Early findings were incorporated back into program improvements in the form of national initiatives, new policies, program training and recommendations, and continuous improvement of local programs. Data were also used in multiple ways to learn more about complex relationships and developmental trajectories of low-income infants and toddlers in a variety of contexts related to poverty. Altogether, new Early Head Start programs demonstrated positive impacts for children and families and larger impacts for specific groups. There were positive effects across program models and diverse population groups (race/ethnicity, teen parents, and older mothers). The Early Head Start interventions studied were especially effective for children in "mixed-model" programs, for African American children, for children with parents who had a moderate number of demographic risks, and for parents who enrolled before the focal child's birth. Although harder to measure, Early Head Start has affected communities, with initiatives and assessments that reach into the Part C, mental health, child care, child welfare, and support systems.

Although impacts of these newly formed programs that were studied in the RCT were significant and widespread, overall effect sizes were modest, which indicates that more needs to be learned and accomplished in interventions to provide fully adequate early intervention for diverse populations of infants and toddlers living in circumstances of extreme poverty and stress. The research we have described provides support for local and national efforts aimed at "earliest" childhood intervention, and there is new information about children that will help programs to more effectively understand the mechanisms of development and intervention services needed for the future. It is also important that research from the Early Head Start experiment continue to inform the field through follow-up studies, ongoing analyses, and developing systems that make the data widely available for further study.

NOTE

1. During the data collection and analyses phases of the Early Head Start Research and Evaluation Project, Helen H. Raikes was a fellow of the Society for Research in Child Development Executive Policy, with oversight of the project at the Administration for Children and Families, U.S. Department of Health and Human Services.

REFERENCES

Abidin, R.R.(1995). *Parenting Stress Index, third edition: Professional manual.* Odessa, FL: Psychological Resources.

Achenbach, T. M. (2000). *Manual for the ASEBA preschool forms and profiles.* Burlington: University of Vermont Department of Psychiatry.

Administration for Children and Families. (1996). Head Start program: Final rule. *Federal Register, 61*(215), 57186–57227.

Administration for Children and Families. (2002a). *Head Start program information report, 2000–2001.* Washington, DC: Department of Health and Human Services.

Administration for Children and Families. (2002b). *Making a difference in the lives of infants and toddlers and their families: The impacts of Early Head Start.* Washington, DC: U.S. Department of Health and Human Services.

Administration for Children and Families. (2003a). *Head Start program information report, 2001–2002.* Washington, DC: Department of Health and Human Services.

Administration for Children and Families. (2003b). *Pathways to quality and full implementation in Early Head Start programs.* Washington, DC: U.S. Department of Health and Human Services.

Administration for Children and Families. (2005a). *Early Promotion and Intervention Research Consortium.* Retrieved March 2, 2005, from http://www.acf.hhs.gov/programs/opre/ehs/ehs_resrch

Administration for Children and Families. (2005b). *Fatherhood Initiative.* Retrieved March 2, 2005, from http://www.fatherhood.hhs.gov/index.shtml

Administration for Children and Families. (2005c). *Head Start program information report, 2003–2004.* Washington, DC: U.S. Department of Health and Human Services.

Administration for Children and Families. (2005d). *The Infant Mental Health Initiative.* Retrieved March 2, 2005, from http://www.zerotothree.org/imh/ (See also http://www.ehsnrc.org/AboutUs/imhi.htm)

Administration on Children, Youth, and Families. (1999a). *Leading the way: Characteristics and early experiences of selected Early Head Start programs: Vol. 1. Cross-site perspectives.* Washington, DC: U.S. Department of Health and Human Services.

Administration on Children, Youth, and Families. (1999b). *Leading the way: Characteristics and early experiences of selected Early Head Start programs: Vol. 2. Program profiles.* Washington, DC: U.S. Department of Health and Human Services.

Administration on Children, Youth, and Families. (2000). *Leading the way: Characteristics and early experiences of selected Early Head Start programs: Vol. 3. Program implementation.* Washington, DC: U.S. Department of Health and Human Services.

Bayley, N. (1993). *Bayley Scales of Infant Development, second edition: Manual.* New York: Psychological Corporation, Harcourt Brace.

Burchinal, M., Roberts, J., Nabors, L., & Bryant, D. (1996). Quality of center child care and infant cognitive and language development. *Child Development, 67,* 606–620.

Caldwell, B.M., & Bradley, R.H. (1984). *Home observation for measurement of the environment: Administration manual* (Rev. ed.). Unpublished manuscript, University of Arkansas at Little Rock.

Cook, T.D., & Campbell, D.T. (1976). The design and conduct of true experiments and quasi-experiments in field settings. In M.D. Dunnette (Ed.), *Handbook of industrial and organizational psychology* (pp. 223–326). Skokie, IL: Rand McNally.

Cost, Quality and Child Outcomes Study Team. (1995). *Cost, quality and child outcomes in child care centers: Public report.* Denver: University of Colorado at Denver.

Dunn, L.M., & Dunn, L.M. (1997). *Peabody Picture Vocabulary Test* (3rd ed.). Circle Pines, MN: American Guidance Service.

Fenson, L., Dale, P.S., Reznick, J.S., Bates, E., Thal, D.J., & Pethick, S.J. (1994). Variability in early communicative development. *Monographs of the Society for Research in Child Development, 59*(5, Serial No. 242).

Gill, S., Greenberg, M., & Vazquez, A. (2002). Changes in the service delivery model and home visitors' job satisfaction and turnover in an Early Head Start Program. *Infant Mental Health Journal, 23,* 1–2, 182–196.

Gish, M. (2004). Head Start issues for the 108th Congress. *CRS Report for Congress.* Washington, DC: Congressional Research Service, Library of Congress.

Hebbeler, K., Spiker, D., Mallik, S., Scarborough, A., & Simeonsson, R. (2003). *Demographic characteristics of children and families entering early intervention.* Retrieved April 23, 2004, from http://www.sri.com/neils/reports.html

Ispa, J.M., Fine, M.A., Halgunseth, L.C., Harper, S., Robinson, J., Boyce, L., et al. (2004). Maternal intrusiveness, maternal warmth, and mother-toddler relationship outcomes: Variation across low-income ethnic and acculturation groups. *Child Development, 75*(6), 1613–1631.

Korfmacher, J., & Spicer, P. (2002). Toward an understanding of the child's experience in a Montessori Early Head Start program. *Infant Mental Health Journal, 23,* 1–2, 197–212.

Love, J.M., Kisker, E.E., Ross, C., Raikes, H., Constantine, J., Boller, K., et al. (in press). The effectiveness of Early Head Start for 3-year-old children and their parents. *Developmental Psychology.*

Love, J.M., Harrison, L., Sagi-Schwartz, A., van Izendoorn, M., Ross, C., Ungerer, J.A., et al. (2003). Child care quality matters: How conclusions may vary with context. *Child Development, 74,* 1021–1033.

Mann, T., Bogle, M., & Parlakian, R., (2004). Early Head Start: An overview. In J. Lombardi & M. Bogle (Eds.), *Beacon of hope* (pp. 1–19). Washington, DC: Zero to Three.

McCall, R.B., & Green, B.L. (2004). Beyond the methodological gold standards of behavior research: Considerations for policy and practice. *Social Policy Report, 28*(2), 1–19.

National Institute of Health and Human Development [NICHD], Early Childhood Child Care Research Network. (1999). Child care and mother-child interactions in the first three years of life. *Developmental Psychology, 35,* 1399–1413.

Pan, B.A., Rowe, M.L., Spier, E., & Tamis-LeMonda, C. (in press). Measuring productive vocabulary of toddlers in low-income families: Concurrent and predictive validity of three sources of data. *Journal of Child Language.*

Radloff, L.S. (1977). The CES-D Scale: A self-report depression scale for research in the general population. *Applied Psychological Measurement, 1,* 385–401.

Raikes, H.H., & Bellotti, J. (in press). Two studies of father involvement in Early Head Start programs: A practitioners' survey and a demonstration program evaluation [Special issue]. *Parenting Science and Practice.*

Raikes, H.H., Love, J., Chazan-Cohen, R., & Brooks-Gunn, J. (2004). What works? Improving the odds for infants and toddlers in low-income families. In J. Lombardi & M. Bogel (Eds.), *Beacon of hope* (pp. 20–44). Washington, DC: Zero to Three.

Raikes, H.H., Roggman, L., Peterson, C., Constantine, J., Brooks-Gunn, J., Schiffman, R., et al. (in review). *Theories of change and outcomes in Early Head Start home-based programs.* Manuscript under review.

Raikes, H.H., Roggman, L., & Summers, J. (2005). Father involvement in Early Head Start programs. *Fathering: A Journal of Theory, Research and Practice about Men as Fathers, 3*(1), 29–58.

Robinson, J., Korfmacher, J., Green, S., Song, N., Soben, R., & Emde, R.N. (2002). Predicting program use and acceptance by parents enrolled in Early Head Start. *NHSA Dialog, 5*(2, 3), 311–324.

Robinson, J.L., & Emde, R., (2004). Mental health moderators of Early Head Start on parenting and child development: Maternal depression and relationship attitudes. *Parenting: Science and Practice, 4*(1), 73–97.

Sameroff, A., & Fiese, B. (2000). Models of development and developmental risk. In C. Zeanah (Ed.), *Handbook for infant mental health* (2nd ed., pp. 3–19). New York: Guilford.

Shonkoff, J.P., & Phillips, D.A. (Eds.) (2000). *From Neurons to Neighborhoods: The Science of Early Childhood Development.* Washington, DC: National Academy Press.

Sonoma State University. (2005). *SpecialQuest.* Retrieved March 2, 2005, from http://www.sonoma.edu/cihs/Hilton_EHS/sqfrontpage.html (See also http://www.acf.hhs.gov/programs/hsb/contacts/hilton.htm and http://www.headstartinfo.org/publications/hsbulletin69/hsb69_17.htm)

Spicer, P., Korfmacher, J., Hudgens, T., & Emde, R.N., (2002). Joining communities: The value of an ethnographic approach in early childhood intervention research. *NHSA Dialog, 5*(2, 3), 340–355.

Tamis-LeMonda, C., Shannon, J., Cabrera, N., & Lamb, M. (2004). Fathers and mothers at play with their 2- and 3-year-olds: Contributions to language and cognitive development. *Child Development, 75,* 1613–1631.

U.S. Department of Health and Human Services. (1990). Head Start research and evaluation: A blueprint for the future. *Recommendations of the advisory panel for the Head Start Evaluation Design Project.* Washington, DC: Author.

U.S. Department of Health and Human Services. (1994). *The statement of the Advisory Committee on Services for Families with Infants and Toddlers.* Washington, DC: Author.

Whiteside-Mansell, L., McKelvey, L., Ayoub, C., Faldowski, R., Hart, A., & Shears, J. (2004, April). Validity of the short form of the parenting stress index for parents of preschoolers. Poster presented at the 14th Biennial Meeting of the Society for Research in Human Development, Park City, UT.

Chapter 9

THE HIGH/SCOPE APPROACH: EVIDENCE THAT PARTICIPATORY LEARNING IN EARLY CHILDHOOD CONTRIBUTES TO HUMAN DEVELOPMENT

Lawrence J. Schweinhart

As special education director of the Ypsilanti, Michigan, public school district in the 1960s, David Weikart encountered daily the school failure of children born in poverty. In this time of the civil rights movement and the man-on-the-moon initiative, this was not a fact of life to be endured but a problem to solve. So, with the High/Scope Perry Preschool program that operated from 1962 to 1967, he began the sequence of work that led to his establishment of the High/Scope Educational Research Foundation in 1970. He established the High/Scope Foundation to pursue the vision of a world in which all educational settings use participatory learning so everyone has a chance to succeed in life and contribute to society. He and his colleagues wanted to assist children with the odds against them to use education to rise above the poverty they were born in, to lift their lives through education. Their methods were curriculum development, research, training, publishing, and communication, primarily applied to early-childhood programs.

This chapter describes five studies that affirm the importance of participatory learning in early childhood. The High/Scope Perry Preschool Study compares the life outcomes of study participants who did and did not participate in such a preschool program. The High/Scope Preschool Curriculum Comparison Study compares the life outcomes of study participants who participated in three types of preschool programs: High/Scope, direct instruction, or traditional nursery school. The Training for Quality Study examines the effects of High/Scope training on teacher trainers, teachers, and children. The Head Start Family and Child Experiences Survey (FACES), conducted by a consortium of research organizations other than High/Scope, examines curriculum and child outcomes in a nationally representative sample of Head Start classrooms. The Preprimary Study of the International Association for the Evaluation of Educational Achievement (IEA) examines early-childhood settings and child outcomes in countries around the world. In addition to their common testimony on the value of participatory learning, these studies also constitute a major portion of the history of the High/Scope Educational Research Foundation.

THE HIGH/SCOPE MODEL OF PRESCHOOL EDUCATION

The model used in all of these studies except the IEA Preprimary Study was the High/Scope open framework of educational ideas and practices based on the natural development of young children. Drawing on the child development ideas of Jean Piaget, it emphasizes the idea that children are *intentional learners,* who learn best from activities that they themselves plan, carry out, and review afterward. Adults introduce new ideas to children through adult-initiated small- and large-group activities. Adults observe, support, and extend the children's play. Adults arrange interest areas in the learning environment; maintain a daily routine that permits children to plan, carry out, and review their own activities; and join in children's activities, asking appropriate questions that extend their plans and help them think about their activities. They add complex language to the discussion to expand the child's vocabulary. Using key experiences derived from child development theory as a framework, adults encourage children to make choices, solve problems, and engage in activities that contribute to their intellectual, social, and physical development.

Although key experiences in child development are used to monitor children's progress, adults do not provide children with prescriptively sequenced lessons that cover a defined subject matter. Instead, they listen closely to children's plans and then actively work with them to extend their activities to challenging levels as appropriate. Adults' questioning style is important, emphasizing questions that initiate conversations with children and drawing out observations and reflections expressed in children's own language. Adults rarely ask questions merely to test children's grasp of letters, numbers, or colors. Instead, they ask for self-generated descriptions or ideas: What happened? How did you make that? Can you show me? Can you help another child? The questioning style permits free conversation between adult and child and serves as a model for conversations among children. This reflective approach permits adults and children to interact as thinkers and doers rather than to assume the traditional school roles of initiating teacher and responding pupil. All are sharing and learning as they work, adults as well as children.

In order to create a setting in which children engage in intentional learning activities, a consistent *daily routine* is maintained that varies only when the child has fair warning that things will be different the next day. Field trips are not surprises, nor are special visits or events initiated in the classroom on the spur of the moment. This adherence to routine gives the child the control that helps develop a sense of responsibility and offers the enjoyment of being independent. The daily routine includes a *plan-do-review* sequence as well as large- and small-group activities. The plan-do-review sequence is the central device that gives children opportunities to express intentions about their activities and reflect on their experience while keeping the adult intimately involved in the process.

THE HIGH/SCOPE PERRY PRESCHOOL STUDY

David Weikart and his colleagues in the Ypsilanti, Michigan, school district operated the High/Scope Perry Preschool program for three- and four-year-olds living in poverty to help them avoid school failure and related problems. Because people differed on whether or not such a program actually did help, they embedded the program in the High/Scope Perry Preschool study to find out.

Design

To conduct this study, they identified 123 young African American children in Ypsilanti living in poverty and assessed to be at high risk of school failure. They randomly assigned about half of them to a no-program group that received no preschool program and the other half to a program group that received a high-quality preschool program at ages three and four. The project staff collected data on both groups annually from ages 3 through 11 and at ages 14, 15, 19, 27, and now at age 40. After each period of data collection, they analyzed the data and wrote a report of the study (Schweinhart et al., 2005).

Findings

The variety of findings of program effects through age 40 spans the domains of education, economic performance, crime prevention, and family and health. All findings reported herein for this study are statistically significant with a probability of less than .05, using a one-tailed test because the obvious direction of the hypothesis is that the preschool program group is doing better than the no-program group, not vice versa. A path model of the study suggests how preschool experience affects age-40 success. Beginning with preschool experience and children's preprogram intellectual performance, the model traces paths to children's postprogram intellectual performance, then to their school achievement and commitment to schooling, then to their educational attainment, then to their adult earnings and lifetime arrests. This model did not differ for males and females. Figure 9.1 presents group differences for these variables.

More of the program group than the no-program group graduated from high school or received a GED (77% vs. 60%). This difference was due to a 42 percentage-point difference between program and no-program females in high school graduation rate (88% vs. 46%). This difference was related to earlier differences between program and no-program females in the rates of treatment for mental impairment (8% vs. 36%) and retention in grade (21% vs. 41%). Earlier, the program group outperformed the no-program group on various intellectual and language tests from their preschool years up to age 7; school achievement tests at 7 to 14; and literacy tests at 19 and 27. The program group had better attitudes toward school than the no-program group as teens, and program-group parents had better attitudes toward their teen children's schooling than did no-program-group parents. The preschool program affected children's performance and attitudes, regardless of their gender, but this common effect seems to have led school staff to track girls but not boys. As will be seen, however, the program had plenty of long-term effects on boys as well.

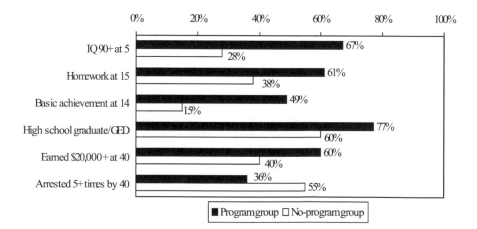

Figure 9.1   Major findings: High/Scope Perry Preschool Study at 40 years of age

More of the program group than the no-program group were employed at 27 (69% vs. 56%) and 40 (76% vs. 62%). The program group had higher median earnings than the no-program group, annually at 27 ($12,000 vs. $10,000) and at 40 ($20,800 vs. $15,300) and monthly at both ages. More of the program group than the no-program group owned their own homes at 27 (27% vs. 5%) and 40 (37% vs. 28%) rather than paying rent, receiving a subsidy, living with others, or being incarcerated. At 40, program males paid more per month for their dwelling than did no-program males. More of the program group than the no-program group had a car at 27 (73% vs. 59%) and 40 (82% vs. 60%). At 40, significantly more of the program group than the no-program group had a savings account (78% vs. 50%). At 27, fewer in the program group than the no-program group reported receiving social services at some time in the previous 10 years (59% vs. 80%). The group difference at 40 had dropped from 21 percentage points to 15 percentage points (71% vs. 86%) and was no longer statistically significant.

During their lives, fewer in the program group than the no-program group were arrested five or more times (36% vs. 55%) or were arrested for violent, property, or drug crimes. Group differences in various types of crime occurred in adolescence, early adulthood, and midlife. By 40, compared to the no-program group, the program group had fewer than 3 of the 78 types of crimes cited at arrest—dangerous drugs, assault and/or battery, and larceny less than $100. Fewer in the program group were sentenced to time in prison or jail by age 40 (28% vs. 52%), particularly from ages 28 to 40 (19% vs. 43%).

More program than no-program males raised their own children (57% vs. 30%). The two oldest children of the program group did not differ significantly from the two oldest children of the no-program group in education, employment, arrests, or welfare status. At 40, more of the program group than the no-program group said they were getting along very well with their family (75% vs. 64%). Fewer program than no-program males reported using sedatives, sleeping pills, or tranquilizers (17% vs. 43%) or marijuana or hashish (48% vs. 71%).

In constant 2000 dollars discounted at 3 percent, the economic return to society for the program was $258,888 per participant on an investment of $15,166 per participant—$17.07 per dollar invested. Of that return, 76 percent went to the general public—$12.90 per dollar invested—and 24 percent went to each participant. Of the public return, 86 percent came from crime savings, and the rest came from education and welfare savings and increased taxes due to higher earnings. A full 92 percent of the public return was due to males because of the large program effect of reducing male crime. This finding for males stands in stark contrast to the large program effect on the high school graduation rates of females. Preschool program participants earned 14 percent more per person than they would have otherwise—$156,490 more over their lifetimes in undiscounted 2000 dollars. Male program participants cost the public 41 percent less in crime costs per person, $732,894 less in undiscounted 2000 dollars over their lifetimes. This cost-benefit analysis is conservative in two respects. It omits hard-to-monetize benefits, such as family, health, and wealth benefits, and it makes conservative assumptions about the earnings profiles and the unit costs of crimes, opting for the data source resulting in smaller group differences when multiple data sources were available.

Validity of the Study

The study's internal validity is strong because of the random assignment of study participants to the program and no-program groups. It is strengthened further by the use of seven covariates representing background characteristics in the age-40 analyses. Additional analyses confirm that major outcomes were not due to placing siblings in the same preschool-experience groups as their older siblings nor to variations among classes of study participants. The study's statistical power is somewhat limited by its sample size of 123 study participants, but the sample size was adequate to identify many statistically significant group differences.

The study's external validity is the extent to which its study participants and program resemble the children and program to which it is generalized. Because this study is rare and relevant to public policy, the demands on its generalizability are great: Head Start, state preschool, and child care programs in the United States and early-childhood programs throughout the world would like to lay claim to such effects.

The effects found in the study generalize to programs that are reasonably similar to the High/Scope Perry Preschool program: preschool education programs run by teachers with bachelors' degrees and certification in education, each serving up to eight children living in low-income families. These programs run two school years at three and four years of age, use the High/Scope educational model, with daily classes of two-and-a-half hours or more and teachers visiting families at least every two weeks.

Because such evidence is reflected neither in the quantity nor in the quality of existing publicly funded preschool programs, we set about to let as many people as possible know about this study. We disseminated the study through publications and presentations for national associations of policymakers, scientists, and educators and for conferences of them in most of the states. We even trained groups of speakers in four states: Michigan, Ohio, North Carolina, and South Carolina. We worked with newspapers and media throughout the country to spread the story. With continuing bipartisan support, overall Head Start funding from 1980 to 2003 increased ninefold from $735 million to $6.7 billion, and funding per child almost quadrupled, from $1,953 to $7,329.

Although many of the features of the study have been the subject of some debate in designing preschool programs, a particularly important question is whether a preschool program must use the High/Scope educational model or some other educational model in order for its participants to experience long-term benefits. This question led to the next study.

THE HIGH/SCOPE PRESCHOOL CURRICULUM COMPARISON STUDY

The High/Scope Preschool Curriculum Comparison Study (Schweinhart & Weikart, 1997a, 1997b) suggests that curriculum has a lot to do with a preschool program's long-term benefits. This study found that young people born in poverty experience fewer emotional problems and felony arrests if they attended a preschool program that used High/Scope rather than direct instruction.

Design

Since 1967, the study has followed the lives of 68 young people born in poverty who were randomly assigned at ages three and four to one of three groups, each experiencing a different curriculum model:

- In the *direct-instruction model,* teachers followed a script to directly teach children academic skills, rewarding them for correct answers to the teacher's questions.
- In the *High/Scope model,* teachers set up the classroom and the daily routine so children could plan, do, and review their own activities and engage in key active-learning experiences.
- In the *traditional nursery school model,* teachers responded to children's self-initiated play in a loosely structured, socially supportive setting.

Program staff implemented the curriculum models independently and to high standards, in two-and-a-half-hour classes held five days a week and one-and-a-half-hour home visits every two weeks when children were three and four years old. Except for the curriculum model, all aspects of the program were nearly identical. The findings presented here are corrected for differences in the gender makeup of the groups.

Findings

Figure 9.2 presents the major findings of this study at age 23. By age 23, the High/Scope and nursery school groups had 10 significant advantages over the direct-instruction group: both groups had two advantages, the High/Scope group alone had another six advantages, and the nursery school group alone had two additional advantages. However, the High/Scope and nursery school groups, after controlling for gender makeup, did not differ significantly from each other on any outcome variable (Schweinhart & Weikart, 1997a).

By age 23, the High/Scope and nursery school groups both had two significant advantages over the direct-instruction group:

- Only 6 percent of either group needed treatment for emotional impairment or disturbance during their schooling, as compared to 47 percent of the direct-instruction group.

- Forty-three percent of the High/Scope group and 44 percent of the nursery school group had done volunteer work, as compared to 11 percent of the direct-instruction group.

The High/Scope group had six additional significant advantages over the direct-instruction group:

- Only 10 percent had ever been arrested for a felony, as compared to 39 percent of the direct-instruction group.

- None had ever been arrested for a property crime, as compared to 38 percent of the direct-instruction group.

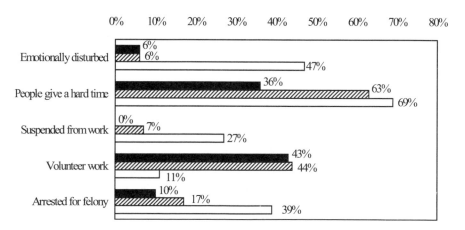

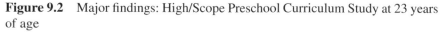

Figure 9.2　Major findings: High/Scope Preschool Curriculum Study at 23 years of age

- At age 15, 23 percent reported that they had engaged in 10 or more acts of misconduct, as compared to 56 percent of the direct-instruction group.

- Thirty-six percent said that various kinds of people gave them a hard time, as compared to 69 percent of the direct-instruction group.

- Thirty-one percent of the group had married and were living with their spouses, as compared to none of the direct-instruction group.

- Seventy percent planned to graduate from college, as compared to 36 percent of the direct-instruction group.

The nursery school group had two additional significant advantages over the direct-instruction group:

- Only 9 percent had been arrested for a felony at ages 22 to 23, as compared to 34 percent of the direct-instruction group.

- None of them had ever been suspended from work, as compared to 27 percent of the direct-instruction group.

Through age 10, the main finding of this study had been that the overall average IQ of the three groups rose 27 points, from a borderline impairment level of 78 to a normal level of 105, after one year of their preschool program and subsequently settled in at an average of 95, still at the normal level. The only curriculum-group difference through age 10 was measured as the preschool programs ended: the average IQ of the direct-instruction group was significantly higher than the average IQ of the nursery school group (103 vs. 93). Throughout their school years, curriculum groups did not differ significantly in school achievement, nor did their high school graduation rates differ significantly. The conclusion at that time was that well-implemented preschool curriculum models, regardless of their theoretical orientation, had similar effects on children's intellectual and academic performance. Time has proved otherwise. Scripted teacher-directed instruction, touted by some as the surest path to school readiness, seems to purchase a temporary improvement in academic performance at the cost of a missed opportunity for long-term improvement.

The High/Scope educational model was originally called the Cognitively Oriented Curriculum (Weikart, Rogers, Adcock, & McClelland, 1971) because it focused on cognitive, logical processes identified in Piaget's theory (Piaget & Inhelder, 1969), such as representation, classification, and seriation. Tests of early-childhood intellectual performance demonstrably tapped these processes in both the Perry study and the curriculum study. So the High/Scope preschool classroom provides a preschool intellectual boost as measured by these tests. It also provides other experiences that facilitate these intellectual processes, such as planning and reviewing one's activities, exploring one's curiosity, and developing a sense of personal control over the events of one's life. This might be called *intellectual performance* broadly defined. It makes sense to combine or supplement this emphasis on intellectual processes with a focus on early literacy or mathematics skills found to predict later achievement, but it does not make sense to replace the first with the second. To do so runs the risk of sacrificing the known long-term effects on school achievement, high school graduation rate, lifetime earnings, and crime prevention.

THE TRAINING FOR QUALITY STUDY

The High/Scope Training for Quality Study (Epstein, 1993) offers evidence of the effectiveness of the High/Scope preschool education model as practiced throughout the United States today. In this multistudy evaluation, we analyzed participant reports of 40 training projects, surveyed 203 certified High/Scope teacher trainers, surveyed and systematically observed the classrooms of 244 High/Scope and 122 comparison teachers, and systematically observed and tested 97 High/Scope and 103 comparison children in these classrooms.

Design

High/Scope trainers identified 244 High/Scope teachers in Michigan, New York, and California who had been employed at their agencies for at least six months, had attended at least four High/Scope workshops, and had received three classroom visits. We selected 122 comparison teachers from lists of licensed child care centers and from agencies nominated by staff or trainers, with efforts to maintain proportions of agency types similar to those of the High/Scope teachers.

The 200 children in the child outcomes study attended preschool programs in 15 agencies in urban, suburban, and rural settings in southeastern Michigan and northwestern Ohio; 46 percent were in Head Start, 19 percent in public schools, and 35 percent in nonprofit centers. Children ranged in age from 2 to 6, average 4.3; 47 percent were male, 53 percent female; 43 percent were white, 32 percent were African American, 5 percent were Hispanic American, and 20 percent were of other ethnic groups. Their fathers and mothers averaged 13.7 years of schooling, identifying these parents as relatively well educated on the average. In both groups, according to Bureau of Labor Statistics codes, fathers' median occupational level was that of laborer, and mothers' median occupational level was that of service worker. Treatment groups did not significantly differ on any of these characteristics.

Findings

The Registry Trainer Survey found that half of High/Scope-certified trainers were in Head Start, 27 percent were in public schools, and 20 percent were in private child care agencies. Eighty-eight percent had completed college, including 37 percent with advanced degrees; 70 percent majored in early childhood. They had a median of 15 years of experience in early childhood. Seventy-eight percent of them were still in the same agency they were in when they received High/Scope certification; 85 percent had teacher-training responsibility, although they only spent an average of eight hours a week training teachers. On average, they made a large-group presentation for 36 staff annually, a hands-on workshop for 15 staff monthly, an observation-and-feedback classroom visit monthly, and an informal classroom visit weekly. The average teacher had attended one presentation and nine workshops and received an observation-and-feedback visit and three informal visits per month.

All the teachers trained had tried out the High/Scope model's room arrangement and daily routine; 91 percent had tried out the key experiences; 63 percent had tried out the child-observation techniques. Eighty-nine percent of them were comfortable and effective with room arrangement; 80 percent were comfortable with the daily routine; 56 percent were comfortable with the key experiences; and 37 percent were comfortable with the child-observation techniques. Trainers said they would show visitors 45 percent of the classrooms of trained teachers as examples of the High/Scope preschool model, an average of four classrooms per trainer.

The High/Scope Registry listed 1,075 early-childhood leaders in 34 states and 10 other countries who successfully completed High/Scope's seven-week Trainer Certification Program in the past decade. The average trainer had trained 15 teaching teams, so an estimated 16,125 early-childhood teaching teams, including 29 percent of all Head Start staff, had received High/Scope model training from these trainers. Because trainers regarded 45 percent of these classrooms as examples of the High/Scope model, they would nominate an estimated 7,256 early-childhood classrooms throughout the United States and around the world as examples of the High/Scope model.

The teacher survey indicated that both High/Scope and comparison classrooms were of high quality. Both groups had at least 10 years of teaching experience. Majorities of both groups had college degrees and early-childhood degrees. Both groups had more than 40 hours of in-service training annually. In both groups, teachers' annual salaries averaged about $20,000 a year, considerably higher than the $9,400 national average for child care teaching staff (Whitebook, Phillips, & Howes, 1993). The few group background differences seemed to compensate for each other: The High/Scope teachers had significantly more teaching experience than comparison teachers (12 vs. 10 years), but significantly fewer High/Scope teachers had college degrees (63% vs. 79%).

While High/Scope and comparison teachers did not differ significantly in their hours of in-service training per year, more High/Scope teachers received significantly more in-service training involving curriculum and teaching practices (91% vs. 71%), child assessment and evaluation (75% vs. 48%), and professional issues (48% vs. 34%). High/Scope teachers placed significantly more importance on the following topics than did comparison teachers: room arrangement, children choosing their own activities, adults participating in children's activities, ongoing training for adults, supervision and evaluation, multicultural awareness, and parent involvement.

High/Scope and comparison *classrooms* differed significantly in classroom environment, daily routine, adult-child interaction, and overall implementation, as assessed by the High/Scope Program Implementation Profile (Schweinhart & Weikart, 1989) adapted for generic use. High/Scope advantages in classroom environment involved dividing the classroom into activity areas, providing adequate work space in each area, arranging and labeling materials, providing enough materials in each area, providing real household and work objects, making materials accessible to children, and providing materials to promote awareness of cultural differences. High/Scope advantages in daily routine involved implementing a consistent daily routine, encouraging children to plan and review activities, and providing opportunities for planning, doing, and reviewing. High/Scope advantages in adult-child interaction differences involved observing and asking questions, participating in children's play, and balancing child and adult talk. Comparison classrooms had no significant advantages over High/Scope classrooms on this instrument. These findings indicate that the High/Scope classrooms were implementing the High/Scope Preschool Curriculum to a significantly greater extent than were the comparison classrooms.

As shown in Figure 9.3, the *children* in High/Scope programs significantly outperformed the children in comparison programs in initiative, social relations, music and movement, and overall child development. High/Scope advantages in initiative involved complex play and cooperating in program routines. High/Scope advantages in social relations involved relating to adults and social problem-solving. High/Scope advantages in music and movement included imitating movements to a steady beat.

Significant positive correlations of .39 to .52 were found between classroom daily routine (measuring children's opportunities to plan activities,

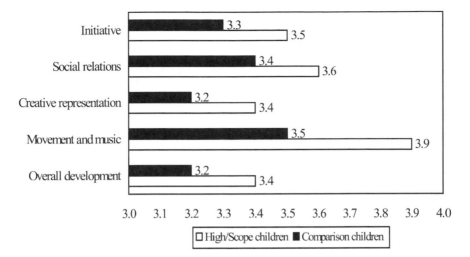

Figure 9.3   Findings: Training for Quality Children's Study

carry out their ideas, and review what they had done each day) and children's overall development, specifically their development of creative representation, initiative, music and movement abilities, and language and literacy.

THE HEAD START FACES STUDY

The Family and Child Experiences Survey (FACES; Zill et al., 2003) is a study of a national random sample of Head Start programs. The first cohort of 3,200 children entered Head Start in fall 1997; the second cohort of 2,800 children entered Head Start in fall 2000.

General Findings

In Head Start, children improved on important aspects of school readiness, narrowing the gap between them and the general population, but still lagging behind. As shown in Figure 9.4, relative to national norms, children made significant gains during the Head Start year, particularly in vocabulary and early writing skills. As shown in Figure 9.5, children in Head Start grew in cooperative classroom behavior—behavior that was helpful, compliant, mature, and interactive—and they exhibited less inattentive, hyperactive behavior, especially if they started out more shy, aggressive, or hyperactive. Teachers rated children as inattentive and hyperactive if the children could not concentrate or pay attention for long, if they were very restless, fidgeted all the time, or could not sit still. The study found that Head Start classrooms were of good quality. Most

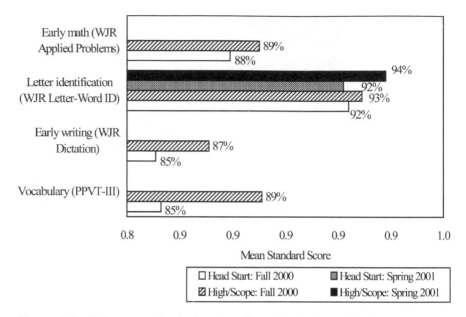

Figure 9.4   Selected academic findings: Head Start FACES Study

programs use a specific curriculum, particularly Creative Curriculum and High/Scope. Use of these curricula and higher teacher salaries were related to child outcomes. Teachers' educational credentials were linked to greater gains in early writing skills. In addition, provision of preschool services for a longer period each day was tied to greater cognitive gains. Based on follow-up of the 1997 cohort, Head Start graduates showed further progress toward national averages during kindergarten, with substantial gains in vocabulary, early mathematics, and early writing skills during kindergarten. Most Head Start graduates could identify most or all of the letters of the alphabet by the end of kindergarten, and more than half could recognize beginning sounds of words.

High/Scope Findings

Conducted independently of the High/Scope Foundation, the FACES study found that four-year-olds in Head Start classes that used the High/Scope model improved from fall to spring in letter- and word-identification skills and cooperative classroom behavior, and they decreased their behavior problems (Zill et al., 2003), as shown in Figures 9.4 and 9.5.

- On a scale of letter and word recognition, children in High/Scope classes registered a highly significant gain (p < .01) of 12.6 scale points, signifi-

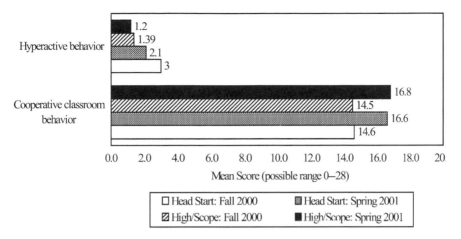

Figures 9.5   Selected social findings: Head Start FACES Study

cantly more (p < .05) than children in classes using Creative Curriculum or other curricula.

- On teacher ratings of cooperative classroom behavior, children in High/ Scope classes experienced a highly significant gain (p < .01) of half a standard deviation, significantly more (p < .05) than children in classes using Creative Curriculum or other curricula.

- On teacher ratings of total behavior problems, particularly problems involving hyperactive behavior, children in High/Scope classes dropped significantly (p < .05) during the year, significantly more (p < .05) than did children in classes using Creative Curriculum or other curricula.

Of the 91 percent of the teachers who used one or more curriculum models, 39 percent used Creative Curriculum, 20 percent used High/ Scope, and 41 percent used some other curriculum, such as High Reach, Scholastic, or Los Cantos Los Ninos. The quality of Creative Curriculum and High/Scope classes was significantly higher than the quality of classes that used other curricula, particularly with respect to language. On the 7-point Early Childhood Environment Rating Scale (Harms, Clifford, & Cryer, 1998), with 5 identified as good, High/Scope classes averaged 5.04, Creative Curriculum classes averaged 5.02, and classes using other curricula averaged 4.55. On its language items, average scores were slightly higher, but the differences were about the same. On a quality composite, the average scores for High/Scope and Creative Curriculum were nearly half a standard deviation higher than the average scores for other curricula—clearly an educationally meaningful difference.

THE IEA PREPRIMARY PROJECT

The IEA Preprimary Project is a multination study of preprimary care and education sponsored by the International Association for the Evaluation of Educational Achievement (IEA; Olmsted & Montie, 2001; Weikart, Olmsted, & Montie, 2003). High/Scope served as the international coordinating center. Working collaboratively with researchers in 15 countries, High/Scope staff were responsible for sampling, instrument development, data analysis, and the writing of five published reports and one in press. The purpose of the study is to identify how process and structural characteristics of community preprimary settings affect children's language and cognitive development at age seven. The study is unique because many diverse countries participated, using common instruments to measure family background, teachers' characteristics, setting structural characteristics, experiences of children, and children's developmental status.

Design

The study is rooted theoretically in the ecological systems model of human development, which views children's behavior and developmental status as being influenced by multiple levels of the environment, some direct and proximal to the child, such as the child's actual experiences in an education or care setting, and some indirect and distal, such as national policy. The study findings focus on the influence of young children's experiences in community preprimary education and care settings on their language and cognitive development at age seven, controlling for family and cultural influences. Both proximal and distal variables are examined within that context.

The target population consisted of children in selected community settings who were approximately four-and-a-half years old. Data for the longitudinal project were collected in early-childhood care and education settings in 10 countries: Finland, Greece, Hong Kong, Indonesia, Ireland, Italy, Poland, Spain, Thailand, and the United States. Each country's research team chose to sample settings that were used by large numbers of families in the community or important for public policy reasons. With expert assistance, each country's research team developed a sampling plan, using probability proportional to size to select settings and systematic sampling procedures to select four children within each classroom. The age-four sample included more than 5,000 children in more than 1,800 settings in 15 countries. Ten of the initial 15 countries followed the children to age seven to collect language and cognitive outcome measures. The median retention rate across countries was 86 percent, ranging from 41 percent to 99 percent. The number of children included in the longitudinal analyses varied from 1,300 to 1,897, depending on the particular analysis.

Working with High/Scope researchers, measures used in the study were developed collaboratively by members of the international team. At age four, data were collected with three observation systems and three questionnaires/interviews. Children's cognitive and language performance was measured at age four and age seven. The observation systems collected time-sampled information about how teachers schedule and manage children's time, what children actually do with their time, and the behaviors teachers use and the nature of their involvement with children.

Interviews were conducted to collect family background information and gather information regarding teachers' and parents' expectations about what is important for preschool-aged children to learn. A questionnaire that focused on the structural characteristics of the settings was administered to teachers and caregivers.

The children were followed until age seven, an age across countries when they had all entered primary school. At that time, cognitive and language measures developed by an international team were administered to assess developmental status.

Based on the structure of the data, with individual children nested within settings and settings nested within countries, a hierarchical linear modeling approach was used for the analysis. Accurate estimation of impacts for variables at different levels was especially important for this study because effects at two levels—settings and countries—were often confounded with one another. Although the relationship between setting variables and children's later development was of primary interest, any such findings would have been hard to interpret if country effects had not been accurately estimated and adjusted for. A three-level approach enabled decomposition of variation of child outcomes into three parts: variation among children within settings, among settings within countries, and among countries. As a result, relationships between care setting variables and children's outcome scores are free of substantial influence from country-level effects.

Selected Findings

Four findings emerged that are consistent across all of the countries included in the data analysis:

- Children's language performance at age seven improves as *the predominant types of children's activities that teachers propose are free rather than personal/social.* From greatest to least contribution, activity types were as follows:

- Free activities, in which teachers let children choose

- Physical/expressive activities (gross- and fine-motor physical activity, dramatic play, arts, crafts, and music)

- Preacademic activities (reading, writing, numbers, mathematics, physical science, and social science)

- Personal/social activities (personal care, group social activities, and discipline)

- Children's language performance at age seven improves as *teachers' years of full-time schooling* increase.

- Children's cognitive performance at age seven improves as they spend *less time in whole-group activities* (the teacher proposes the same activity for all the children in the class—songs, games, listening to a story, working on a craft, or a preacademic activity).

- Children's language performance at age seven improves as the amount and variety of equipment and materials available to children in preschool settings increase.

The wide range of environments throughout the world in which young children grow and learn creates challenging questions for everyone concerned with providing high-quality programs for preprimary children. What are the essential program elements that promote optimum child development? How are these elements delivered in various communities? The findings tell us that teaching practices matter; how teachers set up their classrooms and the activities they propose for children make a difference.

Across diverse countries, child-initiated activities and teachers' education appear to contribute to children's later language performance, and minimization of whole-group activities and a greater number and variety of materials in preschool settings appear to contribute to their later cognitive performance.

Although more research is necessary in the various countries to establish a pattern of cause and effect and explore the learning mechanisms involved, early-childhood educators and policy makers can use these findings to examine local policies and practices and consider if changes are advisable.

SUMMARY

Taken together, these studies make a strong case that participatory learning in early childhood contributes greatly to children's development throughout their lives. The High/Scope Perry Preschool Study presents evidence that a preschool program based on participatory learning prepares young children living in poverty for schooling and leads them to greater commitment to school and school achievement. As a result, they achieve a higher level of educational attainment and greater adult earnings and commit fewer crimes. The High/Scope Preschool Curriculum Comparison Study shows that although preschool programs can do a good job of preparing young children living in poverty for school whether or not they emphasize participatory learning or direct instruction, participatory learning is the crucial ingredient that prevents later emotional problems and commission of crimes. The Training for Quality Study shows that we can train teacher trainers who can train teachers to implement successful preschool programs based on young children's participatory learning; in other words, these programs can go beyond isolated models to full-scale service programs. Conducted independently of the High/Scope Foundation in typical Head Start classrooms, the Head Start FACES Study shows that Head Start teachers who use the High/Scope model of participatory learning contribute to children's literacy and social skills. The IEA Preprimary Study shows evidence of a few universals in preschool education: Children's freely chosen activities, the time they spend in activities other than whole-group activities, the amount and variety of equipment and materials available to them, and the educational attainment of their teachers all contribute to their intellectual growth.

CONCLUSION

Participatory learning is process, not content. Thus, it is consistent with whatever content is determined to be the appropriate content. Early childhood is a formative period for language, literacy, and mathematics skills. Such content is ideal for participatory learning. As process, participatory learning is distinguished from direct instruction. The attraction and apparent advantage of direct instruction is that it is very efficient, focused precisely on specific learning objectives. However, this advantage also has its disadvantage. Its precise focus limits the generalizability of direct-instruction learning to other desirable skills that are not specifically targeted. When direct instruction focuses on language and literacy skills, it does so by eliminating spontaneous conversations between children and adults and among children themselves that give reality to their language development. It eliminates the give-and-take of unscripted interpersonal interaction that gives reality to children's ethical and moral values. There is nothing wrong with direct instruction in early childhood. It is just not enough.

Today in the United States, early childhood programs are coming of age. They are making the transition from cottage industry (i.e., work in homes) to full-fledged public institutionalization. As such, they are entering the domain of the nation's schools—public schools, private schools, elementary, secondary, and higher education schools. The nation's early-childhood policy issues are becoming *the* educational policy issues. Early-childhood programs become a key element in addressing the nation's literacy crisis. The question is no longer whether or not to invest in early-childhood programs, but how to do so. What is the best balance of federal, state, and local funding? Should public funding go to schools and centers or to parents through vouchers?

The purpose of early-childhood programs is the most basic issue of all. Should they extend dominant school traditions to younger children? Or should they extend family nurturance upward? Surely, the best answer to these questions is that they should find the right balance between academic content demands and child-centered nurturance. A preschool program that emphasizes direct instruction only is heavy on academic content demands and light on child-centered nurturance. The reverse is true for a child care or nursery school emphasis that eschews academic demands. Participatory learning achieves a good balance by integrating academic content demands with child-centered nurturance. One might say that participatory learning is the way to support children's development.

This thinking has clear implications for appropriate assessment of young children. It is easy for early-childhood assessment to focus only on academic content demands; indeed, that is its primary purpose for older students. Further, early-childhood assessment standards of reliability and validity are most easily met in the assessment of academic content. But if early-childhood assessment is to strike a good balance between academic content demands and child-centered nurturance, it must also assess the social and interpersonal aspects of children's behavior; that is to say, it must assess all of children's development.

At this crossroads in the history of early-childhood education, three paths extend. One is to continue to pay too little for early-childhood programs to maintain high quality and thereby to squander one of our best chances to enable young children to achieve their full potential. A second path is to convert early-childhood programs to academically focused, teacher-directed programs that purchase long-term academic success by allowing other aspects of early-childhood development to go wanting. This path has the advantage of proving itself quickly with hard-nosed research. It has the disadvantage of squandering the opportunity to develop children's character, motivation, and social skills. The third path is the middle path: investing enough in early-childhood programs to let well-trained early-childhood teachers engage in the artistry of early-childhood education, educating young children to be whole and balanced high achievers and high producers who care about other people and take initiative and responsibility for the world in which they live. This is really the only path worth taking.

REFERENCES

Epstein, A. S. (1993). *Training for quality: Improving early childhood programs through systematic inservice training.* Ypsilanti, MI: High/Scope Press.

Harms, T., Clifford, R. M., & Cryer, D. (1998). *Early Childhood Environment Rating Scale* (Rev. ed.). New York: Teachers College Press.

Olmsted, P., & Montie, J. (Eds.). (2001). *What do early childhood settings look like? Structural characteristics of early childhood settings in 15 countries.* Ypsilanti, MI: High/Scope Press.

Piaget, J., & Inhelder, B. (1969). *The psychology of the child.* New York: Basic Books.

Schweinhart, L. J., Montie, J., Xiang, Z., Barnett, W. S., Belfield, C., & Nores, M. (2005). *Lifetime effects: The High/Scope Perry Preschool Study through age 40* (Monographs of the High/Scope Educational Research Foundation, 13). Ypsilanti, MI: High/Scope Press.

Schweinhart, L. J., & Weikart, D. P. (1989). The High/Scope Perry Preschool Study: Implications for early childhood care and education. *Prevention in Human Services, 7*(1), 109–132.

Schweinhart, L. J., & Weikart, D. P. (1997a). The High/Scope Preschool Curriculum Comparison Study through age 23. *Early Childhood Research Quarterly, 12,* 117–143.

Schweinhart, L. J., & Weikart, D. P. (1997b). *Lasting differences: The High/Scope Preschool Curriculum Comparison Study through age 23* (Monographs of the High/Scope Educational Research Foundation, 12). Ypsilanti, MI: High/Scope Press.

Weikart, D. P., Olmsted, P. P., & Montie, J. (Eds.). (2003). *A world of preschool experience: Observations in 15 countries.* Ypsilanti, MI: High/Scope Press.

Weikart, D. P., Rogers, L., Adcock, C., & McClelland, D. (1971). *The Cognitively Oriented Curriculum: A framework for preschool teachers.* Urbana: University of Illinois.

Whitebook, M., Phillips, D., & Howes, C. (1993). *National Child Care Staffing Study revisited: Four years in the life of center-based child care.* Oakland, CA: Child Care Employee Project. Retrieved July 11, 2004, from http://www.ccw.org/pubs/nccssrevisit.pdf

Zill, N., Resnick, G., Kim, K., O'Donnell, K., Sorongon, A., McKey, R. H., et al. (2003, May). *Head Start FACES (2000): A whole child perspective on program performance—Fourth progress report.* Prepared for the Administration for Children and Families, U.S. Department of Health and Human Services (DHHS) under contract HHS-105-96-1912, Head Start Quality Research Consortium's Performance Measures Center. Retrieved July 11, 2004, from http://www.acf.hhs.gov/programs/core/ongoing_research/faces/faces00_4thprogress/faces00_4thprogress.pdf

Chapter 10

IMPACTS OF THE CHICAGO CHILD–PARENT CENTERS ON CHILD AND FAMILY DEVELOPMENT

Arthur J. Reynolds and Judy A. Temple

Early-childhood programs are a centerpiece of educational reforms in states and localities across the United States. The main attraction is their potential for prevention and cost-effectiveness, especially when compared to the well-known limits of remediation and treatment. In the justice system and even in schools, most services and interventions are to treat families and children after problems have occurred rather than to prevent the need for services or provide early intervention. Early-childhood programs in this chapter are defined as the provision of educational, family, health, and/or social services during any of the first five years of life, especially to children at risk of poor outcomes due to socioenvironmental disadvantages or developmental disabilities.

In the past two decades, scores of studies have demonstrated the short- and long-term positive effects of participation in early-childhood intervention for many child-development outcomes, including cognitive skills, school readiness and achievement, need for remedial education and social services, delinquency behavior, educational attainment, and economic well-being (Barnett, 1995; Currie, 2001; Karoly et al., 1998; Reynolds, Wang, & Walberg, 2003).

Funding support has been provided by grants from the National Institute of Child Health and Human Development (no. R01HD34294) and the Doris Duke Charitable Foundation (no. 20030035). Address correspondence to Arthur Reynolds, Waisman Center and School of Social Work, University of Wisconsin-Madison, 1500 Highland Avenue, Madison, WI 53705, or areynolds@waisman.wisc.edu.

Four limitations in the knowledge base, however, have reduced confidence in findings for social policy. First, most of the evidence for the link between preschool participation and long-term effects on well-being, such as reduced need for remedial services, lower delinquency and crime, and higher educational attainment, comes from model demonstration programs rather than established, large-scale programs run by human service agencies and schools. Evidence from large-scale, established programs is needed to best assess the effectiveness of current state and federal programs. Few large-scale studies have investigated links between participation in early intervention and delinquency, educational attainment, and child maltreatment, among others (Reynolds, 2000). A second limitation of existing research is that few studies have demonstrated the cost-effectiveness of early intervention. No studies of large-scale public programs have investigated cost-effectiveness. In an age of growing budget deficits and increasing fiscal uncertainties, identification of programs that provide the greatest returns to society is a high priority. The third limitation of research on early intervention is that the personal and environmental conditions that contribute to long-term intervention effects are not well understood. Are the effects of preschool participation due to the cognitive-scholastic advantage children receive, to enhanced family support behavior, or to improved social adjustment in the program? Studies that comprehensively examine these and other mediators have not been conducted until recently yet would enhance understanding of how to strengthen the maintenance of effects over time (Reynolds, 2000; Reynolds & Temple, 2005). The final limitation of the research is that family outcomes of early intervention have been investigated much less frequently. Although the primary focus of most programs is to enhance child development, family services can be substantial, and impacts on family socialization, parenting, and other families' outcomes are possible.

In this chapter, we present evidence about the effects of a school-based early-childhood intervention on children's well-being in the short and long term using data from the Chicago Longitudinal Study. The federally funded Chicago Child–Parent Centers provide education and family support services to low-income children from preschool to third grade. The centers are the nation's second oldest federally funded preschool program. Since 1967 more than 100,000 families have been served. Program effects are summarized up to age 22 for preschool, school-age, and extended-intervention components. Findings are summarized about the program's cost-effectiveness, the first such analysis for a public early-childhood program. Finally, the personal, family, and school factors that mediate the effects of program participation on long-term outcomes are identified. This is followed by a section on implications for policy and program development.

CHICAGO LONGITUDINAL STUDY

The Chicago Longitudinal Study (CLS, 1999; Reynolds, 2000) is an ongoing investigation of a complete cohort of 1,539 low-income children (93% African American) who participated in the Child–Parent Centers (CPC) program beginning in 1983–1984 and a comparison group of children the same age who enrolled in alternative kindergarten programs without CPC preschool experience. The 989 program and 550 comparison-group participants were born in 1980 or 1979, resided in high-poverty neighborhoods, and attended the Chicago Public Schools. In this matched-group, quasi-experimental study, the comparison group attended full-day kindergartens in randomly selected schools participating in a K–8 intervention project. The major goals of the CLS are to (1) evaluate the effects of the CPC program, including its timing and duration; (2) identify which subgroups of children and families benefit most from program participation; (3) identify the mechanisms through which the effects of participation are achieved; (4) determine the economic benefits of participation; and (5) investigate the contribution of a variety of individual, family, and school factors on children's well-being, especially those that are modifiable. In this chapter, our focus is the main effects of participation, cost effectiveness, and the identification of mediators of long-term effects.

The study began in 1985 as an internal evaluation of the effects of government-funded early-childhood programs in the Department of Research and Evaluation at the Chicago Board of Education. This led to a university-community collaborative study funded primarily by the National Institutes of Health and U.S. Department of Education with extensive involvement by teachers, managers, and principals. Collaborative activities included developing survey instruments, assisting in data collection and insuring high response rates, communicating with schools and families, identifying primary outcome measures, and disseminating and utilizing study findings. The Chicago schools also were invaluable in helping the study investigators secure access to data from the following sources: school records and standardized test scores, the Department of Children and Family Services (DCFS), county juvenile courts, Department of Human Services, Department of Public Health, Departments of Corrections, and from colleges and universities.

Over the 20 years of the study, extensive information on child and family well-being has been collected through school records, standardized test scores, surveys and interviews of children, parents and teachers, social service records, justice system records, and on postsecondary education. These data provide a unique opportunity to investigate the relation between program participation and later well-being and the environmental conditions and personal experiences that contribute to social and educational success. By age 21, data were obtained on educational attainment for 1,314 (or 85.4%) of the original study sample. This is 86.8 percent and 82.9 percent of the original program and comparison groups, respectively. For juvenile delinquency, sample recovery was 1,404 (or 91.2%). No group differences in rates of attrition have been found.

As shown in Table 10.1, the program and comparison groups in the follow-up sample were similar on many characteristics. An overall summary is represented by the family risk index, a sum of six factors that are associated with lower levels of well-being (e.g., low parent education, single-parent family status, not employed). Among the follow-up sample, the intervention group had a higher proportion of girls, a higher proportion of parents who had completed high school, and fewer siblings. Alternatively, the intervention group was more likely than the comparison group to reside in higher-poverty neighborhoods. The latter differences are the result of the centers being located in the most disadvantaged neighborhoods and that school personnel enroll children with the most educational disadvantages. Because the comparison group participated in alternative interventions, estimates are likely to be conservative.

The study has two limitations. First, generalizability of findings is limited to children and families with similar socioeconomic characteristics, primarily low-income children in large urban areas. The CPC program's long history of successful implementation also restricts generalizability to programs that are relatively established and high in quality. Second, because the study formally began during children's kindergarten year, the amount of data available during the preschool years is limited. Nevertheless, demographic data from birth records, school administrative data on program enrollment and attendance, and teacher retrospective reports on preschool learning activities provide valuable information on children's early-learning context. Inferences about the impact of the program in this matched-group design are strengthened as a consequence of the robustness of findings to alternative model specifications (Reynolds, 2000; Reynolds, Temple, Robertson, & Mann, 2002).

CHILD–PARENT CENTER PROGRAM

The CPC program (Sullivan, 1971) is a center-based early intervention that provides comprehensive educational and family support services to economically disadvantaged children and their parents from preschool to early elementary school. It began in 1967 through funding from the Elementary

Table 10.1

Sample Sizes and Characteristics for Program and Comparison Groups in the Chicago Longitudinal Study

Sample Characteristic	CPC Intervention Group	Comparison Group
Original sample size	989	550
Preschool participation, %	100	14.8 (Head Start)
Kindergarten participation, %	100	100
School-age participation, %	69.2	30.2
Child and Family Characteristics		
Female child, %*	52.3	46.3
African American child, %	94.0	92.6
Family risk index (0–6, mean)	3.6	3.6
Reside in high-poverty school area, %+*	77.1	71.9
Eligible for subsidized lunches, %+	92.3	92.8
Parent completed high school, %+*	66.1	59.3
Single parent status, %+	69.6	65.7
Parent not employed by child's age 12, %+	64.9	60.8
Number of siblings, mean+*	2.6	2.8
Child maltreatment report by age 4, %	1.1	1.3
Parent <20 years at child's birth, % birth	23.2	19.2
Sample Sizes for Major Outcomes		
Educational attainment at age 21	858	456
Juvenile arrest by age 18	911	493
Child abuse and neglect, ages 4–17	913	495
School remedial services, ages 6–18	841	445
Known status for two or more outcomes	934	504

Note: Preschool participation of the comparison group was in Head Start. CPC participation began at age three and could continue to age nine (third grade) in selected elementary schools. All children were eligible for participation in the school-age component regardless of preschool status.
+ Included in family risk index.
* Group difference significant at the .05 level.

and Secondary Education Act of 1965. Title I of the act provided grants to local public school districts serving high concentrations of children from low-income families. By the mid-1980s, 25 centers were in operation. As shown in Figure 10.1, the centers provide comprehensive services under the direction of the head teacher and in collaboration with the elementary school principal. Other primary staffs in each center are the parent-resource teacher, the school-community representative, bachelor's level classroom teachers, aides, nurses, speech therapists, and school psychologists. The major rationale of the program is that the foundation for school success is facilitated by the presence of a stable and enriched learning environment

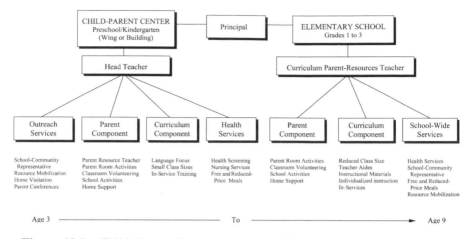

Figure 10.1   Child–Parent Center program model

during the entire early-childhood period (ages three to nine) and when parents are active participants in their children's education.

Five program features are emphasized: early intervention, parent involvement, a structured language/basic skills learning approach, health and social services, and program continuity between the preschool and early school-age years. The program theory is that children's readiness for school entry and beyond can be enriched through systematic language-learning activities and opportunities for family support experiences through direct parent involvement in the centers. Classroom teachers in preschool and kindergarten used a mix of teacher-directed and child-initiated instructional approaches, which varied across centers (Graue, Clements, Reynolds, & Niles, 2004). Class sizes in preschool were limited to 17 children taught by two staff (teacher and an aide). In kindergarten through third grades, the ratios were 25 to 2. The typical class sizes in first to third grade in Chicago is 35 to 40 with no aide.

Sullivan (1971) described the philosophy of the Child–Parent Centers as strengthening the family-school relationship: "In a success-oriented environment in which young children can see themselves as important, they are 'turned on' for learning. Attitudes toward themselves and others, interest in learning, increased activity, conversation, and enthusiasm are all evidences of the change. Parents are increasingly aware of the role of the home in preparing children for school and have renewed hope that education will develop the full potential of their children" (p. 70).

The unique feature of the parent program is the parent-resource room, which is physically located in the center adjacent to the classrooms. The full-time parent-resource teacher organizes the parent room in order to implement parent educational activities, initiate interactions among parents, and foster parent–child interactions. With funds for materials, supplies, and speakers, areas of training include consumer education, nutrition, personal development, health and safety, and homemaking arts. Parents may also attend GED classes at the centers. Staff also assess the service needs of parents and children and provide referrals to health, mental health, vocational, and social services.

PROGRAM PARTICIPATION ENHANCES CHILDREN'S WELL-BEING

We summarize many project findings on program group differences for five domains of child-development and family outcomes (for these and other results, see Reynolds, 2000; Reynolds, Temple, Robertson, & Mann, 2001; Reynolds et al., 2002). All estimated program effects are adjusted for differences in gender and racial/ethnic composition, family risk status, child abuse/neglect history, program sites, and earlier/later program participation (preschool or school-age). Group differences for extended intervention were estimated separately and added kindergarten reading achievement as a covariate in place of earlier/later intervention.

Overall, preschool participation at ages 3 or 4 is associated with better educational and social outcomes spanning ages 5 to 21, up to 18 years after the end of intervention. School-age participation in first to third grades and extended program participation in preschool and school-age programs for four to six years also were associated with child-development and family outcomes over time. These findings are described briefly by outcome domain.

School Readiness and Achievement

Preschool. Relative to the comparison group, CPC preschool participants began kindergarten at significantly higher levels of school readiness as assessed by the ITBS cognitive composite (mean standard scores of 49.6 vs. 43.3, respectively). This difference translates to an effect size of .61 standard deviations. Alternatively, nearly twice as many program participants (46.7%) as the comparison group (25.1%) scored at or above national norms on the cognitive composite.

The performance advantage of the preschool group in reading achievement and math achievement in kindergarten persisted to age 15 (ninth grade) when annual testing in reading and math ceased (math achievement findings are not shown in Table 10.2). As expected, the program had the largest impact immediately (see also Reynolds, 2000).

School-Age and Extended Intervention. Both intervention components were associated with greater reading and math achievement. Advantages for school-age intervention continued to the end of third grade, whereas those of extended intervention persisted to age 15 (see Table 10.2). This pattern of findings indicates that school-age intervention in conjunction with preschool intervention provides the most optimal effects. Nevertheless, both intervention groups had significantly higher passing rates on a test of consumer skills, which was required for high school graduation in Chicago.

Remedial Education

Preschool. Participation also was associated with significantly lower rates of grade retention and special education placement. The 23 percent rate of grade retention for the preschool group was 40 percent lower than the 38.4 percent rate for the comparison group. Preschool participants had a 41 percent lower rate of special education over ages 6 to 18 (14.4% vs. 24.6%). Program participants spent fewer years in special education as well.

School-Age and Extended Intervention. School-age intervention alone and extended intervention into the primary grades also were linked to significantly lower rates of remedial education. Percentage reductions over the comparison groups were, respectively, 28 percent and 35 percent. These findings are consistent with previous literature (Barnett, 1995; Reynolds, 2000).

Family Support Behavior

Preschool. Program participation led to improved parenting practices. Preschool participants had higher ratings of parent involvement in school measured by the number of positive ratings by teachers and parents over ages 8 to 12 (range = 0 to 5). For example, 30.9 percent of program participants had three or more positive ratings of involvement versus 21 percent for the comparison group.

CPC preschool participation was associated with significantly lower rates of substantiated reports of child maltreatment by age 17 through both court petitions (5.0% vs. 10.5%, a 52% reduction) and substantiated DCFS reports (6.9% vs. 14.2%, a 52% reduction). Two years of preschool yielded a greater reduction in child maltreatment than did one year.

School-Age and Extended Intervention. School-age participation was associated with only increased levels of parent involvement in school between ages 8 and 12 (teacher and parent reports). Extended intervention was linked to higher levels of parent involvement in school and to

Table 10.2
Sample Sizes and Characteristics for Program and Comparison Groups in the Chicago Longitudinal Study

Domain and Measure	N	Preschool Group	Comparison Group	Diff.	School-Age Group	Comparison Group	Diff.
School Achievement							
Age 5 ITBS cognitive development	1,102	49.6	43.3	6.3***	—	—	
Age 6 ITBS word analysis	1,531	66.0	59.8	6.2***	—	—	
Age 9 ITBS reading achievement	1,285	98.2	93.5	4.7***	98.4	93.4	5.0***
Age 14 ITBS reading achievement	1,158	147.1	141.6	5.5***	145.0	143.4	1.6*
Age 14/15 consumer skills, % passing	1,158	62.5	52.3	10.2***	61.0	53.8	7.2***
Family Support for Education							
Number of positive ratings (0–5) of parent involvement in school by parents/teachers, ages 8–12	1,164	1.8	1.6	0.2**	1.8	1.6	0.2***
School Remedial Services							
Grade retention by age 15, %	1,281	23.0	38.4	-15.4***	23.8	34.3	-10.5***
Special education by age 18, %	1,281	14.4	24.6	-10.2***	15.4	21.3	-5.9**
Number of years of special education from ages 6 to 18	1,281	0.7	1.4	-0.70*	0.8	1.2	-0.4*
Child Maltreatment (Substantiated)							
Abuse/neglect, ages 4-17, court reports, %	1,408	5.0	10.3	-5.3***	6.3	7.7	-1.4
Juvenile Arrest by Age 18							
Petition to juvenile court, %	1,404	16.9	25.1	-8.2***	19.8	19.8	0.0
Petition to juvenile court for violent offense, %	1,404	9.0	15.3	-6.3***	10.8	11.8	-1.0
Number of petitions to juvenile court	1,404	0.5	0.8	-0.33*	0.6	0.6	.00
Educational Attainment by Age 21							
High school completion, March 2001	1,314	61.9	51.4	10.5***	58.3	58.3	0.0
Highest grade completed, March 2001	1,293	11.2	10.9	0.36**	11.1	11.13	0.0

(Continued)

Table 10.2
Sample Sizes and Characteristics for Program and Comparison Groups in the Chicago Longitudinal Study (Continued)

Domain and Measure	Extended Intervention Group(n = 491)	Nonextended Intervention Group(n = 480)	Diff.
School Achievement			
Age 9 ITBS reading achievement	98.4	93.4	5.0***
Age 14 ITBS reading achievement	146.7	143.7	4.0**
Age 14/15 consumer skills, % passing	63.7	57.7	6.0**
Family Support for Education			
Number of positive ratings (0–5) of parent involvement in school by parents/teachers, ages 8–12	2.2	1.6	0.6***
School Remedial Services			
Grade retention by age 15, %	21.9	32.3	–10.4***
Special education by age 18, %	13.5	20.7	–7.2***
Number of years of special education from ages 6 to 18	0.6	1.2	–0.7*
Child Maltreatment (Substantiated)			
Abuse/neglect, age 6–17, court reports, %	4.4	7.7	–3.3**
Juvenile Arrests by Age 18			
Petitions to juvenile court, %	19.2	20.1	–0.9
Petition to juvenile court for violent offense, %	9.3	12.4	–3.1*
Number of arrests	0.5	0.6	–0.1
Educational Attainment by Age 21			
High school completion, March 2001	59.4	57.2	2.2
Highest grade completed, March 2001	11.1	11.0	0.1

Note: Coefficients for dichotomous and count data are from probit and negative binomial regression analysis transformed to marginal effects, and they are adjusted for sex of child, race/ethnicity, the risk index, and program sites.

* p < .10
*** p < .05
*** p < .01

significantly lower rates of substantiated child maltreatment by age 17 (4.4% vs. 7.7%, a 43% reduction). This is the first school-based program demonstrating effectiveness in preventing child maltreatment.

Juvenile Delinquency

Preschool. Preschool participants had a significantly lower rate of petitions to the juvenile court by age 18 than their comparison cohort (16.9% vs. 25.1%, a 33% reduction). They also had a significantly lower rate of multiple arrests (9.5% vs. 12.8%, a 26% reduction), arrests for violent offenses (9.0% vs. 15.3%, a 41% reduction), as well as fewer arrests. This is the first study of a large-scale program to show links to delinquency prevention (Reynolds et al., 2001).

School-Age and Extended Intervention. Neither component of the CPC program was consistently associated with lower rates of juvenile arrest. However, participation in extended intervention was linked to a lower rate of official juvenile arrest for violent offenses (9.3% vs. 12.4%, a 25% reduction, p = .099).

Educational Attainment

Preschool. Preschool participation also was linked to greater educational attainment by age 21. CPC participants had a 20 percent higher rate of high school completion (graduation or GED; 61.9% vs. 51.4%). They also had a higher mean number of years of completed education (11.2 years vs. 10.9 years). Only model programs have shown these impacts previously (Consortium for Longitudinal Studies, 1983; Schweinhart, Barnes, & Weikart, 1993).

School-Age and Extended Intervention. Neither component was associated with a higher rate of high school completion and more years of completed schooling at age 21. Extended intervention was linked to a higher rate of school completion up to age 20, however (Reynolds et al., 2001). Note that these findings and other earlier findings assess the impact of extended intervention above and beyond the impact of fewer years of intervention as well as kindergarten achievement. Extended program participants have significantly higher levels of educational attainment than children with no CPC intervention and without controlling for kindergarten achievement, which introduces a conservative bias.

BENEFITS OF PROGRAM PARTICIPATION EXCEED COSTS

Cost-benefit analysis is ready-made for translating evaluation findings into language relevant to the policy-making process. It assesses both effectiveness and efficiency, the latter indicating the largest return at the lowest cost. At a minimum, the economic benefit should equal the amount invested in the program—a return of at least one dollar per dollar invested. The use of cost-benefit analysis in prioritizing funding for early education is now prominent.

Chicago study investigators conducted the first benefit-cost analysis of a large-scale public early-childhood program. Based on the previous findings and following standard procedures of cost-benefit analysis, the present value of program benefits was estimated in 2004 dollars for six main categories: (1) reductions in expenditures for remedial education, (2) reductions in criminal justice system expenditures for both juvenile and adult arrest and treatment, (3) reductions in child welfare system expenditures, (4) averted tangible expenditures to crime victims and to victims of child maltreatment, (5) averted tangible expenditures to victims of child maltreatment, and (6) increases in projected earnings of program participants and tax revenues as a result of higher levels of educational attainment (for details, see Reynolds et al., 2002).

At a cost of $7,755 per child for one-and-a-half years of half-day preschool, the program generated a return to society by age 21 of $55,348 per child (2004 dollars). About half of the benefits were to the general public (taxpayers and crime victims) and half to program participants.[1] The largest benefit was program participants' increased earnings capacity projected from higher educational attainment. The largest categories of public benefits, which excluded individual earnings, were increased taxes on earnings projected from educational attainment (28%) and savings to the criminal justice system in adolescence and adulthood due to lower rates of arrest (28%). Reductions in expenditures for school remedial services (18%) and savings on tangible costs to crime victims (24%) also provided significant benefits to the public.

The CPC school-age program, with an average cost per child of $3,339, had an estimated return of $5,730 per child. The largest benefit categories were savings associated with remedial education. At an average cost of $4,702 per child, the CPC extended intervention had an economic return of $28,708 per child. The largest benefit categories were savings in remedial education, savings in the criminal justice system and to crime victims, and increased economic well-being. Figure 10.2 shows the categorical breakdown of economic benefits and costs per program participant for preschool and for extended program participation.

Overall, each dollar invested in the CPC preschool program returned $7.14 to society at large in government savings on remedial education and justice system treatment and in increased economic well-being. The CPC school-age program and the CPC extended-intervention program

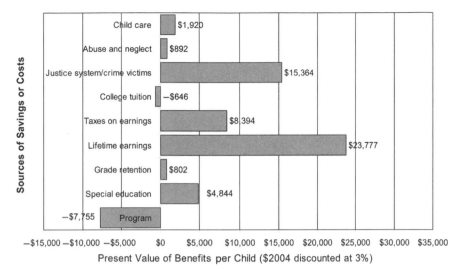

Figure 10.2a   Breakdown of benefits and costs for CPC preschool participa-

(preschool + school-age participation for four to six years) also had positive economic returns. The school-age program had a return of $1.66 per dollar invested, and the extended-intervention program had a return of $6.11 per dollar invested relative to less-extensive program participation. None of these estimates include intangible savings to crime victims for pain and suffering. Adding these savings yields economic returns per dollar invested of $10.15, $2.12, and $9.05, respectively for preschool, school-age, and extended program participation.

The CPC preschool findings are similar to those of other high-quality early-childhood interventions, including the Abecedarian Project, the High/Scope Perry Preschool Program, and Perinatal Early Infancy Project (Campbell & Ramey, 1995; Olds et al., 1997; Schweinhart et al., 1993) despite the significant differences between programs in their timing and duration, geography, social context, time period, and content. As prevention programs, the full economic benefits are achieved many years after the end of the program. This consistent pattern of effects from different programs strengthens the generalizability of findings to contemporary programs and contexts.

Because the Child–Parent Center study is the first cost-benefit analysis of a public preschool program, the findings increase the generalizability of results to publicly funded programs, including emerging universal access programs. Findings also indicate that school-based prevention programs during early childhood can lead to reduced child maltreatment and delinquency. These findings are of special significance given the paucity

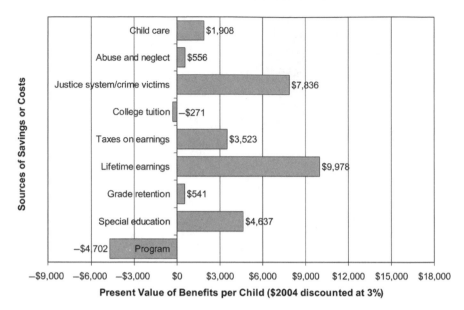

Figure 10.2b Breakdown of benefits and costs for CPC extended program participation

of evidence that treatment programs to prevent maltreatment and delinquency are effective and cost-effective (MacLeod & Nelson, 2000; Zigler, Taussig, & Black, 1992). The implication of the Chicago study findings is that early-education programs that provide comprehensive family services have the possibility of reducing the later risk of child abuse and neglect.

MULTIPLE SOURCES OF LONG-TERM PROGRAM BENEFITS

Which child, family, and school processes explain the long-term benefits of program participation? Although it is difficult to determine the precise sources of benefits, one approach is to investigate the extent to which the main effects of participation are mediated by intervening factors after the end of participation. Very few studies have investigated these sources systematically. Their identification can help direct additional intervention services to maintain or enhance the effects of early intervention. Five hypotheses were expected to account for the long-term effects of participation in intervention. These include the cognitive advantage, family support, social adjustment, motivational advantage, and school support hypotheses (see Reynolds, 2000; Reynolds, Ou, & Topitzes, 2004).

Figure 10.3 shows the five hypotheses and their corresponding indicators, as identified in the accumulated literature, that were predicted

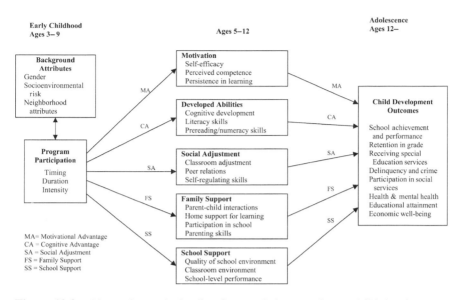

Figure 10.3   Alternative paths leading from early intervention to child-development outcomes

to explain the link between early intervention and competence outcomes. In the cognitive advantage hypothesis, for example, the long-term effects of intervention are due to the initial improvement in children's cognitive development, which leads to cumulative advantages over time. In the family support hypothesis, enduring intervention effects are due to the enhancement of family support behavior, such as parental involvement in children's learning and schooling. To identify the contributions of each hypothesis, indicators were entered together in a multi-equation structural equation model estimated in LISREL.

Results of a structural equation model based on the hypotheses in Figure 10.3 indicated the following results for the links between preschool participation, educational attainment, and juvenile arrest (see Reynolds et al., 2004). The contribution of the hypotheses is described as the percentage of the indirect effect of preschool attributed to the particular hypothesis. In other words, these findings indicate the extent to which the long-term effects of intervention are accounted for by the intervening factors.

For educational attainment, the family support hypothesis, measured by parent involvement ratings and incidence of child maltreatment, accounted for 26 percent of the indirect effect of preschool on high school completion. The school support hypothesis, measured by school mobility and attendance in magnet elementary schools, accounted for 30 percent of the indirect effect. The cognitive advantage hypothesis, measured by literacy scores in kindergarten, accounted for 32 percent of the indirect effect as the higher scores of preschool participants enhanced their later educational success. The motivational advantage hypothesis accounted for 8 percent. Altogether, the mediators accounted for 58 percent of the main effect of preschool participation on high school completion.

The pattern of contributions in explaining program effects for juvenile arrest was somewhat different and favored the school support hypothesis. The family support hypothesis accounted for 22 percent of the indirect effect of preschool on juvenile arrest. For example, program participation was directly associated with higher levels of parent involvement, and these higher levels of involvement were significantly linked to school completion. The school support hypothesis and cognitive advantage hypothesis accounted for, respectively, 50 percent and 19 percent of the total indirect effect. Enrollment in magnet schools, a measure of school quality, was the main contributor to the school support findings. This may be due to the greater presence of peers who are committed to prosocial skills. The motivational advantage hypothesis accounted for just 2 percent of the indirect effect. Altogether, the mediators accounted for 79 percent of the main effect of preschool participation on official juvenile arrest.

Overall, these findings indicate that these three hypotheses substantially accounted for the long-term effects of intervention for two major outcomes. Promoting educational enrichment and family support behavior in the early years of life and enhancing the quality of the postprogram school and community environment are likely to yield enduring effects of intervention. Notably, the motivational advantage and social adjustment hypotheses accounted for smaller effects, but they did contribute to model fit. Further analyses of these and other hypotheses are needed to confirm the pattern of contributions from the mediators.

CONCLUSION AND IMPLICATIONS

Findings from the Chicago Longitudinal Study and from other projects indicate that greater investments in high-quality programs that provide child education and intensive resources for parent involvement are needed. Because nearly one-half of all eligible children do not enroll in center-based early-care and education programs and the quality of services that many receive is not high, programs with demonstrated effectiveness like the Child–Parent Centers warrant expansion and provide models for the design of universal access programs.

Research on the CPC program and other early-childhood interventions suggests that effectiveness can be enhanced by greater attention to four program characteristics. Based in part on the findings of the study, greater investments have been made in early-childhood programs in Chicago and other cities.

First, a system of intervention is in place beginning at age three and continuing to the early school grades. This single administrative system promotes stability in children's learning environment that can provide smooth transitions from preschool to kindergarten and from kindergarten to the early grades. This is a so-called first-decade strategy for promoting children's learning (Reynolds et al., 2003). Today, most preschool programs are not integrated within public schools, and children usually change schools more than once by the early grades. In the movement to universal access to early education, schools could take a leadership role in partnership with community agencies. More generally, programs that provide coordinated, or wraparound, services may be more effective under a centralized leadership structure rather than under a case-management framework.

A second distinctive feature is that as a public school program, all teachers have bachelor's degrees and certification in early-childhood education. They are compensated well, and turnover is minimal. It is no coincidence that the Chicago program and other successful early interventions (Schweinhart et al., 1993) were run by staff with at least bachelor's degrees and certification in their specialties. In most early-care and Head Start programs, staff do not have this level of education, training, and compensation, and turnover is high. In contemporary education programs, greater commitment to preservice and ongoing professional training is needed.

Third, educational content should be responsive to all of children's learning needs, but special emphasis should be given to literacy and school readiness through a structured but diverse set of learning activities. From its inception, the CPC program has emphasized the development of literacy skills necessary for successful progress. They do this with a blend of instructional activities that include phonics training, field trips, and individualized learning activities (Reynolds, 2000; Sullivan, 1971). Extrapolating these findings to other educational and child welfare programs, programs are more likely to have enduring effects if they provide services that are intensive and are dedicated to the enhancement of specific behavior skills (Heckman, 2000).

Finally, as a child-development program, comprehensive family services provide many opportunities for positive learning experiences in school and at home. Because each center has a staffed parent-resource room and provides school-community outreach, parental involvement is more intensive than in other programs. Health services also are provided with referrals to community clinics and agencies for job training and other social services. Those with special needs or most at risk benefit from intensive and comprehensive services. Also, opportunities are needed for parents to enhance their own educational and personal development. Thus, the centers show that literacy education and comprehensive family services can be integrated successfully.

Compare the evidence from early-childhood interventions to that of other social programs that take up the largest share of government expenditures. Small class sizes are associated with increased school achievement, but impacts are not large or enduring. The benefits of remedial education such as tutoring and summer school are, at best, inconsistent and short-lived. The track record of child welfare treatment, delinquency, and dropout prevention programs is weak, and given their treatment focus, even the best have low cost-effectiveness (Heckman, 2000). Certainly, many of these programs have an important role to play, but preventive investments in early education have demonstrated the largest and most enduring benefits. They deserve a greater share of public investments. The percentage of the total expenditures spent on social programs that goes to prevention services is less than 1 percent (National Science and Technology Council, 1997).

Besides incorporating these features into Head Start and Title I programs, we offer four recommendations for improving the effectiveness of early-childhood education. The first is to increase the amount of Title I funds that go to preschools. In 2000, only 5 percent of federal Title I dollars provided to school districts went to preschool programs. Given established evidence on the long-term effects and economic returns of preschool programs, this percentage should be significantly higher. The second recommendation is to increase the number of Head Start programs administered by public schools. Only about one-third of grantees are schools. This strategy would improve coordination of services with public schools, which is a goal that has been expressed consistently by the U.S. secretaries of Education and Health and Human Services. Third, full-day programs should be widely available beginning at age three and continue through kindergarten. As program length increases, so does children's school performance. Programs that extend to the primary grades will help reinforce learning gains. Finally, greater investments in research are needed to evaluate new and established programs. The research and evaluation budgets of Head Start and Title I are each less than one-third of 1 percent of total expenditures. More evaluation research is required to know what works and what works better. Of the approximately \$550 billion to \$600 billion spent on K–16 education and social programs for children and youth each year, only one-third of 1 percent goes to research and development (National Science and Technology Council, 1997).

Until recently, the empirical evidence of the long-term effects and cost-effectiveness of public programs has been very limited. As described in this chapter, the Child–Parent Centers provide one model for improving children's well-being. As communities increase access to early education, public schools appear to be a location of choice for organizing educational, social, and family services. The major challenge for the future is how the recommendations and principles derived from the extensive knowledge base on early education can be best tailored to the needs of children and families. Unlike a decade ago, scientific support for the benefits of a wide variety of programs, both pilot and large-scale, is strong. The Child–Parent Centers are not perfect, but they illustrate that the principles of comprehensive services and early literacy within a school-based program can be integrated successfully in ways that strengthen effectiveness. One main lesson from the accumulated research on the project is that public schools are well positioned to take a leadership role in organizing systems of early care and education that is tailored to the needs of families and in which all children have the opportunity to participate.

NOTE

1. Reynolds, Temple, Robertson, & Mann (2002) reported economic benefits and costs in 1998 dollars. In the 2002 study, intangible crime victim savings were estimated but were not included in the main study findings. Adding them would yield, in 2004 dollars per child, \$78,732 total benefits to society for preschool, \$7,328 for school-age, and \$42,566 for extended intervention.

REFERENCES

Barnett, W. S. (1995). Long-term effects of early childhood programs on cognitive and school outcomes. *The Future of Children, 5*(3), 25–50.

Campbell, F. A., & Ramey, C. T. (1995). Cognitive and school outcomes for high risk African-American students at middle adolescence: Positive effects of early intervention. *American Educational Research Journal, 32,* 743–772.

Chicago Longitudinal Study. (1999). *Chicago Longitudinal Study: User's guide* (Vol. 6). Madison: Waisman Center, University of Wisconsin.

Consortium for Longitudinal Studies. (1983). *As the twig is bent ... lasting effects of preschool programs.* Hillsdale, NJ: Erlbaum.

Currie, J. (2001). Early childhood education programs. *Journal of Economic Perspectives, 15,* 213–238.

Graue, E., Clements, M.A., Reynolds, A.J., & Niles, M. (2004). More than teacher directed or child initiated: Preschool curriculum, parent involvement, and child outcomes in the Chicago Longitudinal Study. *Education Policy Analysis Archives, 12*(75). Retrieved September 15, 2005 from http://epaa.asu.edu/epaa/v12n72/v12n72.pdf.

Heckman, J. (2000). Policies to foster human capital. *Research in Economics, 54,* 3–56.

Karoly, L.A., Greenwood, P.W., Everingham, S.S., Houbé, J.M., Kilburn, R.C., Rydell, P., et al. (1998). *Investing in our children: What we know and don't know about the costs and benefits of early childhood interventions.* Santa Monica, CA: RAND.

MacLeod, J., & Nelson, G. (2000). Programs for the promotion of family wellness and the prevention of child maltreatment: A meta-analytic review. *Child Abuse & Neglect, 24,* 1127–1149.

National Science and Technology Council. (1997). *Investing in our future: A national research initiative for America's children for the 21st century.* Washington, DC: Executive Office of the President, Office of Science and Technology Policy, Committee on Fundamental Science, and the Committee on Health, Safety, and Food.

Olds, D.L., Eckenrode, J., Henderson, C.R., Kitzman, H., Powers, J., Cole, R., et al. (1997). Long-term effects of home visitation on maternal life course and child abuse and neglect. Fifteen-year follow-up of a randomized trial. *Journal of the American Medical Association, 278*(8), 637–643.

Reynolds, A. J. (2000). *Success in early intervention: The Chicago Child–Parent Centers.* Lincoln: University of Nebraska Press.

Reynolds, A.J., Ou, S., & Topitzes, J.W. (2004). Paths of effects of early intervention on educational attainment and juvenile arrest: A confirmatory analysis of the Chicago Child–Parent Center. *Child Development, 75,* 1299–1328.

Reynolds, A.J., & Temple, J.A. (2005). Priorities for a new century of early childhood programs. *Infants & Young Children, 18,* 104–118.

Reynolds, A.J., Temple, J.A., Robertson, D.L., & Mann, E.A. (2001). Long-term effects of an early childhood intervention on educational achievement and juvenile arrest: A 15-year follow-up of low-income children in public schools. *Journal of the American Medical Association, 285*(18), 2339–2346.

Reynolds, A.J., Temple, J.A., Robertson, D.L., & Mann, E.A. (2002). Age 21 cost-benefit analysis of the Title I Chicago Child–Parent Centers. *Educational Evaluation and Policy Analysis, 24,* 267–303.

Reynolds, A.J., Wang, M.C., & Walberg, H.J. (Eds.). (2003). *Early childhood programs for a new century.* Washington, DC: CWLA Press.

Schweinhart, L. J., Barnes, H. V., & Weikart, D. P. (1993). *Significant benefits: The High-Scope Perry Preschool Study through Age 27.* Ypsilanti, MI: High/Scope Press.

Sullivan, L. M. (1971). *Let us not underestimate the children.* Glenview, IL: Scott, Forsman.

Zigler, E., Taussig, C., & Black, K. (1992). Early childhood intervention: A promising preventive for juvenile delinquency. *American Psychologist, 47,* 997–1006.

PREVENTION AND PROMOTION AT PRESCHOOL AGE AND BEYOND

Chapter 11

LOW-INCOME CHILDREN IN HEAD START AND BEYOND: FINDINGS FROM FACES

Nicholas Zill and Gary Resnick

INTRODUCTION

In this chapter we describe the national Head Start program and its goals of providing high-quality preschool education to improve disadvantaged children's emergent literacy. We then describe the Family and Child Experiences Survey (FACES) and present a conceptual framework that guides the FACES research effort. The conceptual framework then leads into the research questions that are the focus of data presented in this chapter.

The FACES research project was sponsored by the ACYF, U.S. Department of Health and Human Services (DHHS) under contract no. HHHS-105-96-1912, Head Start Quality Research Consortium's Performance Measurement Center.

The authors are grateful to the Child Outcomes Research and Evaluation, Office of Planning, Research and Evaluation, ACYF, U.S. Department of Health and Human Services, Washington, DC, for their continuing support of this project.

The authors also acknowledge key members of the FACES project team, including Peggy Hunker, Kwang Kim, and Alberto Sorongon, Westat; Ruth Hubbell-McKey (co-project director), Shefali Pai-Samant, and Cheryl Clark, Xtria; and Robert O'Brien and Mary Ann D'Elio, The CDM Group. As well, the authors wish to thank the statistical programming assistance provided by members of Westat's programming group, including John Brown (manager), Ban Cheah, and Kristen Madden.

Some results discussed in this chapter were previously presented at the Society for Research in Child Development Biennial Meeting in Atlanta, Georgia, April 7–10, 2005.

Correspondence about this chapter should be addressed to: Gary Resnick, Child and Family Studies, Westat, 1550 Research Blvd., Rockville, MD 20850.

HEAD START AND EMERGENT LITERACY

Program Design and Development

Head Start was founded on the premise that children from low-income families did not get the same intellectual stimulation and encouragement of learning before starting school that more privileged children received. Furthermore, low-income parents had fewer resources to obtain high-quality child care and preschool services for their children. When it began in 1965, the early-education and child care landscape was very different than it is today. Publicly funded preschool and kindergarten programs were not widely available, nor were private programs, at least not at prices that low-income families could afford.

Head Start was designed as a federal program to fund local agencies to run primarily center-based comprehensive child development programs. Local agencies had great latitude to tailor the services to the needs of the communities they served, while meeting the overall mandate to improve learning experiences for low-income children, and provide parent educational services, social services, and preventive health services that poor families often could not afford for their offspring, such as nutritious meals, health checkups, vaccinations, and dental care. Marian Wright Edelman once noted that Head Start is not one program but rather a family of programs (Edelman, 1981). Head Start has spawned many spin-off demonstrations, including the Parent–Child Centers, the Child and Family Resource Program, the Home Start demonstration, the National Transition Study, and Early Head Start, which have expanded the services provided beyond its original mandate. These expansions indicate an important strength of Head Start: its ability to adapt to the changing goals and needs of families living in poverty.

Head Start was designed originally from policy proposals based on scientific advances, but it was not based on an extensive body of research. A small set of intervention studies focused on educational enrichment for mentally retarded children served as the basis for the program design. Outcomes focused on intellectual performance as the target shifted from mental retardation to *social* disadvantage. There was always concern about variations in the quality of local Head Start programs and the possible linkage of those variations to child and family outcomes. By the mid-1980s the program goals evolved to focus on family outcomes, providing multiple services for children and families and including success in children's social-emotional development as a program objective in addition to cognitive and literacy outcomes (Valentine & Zigler, 1983).

There has been consistent support for several of the premises underlying the Head Start program. Evidence that low-income families provide less intellectual stimulation to their young children than higher-income families has been found in large-scale population studies in the United States (Bradley et al, 1989; Nord, Lennon, Liu, & Chandler, 1999; Zill, Collins, West, & Hausken, 1995; Zill, Moore, Smith, Stief, & Coiro, 1995) and in smaller-scale, in-home observational studies (Beals, 1993; Dickinson & Tabors, 2001; Hart & Risley, 1995). Longitudinal studies showed that high-quality, intensive early-childhood education programs could effectively improve children's cognitive, language, and social outcomes. Influential studies by the Consortium for Longitudinal Studies, Ira Gordon's Parent Education Program, Francis Palmer's Harlem Training Project, and the High/Scope Perry Preschool Project demonstrated the positive effects of early-childhood education for children living in poverty (Consortium for Longitudinal Studies, 1983; Lazar, Darlington, Murray, Royce, & Snipper, 1982).

Head Start became one of the most widely recognized and popular federal programs, providing services in 2003 to approximately 900,000 children and their families at an annual cost of nearly $6 billion. Congress reauthorized the program in 1998 and in the following year appropriated an additional $1 billion to provide services to still more children and improve the quality of those services. There has long been a role for Head Start as a national laboratory for studying best practices in early-childhood education and family-support services in low-income communities. Earlier efforts such as the National Head Start Transition Study and the more recent Early Head Start Research Study, the Quality Research Centers Consortium, and the National Head Start Impact Study (HSIS) have improved the reputation of Head Start as a source of evidence-based educational programming for families in poverty.

While expanding its clientele, Head Start has undergone a philosophical shift from emphasizing children's cognitive and language development to bolstering children's social skills. Promotion of heavily didactic activities, such as teaching children letters and numbers, has given way to more play-oriented and discovery-learning activities. Recently, some have criticized Head Start for going too far in socialization, whole language, and discovery-learning directions to the neglect of providing grounding in print awareness, phonemic sensitivity, or word-decoding skills.

In the 1998 reauthorization legislation, Congress mandated a set of preliteracy skills that children should accomplish by the end of their participation in Head Start. These skills were modeled on the Developmental Accomplishments of Literacy Acquisition for three- to four-year-olds from the report of the National Academy of Sciences Committee on the Prevention of Reading Difficulties in Young Children (Snow, Burns, & Griffin, 1998, Table 2.1, p. 61), including the ability to identify 10 letters of the alphabet. This chapter summarizes evidence from a national Head Start sample of the extent to which the programs are meeting those mandated goals, both in preschool and in kindergarten.

Evaluation of Effectiveness

Despite the prominence and growth of the program, there has been little large-scale research on Head Start's quality or outcomes for children and families, although numerous smaller-scale studies examined its efficacy. Early studies such as the well-known Westinghouse study did not take into account the differing levels of quality among local sites, and concerns have long been raised about local program quality. In 1985, the Head Start Evaluation, Synthesis and Utilization Project (McKey, Condelli, Ganson, McConkey, & Plantz, 1985), concluded from meta-analyses of more than 75 research studies that Head Start produced immediate, meaningful gains in all areas of cognitive development as well as in social behavior, achievement motivation, and health status. However, even early evaluations reported that initial cognitive and socioemotional gains of Head Start children appeared to fade over time (Datta, 1986). The so-called fade-out effect has been attributed to lack of supportive school experiences and home environments when children leave Head Start (Lee, Brooks-Gunn, Schnur, & Liaw, 1991).

Some large-scale attempts to assess the efficacy of Head Start have been challenged on methodological grounds. The ETS Head Start study by the Educational Testing Service eliminated from testing children who had been retained in grade or placed in special education classes, producing biases against finding significant differences between control and program groups, and it has been argued that the fade-out effect may be an artifact of selective attrition as cohorts age over time (Barnett, 1998). Currie and Thomas (1995, 1999) used data from the National Longitudinal Survey of Youth (NLSY) to compare the outcomes of Head Start children to those of siblings served at other preschools or not at all. They reported large significant gains in receptive vocabulary for both white and African American children attending Head Start over their siblings as well as gains for Hispanic children, but the gains of African American children faded by age eight. However, serious methodological issues cast doubt on the validity of the findings (Barnett & Camilli, 1997). Barnett and Camilli concluded that the NLSY data set had limited utility for estimating Head Start effects.

Largely in response to questions about the efficacy of Head Start, and to collect data for program improvement, the Head Start Family and Child Experiences Survey (FACES) was established in 1996. FACES is a major activity within the Head Start Performance Measurement Center

(HSPMC), which helps monitor the quality and effectiveness of Head Start and guides agency efforts to improve program performance. The study collects data from representative samples of Head Start parents, observations of Head Start classrooms and home-based programs in operation, and assessments of intellectual, social, and emotional development of representative samples of the children served. Data collection is done on a recurring basis in order to monitor how program performance changes over time.

There are limitations in the design and mandate of FACES. FACES employs tests with national norms but does not include nonpoor control groups or a comparison group of children from low-income families who do not attend Head Start. Programs are selected for study using probability sampling methods; hence, FACES is not a study of so-called best practices. Neither are programs selected on the basis of curriculum or level of performance. The purpose of FACES is to provide longitudinal findings and secular trend data on the program performance of Head Start.

The ultimate goal of Head Start is to promote the school readiness of children (Administration on Children, Youth and Families [ACYF], 1997). Emergent literacy skills usually acquired during the preschool years have shown to be critical stepping-stones for reading and language achievement in elementary school (Snow, Barnes, Chandler, Goodman, & Hemphill, 1991). FACES measures school readiness using a whole-child perspective (Goal One Technical Planning Group, 1991, 1993) that defines school readiness in five developmental domains: physical well-being and motor development, social and emotional development, approaches to learning, language usage and emerging literacy, and cognition and general knowledge. The battery of FACES measures covers all of these domains and recognizes their interrelatedness.

Progress in children's cognitive, language, and social development is essential for determining the efficacy of preschool educational programs like Head Start and for making program improvements. Consistent findings in the research literature show that the contribution of classroom quality to raising children's achievement is significant but relatively modest (Peisner-Feinberg & Burchinal, 1997). High quality in community child care settings has been related to better child outcomes in the short term, after controlling for child and family background factors (Bryant, Burchinal, Lau, & Sparling, 1994; National Institute of Child Health and Human Development [NICHD] Early Child Care Research Network [ECCRN], 2000; Phillips, McCartney, & Scarr, 1987; Whitebook, Howes, & Phillips, 1989). There are notable exceptions for which quality was not related to children's developmental outcomes (e.g., Kontos & Fiene, 1987), but this finding could be attributed to small classroom samples, a relatively restricted range of quality across study centers, or both (Peisner-Feinberg et al., 2001). Recently, promising evidence shows that, despite modest immediate effects for quality, long-term effects may extend into the second grade, and these effects are strongest for children living in families most at risk. Several recent national studies, including the NICHD Study of Early Child Care (Vendell, Shumow, & Posner, 2005), the six-state study of early-childhood education by the National Center for Education, Development, and Learning (Burchinal & Cryer, 2003), and the British national longitudinal study (Sammons, Elliot, Melhish, Siraj-Blatchford, & Taggart, 2004), support earlier findings that quality predicts children's emergent literacy skills beyond kindergarten and first grade but that the relationships are modest at best. Hence, the premium that is placed on monitoring the compliance of Head Start centers in meeting the program standards for quality.

Factors "beyond the classroom door" may have potentially powerful influences on children's experiences of quality child care, such as the availability of additional resources and the broader context within which these programs are situated (Blau, 1997; Hofferth & Chaplin, 1998). Program management styles, resources, and the demographics of the community may influence decisions about quality made by center directors and, indirectly, by teachers in individual classrooms.

This chapter analyzes changes in children's emergent literacy skills during their participation in Head Start and into kindergarten but also examines factors at the program, center, and classroom levels that may enhance or constrain children's acquisition of emergent literacy and numeracy skills.

CONCEPTUAL FRAMEWORK OF FACES

The conceptual model that underlies the FACES battery assumes that a multitude of influences shape children's emergent literacy and cognitive development, including the children's Head Start experiences in moderating or compensating for deficiencies in their home environments. Emergent literacy is defined as the skills, knowledge, and attitudes that are considered to be developmental precursors to reading and writing and, more broadly, school achievement (Whitehurst & Lonigan, 1998).

Both emergent literacy and school readiness are hypothesized to depend on child care and preschool education, including Head Start, as well as on family backgrounds and home environments. A center-based learning environment such as Head Start should benefit the development of all children but especially those from disadvantaged family environments

(NICHD ECCRN, 2000). Parent involvement in their children's educational experiences may also be an important factor and one that programs can foster. The nature and quality of a Head Start learning environment depends on the training and experience of teachers in the program; the resources available to them in terms of facilities, materials, and teaching assistants as well as the educational philosophy to which the program adheres; and the kind of curriculum centers and teachers are encouraged to follow. Children are expected to do better in programs that employ well-designed curricula that are comprehensive and integrated in their educational activities and assessment methods. Adequate training for the teachers and support for the curriculum are especially important. It also stands to reason that children will progress most in those areas of development that are featured most prominently in the basic philosophy and curriculum of choice at the center.

Research Questions

Several questions about how Head Start preschool programs function to enhance developmental growth have guided our research:

- What is the typical process and structural quality of Head Start classrooms as early learning environments?
- How much variation in quality is there across different programs and classes and between classes within the same programs?
- How is classroom quality related to program and teacher characteristics?
- What skill levels do Head Start children have when they enter and leave the program during the same school year?
- How large are the gains children make while in Head Start?
- What are the skill levels of Head Start graduates in the initial year of elementary school?
- How much variation is there in children's skill levels and gains across Head Start programs and classes and between classes within the same programs?
- Are variations in skill levels and gains related to variations in program quality?

In this chapter we summarize findings based on children, classrooms, and programs involved in the FACES 2000 and FACES 2003 cohorts that were assessed in English in both the fall and spring of the Head Start year and in the spring of their kindergarten year. Information about the skills and knowledge of children whose knowledge of English was insufficient for testing in English in the fall (and thus were initially assessed in Spanish) is available in other FACES reports (e.g., ACYF, 2003). This summary is drawn from a variety of reports and presentations that provide greater detail about the findings. Our primary purpose here is to summarize what we know from FACES about the National Head Start program.

Methods

In this section we describe the sample, measures, and analytic plan of FACES generally, emphasizing those measures and analyses designed to answer the research questions posed previously. Readers are encouraged to find more detailed descriptions of the sample, measures, procedures, and analytic methods in the *FACES 2000 Technical Report* (ACYF, in press) as well as in the *Fourth Progress Report* (ACYF, 2003) and the *Fifth Progress Report* for the FACES 2003 cohort (forthcoming).

Study Sample. The first cohort of FACES was examined in fall 1997, following a spring 1997 national field test. The fall 1997 cohort consisted of a nationally representative sample of 3,200 children and their families, measured in fall 1997 and spring 1998 of the children's Head Start year and upon entry into kindergarten, in spring 1999 and spring 2000, and into first grade, in spring 2001 for some children.[1] In order to conduct longitudinal, ongoing accountability measurements for program improvement, new national cohorts were examined in 2000 and 2003. In fall 2000, we examined a second national cohort, called FACES 2000, that consisted of 2,800 children and their families in 43 different Head Start programs across the nation.[2] A third national cohort, FACES 2003, was examined in fall 2003, with a nationally representative sample of approximately 2,800 three- and four-year-old children and their families from approximately 70 different Head Start programs. This chapter focuses on findings from the second and third FACES cohorts, FACES 2000 and 2003.

The sample plans for the second and third cohorts were identical, with the exception that in the third cohort (FACES 2003) more programs were selected. The Head Start children for each cohort were selected in two stages, with the first stage sampling units comprising Head Start programs listed in the Program Information Record (PIR) and the second stage units comprising classes within sampled programs. In each sampled classroom, all eligible children entering their first year of Head Start were taken into the sample. Additionally, the FACES 2003 cohort was selected to minimize the overlap with the programs sampled in the prior FACES cohorts, and as a result, the 68 programs sampled for the third FACES cohort did not overlap with the previous program samples. In FACES 2000, there were 43 programs, 286 classrooms, and 2,790 first-year children and their families. In FACES 2003, there were 63 programs, 175 centers, and a total of 2,816 first-year children and their families in the final sample.

Measures. FACES was designed to assess children's cognitive and socioemotional development in a direct, one-on-one test battery that emphasized cognitive, language, and emergent literacy skills. To measure children's socioemotional development, FACES relies on developmental reports and behavior ratings from teachers, parents, and test administrators. FACES also obtains multiple measures about classroom quality and program operations, including interviews with center directors, education coordinators, and teachers; observations of facilities, contents and activities in classrooms; and an extensive interview with parents at the beginning and end of the year concerning their activities with children, sociodemographic information, and satisfaction with Head Start.

Many measures used in the second and third cohorts were identical. Complete descriptions of all the FACES 2000 measures can be found in the *Fourth Progress Report* (ACYF, 2003) and in Zill and Resnick (2005). Descriptions of all FACES 2003 measures are available in the *Fifth Progress Report* (ACYF, in press).

CHILD ASSESSMENT BATTERY, FACES 2000, AND FACES 2003

The entire child assessment battery can be found in prior FACES reports (ACYF, 2003) and at the following Web site: http://www.acf.hhs.gov/programs/opre/hs/faces/instruments/child_instru97/instru97_index.html.

Zill and Resnick (2005) discuss the rationale for selecting all measures in the battery.

The battery consists of tasks assessing both so-called outside-in and inside-out emergent literacy skills (Whitehurst & Lonigan, 1998). Briefly, *outside-in* skills refer to children's general knowledge of the outside world and oral language skills, including knowledge of vocabulary, oral grammar, and narrative or story conventions. *Inside-out* skills refer to the ability to decode written text into spoken sounds, words, and phrases using knowledge of phonics, punctuation, spelling, and conventions of English print. Both kinds of emergent literacy skills at preschool and kindergarten age appear to strongly predict reading achievement in middle and late elementary school (Dickinson & Tabors, 2001; Snow, Tabors, Nicholson, & Kurland, 1991; Snow, Tabors, Nicholson, & Kurland, 1995).

The FACES measures include norm-referenced and criterion-referenced tests, both of which predict later school achievement, especially reading proficiency and oral language skills (Horn & Packard, 1985; Pianta & McCoy, 1997; Snow et al., 1991; Snow, Tabors, Nicholson, Kurland,

1995). The norm-referenced measures are based on a nationally representative sample of U.S. children of the same age and from all family
income groups. The criterion-referenced measures do not have national
norms but cover areas often included in assessing school readiness and
academic progress. Tasks in the FACES battery can be plotted by skill
area (inside-out/outside-in/numeracy) and test type (norm- vs. criterion-
referenced; see Table 11.1).

Continuity and Change in Child Assessments across Two Cohorts

Table 11.1 provides comparisons of the FACES 2000 and FACES
2003 cohorts. Modifications in the battery for FACES 2003 are detailed
in the *Fifth Progress Report* (ACYF, in press). We will discuss here the
key changes from the 2000 to the 2003 assessments. In FACES 2000,
Spanish-speaking children were assessed in Spanish unless their teachers
reported they had sufficient command of English to be assessed in that
language. By spring 2001, language-minority children in the FACES 2000
sample were assessed in English. Results of Spanish-only and bilingual
child assessments for FACES 2000 are described in the *Fourth Progress
Report* (ACYF, 2001a, 2003). In FACES 2003, all children were administered the Comprehension of Spoken English task to screen for English
language ability. Children scoring above a certain threshold on the task
were given the English assessment in fall 2003 as well as two Spanish-
only tests, the TVIP and the Spanish Letter-Word Identification test from
the Woodcock-Munoz Batteria.

Fall 2003 assessments used a shortened 48-item adaptation of the
Peabody Picture Vocabulary Test-III (PPVT-III), developed through Item-
Response Theory (IRT) analyses of an extensive database collected on
national samples of Head Start children in the previous cohorts of FACES.
A shortened version of the Spanish-language test, Test de Vocabulario en
Imagenes Peabody (TVIP), was developed for testing FACES 2003 chil-
dren whose primary language was Spanish.

FACES 2003 employed the Woodcock-Johnson Psychoeducational
Battery, third edition (WJ-III), a revision of the FACES 2000 test battery.
With some modifications of the original items, the same three subscales
are available in the third edition: Letter-Word Identification, Spelling
(originally termed *Dictation*), and Applied Problems. To allow for continued comparisons with previous FACES cohorts, the two editions (third
edition and revised edition) were calibrated by using IRT analytic methods for developing equivalencies between the subset of items common to
the two versions. The third edition Spanish version was not available for

Table 11.1
Summary of FACES Child Assessment Battery Subtasks by Skill Area and Test Type

	Type of Test			
	Norm-Referenced		*Criterion-Referenced*	
Skill Area	*FACES 2000*	*FACES 2003*	*FACES 2000*	*FACES 2003*
Outside-In Emergent Literacy Skills	Peabody Picture Vocabulary Test, 3rd ed. (PPVT-III)	PPVT-III Adaptive Version	• Story and Print Concepts Task "Where's My Teddy?" • Social Awareness • Color Names section of the Color Names and One-to-One Counting task	• Story and Print Concepts Task "Little Bear" • Social Awareness • Color Names section of the Color Names task
Inside-Out Emergent Literacy Skills	Letter-Word Identification and Dictation Subtasks of the Woodcock-Johnson Psycho-Educational Battery-Revised (WJ-R)	Letter-Word Identification and Dictation Subtasks of the Woodcock-Johnson Psycho-Educational Battery-Third Edition (WJ-III)	McCarthy Draw-a-Design from the McCarthy Scales of Children's Abilities (McCarthy, 1972)	• McCarthy Draw-a-Design from the McCarthy Scales of Children's Abilities (McCarthy, 1972) • Elision subtest of the Preschool Comprehensive Test of Phonological Processing (Pre-CTOPP)
Emergent Numeracy Skills	Applied Problems subtask of the Woodcock-Johnson Psycho-Educational Battery-Revised (WJ-R)	Applied Problems subtask of the Woodcock-Johnson Psycho-Educational Battery-Third Edition (WJ-III)	Counting section of the Color Names and One-to-One Counting task (FACES)	• Counting Blocks task

assessing Spanish-speaking children, so the Spanish version of the revised edition (WJ-R) was used.

In FACES 2003, a new measure of phonemic awareness was employed, the Elision subtest of the Preschool Comprehensive Test of Phonological Processing (Pre-CTOPP), developed by Lonigan and associates; it is also used in the National Head Start Impact Study (NHSIS). Finally, the revised FACES 2003 Story and Print Concepts task used a new storybook and questions tapping story comprehension that were revised to fit the content of the new story book. The Spanish battery used a Spanish version of the text: Osito.

Research staff trained and periodically monitored all child assessors to ensure the tests were administered in a standardized method, and assessors did not engage in coaching or give nonneutral praise. The direct child assessment usually required 30 to 40 minutes per child.

Measures of Children's Social-Emotional Skills

Measures of children's social-emotional skills in FACES relied on reports from both teachers and parents. These measures are described in previous FACES reports (ACYF, 2003) and on the Web site listed earlier. Table 11.2 summarizes the measures by cohort and reporting source (teacher or parent). FACES 2003 replaced some positive classroom behavior teacher-rated items from the FACES 2000 Social Skills Rating Scale (SSRS) with the Preschool Learning Behavior Scale (PLBS; Fantuzzo, Manz, & McDermott, 1998) in order to achieve greater variation in children's behavior and to measure approaches to learning. Teachers also rated each study child on overall health and any developmental conditions or special needs concerns and whether or not such needs were identified prior to entering preschool. (At the spring data collection we asked if the child was subsequently identified while in Head Start.)

Measures of Program and Classroom Quality

Classroom quality measures of processes and structure used for both cohorts, fall and spring (Head Start classrooms only), included:

- Early Childhood Environment Rating Scale-Revised (ECERS-R; Harms, Clifford, & Cryer, 1998),
- ECERS-R Language Scale,
- Learning Environment Scale of the Assessment Profile for Early Childhood Programs: Research Edition I (Abbott-Shim, Lambert, & McCarty, 2000),

Table 11.2
Summary of Child Socioemotional Measures by Cohort and Source

Construct	FACES 2000		FACES 2003	
	Teacher	*Parent*	*Teacher*	*Parent*
Social skills	SSRS/PMS (12 items)	SSRS/PMS (7 items)	SSRS/PMS (12 items)	SSRS/PMS (7 items)
Behavior problems	CBCL (14 items)	CBCL (12 items)	CBCL (14 items)	CBCL (8 items)
Approaches to learning	COR (12 items)	—	PLBS (29 items)	PLBS (6 items)
Child health and disabilities	—	Disabilities (12 items) Health (2 items)	Disabilities (5 items)	Disabilities (12 items) Health (2 items)

Note: SSRS = Social Skills Rating System; PMS = Personal Maturity Scale; CBCL = Child Behavior Checklist; PLBS = Preschool Learning Behavior Scale.

- Arnett Caregiver Interaction Scale (Arnett, 1989), and
- child-adult ratio calculated from two separate enumerations made by observers during the classroom day.

FACES 2000 used two other assessment profile scales: the Scheduling and Individualizing scales and a Quality Composite variable created using principal components factor analyses to combine the ECERS-R Language Scale with the Learning Environment and Scheduling scales. FACES 2003 dropped the Scheduling and Individual scales and revised the Quality Composite score to include only the Learning Environment and ECERS-R Language scales. The observational measures of quality yielded independent interobserver agreements between 80 percent and 94 percent in fall 2000 and fall 2003; interrater reliability on the ECERS-R improved from 80 percent in fall 2000 to 90 percent in fall 2003. Most measures of classroom quality were common to both cohorts. FACES 2003 research staff field-tested the Instructional Support items from the Classroom Assessment Scoring System (CLASS) developed by La Paro, Pianta, and Stuhlman (2004). The field test was conducted on only a small number of classrooms (n = 21) by the FACES quality-control visitors who also assessed the reliability of the FACES field observers using the core observational measures. The limited results from this small sample are presented here for descriptive purposes.

We interviewed Lead Head Start classroom teachers to collect teacher background information (experience and qualifications) and detailed information about their curriculum, classroom activities, attitudes, and knowledge about early-childhood education practices, using 10 items adapted from the Teacher Beliefs Scale (Burts, Hart, Charlesworth, & Kirk, 1990). All of this information is available at the Web site listed earlier, in the *Fourth Progress Report* (ACYF, 2003), and in the *Fifth Progress Report* (in press).

RESULTS

Analysis Method

We used a series of complex statistical models to answer the research questions and test the conceptual model regarding the role of classroom and program factors in shaping children's skill levels and gains over time. The first models test the relationships between program and class features, child and family characteristics, and school readiness outcomes. The next set of models determines children's readiness levels at the end of Head Start program participation and readiness gains from fall to spring of their

Head Start year. All analyses employed Hierarchical Linear Modeling using the SAS PROC MIXED computer program (Bryk & Raudenbush, 1992; Singer, 1998). Multilevel modeling shows how average achievement scores of a sample of classes, schools, or other educational units (Head Start programs and classes in this case) relate to characteristics of those units, such as program demographics and classroom quality. This modeling can simultaneously examine how achievement scores of individual children in each program and class relate to child attributes, such as race or home literacy activities. This method provides a numerical estimate of program and class comparisons in average scores, relative to the individual variations in scores across children within classes. This reveals how much program quality contributes to children's achievement levels and gains during the Head Start year and into spring of the kindergarten year.

Standardized difference scores between fall and spring measure each child's gains in word vocabulary, letter-word identification, early writing, early math skills, and in the criterion-referenced book knowledge, counting, social awareness, color naming, and design copying measures. In a sense, each child serves as his or her own matched control subject for progress toward school readiness.[3]

Effect sizes estimate the meaningfulness of significant findings because differences in large-scale studies may be statistically reliable, but the size of the effect may be too small to be meaningful for educational programming purposes.[4] For small samples, effect sizes must be large in order to detect meaningful differences, but for large samples, as in this study, a very small effect size can be statistically significant though not meaningful for planning policies or programs (for details on effect size, see Cohen, 1995; Rosenthal & Rosnow, 1984). All of our analyses conducted statistical tests on weighted data using WesVarPC software, which adjusts standard errors for effects of sample clustering and differential sampling rates, allowing us to interpret results for the Head Start population as a whole (Brick & Morganstein, 1997). We used the more recent FACES 2003 data sets whenever possible; in some cases both data sets were used to detect which findings were replicated across cohorts. Because FACES 2003 kindergarten data are not yet available, analyses of gains through kindergarten rely solely on the FACES 2000 data set, with children's gain scores from fall to spring of their Head Start year and then from spring of Head Start to spring of kindergarten.

Variations between Programs and Classrooms in Head Start

Quality of Classrooms. The quality of Head Start classrooms in both assessments was good, indeed *above* that usually found among center-based preschools. The overall average ECERS-R score for 324 classrooms observed in fall 2003 was 4.81 (with a standard deviation of 0.91), compared with an average score of 4.78 (standard deviation of 0.90) for 258 classrooms in fall 2000. Four items constituting the ECERS-R Language Scale yielded an average score of 5.81 on a 7-point scale for fall 2003, indicating good quality of language materials and activities to stimulate emergent literacy and generally higher quality than that found for the ECERS-R mean score across all items. The standard deviation of 1.14 for the Language subscale indicates a greater range of variation in the quality of these language items than what was found for the ECERS-R total score.

We grouped classrooms for overall environmental quality on the ECERS-R 7-point scale where scores of 1, 3, 5, and 7 denote *inadequate, minimal, good,* and *excellent* quality, respectively.[5] Few classrooms in either cohort were scored as inadequate or minimal in quality, but slightly more Head Start classrooms were rated lower in quality in the latest (2003) cohort, although the differences were not statistically significant. The number of classrooms rated excellent (ECERS-R scores of 6 or higher) increased across the two cohorts, which suggests greater variation in quality among Head Start classrooms in 2003 than in 2000.

A variety of studies in different child care settings have used either the ECERS-R or the original ECERS, so we charted the mean and variability in scores reported in published findings (Figure 11.1). The average score for Head Start classrooms was higher, but the variation was less for Head Start classrooms than was found in those other settings.

Scores for other process and structural measures of classroom quality appear consistent across both cohorts and support the conclusion that quality in Head Start classrooms is consistently good. The Assessment Profile Learning Environment Scale indicates that Head Start classrooms in fall 2000 and fall 2003 achieved 80 percent and 77 percent, respectively, of the maximum obtainable score. Classrooms appear to have a range of learning materials and activities to stimulate development and good use of language-based materials. Scores on the Arnett Caregiver Interaction Scale (CIS) showed that Head Start teachers are sensitive and responsive. CIS scores averaged 71.5 (SD = 12.2) in 2000 and 74.3 (SD = 11.03) in 2003, indicating a slight but nonsignificant increase in teacher sensitivity and responsiveness in 2003. Based on a maximum attainable score of 90 for the total CIS, Head Start teachers were scored positive for 79.4 percent (in fall 2000) and 82.5 percent (in fall 2003) of the maximum score.

There were 5.4 children per adult on average in fall 2003, which was identical to the 5.4 ratio for 2000. Classrooms in 2003 averaged 6.3 children per paid staff member, compared with 6.5 children per paid staff in

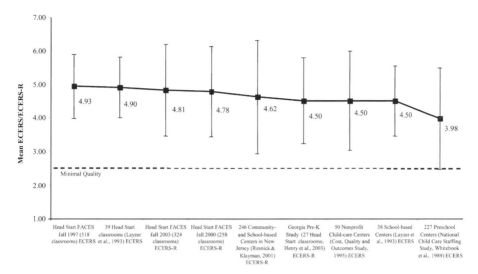

Figure 11.1   Classroom quality in Head Start in FACES 1997, 2000, and 2003 and comparisons with other preschool and child care settings

2000. These differences suggest slight improvement in the use of volunteers because lower ratios indicate more adult support. These ratios are far better than the National Association for the Education of Young Children (NAEYC) accreditation standard of 8 or fewer three-year-olds or 10 or fewer four-year-olds for each adult and exceed the Head Start Program Performance Standards of 7.5 to 8.5 or fewer three-year-olds or 10 or fewer four-year-olds per adult.

The field test of the Classroom Assessment Scoring System (CLASS), conducted in fall 2003 on a small number of FACES classrooms (n = 21), suggested that Head Start children scored at the midlevel for child engagement, productivity, and instructional learning formats, indicating that teachers are generally able to maximize the instructional time to optimize learning, that children are focused and participating in learning activities, and that a variety of learning modalities are used to encourage children's active involvement. However, the field test also showed that teachers focus on learning specific facts or skills, moving through activities in a perfunctory manner and not soliciting ideas from children or following up for elaborations of children's questions or ideas. Teachers' feedback for children mainly focused on correct answers rather than on extending or elaborating on children's ideas, which would encourage further participation in activities and reinforce the learning process. Scores from the 21 FACES classrooms were highly comparable to published norms from the developers of the CLASS (La Paro et al., 2004). The CLASS measure offers useful insight about teachers' instructional strategies that goes beyond other measures of quality to focus on how teachers use the learning process to promote so-called intentionality and maximize children's learning. Our results suggest that more could be done to assist teachers to encourage logical thinking skills and higher-order reasoning during learning activities.

Quality between Programs and Classrooms and Relationships to Teacher. To determine how much Head Start programs differed in average quality, the total variability in classroom quality scores was divided into two components: the variation between programs in the average classroom quality scores, and the variation among classrooms within the same program. If classrooms with differing levels of quality were randomly distributed across Head Start programs, one would expect most of the quality variations to fall *inside* the programs component, but if the programs differed significantly in classroom quality, then most of the variation would fall *between* the programs (Bryk & Raudenbush, 1992). Such an approach was used effectively to study characteristics of school organization on teachers' sense of efficacy (Bryk & Driscoll, 1988) and the effects of school characteristics on individual children's achievement (Lee & Bryk, 1989).

A sequence of hierarchical linear regression models was run for each of the six key indicators of quality (ECERS-R total scores, ECERS-R Language Scale, Arnett Caregiver Interaction Scale, Assessment Profile Individualizing subscale, child-adult ratio, and Quality Composite score). The first (random) model partitioned the variations *within* classrooms separately from the variations *between* classrooms. The second model introduced the classroom level *teacher* factors: teacher education, years of Head Start teaching experience, membership in early-childhood professional associations, ethnicity, and beliefs about developmentally appropriate practices. The third model tested the effect of *program* factors: family incomes and parental education of the clients, proportion of nonminority students, use of Creative or High/Scope curriculum, and average teacher salaries at the center (keeping classroom predictors separate). The fourth model combined the classroom teacher factors (from the second model) with the program factors (from the third model) to distill the values of each component for predicting classroom quality.

Most of the variation in classroom quality was attributable to the differences *between* programs rather than to variations among classrooms within the same program. Program factors accounted for 30 percent of the variation in ECERS-R total quality scores, 22 percent of the ECERS-R Language Scale score variation, and 26 percent of the variation in Arnett CIS scores. Lesser predictive power was found for the Assessment Profile scales, the Quality Composite, or the child-adult ratio. Full results may be found in a technical report (ACYF, in press).

These results suggest that Head Start programs with a common integrated curriculum across classrooms and that pay their teachers well have sufficient resources to ensure high classroom quality through the abilities of teachers hired, their experience and attitudes, and their knowledge. The program and classroom factors included in these models offer convincing evidence of the process aspects of child care quality, such as learning materials, systematic language activities, and teacher-child interactions, but they do less well at predicting the more structural aspects of quality, such as child-adult ratios.

Cognitive Skill Levels across Programs and Classes. Next, we inquire how much children's skill levels vary between programs as opposed to between classrooms within the program. The primary measures of interest were the cognitive assessment scores measured in fall 2003 and spring 2004 and the gains each child made during that period. These analyses included only children assessed in English in both periods. For these analyses we partitioned the variation in emergent literacy into three components: (1) variation between *programs,* (2) variation between *classrooms,* and (3) variation between *children.*

If children with differing levels of initial achievement were randomly distributed across Head Start programs and classrooms, most of the variation would be found in the third rubric. On the other hand, if some process were systematically sorting children into different programs or classrooms according to their initial achievement levels, or if programs and/or classrooms differed substantially in the efficacy of their instructional activities, then one might expect substantial variation between *programs* (the first rubric) and/or between *classrooms* (the second rubric). Using the FACES 2003 national sample from 60 programs, each analytic model tested the three components of variation in cognitive skills (Singer, 1998).

Program variables included the curriculum employed, average teacher salary levels, and average demographic and social-class characteristics of the families served. *Classroom* variables consisted of measures of teacher preparation, teacher background characteristics, if the class was of full-day or part-day duration, and indicators of classroom quality such as the ECERS-R Language Scale and Caregiver Interaction Scale. *Child* variables included demographic characteristics of the child; socioeconomic, cultural, and structural characteristics of the family; parent literacy levels; disability status of the child; and the frequency of parental reading to the child.

Statistical tests indicated substantial variation in the cognitive skill levels reached by the end of the Head Start year and into kindergarten. In the children's spring 2004 scores (at the end of their Head Start year),

71 percent of variation in vocabulary scores and 84 percent of the variation in prereading (letter-word identification) scores was found to be *within* classroom variation, which indicates stronger differences between children than between programs or classrooms. These cognitive skills and gains were more dependent on the socioeconomic, ethnic, and family background characteristics of the children than on teacher qualifications or program quality. However, partitioning the remaining variation *not* accounted for by the children themselves showed some lesser influences of such factors as instructional activities, program management, and classroom quality. Details of these analyses may be found in the *FACES 2000 Technical Report* (ACYF, in press) and in the *Fifth Progress Report* (ACYF, forthcoming) and finally Zill and Resnick (2005).

Children's Emergent Literacy Skills

Head Start in Comparison with National Norms. One of the goals of Head Start is to provide disadvantaged children with compensatory learning experiences that will enhance children's school readiness and prepare them for entry into kindergarten. Skills related to literacy, including vocabulary, letter recognition, writing, and numeracy, are considered central to school readiness. To determine whether or not Head Start children's school readiness skills improve, a primary focus of FACES is to measure the knowledge and skills that children bring with them when they begin the Head Start program and how they varied across academic skills areas. The fall 2003 assessment scores provide a baseline measure of children's skills at the time of entry into Head Start. These scores can then be compared with the national norms for these standardized assessments. These assessments follow the convention of a mean of 100 at each age grouping with a standard deviation of 15. In order to make these comparisons, FACES used weighted data to obtain IRT True Scores, which were converted into standard scores (i.e., a mean of 100 and standard deviation of 15) based on the publisher conversion tables for children of the same age.

The majority of children who entered Head Start in fall 2003 came into the program with early literacy and numeracy skills that were less developed than those of most children of the same age (Figure 11.2). Based on standard scores (with an overall mean of 100 and a standard deviation of 15), the literacy and number skills of the average Head Start child entering the program were from half a standard deviation to a full standard deviation below national averages.

Earlier studies have found that the standard scores of low-income children without preschool experience on tests such as the PPVT are

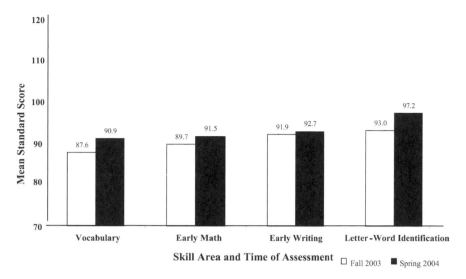

Figure 11.2   Mean standard scores of Head Start children in fall 2003 and spring 2004, by skill area (FACES 2003)

typically in the 82 to 85 range (Haskins, 1989; McKey et al, 1985; White, 1986). For some especially disadvantaged low-income populations, average standard scores of preschool children in the high 70s have been reported. For example, in the evaluation study of the Comprehensive Child Development Program recently completed by Abt Associates, average standard scores on the PPVT-R for 1,110 control-group children aged four years was 77.3. Thus, the average entry-level scores of children in the Head Start FACES 2003 sample were at these levels for vocabulary (PPVT-III) and early math (Woodcock-Johnson III Applied Problems) but were somewhat higher for early writing (Woodcock-Johnson III Spelling) and were closer to the national norms for Woodcock-Johnson III Letter-Word Identification.

Children's Gains during Head Start. Children in Head Start showed significant advances in some emergent literacy skills between the beginning and end of the program year but continued to lag behind national norms (Figure 11.2). The gains were also in line with earlier findings on the immediate effects of Head Start on children's intellectual performance (Haskins, 1989, p. 277; McKey et al., 1985). Most gains in the norm-referenced measures were relatively modest in magnitude but fell within the range that has been deemed *educationally meaningful* (Rosenthal & Rosnow, 1984). Educationally meaningful results explain a sufficiently large amount of the variation in scores to have meaningful programmatic or policy implications.

On the other hand, the vocabulary gains found in Head Start were about half the size of standard-score gains in IQ and achievement obtained in earlier studies of more intensive interventions with children from disadvantaged families (Barnett, 1998, pp. 13–14). Barnett (1998), citing studies from the intervention literature by White and Casto (1985), McKey et al. (1985), and Ramey, Bryant, and Suarez (1985), reported gains of one-half of a standard deviation or approximately 8 standard score points. Barnett concludes that short-term effects are larger for intensive, high-quality, and well-designed interventions compared with other child care programs.

Gains in letter-word identification have increased across the three cohorts of FACES, but no similar increase was found for gains in vocabulary scores (Figure 11.3). These data are based on the fall-to-spring gains expressed as percentages of the fall standard deviations, after equating the scale scores of the measures using IRT methods.

Children's Skills at the end of Kindergarten in Comparison with National Norms. Measures of children's literacy skills in the spring of their kindergarten year included:

- Vocabulary: PPVT-III (N = 1,433)
- Early Reading: ECLS-K Reading Assessment (N = 1,894)
- Early Writing: WJ-R Dictation Test (N = 1,340)
- Early Math: WJ-R Applied Problems Test (N = 1,387)
- General Knowledge: ECLS-K (N = 1,874).

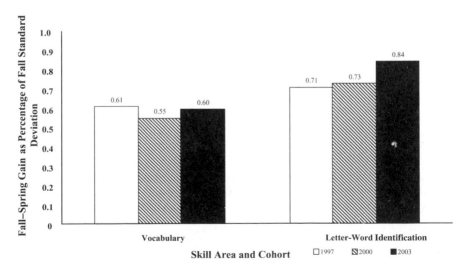

Figure 11.3 Fall–spring IRT Scale score gains in vocabulary and letter-word identification (FACES 1997, 2000, 2003)

FACES 2003 kindergarten data are still being collected, so we use FACES 2000 data, focusing only on those children assessed in English at all time periods. Looking just at the average standard scores in spring of the children's kindergarten year, we find that the average Head Start graduate comes close to national norms in decoding, or inside-out, skills (recognizing letters and letter sounds and writing letters on demand) but continues to lag significantly below national norms in outside-in skill areas (vocabulary, general knowledge, and solving simple math word problems; Figure 11.4).

Graduates all showed significant gains in these skills during the Head Start year and from spring of their Head Start year to spring of kindergarten, but the size of the gains were uneven. For gains made during the Head Start year the largest effect size was for vocabulary (0.25), and effect sizes were much lower for other skill areas (0.13 for prewriting, 0.07 for early math and 0.03 for prereading). Gains made by spring of their kindergarten year were much larger on the basis of effect size and showed that the highest gains were made for prewriting (0.81) and prereading (0.43) followed by early math (0.39) and finally vocabulary (0.26). It is important to note that vocabulary gains by Head Start graduates in kindergarten were much less than those in other skills areas and only comparable to the gains made while in Head Start. Meanwhile, Head Start graduates made large gains at kindergarten in other skill areas, most notably the inside-out skill areas of prewriting and prereading.

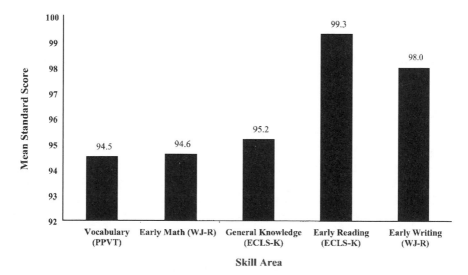

Figure 11.4   Mean standard scores of Head Start graduates at end of kindergarten, by skill area (FACES 2000)

Put another way, more of the gap between initial skill levels and national norms was made up by kindergarten in the prereading (90%) and prewriting (86%) skills. Much less of the gap was bridged for early math (52%) and vocabulary (41%), which highlights the discrepancy in gains made by Head Start graduates by the end of kindergarten in inside-out or decoding skills compared with the outside-in literacy skills, such as word knowledge and numeracy. These results suggest that Head Start graduates were ready to learn in the sense that they made significant progress toward national norms in kindergarten, especially in early reading and writing skills, but graduates remained below national norms in vocabulary, general knowledge, and early math at the end of kindergarten.

Program and Classroom Factors Associated with Head Start Children's Skills. Having established that Head Start children made significant (albeit modest) progress in emergent literacy skill development, we conducted a series of analyses to ascertain the relative weights that could be assigned to account for those gains. Specifically, we were interested in whether or not the results could be explained *entirely* by demographic and socioeconomic characteristics of program participants or whether or not program quality and process factors (such as facilities, curriculum, and teacher experience, credentials, and knowledge or belief) contributed significantly to the predictions.

For each dependent variable (consisting of the child's literacy skills), two models were tested, looking at the child's skills upon graduation from Head Start (spring of their Head Start year) and the gains in skills the children made from fall to spring of their Head Start year. Comparing the percentage of variation in gain scores and spring levels for the key literacy measures, we found that most of the variation was attributable to child variables rather than to program or classroom factors (Figure 11.5). Forty-one percent of the levels in vocabulary scores at the end of the Head Start year were attributable to child and family background factors, and only 5.5 percent could be ascribed to program or classroom factors. As in the previous findings, the traceable influence of programs and classrooms was quite limited when matched against the background features of the children served and their families.

On the other hand, when testing the influence of specific program and classroom factors, the following variables seemed to make a difference for children's progress and may be worthy of further investigation:

1. programs having higher teacher salaries,
2. higher scores on the Caregiver Interaction Scale tapping teacher sensitivity,
3. teachers with associate's degree or higher, and
4. parents reporting that they read to their children more frequently.

These results are discussed in greater detail elsewhere (*Fifth Progress Report,* ACYF, forthcoming), but in general, the average annual lead teacher salary was associated with higher spring scores in vocabulary, letter-word identification, and early math and with greater gains in letter recognition. Higher Caregiver Interaction Scale scores, indicating greater teacher sensitivity and responsiveness, were associated with children's spring vocabulary, early math scores, and higher positive scores on teacher-reported approaches to learning (as measured by the PLBS). It is interesting to note that similar relationships between teacher sensitivity and children's literacy gains or social behavior were *not* found for the FACES 2000 cohort. Classrooms with teachers having a four-year college degree or an associate's degree in education or a closely related field tended to have children with higher early-writing scores in spring of their Head Start year.

Parents were asked if they read to their children *not at all, once or twice, three to six times,* or *every day* during the previous week. Parental responses to the question were entered into the regression analyses as a set of dichotomous variables, with the most frequent response, three to six times, as the omitted reference category. The reading responses were entered as child-level independent variables.

Children whose parents reported reading to their children every day had significantly higher mean vocabulary scores in spring of their Head Start year than did children whose parents reported reading three to six times. Spring early-writing scores were significantly lower among children

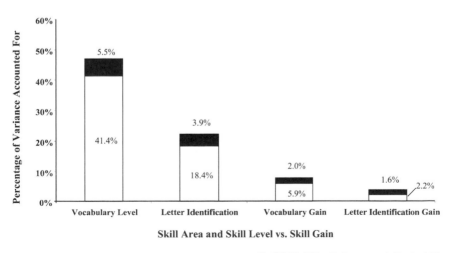

Figure 11.5 Percentage of variance in assessment scores accounted for by child-level variables and program and class-level variables

whose parents read once or twice compared to those who read three to six times. Further, children whose parents reported reading to their children once or twice per week had significantly lower mean scores for approaches to learning than children whose parents reported reading three to six times in the last week. Significant effects of parental reading were obtained even after controlling for parent education level, the mother's score on a measure of adult literacy (the K-FAST), and an indicator of the presence of books in the home. Although these analyses do not address whether or not Head Start programs have an impact on parental reading to children in the home, they do support the notion that programs that are able to effectively encourage parents to engage in such activities show greater school readiness in their children by the end of the Head Start year.

These results are similar to those in FACES 2000, which found that frequency of parents reading to their children was related to children's school readiness *during* Head Start. Regression analyses showed that frequent parental reading to children was correlated with higher spring scores as well as greater gains from fall to spring on the vocabulary task. Similar findings associated parental reading to their children with higher spring scores (and greater gains) in letter-word identification skills (ACYF, 2003).

However, some program and classroom factors did *not* show significant relationships with children's academic progress and literacy gains, as initially hypothesized. The High/Scope and Creative Curricula are comprehensive, integrated preschool curricula that have a long history of research and development. These are among the most popular integrated curricula employed in Head Start programs. We hypothesized that children in programs that used an integrated curriculum such as these would make more progress in school readiness skills than children in programs that used other curricula, and such an association was found for the FACES 2000 data (ACYF, 2003). However, the replication studies with FACES 2003 data did not find any significant associations between gains in school readiness skills and curriculum.

We also explored whether or not children benefited more from the program in terms of academic achievement if they attended full-day classes. Children in FACES 2000 who did attend full-day Head Start programs made greater gains in several areas than children who attended part-day (ACYF, 2003). However, the parallel analyses with the FACES 2003 data did not replicate those findings.

Process quality has been widely considered as an important influence on children's emergent literacy gains in early-childhood education programs. There are consistent findings in the research literature showing that the contribution of classroom quality to raising children's achievement is significant but relatively modest (Peisner-Feinberg & Burchinal, 1997).

High quality in community child care settings has been related to better child outcomes in the short term, after controlling for child and family background factors (Bryant et al., 1994; NICHD ECCRN, 2000; Phillips et al., 1987; Whitebook et al., 1989).

We hypothesized that providing children with higher-quality classrooms and with greater frequency and quality of Head Start classroom activities that promote growth in language skills would result in greater gains for children. However, the regression studies yielded mixed results. Supporting the initial hypotheses, higher ECERS-R Language Scale scores were associated with higher fall-to-spring gains in positive approaches to learning, but there were no associations between the ECERS-R Language, ECERS-R, Quality Composite, or Assessment Profile Learning Environment scores and children's emergent literacy skills at graduation or in fall-to-spring gains. In FACES 2000, the ECERS-R Language Scale was not associated with higher spring scores or greater fall-to-spring gain scores on any of the school readiness measures (for details, see ACYF, 2003). Earlier reports for the first FACES cohort initiated in 1997 found weak relationships between process measures of quality and children's graduation levels and no relationships with children's fall-to-spring gains. In general, FACES has found only weak or nonexistent relationships between traditional measures of early-childhood program quality and the gains Head Start children make in either the cognitive or social-emotional realms. Additionally, some findings with regard to social competence appeared to be counterintuitive, for example, that classrooms with higher child-adult ratios, indicating lower quality, had children with higher teacher-rated cooperative classroom behavior scores. These results are presented in the *Fifth Progress Report* (ACYF, forthcoming).

There appear to be a number of reasons for the discrepancy in the FACES findings, relative to other studies, regarding the relationship between classroom quality and children's emergent literacy. As reported earlier in this chapter, Head Start classrooms generally are of good quality, and there is a more limited range of variation in quality, relative to other early-childhood education settings. The limited variation in quality places constraints on the magnitude of any potential relationship between quality and children's outcomes. Further, classroom quality may be a necessary but not sufficient condition for promoting significant gains in specific cognitive or behavioral areas.

CONCLUSIONS

What have we learned about the national Head Start program that could reassure U.S. taxpayers that $6,843,114,000.00 has been well spent in 2005 for this most ambitious early-childhood intervention in history? And what have we learned that might justify our national congressional representatives increasing that appropriation by more than 1.01022 percent in the *next* fiscal year? We have explored *process* and structural *quality* in broad, nationally representative samples of Head Start classrooms. We have focused special attention on the emergent literacy skills acquired by children over the course of their Head Start year(s) and into kindergarten. Results have shown that classroom quality in Head Start is generally *good,* even slightly better than the average for child care settings nationally and with an encouragingly *limited range in quality.* That is all good news that should be gratifying to supporters of the program and to the tens of thousands of Head Start teachers, administrators, volunteers, and parents who have invested their time, their energy, their money, and their hopes in this remarkably charitable leap of faith in our children and our future. The data have spoken soberly and objectively, testifying that the program works and many of our neediest children benefit from it.

What have we learned that has surprised us or given us pause for concern? Analyses have shown that demographic and family background characteristics of the children accounted for more of the progress in child achievements and emergent literacy skills than either program or classroom features at the Head Start sites. We interpret this to mean that the cognitive (and probably other) gains children make in Head Start depend on the nature and quality of the learning environment *both* at home and in child care settings. Like any other child care or preschool program, Head Start must work with what parents and other caretakers bring to its doorstep.

Children in Head Start *do* make some gains in emergent literacy, but these gains are relatively modest, which suggests that much more can be accomplished. It would appear that outside-in skills such as vocabulary, book knowledge, and color naming are those most likely to show improvement among Head Start children, as compared with the inside-out skills such as letter-word identification, psychomotor tasks, and early writing. (These latter two skills showed improvement but not as much progress as the outside-in skills.) Head Start graduates were ready to learn in the sense that they made significant progress toward national norms in kindergarten, especially in early reading and writing skills, but graduates remained *below* national norms in vocabulary, general knowledge, and early math at the end of kindergarten. All of that beckons us (like Avis) to try harder and do better.

The gains made by Head Start children are smaller than those reported in the literature for more intensive, so-called model, research and demonstration programs, such as the Perry Preschool and Abecedarian Projects. However, many writers have noted the differences when comparing studies involving model research and large, government-funded demonstration programs "taken to scale." Many of the positive effects of early-childhood education programs may be attributed to the intensity and control available in programs of modest scope. The dissemination of a promising program model to a larger scale at the state or national levels often results in what Heather Weiss termed the *demonstration dilution effect* (Weiss, Resnick & Hausman, 1987). Thus, it is possible that the discrepancies between results obtained by Head Start and model programs could be attributed—at least in part—to the greater intensity and quality of the model programs as well as to the fact that children start earlier and stay longer in those programs than do children in Head Start. On the other hand, many studies that tested model demonstration programs began their research during the early years of program implementation, when programs may not have been fully operational (Reynolds, 1995). Head Start represents an established program that, with perhaps more modest resources than many model demonstration programs, does have an extensive implementation history and can tailor its services to the needs and aspirations of children and families. Clearly, it is important to consider the contextual differences in which model programs and Head Start operate in order to understand the potentially discrepant research evidence.

Our results resoundingly demonstrate that it *really* matters how much is paid to Head Start teachers and staff members and how well they are qualified by education and training to do their jobs. On the other hand, results from FACES 2003 also suggest that increasing teacher qualifications and improving general classroom quality may not *necessarily* be sufficient to produce greater school readiness gains for Head Start children. What seems essential is system-wide adoption of instructional methods with proven effectiveness in boosting specific elements of school readiness, such as outside-in skills. Small-scale studies have shown that this can be accomplished with respect to specific aspects of early literacy, particularly in the areas of alphabetic skills (Spira, Bracken, & Fischel, 2005), vocabulary knowledge (Wasik & Bond, 2001), and phonemic awareness (Anthony & Lonigan, 2004). However, boosting outside-in skills such as vocabulary may be more challenging than strengthening inside-out skills such as letter knowledge.

One of the possible reasons why it may be harder to boost outside-in skills is that programs are working against children's home educational experiences, which appear to exert powerful influence either to hold children back or to enhance their learning. In particular, parental reading to children seems to be an *extremely* important factor in shaping children's literacy skills. Parents and the home environment may enable or constrain the effects of exposure in Head Start classrooms to language and literacy learning. This underlines how important it is to coordinate the programmatic initiatives and objectives of Head Start with the values and activities of parents in the home environment. The size of program effects may depend *crucially* on the disparities between the quality of the learning environment provided by Head Start and the quality of the learning environment in the child's home and community (Barnett, 1998).

System-wide improvements that target outside-in literacy skills may require considerable effort to change the culture of many Head Start programs. In recent years, there have been a variety of federal government initiatives aimed at improving the quality of Head Start programs, including renewed emphasis on enhancing children's learning of emergent literacy and numeracy skills (ACYF, 2001b). We mentioned earlier the philosophical shift in Head Start programming away from heavily didactic activities, such as teaching children letters and numbers, and toward encouragement of more play-oriented and discovery-learning activities; this may cause programs to resist adopting some systemic interventions that have proven effectiveness. Although we see a place for socialization, whole language, and discovery-learning activities, these perhaps should not be exaggerated to the detriment of giving children firm grounding in print awareness, phonemic sensitivity, or word-decoding skills. Intervention research into methods for boosting language and literacy is at an important crossroads in development, with many important studies currently under way that may *not* inform practice for several more years. Longer-term follow-up studies are needed to establish if—and how—early gains may have lasting benefits for children's achievement.

As noted previously (Resnick & Zill, 2003), variations in the effectiveness of Head Start services may be explained in large part by characteristics of the families and children they serve, by the curriculum used in the program, and by teacher qualifications and attitudes about early-childhood educational practices. Improvements in quality at the classroom level may bring only limited benefits without systemic changes in the Head Start program. These changes require resources in order to institute effective, literacy-focused interventions while also improving the educational qualifications of teaching staff and upgrading the quality of learning environments in the classrooms. Some lower-quality Head Start programs do not have sufficient resources to make those necessary changes. We do not yet fully understand the relationship between classroom quality and the effects of a systematic, results-focused literacy intervention. Finally, we do not yet know how best to boost home literacy activities, although emerging studies from the Department of Education's Preschool

Curriculum Evaluation Research (PCER) initiative may shed some light on this issue.

These are some of the challenges that face the current movement toward earlier and more effective childhood intervention. The direction is clearly marked, but we still need to connect the dots.

NOTES

1. Details of the first cohort design, measures, and findings are described in *Head Start FACES: Longitudinal Findings on Program Performance. Third Progress Report* (Administration on Children, Youth and Families, 2001a), available from www.acf.hhs.gov/programs/core/ongoing_research/faces/faces_pubs_reports.html

2. Details of the second cohort design, measures, and findings are available in *Head Start FACES 2000: A Whole Child Perspective on Program Performance. Fourth Progress Report* (Administration on Children, Youth and Families, 2003), available from http://www.acf.dhhs.gov/programs/core/ongoing_research/faces/faces00_4thprogress/faces00_title.html.

3. Much has been written about the unreliability of difference scores derived from subtracting the Time 2 score from the Time 1 score when trying to estimate individual differences in growth. However, according to Willett (1989), the reliability in the difference score can actually be quite high under some conditions, particularly those favored by large-scale population-based survey methods. Difference scores for measuring change over two data points are not intrinsically as unreliable as the psychometric literature has argued, and the difference score can be "an appealing and unbiased measure" of individual growth (Willett, 1989).

4. The effect size is defined as an estimate of the magnitude of the relationship or difference between two or more variables. In this study, effect sizes were calculated as *Cohen's d,* which was defined as the mean difference divided by the standard deviation for the underlying distribution, and is expressed in standard score units. Effect sizes of approximately .20 are considered small, such as the difference in mean IQ between twins and nontwins (for details, see Cohen, 1977). Moderate effect sizes typically approximate .50 and are conceived as those differences large enough to be clearly visible in behavior or attitudes. Large effect sizes are those higher than .80 and are represented, for example, by the mean IQ difference between holders of a PhD degree and typical college freshman. However, the delineation of thresholds for considering an effect size to be small, moderate, or large may vary depending on the research question being asked and the methodological rigor of the study (Cohen, 1977). In this study, the weighted means and standard deviations were used, so they are already adjusted for the underlying FACES population, reflecting the probability sample that was drawn.

5. The groups were defined along the midpoints of each whole score, as follows: 1–1.49 = 1, 1.5–2.49 = 2, 2.50–3.49 = 3, 3.5–4.49 = 4, 4.5–5.49 = 5, 5.5–6.49 = 6, 6.5–7 = 7.

REFERENCES

Abbott-Shim, M., Lambert, R., & McCarty, F. (2000). Structural model of Head Start classroom quality. *Early Childhood Research Quarterly, 15,* 1, 115–134.

Administration on Children, Youth and Families (ACYF). (1997). First progress report on the *Head Start Program Performance Measures.* Washington, DC: U.S. Department of Health and Human Services. Retrieved June 23, 2005, from http://www.acf.dhhs.gov/programs/core/pubs_reports/faces/meas_one_toc.html

Administration on Children, Youth and Families (ACYF). (2001a). *Head Start FACES: Longitudinal findings on program performance. Third progress report.* Washington, DC: U.S. Department of Health and Human Services. Retrieved June 23, 2005, from http://www.acf.dhhs.gov/programs/core/pubs_reports/faces/meas_99_intro.html

Administration on Children, Youth and Families (ACYF). (2001b). *Reaching out to families: Head Start recruitment and enrollment practices.* Washington, DC: U.S. Department of Health and Human Services. Retrieved June 23, 2005, from http://www.acf.dhhs.gov/programs/core/ongoing_research/faces/reaching_out_families/reaching_title.html

Administration on Children, Youth and Families (ACYF). (2003). *Head Start FACES 2000: A whole child perspective on program performance. Fourth progress report.* Washington, DC: U.S. Department of Health and Human Services. Retrieved June 23, 2005, from http://www.acf.dhhs.gov/programs/core/ongoing_research/faces/faces00_4thprogress/faces00_title.html

Administration on Children, Youth and Families (ACYF). (in press). *FACES 2000 technical report.* Washington, DC: U.S. Department of Health and Human Services.

Administration on Children, Youth and Families. (forthcoming). *Head Start FACES 2003: Fifth progress report.* Washington, DC: U.S. Department of Health and Human Services.

Anthony, J.L., & Lonigan, C.J. (2004). The nature of phonological awareness: Converging evidence from four studies of preschool and early grade school children. *Journal of Educational Psychology, 96*(1), 43–55.

Arnett, J. (1989). Caregivers in day-care centers: Does training matter? *Journal of Applied Developmental Psychology, 10,* 541–552.

Barnett, W.S. (1998). Long-term effects on cognitive development and school success. In W.S. Barnett & S.S. Babcock (Eds.), *Early care and education for children in poverty* (pp. 11–44). Albany: State University of New York Press.

Barnett, W.S., & Camilli, G. (1997). *Definite results from loose data: A response to "Does Head Start make a difference?"* Updated version of paper presented at the Seminar on Labor and Industrial Relations. Princeton University. New Brunswick, NJ: Rutgers University, Graduate School of Education.

Beals, D. E. (1993). Explanations in low-income families' mealtime conversations. *Applied Psycholinguistics, 14*(4), 489–513.

Blau, D. (1997). The production of quality in child care centers. *Journal of Human Resources, 32,* 354–387.

Bradley, R. H., Caldwell, B. M., Rock, S. L., Ramey, C. T., Barnard, K. E., Gray, C., et al. (1989). Home environment and cognitive development in the first 3 years of life: A collaborative study involving six sites and three ethnic groups in North America. *Developmental Psychology, 25*(2), 217–235.

Brick, J. M., & Morganstein, D. (1997). Computing sampling errors from clustered unequally weighted data using replication: WesVarPC. *Bulletin of the International Statistical Institute, Proceedings, Book 1,* 479–482.

Bryant, D., Burchinal, M., Lau, L., & Sparling, J. (1994). Family and classroom correlates of Head Start children's developmental outcomes. *Early Childhood Research Quarterly, 9,* 289–309.

Bryk, A. S., & Driscoll, M. E. (1988). *An empirical investigation of school as a community.* Madison: University of Wisconsin Research Center on Effective Secondary Schools.

Bryk, A. S., & Raudenbush, S. W. (1992). *Hierarchical linear models: Applications and data analysis methods.* Newbury Park, CA: Sage.

Burchinal, M. R., & Cryer, D. (2003). Diversity, child care quality, and developmental outcomes. *Early Childhood Research Quarterly, 18*(4), 401–426.

Burts, D. C., Hart, C. H., Charlesworth, R., & Kirk, L. (1990). A comparison of frequencies of stress behaviors observed in kindergarten children in classrooms with developmentally appropriate versus developmentally inappropriate practices. *Early Childhood Research Quarterly, 5,* 407–423.

Cohen, J. (1977). *Statistical power analysis for the behavioral sciences.* New York: Academic Press.

Cohen, M. (1995). Sample sizes for survey data analyzed with hierarchical linear models. *Proceedings of the Section on Survey Research Methods of the American Statistical Association,* 690–693.

Consortium for Longitudinal Studies. (1983). *As the twig is bent... Lasting effects of preschool programs.* Hillsdale, NJ: Erlbaum.

Currie, J., & Thomas, D. (1995). Does Head Start make a difference? *American Economic Review, 85,* 341–364.

Currie, J., & Thomas, D. (1999). Does Head Start help Hispanic children? *Journal of Public Economics, 74*(2), 235–262.

Datta, L. E. (1986). Benefits without gains: The paradox of the cognitive effects of early childhood programs and implications for policy. *Special Services in the Schools, 3*(1–2), 103–126.

Dickinson, D. K., & Tabors, P. O. (Eds.). (2001). *Beginning literacy with language.* Baltimore: Paul H. Brookes.

Edelman, M. W. (1981). Who is for children? *American Psychologist, 36*(2), 109–116.

Fantuzzo, J., Manz, P.H., & McDermott, P. (1998). Preschool version of the social skills rating system: An empirical analysis of its use with low-income children. *Journal of School Psychology, 36*(2), 199–214.

Goal One Technical Planning Group. (1991). The Goal One technical planning subgroup report on school readiness. In National Education Goals Panel (Ed.), *Potential strategies for long-term indicator development: Reports of the technical planning subgroups* (Report no. 91-0, pp. 1–18). Washington, DC: National Education Goals Panel.

Goal One Technical Planning Group. (1993). Reconsidering children's early development and learning: Toward shared beliefs and vocabulary. Draft report to the National Education Goals Panel. Washington, DC: National Education Goals Panel.

Harms, T., Clifford, R.M., & Cryer, D. (1998). *Early childhood environment rating scale* (Rev. ed.). New York: Teachers College Press.

Hart, B., & Risley, T.R. (1995). *Meaningful differences in the everyday experience of young American children.* Baltimore: Paul H. Brookes.

Haskins, R. (1989). Beyond metaphor: The efficacy of early childhood education. *American Psychologist, 44*(2), 274–282.

Hofferth, S.I., & Chaplin, D.D. (1998). State regulations and child care choice. *Population Research and Policy Review, 17,* 111–140.

Horn, W.F., & Packard, T. (1985). Early identification of learning problems: A meta-analysis. *Journal of Educational Psychology, 77,* 597–607.

Kontos, S., & Fiene, R. (1987). Childcare quality, compliance with regulations, and children's development: The Pennsylvania Study. In D. Phillips (Ed.), *Quality, child care: What does the research tell us?* (pp. 57–79). Washington, DC: National Association for the Education of Young Children.

La Paro, K.M., Pianta, R.C., & Stuhlman, M. (2004). The classroom assessment scoring system: Findings from the prekindergarten year. *Elementary School Journal, 104*(5), 409–426.

Lazar, I., Darlington, R., Murray, H., Royce, J., & Snipper, A. (1982). Lasting effects of early education: A report from the Consortium for Longitudinal Studies. *Monographs of the Society for Research in Child Development, 47*(Series no. 195), 2–3.

Lee, V.E., Brooks-Gunn, J., Schnur, E., & Liaw, F.R. (1991). Are Head Start effects sustained? A longitudinal follow-up comparison of disadvantaged children attending Head Start, no preschool, and other preschool programs. *Annual Progress in Child Psychiatry & Child Development,* 600–618.

Lee, V., & Bryk, A. (1989). A multilevel model of the social distribution of educational achievement. *Sociology of Education, 62,* 172–192.

McCarthy, D. (1972). *McCarthy Scales of Children's Abilities.* San Antonio, TX: The Psychological Corporation. McKey, R.H., Condelli, L., Ganson, H., Barrett, B.J., McConkey, C., & Plantz, M.C. (1985). *The impact of Head Start on children, families, and communities* (DHHS Publication no. OHDS 85-31193). Washington, DC: U.S. Government Printing Office.

McKey, R. H., Condelli, L., Ganson, H., McConkey, C., & Plantz, M. (1985). *The impact of Head Start on children, families, and communities: Final report of Head Start evaluation, synthesis, and utilization project.* Washington, D.C.: U.S. Department of Health and Human Services.

National Institute of Child Health and Human Development (NICDH), Early Child Care Research Network (ECCRN). (2000). The relation of child-care to cognitive and language development. *Child Development, 71,* 823–839.

Nord, C. W., Lennon, J., Liu, B., & Chandler, K. (1999, November). *Home literacy activities and signs of children's emerging literacy.* Washington, DC: U.S. Department of Education, Office of Educational Research and Improvement, National Center for Education Statistics. Retrieved June 23, 2005, from http://nces.ed.gov/pubs2000/2000026.pdf

Peisner-Feinberg, E. S., & Burchinal, M. R. (1997). Relations between preschool children's child-care experiences and concurrent development: The Cost, Quality and Outcomes Study. *Merrill-Palmer Quarterly, 43*(3), 451–477.

Peisner-Feinberg, E. S., Burchinal, M. R., Clifford, R. M., Culkin, M. L., Howes, C., Kagan, S. L., et al. (2001). The relation of preschool child-care quality to children's cognitive and social developmental trajectories through second grade. *Child Development, 72*(5), 1534–1553.

Phillips, D., McCartney, K., & Scarr, S. (1987). Childcare quality and children's social development. *Developmental Psychology, 23,* 537–543.

Pianta, R. C., & McCoy, S. J. (1997). The first day of school: The predictive validity of early school screening. *Journal of Applied Developmental Psychology, 18,* 1–22.

Ramey, C. T., Bryant, D. M., & Suarez, T. M. (1985). Preschool compensatory education and the modifiability of intelligence: A critical review. *Current Topics in Human Intelligence, 1,* 247–296.

Resnick, G., McKey, R. H., & Klayman, D. (2001). *The evaluation of early childhood education programming in the 30 Abbott School Districts: First-year report on program implementation and descriptions of children and families.* Trenton, NJ: New Jersey Department of Human Services and New Jersey Department of Education.

Resnick, G., & Zill, N. (2003, April). *Understanding quality in Head Start classrooms: The role of teacher and program-level factors.* Paper presented at the Biennial Meeting of the Society for Research in Child Development, Tampa, FL, April 24–27, 2003.

Reynolds, A. T. (1995). One year of preschool or two: Does it matter? *Early Childhood Research Quarterly, 10,* 1–31.

Rosenthal, R., & Rosnow, R. L. (1984). *Essentials of behavioral analysis: Methods and data analysis.* New York: McGraw-Hill.

Sammons, P., Elliot, K., Melhish, E., Siraj-Blatchford, I., & Taggart, B. (2004). The impact of pre-school on young children's cognitive attainments at entry to reception. *British Educational Research Journal, 30*(5), 691–712.

Singer, J. (1998). Using SAS PROC MIXED to fit multilevel models, hierarchical models, and individual growth models. *Journal of Educational and Behavioral Statistics, 24*(4), 323–355.

Snow, C.E., Barnes, W., Chandler, J., Goodman, L., & Hemphill, L. (1991). *Unfulfilled expectations: Home and school influences on literacy.* Cambridge, MA: Harvard University Press.

Snow, C.E., Burns, M.S., & Griffin, P. (Eds.). (1998). *Preventing reading difficulties in young children.* Washington, DC: National Academy Press.

Snow, C.E., Tabors, P.O., Nicholson, P.A., & Kurland, B.F. (1995). SHELL: Oral language and early literacy skills in kindergarten and first-grade children. *Journal of Research in Early Childhood Education, 10*(1), 37–48.

Spira, E.G., Bracken, S.S., & Fischel, J.E. (2005). Predicting improvement after first-grade reading difficulties: The effects of oral language, emergent literacy, and behavior skills. *Developmental Psychology, 41*(1), 225–234.

Valentine, J., & Zigler, E.F. (1983). Head Start: A case study in development of social policy for children and families. In E.F. Zigler, S.L. Kagan, & E. Klugman (Eds.), *Children, families, and government: Perspectives on American social policy* (pp. 266–280). Cambridge, MA: Cambridge University Press.

Vendell, D.L., Shumow, L., & Posner, J. (2005). After-school programs for low-income children: Differences in program quality. In J.L. Mahoney & R.W. Larson (Eds.), *Organized activities as contexts of development: Extracurricular activities, after-school and community programs* (pp. 437–456). Mahwah, NJ: Erlbaum.

Wasik, B.A., & Bond, M.A. (2001). Beyond the pages of a book: Interactive book reading and language development in preschool classrooms. *Journal of Educational Psychology, 93*(2), 243–250.

Weiss, H.B., Resnick, G., & Hausman, B. (1987, unpublished). The place of family support and education programs on the social policy agenda. *Harvard Occasional Papers Series.* Cambridge, MA: Harvard Family Research Project.

White, K.R. (1986). Efficacy of early intervention. *Journal of Special Education, 19,* 401–416.

White, K.R., & Casto, G. (1985). An integrative review of early intervention efficacy studies with at-risk children: Implications for the handicapped. *Analysis & Intervention in Developmental Disabilities, 5*(1–2), 7–31.

Whitebook, M., Howes, C., & Phillips, D. (1989). *Who cares? Childcare teachers and the quality of care in America.* Final report of the National Child Care Staffing Study. Oakland, CA: Child Care Employee Project.

Whitehurst, G.J., & Lonigan, C.J. (1998). Child development and emergent literacy. *Child Development, 69*(3), 848–872.

Willett, J. (1989). Some results on reliability for the longitudinal measurement of change: Implications for the design of studies of individual growth. *Educational & Psychological Measurement, 49*(3), 587–602.

Zill, N., Collins, M., West, J., & Hausken, E.G. (1995). *Approaching kindergarten: A look at preschoolers in the United States.* Washington, DC: U.S. Department of Education, Office of Educational Research and Improvement, National Center for Education Statistics, National Household Education Survey.

Zill, N., Moore, K.A., Smith, E.W., Stief, T., & Coiro, M.J. (1995). The life circumstances and development of children in welfare families: A profile based on national survey data. In P.L. Chase-Lansdale & J. Brooks-Gunn (Eds.), *Escape from poverty: What makes a difference for children?* (pp. 38–59). New York: Cambridge University Press.

Zill, N. and Resnick, G. (2005). Emergent literacy of low-income children in Head Start: Relationships with child and family characteristics, program factors and classroom quality. In Dickinson, D. and Neumann, S. (Eds.). *Handbook of Early Literacy Research, vol. 2.* New York: Guilford Publications.

Chapter 12

EARLY LEARNING AND SCHOOL READINESS: CAN EARLY INTERVENTION MAKE A DIFFERENCE?

Craig T. Ramey and Sharon Landesman Ramey

WHAT INFLUENCES YOUNG CHILDREN'S ACADEMIC ACHIEVEMENT?

Beyond any doubt, there are powerful and long-lasting environmental influences on children's academic achievement (Borkowski, Ramey, & Bristol-Power, 2002; Ramey & Ramey, 2004; Shonkoff & Phillips, 2000). The two best-documented and largest influences on a child's language and intellectual competence at time of entry into kindergarten are: (1) parental cognitive competence, as indexed by parent education, tested intelligence, and/or tested language skills; and (2) extensive exposure to high-quality learning opportunities, at home and/or in high-quality center-based preschool programs. Hundreds of scientific studies substantiate these major conclusions (Ramey & Ramey, 1998a), including recent large-scale and carefully conducted observational studies (e.g., NICHD Early Child Care Research Network, 2005; Reynolds & Temple, this volume) and experimental studies (e.g., Ramey, Ramey, & Lanzi, 2004, in press; Schweinhart, this volume). These studies support conclusions consistent with the landmark studies from the 1930s through 1960s about the lasting impact of early environmental deprivation versus enrichment (Ramey & Sackett, 2000; Shonkoff & Phillips, 2000). Indeed, the strong scientific support about the importance of parental educational attainment and intelligence and the value of providing educationally enriching experiences has been the basis for launching major federal, state, and philanthropic programs that now invest many billions of dollars annually in efforts intended to improve the intellectual development and school performance of children living in poverty. Among the best known are Head Start, Early Head Start, Even Start, Title I programs, and Good Start/Grow Smart.

There is little controversy about the conclusion that children from very low-resource families are at great risk for poor academic progress; in contrast, there still are vigorous debates within the political and scientific arenas concerning whether or not investment in early educational interventions produces major benefits (e.g., Bruer, 1999; Herrnstein & Murray, 1994). By posing extreme questions such as "Are the first three years the only years that matter?" "Are we forcing children to learn too early?" "Will academically stimulating preschool programs prevent children from playing and learning social skills?" critics create an aura of uncertainty that the life course of at-risk children can be altered. In this chapter, we begin by sharing our insights into why the scientific evidence continues to be debated, ignored, or distorted. Second, we provide an up-to-date summary of key scientific findings from our own experimental studies, here and abroad, regarding educational interventions to promote positive health and education outcomes in vulnerable young children. We emphasize the consistency of findings and the pattern of benefits to children over their life course. Further, we note that some children benefit more than others do and suggest mechanisms that account for these differential benefits. Third, we identify those program features we judge to be essential to produce measurable benefits in children's academic and school performance and note that our research also supports the idea of spillover effects—that is, unintended benefits that improve parent and family well-being. Fourth, we report, with sadness and our own sense of moral obligation, from firsthand observations that there currently is widespread neglect as well as poor-quality instruction in many preschool, child care, and Head Start programs. These include programs designed to implement evidence-based practices but that fail to understand adequately what young children need to promote language, early literacy and math skills, and good social-negotiation and problem-solving skills. We conclude by identifying strategies we think are promising to produce effective and timely correction of a nationally unacceptable situation in which many children are in harm's way.

WHY THE DEBATE CONTINUES ABOUT THE VALUE OF EARLY INTERVENTIONS AND HOW TO SHIFT IT TO BE PRODUCTIVE

For five decades, there have been strong national and local efforts to reduce educational disparities, including major efforts to eliminate segregated education and to improve the quality of public education. These include the U.S. Supreme Court's 1954 landmark decision *Brown v. Board of Education,* the launching of the War on Poverty, and efforts by First Ladies Barbara Bush to launch family literacy programs, Hilary Rodham Clinton (1996) to promote understanding of the importance of early-childhood learning, and Laura Bush to promote early literacy and language programs, including the Good Start, Grow Smart program. The effects of the abysmal and shameful history of racism in the United States are far from eliminated, however, by these efforts (Donovan & Cross, 2002). Since 1968, when Klaus and Gray published the first article describing positive results from an experimental study (randomized controlled trial) in Tennessee that provided systematic educational enrichment to children from extremely economically impoverished homes, there has been a steady reporting of positive outcomes attributed to providing high-quality instructional supports to children prior to school entry. Why then does the debate still continue as though there is an unresolved question about the potential of such planned early educational interventions to produce meaningful gains?

Having been so close to these debates, literally and figuratively being on the center stage, in the front rows, and in the hallways, we have observed multiple (and surprisingly divergent) forces that sustain the debates that we judge to be misguided and largely misinformed. The consequences of allowing such debates to continue are serious, because they erode confidence in the importance and urgency of ensuring that all young children receive high-quality early care and supports for learning. At the same time, a naive and uncritical belief that any program or outreach effort is likely to have at least some positive effects, and certainly no harmful effects, is unwarranted and potentially dangerous.

The critics who claim either that early intervention does not work, or that the effects are very small and not long lasting, come from five major groups: (1) academic and scientific circles, where skepticism is considered a sign of intellectual prowess and where the most vocal critics have been individuals who have never conducted treatment or intervention research; (2) socially and fiscally conservative groups that are reluctant to spend more money in efforts to alter the life course of poor people—some because they believe that social class order is a natural, unavoidable, and maybe even good condition and others because they believe government-led programs will erode responsibility and self-initiative in families and local communities; (3) religious groups that believe it is fundamentally wrong to interfere with any aspect of parenting and family life, particularly in the early formative years; (4) groups seeking support for alternative programs (e.g., improving middle or high school education, home visiting programs) that perceive a major threat from expansion of early educational initiatives; and (5) some individuals, programs, and advocacy groups currently supported by one or more of the many early-childhood initiatives that do not want their programs to be closely monitored or evaluated for fear that inadequacies will be revealed, and some entire programs found seriously deficient or harmful to children. These five groups often participate in maintaining the public and policy debates, with quite different motives but an awareness that they mutually benefit from one another as they support the aura of uncertainty about what, if anything, should be done to improve societal investments in very young children's well-being. From our vantage point, these debates essentially cancel out any major new investments and eliminate thoughtful plans to be innovative in combining funding streams, establishing national standards for care and early education, and developing effective systems of monitoring and improving the quality of programs for vulnerable young children and their families.

We acknowledge that the scientific and scholarly critics have legitimate concerns about some very important and still-unanswered questions, such as exactly what amounts and types of learning supports are needed at particular ages, whether or not programs segregated by poverty status are less effective or maybe harmful compared to programs that are economically as well as racially and ethnically integrated, and whether or not biological factors (including controversial genetic influences) are contributing to differential needs and benefits. Unfortunately, however, some academically affiliated individuals have used their credentials and perceived status to promote seriously distorted conclusions from the scientific evidence. Why? Part of the answer is that authors who claim that the status quo in the United States cannot or should not be changed (e.g., Herrnstein & Murray's *The Bell Curve,* 1994) or that the early years of life are not of much consequence (e.g., Bruer's *Myth of the First Three Years,* 1999), garner tremendous national media attention and then receive large royalties and speaking fees related to their extreme claims. Substantial financial incentives are offered by those groups (identified above) that welcome having outsiders—with apparent scholarly backing—who independently assert that efforts to promote the well-being of poor and minority children are doomed. The prominence achieved by these naysayers is possible, in part, because the results of the research are, in fact, complex and widely scattered in journals, books, and project reports; the early educational intervention studies have had some notable limitations and flaws; and their writings are so skillful that it is virtually impossible for even a highly intelligent, but nonspecialist reader to recognize the extent to which these authors have distorted, selectively ignored, and oversimplified the scientific evidence. Besides, these authors' posture as brave mavericks is highly appealing, and the more scholarly scientists in the field have very little "news" because the evidence affirming positive outcomes has been reported many times before.

In seeking to redirect the debates in the realms of public policy, early-childhood and educational "best practices," and the human life sciences, we review the evidence from our own research in the next section, with particular attention to underscoring both the consistencies in major conclusions and the pressing, but not yet answered, questions.

EXPERIMENTAL STUDIES REGARDING EDUCATIONAL INTERVENTIONS FOR VULNERABLE YOUNG CHILDREN

Over the past 35 years, we have been engaged in multiple research studies that test the basic hypothesis that the course of a child's life can be altered in a positive direction by systematically providing enriching experiences. Our research studies have been conducted on children from environments that are very high risk as indexed by multiple factors, children with risk conditions and disabilities recognized at or near birth, and children who have suffered from natural disaster, including deprivation in orphanages.

Science promotes knowledge through a rigorous process of designing and conducting research that gathers evidence in ways that are as objective and valid (accurate) as possible and then actively analyzes the evidence to help inform understanding of a given phenomenon. In this section, we provide examples of major findings from our own studies that have used an experimental (rather than descriptive or naturalistic) design—that is, studies with a randomized controlled trial methodology in which children and families have an equal chance of being assigned to the educational intervention group or the comparison group. In our research, we adopted an approach that uses no untreated control groups, but rather we provide additional health and social supports to participants in the comparison condition. This variation in research design is important to understanding what is revealed by the scientific findings from these studies. We have been seeking to test the idea that the educational intervention itself is the primary change agent (in other words, educational enrichment experiences are what directly alter children's development); thus, we judge as essential that other risk factors be ruled out—specifically, inadequate early nutrition, failure to receive well-child health care and immunizations, and serious family disturbances such as violence, substance abuse, and inadequate housing. Accordingly, the studies we have conducted include a comparison group that received assistance in nutrition, health care, and social services throughout the time they participated in the project.

The educational intervention group also received these basic nutritional, health, and social services plus the educational intervention being tested for efficacy.

The primary educational interventions we have developed and evaluated provide direct support to children on a consistent, daily, and extended basis. In developmental and educational terms, these supports can be characterized as responsive and stimulating care, individualized, fun and natural for both children and adults, and educationally rich in terms of preparing a young child for the anticipated language, cognitive, and social demands in school and later life. All of our studies used and implemented a formal, well-documented, written curriculum or treatment protocol (so that the educational intervention can be fully understood and, if desired, replicated exactly or modified for special populations).

Two other features about our research warrant mention here. First, the educational interventions are ones that we and our colleagues designed, based on both theory and previous research results about how to promote early learning, and that we had fully controlled in terms of staffing, training, supplies, and daily operations. We monitored our programs constantly and systematically documented them in terms of the provision of the planned and individualized educational treatment activities. That is, we did not start with existing programs and staff and seek to improve their quality, nor did we rely on others to try to implement our curriculum on their own. Frequently, the general public thinks that some of our interventions were Head Start or Head Start-like programs. This is not correct, even though the findings from these studies are among those most frequently cited by Head Start and Early Head Start supporters. (For those seeking more information about Head Start and Early Head Start, programs that have national standards but are highly variable in the types, amounts, and quality of supports they actually provide to children living in poverty, we recommend reading Zigler & Styfco's *The Head Start Debates,* 2004). Some critics point out that our programs may have had close-to-ideal conditions, because they were not part of an externally regulated ongoing program, and, therefore, these findings are unlikely to be found elsewhere. We recognize that the greatest challenge for the field of early intervention lies in determining how to ensure that "real-world" programs adhere to high standards for performance at all times, in order to ensure benefits for participating children and their families.

A second important feature is that our research was peer-reviewed from the beginning, and throughout its long-term follow-up periods, and adhered to high scientific standards and university scrutiny to prevent potential bias in collecting outcome data and documenting program delivery. For example, each time children and parents were assessed, the assessors were rigorously trained in the data-collection procedures, had no information about the child's or family's history or previous performance, and had not been part of the treatment intervention. Such features collectively serve to strengthen confidence in the objectivity and accuracy of the reported and peer-reviewed findings.

The Historical Context for the Abecedarian Project and Its Replication Studies

The historical context for launching the Abecedarian Project in the early 1970s is remarkably similar to today's context in that school readiness and school achievement were at the forefront of our country's domestic social policy concerns (Ramey & Ramey, 1998b). How can we help all children in the United States to truly succeed in school and in life? A well-educated citizenry has always been an American ideal, promoted as vital to the future of our democracy as well as a productive and economically strong nation. Alarmingly high numbers of children, then as now, were starting public kindergarten with major delays in language and basic academic skills. Waiting until these children "failed" in school, often by repeating one or more grades and then by being shifted into special education classes where educational expectations were further lowered and instruction in academic content areas was reduced, established a predictable cycle associated with early school dropout, marginal skill sets in adolescence and early adulthood, increased likelihood of engaging in risk-taking behaviors destructive to self and society, and failure to become economically self-sufficient. The idea of preventing this cycle of downward decline in the first two decades of life was not novel, but there was a need to carefully test if a planned treatment or intervention could suffice to counter or minimize the cumulative toll of many negative environmental and likely biological influences on high-risk children. Although critics correctly point out that the most-cited research findings (including those from the Abecedarian Project) used in today's policy arenas derive from "old research," this is simply because measuring long-term outcomes in children takes several decades. Moreover, the issue of so many children arriving at public school with major developmental delays in language and cognitive skills is as pressing now as it was three decades ago, despite tremendous changes in our nation's demography.

Are conditions of poverty, racism, segregation, violence, and public schools worse or better today than in the 1970s, the 1980s, or the 1990s? From our perspective as scientists, the nature and severity of entrenched poverty always have varied considerably from place to place and time to time, yet the consequences for children appear quite similar—namely, they receive extremely low levels of environmental support and few learning opportunities, which contribute to serious delays in their cognitive and language development. Indeed, even in the extremely impoverished Romanian orphanages where we conducted research (see following section), the absences in terms of responsive care, frequent individualized verbal and social exchanges, and systematic efforts to promote learning and intellectual competence were shockingly similar to those we observed in very low-resource homes and child care settings in both inner city and rural settings in the United States. Although the particular context for our first project was a small university town in North Carolina, with a good public educational system and a small proportion of children born into poverty, we subsequently expanded our scientific inquiry into many diverse settings—all with the same goal of answering the straightforward question "To what extent can children's downward spiral be prevented and their lifelong learning be promoted?"

The Abecedarian Study

The first study we began is known as the Abecedarian (pronounced *Ab'-a-sa-dare-ee-an,* similar to ABCDarian) or the ABC Study. The word *Abecedarian* comes from Latin and means "one who learns the basics, such as the alphabet." Originally, the ABC Study was conceptualized as a scientific study that would enroll children from all walks of life, including children from very high-resource families. Funding priorities, then as now, however, did not support the importance of learning how to sustain and enhance high academic competence in children from nonrisk or advantaged families. Thus, in the early 1970s, we began the process of enrolling 111 children in the Abecedarian Study, based on systematic risk screening conducted in the Health Department, the Department of Social Services, and the local maternity hospital. All enrolled families had a composite Risk Index indicative of very low resources and multiple disadvantages: Family incomes averaged well below 50 percent of the federal poverty line; mothers' education averaged about 10 years of education (mothers with any college experience were excluded); low maternal intellectual attainment (with a mean maternal full-scale WAIS IQ score near 80); and mostly unemployed, single parents (although many were not receiving public welfare). At birth, all of the children were judged to be healthy, full-term, and normal birth weight. Mothers granted informed consent to be in the study and to be randomly assigned to one of the two groups (described later).

Table 12.1 outlines the two major preschool groups in the Abecedarian, or ABC, Project. Both the treatment group and the control group were provided adequate nutrition in the form of free, unlimited supplies of formula (no mother chose to breast-feed), social services for the family and referrals as needed (such as for housing, job-training, mental health, and substance abuse problems), and free or reduced-cost medical care throughout the first five years of life (consistent with the highest levels of professionally recommended pediatric care). Thus, the ABC comparison-group children and their families were not "untreated"; further, throughout the study, whenever children's performance on outcome measures indicated clinical problems or potential concerns, the project staff made referrals and assisted with obtaining appropriate follow-up evaluations and treatment. Thus, a potential criticism of the ABC study is that it probably is underestimating the benefits of early intervention, because the comparison children and their families did receive some systematic and ongoing help. The scientific comparison of the group receiving educational intervention along with nutrition, health, and social services versus the nutrition, health, and social services group thus represents a scientifically cautious estimate of how much the combined package of supports helped the children and their parents. We think this was both ethically and scientifically desirable.

What Was the ABC Educational Program and Curriculum? The educational experimental group children were enrolled in a specially created early-childhood center by the time they were six months of age. This preschool program was a full-day program (most children spent 8 to 10 hours per day in the program), 5 days per week, 50 weeks per year. Children

Table 12.1
Supports in the First Five Years of Life Provided to Children in the Two Abecedarian Groups

Treatment Group	*Control Group*
• Adequate nutrition	• Adequate nutrition
• Supportive social services	• Supportive social services
• Free primary health care	• Low-cost or free primary health care
• Preschool treatment:	
Intensive (full day, 5 days/week,	
50 weeks/year, 5 years)	
Learningames Curriculum	
Cognitive fine motor	
Social self	
Motor	
Language	
Individualized pace	

Source: Campbell & Ramey (1995).

received free transportation to the program, and all children attended until they entered public kindergarten. The specially developed curriculum, known as Learningames (Sparling & Lewis, 1979, 1984) and later as Partners for Learning (Sparling, Lewis, & Ramey, 1995), was informed by developmental theory and the burgeoning scientific evidence about how infants and toddlers learn. The ABC Learningames curriculum had more than 500 specified activities for teachers to provide for children in the areas of cognition, fine motor development, social and self-development, motor development, and language. These learning activities had been pretested on an independent sample of infants and toddlers and emphasized learning using natural everyday objects and situations in the developmental domains of language, general cognition, personal and social development, and gross and fine motor development. Teacher to child ratios were 1:3 for the first year of life, 1:4 for the second year of life, 1:5 for three-year-olds, 1:6 for four-year-olds, and 1:7 for five-year-olds. Each classroom had a teacher and an aide, with classroom size limited to double the ratios for each age (e.g., 6 infants with 2 adults, 14 five-year-olds with 2 adults). Both teachers and aides received intensive preservice and weekly in-service training throughout the project. Generally, the teachers had four-year college degrees (mostly in education, some with master's degrees), and aides did not. About half of the teaching staff were African American, half not; some were hired through a Job Corps program. The teaching staff was highly skilled at individualizing the Learningames curriculum in the way it was designed: namely, to have children, from early infancy on, receive continuous exposure to challenging learning activities, based largely on Hunt's (1961) *concept of the match.* The concept of the match was part of a theory about motivation, curiosity, and learning that hypothesized that children needed a mix of the familiar and the unfamiliar in order to engage their attention and create an environmental press to acquire increasingly more complex and refined skills. That is, children were not placed in a rigid group curriculum that might have been either too advanced for some or too simple for others. In addition, we designed a special English language curriculum for all five years that emphasized engaging infants in responsive talk, conversational exchanges rather than directive language, and building a large vocabulary, with later introduction of phonics-based activities and early or prereading activities (McGinness & Ramey, 1981; Ramey, McGinness, Cross, Collier, & Barrie-Blackley, 1981) and use of a new IBM-generated program known as Writing to Read for four- and five-year-olds.

The Abecedarian Study Preschool Results. We measured many aspects of children's growth and development during the preschool years. In this article we concentrate on the early outcomes most strongly linked with school readiness, academic achievement, and later school success.

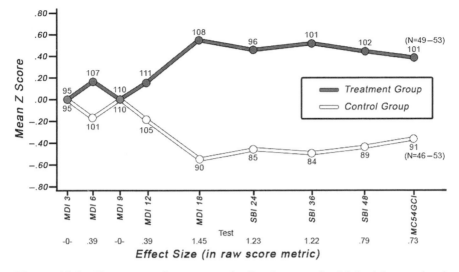

Figure 12.1 Z scores and mean standardized scores for high-risk preschool treatment and control children in the Abecedarian Project at nine preschool measurement occasions (from Ramey et al., 2000)

Figure 12.1 (adapted from Ramey et al., 2000) shows the results of individual cognitive assessments in which a score of 100 represents the national average and the standard deviation is 15 to 16 points. We standardized the scores by summing over both groups and have plotted the mean scores of each group at each age in a common Z-score metric. Above and below each age point, we include the mean developmental quotient or IQ score for each group. The difference between the lines at each point represents the effect size of the treatment, by comparing scores of children in the treatment group relative to those in the control group. In the field of education, an effect size of .25 or greater is widely accepted as practically beneficial and worthy of being the basis for recommending changes in practice and policy. As discussed later, effect sizes exceeded this level after the first year of life at all tested ages, regardless of the particular test of intelligence or general development used.

As Figure 12.1 illustrates, both groups performed similarly during the first nine months of life, and both performed slightly above national average. In the second year of life, there is a precipitous decline in the performance of the control-group children, such that by 18 months old they perform below the low end of the normal range on the Bayley Scales of Infant Development. This decline was prevented in the ABC Educational Intervention group. Throughout the remainder of this preschool period, using two different types of developmental assessments (the Stanford,

Binet IQ and the McCarthy General Cognitive Index), the ABC group averaged approximately 14 IQ points higher than did the control children. The effect sizes, shown on the x-axis, indicated the magnitude of the statistically significant differences. The effect size from 18 months through 4.5 years ranged from .73 to 1.45 with a mean of 1.08, differences that are considered very strong and likely to reflect meaningful benefits in children's everyday lives. We note that this magnitude of difference is exactly the same as that repeatedly reported as the average difference in cognitive and language performance between white/non-Hispanic and African American children in population-based studies in the United States (Herrnstein & Murray, 1994). In the Abecedarian Project, 98 percent of children in both the experimental and comparison groups were African American. The implication of these experimentally produced differences is that early learning experiences clearly serve a major role in reported population differences between blacks and whites. Further, providing enrichment of learning experiences suffices to overcome the typical decline or delays produced by inadequate environmental supports in the first five years of life.

Figure 12.2 displays the scientific findings, in terms of the clinical cut-offs for normal versus below normal range of tested intelligence (Martin, Ramey, & Ramey, 1990). The picture shows that the educational intervention serves to allow children to maintain the normal-range development they showed in the first year of life—and prevents the decline to below

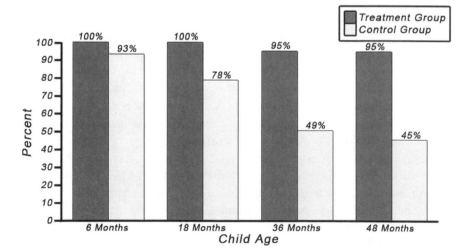

Figure 12.2   Percent of Abecedarian sample in normal IQ range (>84) by age (longitudinal analysis; from Martin, Ramey, & Ramey, 1990)

average levels that characterizes more than 50 percent of the children in the comparison group. In separate analyses, we have discovered that within the comparison group of children, some families (about half) sought and obtained preschool experiences for their children and that their children performed intermediate to those in the ABC educational intervention group and other comparison children who did not receive any center-based care (Burchinal, Campbell, Bryant, Wasik, & Ramey, 1997). Another way of expressing this finding is that the comparison group of children would appear to be even lower in their cognitive performance if we had excluded those comparison children who received extra educational experiences in other community child care centers. By age four, only 45 percent of the comparison children earned scores of 85 points or higher, even though 90 percent were in the normal range in the first year of life; in marked contrast, more than 95 percent of the children in the ABC treatment group were in the normal range of cognitive abilities at all tested ages. This finding underscores the practical magnitude of the treatment group differences and illustrates the role of positive experiences in preventing intellectual disabilities.

School-Age and Young Adult Results of the Abecedarian Program. The Abecedarian children's performance during their K–12 years was followed in terms of key academic indicators. These data are presented in detail in Ramey and Ramey (2000) and Campbell, Pungello, Miller-Johnson, Burchinal, and Ramey (2001). Reading achievement scores on the Woodcock-Johnson Test for those who received the ABC preschool treatment were significantly higher at every age tested, including age 21. Similarly, their math achievement scores also were significantly higher at all tested ages.

In addition to performance on standardized and individually administered tests, the children's real-world school performance is of paramount interest; we identified major markers of school adjustment that have practical and social significance—namely, advancing to the next grade and placement in special education versus continuing in regular education classes (Ramey & Ramey, 2000). Figure 12.3 summarizes the rates of retention in grade by age 15 (i.e., failing at least one grade) and placement in special education. For the comparison group, nearly 6 of 10 children failed at least one grade (for many, they repeated two grades by the time they were 15), whereas this was reduced by about half for the children in the educational intervention group. We do note, however, that grade repetition was not completely eliminated for those who received the early intervention, a finding we think reflects the fact that these children attended schools in which the average levels of achievement were extraordinarily high (above the 90th percentile) among their

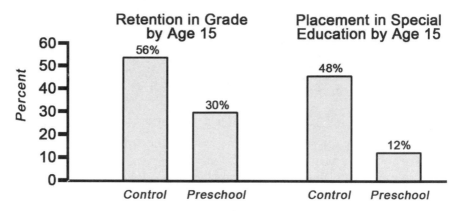

Figure 12.3   Retention in grade and placement in special education by age 15

classmates, many of whom were children of university professors in this small town. Interestingly, the impact of early educational intervention or placement in special education was even more dramatic: Almost 50 percent of the comparison children had been placed in special education by the age of 15 (often after repeated academic failures and social adjustment problems), compared to only 12 percent of those in the ABC education group. This is close to the national average of 11 percent placement in special education. In general, special education costs are projected to be approximately two-and-a-half times the cost of regular education, and children in special education are entitled to free public education for an extra three years (until the age of 22). The stigmatization associated with special education has been considerable for many children, particularly those from low-income and/or minority families who do not have medically diagnosed disabilities (e.g., Donovan & Cross, 2002). Thus, the benefits can be measured at both the individual psychological level and in terms of societal cost savings.

We have had the rare opportunity to be able to follow 99 percent of the living children into adulthood. Key results when they were 21 years old (Campbell, Ramey, Pungello, Sparling, & Miller-Johnson, 2002) confirm significant benefits. Not only were treated children still performing better on intelligence and reading and math assessments, but almost 70 percent of those who received the preschool treatment were engaged in skilled jobs (above entry-level positions) or enrolled in higher education, in contrast to only 40 percent of those in the control group. What was particularly noteworthy was that the educational intervention children were three times more likely to attend a four-year college than were control-group children: 36 percent versus 12 percent. Another young adult advantage was the delay of almost two years in their age of having a first child—waiting until after high school completion. These practical positive outcomes appear to be mediated by improved cognitive, linguistic, and social competence (Burchinal et al., 1997).

Summary of Abecedarian Results. The key findings from the ABC/ Abecedarian Project are consistent and encouraging. From 18 months through 21 years of age, the benefits include the children's higher IQ and reading and math scores; an improved understanding of their role in the educational process, reflected in improved "academic locus-of-control" scores (Walden & Ramey, 1983) in which the children equate their effort and learning with their grades and achievement (rather than attributing them to factors such as teacher bias, chance, or luck); increased social competence, more years of education, and greater likelihood of full-time and higher-status employment. The rates of grade repetition, special education placement, teen pregnancy, and smoking and drug use were all significantly lower than in the control group. We believe that these findings and those from other early intervention research programs have established that early intervention can be a major positive factor in altering the developmental course of high-risk children. Not all early intervention programs have produced such positive results, however.

Replication of Abecedarian Benefits in the Preschool Years

The hallmark of science is replicability of procedures and findings. The ABC Project was replicated beginning in 1977 and 1978 in North Carolina in Project CARE (Ramey, Bryant, Sparling, & Wasik, 1985; Wasik, Ramey, Bryant, & Sparling, 1990) and then later replicated in a multisite randomized, controlled study of 985 low-birth-weight, premature infants in eight different sites (Ramey et al., 1992). In each of these nine replication studies, significant benefits of the preschool educational treatment obtained (Ramey & Ramey, 2000; Ramey & Ramey, 2004). These projects used the same adult-to-child ratios, the same educational curriculum and training supports for teachers and aides, and also documented the individualization of the educational intervention in a manner consistent with the ABC Project. In fact, the magnitude of the measured differences—averaging between the performance of the experimental and comparison-group children—is almost identical across these studies, despite differences in when the research was conducted (from the 1970s through the early 1990s), the use of newly standardized tests with updated national norms, and differences in the ethnic, racial, geographic, and birth characteristics of children.

We show a graph that presents comparable findings at age three from these replication studies. Figure 12.4 compares the differences in test performance for children in Project CARE (also in North Carolina, started in 1977) who received the identical preschool experience for the first five years of life as those in the ABC Project as well as findings from the Infant Health and Development Program (IHDP; Liaw & Brooks-Gunn, 1993) conducted in eight different cities where two groups of low-birth-weight infants received a highly similar ABC educational intervention. In this figure, the test scores are for the heavier low-birth-weight infants (2,000g–2,500g) that constitute the majority of low-birth-weight infants born in the United States. These heavier low-birth-weight children come disproportionately from minority, low-income, and low-education families and thus are most like the children served in the original ABC Project. The IHDP eight-site replication, however, differed in several other ways from the ABC Project. The IHDP center-based educational program did not begin until children were 12 months of age; there was a formal home visiting program, begun just after birth with weekly home visits in the first year of life to teach mothers a variety of skills, from problem solving related to their own lives to being able to stimulate their children's development in the same domains as the Partners for Learning curriculum; followed by bimonthly then monthly visits in years two and three; and the IHDP educational intervention ended when the children were 36 months old (correcting for gestational age). This earlier end was based on a plan (that did not fully materialize) that almost all of the children would naturally transition into Head Start programs or into other community

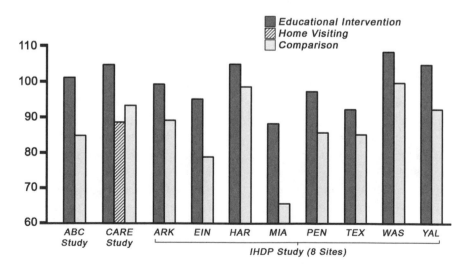

Figure 12.4   Stanford-Binet IQ scores at 36 months

preschools that would provide high-quality instruction when children were four and five years old. Despite these differences, Figure 12.4 shows that in all nine of these replication studies, there were significant and large differences in cognitive attainment at age three, with an average of about 13 IQ points across these nine replications. (In the section on differential benefits, we discuss a somewhat different pattern of results—the results for the more biologically impaired children who made up the lighter low-birth-weight group—as well as the failure to produce benefits for a highly intensive home visiting group in Project CARE.)

In 1990, after Communist rule had been overthrown in Romania, we were asked to help plan for the rehabilitation of children who had suffered extreme deprivation in the Romanian leagans (institutions depicted as orphanages in Western media). These efforts included international exchange programs; rebuilding the professions of pediatrics, nursing, special education, and psychology that had been forbidden areas of study for three decades; and conducting scientific research to answer key questions about the extent of recoverability among children who had been institutionalized for different lengths of time. J. Sparling, the lead author of the ABC and IHDP curricula, coordinated the translation and adaptation of Partners for Learning into Romanian and trained the teachers who implemented the intervention. We conducted two randomized controlled trials in which the educational intervention was offered for 6 hours a day, 5 days a week, for 12 or 13 consecutive months. Children in the comparison group were provided enrichment materials and books, and their care providers were eligible to attend professional development workshops. No children were prevented from being placed in more optimal settings or from being adopted during the course of the study. Figure 12.5 displays findings for the outcomes of language and personal-social development. What is noteworthy in this group of children, who had been institutionalized for all or almost all of their first 15 months of life, is that their initial levels of performance had been delayed by about half—that is, they demonstrated the developmental level of a typical seven- to eight-month-old infant (using U.S. norms, the only ones available). After 13 months of daily educational enrichment, children in the educational intervention group advanced their skills 15 months in personal-social and 10 months in language. The comparison group, however, although they showed some progress, actually became more delayed in their overall development by the end of the study, with the most profound delays occurring in language development, in which they lagged by more than a full year by the time they were just older than two years old. This precipitous decline in language development in the second year of life is similar to that observed

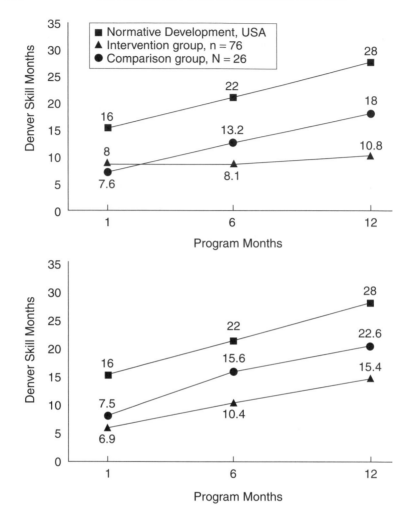

Figure 12.5   Language and personal social development

in the ABC comparison children who received low levels of stimulation in their natural environments (as documented independently through multiple visits to conduct standardized home assessments). In a recent article, we conclude (Sparling, Dragomir, Ramey, & Fiorescu, 2005) that early deprivation does not permanently impair children's ability to learn or to benefit from educational experiences that are developmentally well matched to their needs, but the educational enrichment we provided was insufficient to overcome the toll already taken at the time the intervention began.

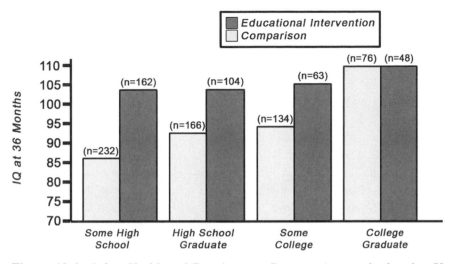

Figure 12.6   Infant Health and Development Program (maternal education X treatment group; adapted from Ramey & Ramey, 1998a)

Differential Benefits of Early Education. One of the most pressing public policy issues is which young children need and can benefit from Abecedarian-style educational enrichment. For instance, do all premature and low-birth-weight infants need a special early educational intervention program like IHDP, or are family resources an important contributing factor to degree of developmental risk? The findings from the Infant Health and Development Program in eight sites are informative. As shown in Figure 12.6, the 608 comparison-group children reveal the well-established effects of maternal education on children's intellectual and cognitive performance. That is, the comparison children whose mothers have less than a high school degree performed at the very lowest levels, with an average IQ around 85—the same average that appears for children in most all inner-city schools throughout the United States. In the comparison, the next most cognitively capable children were those whose mothers had a high school education, followed by the group whose mothers had some college education, and then the highest-performing group—exceeding the national average of 100—were children whose mothers had a four-year college degree or higher. This stepwise and orderly difference reflects what is termed the *achievement gap* when children enter school, and the well known social class differences documented for decades throughout the United States. The expected pattern, however, is essentially eliminated for three of the four maternal education groups when their premature, low-birth-weight infants received the IHDP early-childhood education. Essentially, the provision of the ABC preschool program "leveled the playing field" for these children by supporting their performance at levels very close to or just higher than the national average. Notice, however, that there is one group of children who did not display significant benefits of the preschool treatment: namely, those children whose parents were college graduates. For this group, the children fared quite well regardless of whether or not they participated in the planned educational intervention or the natural stimulation and programs that parents in the comparison group provided for their infants. This indicates that not all children need to have additional systematic education or enrichment in the form of a planned preschool program, a finding confirmed in other studies as well. Rather, those children whose families have the lowest resources—best estimated by their parents' own educational and intellectual skills—are those who have the greatest need and appear likely to benefit the most from systematic provision of enriched learning opportunities. It is also important to note that there was no negative effect of the treatment on the intellectual performance of children from high-resource families. This is important because such families may seek high-quality care for their children for reasons other than educational enrichment—such as employment of the mothers.

In the Infant Health and Development Program, the educational intervention also was provided for a group of more biologically vulnerable infants, those whose birth weights were below 2,000g. For the lighter low-birth-weight infants, the educational intervention produced significant benefits in seven of the eight sites, and the overall average magnitude of benefits as measured at age three in terms of IQ points was about half that detected for the heavier low-birth-weight children (Liaw & Brooks-Gunn, 1993). This differential level of benefits is attributable, we think, to three factors: (1) these children may have had increased special learning needs that were not as readily met by the standard educational program (partially confirmed by their average lower levels of performance in both the comparison and educational intervention groups); (2) these children included a greater proportion from higher-income and higher-education families, and therefore it is less likely that lack of appropriate environmental learning opportunities was the major source of their lower cognitive attainment; and (3) in the one site that did not show benefits, the comparison children were eligible for participation in the state early intervention program, which essentially provided equal types of early supports for these premature, low-birth-weight infants. Children in both groups in this site (Boston) performed at high levels, compared to children in the other seven sites.

Finally, we have reported elsewhere that in the ABC Project, Project CARE, and IHDP, the children who appear to benefit at particularly high levels are those with mothers whose full-scale WAIS IQ scores or Peabody

Picture Vocabulary Test scores fall below 70, the range considered *significantly subnormal* (consistent with a diagnosis of mental retardation if accompanied by major problems in adaptive behavior; Ramey, Echols, Ramey, & Newell, 2001). For example, in the ABC Study, the children's own IQ scores average more than 25 points higher than their mothers' at the time children are ready to enter public school. In essence, the educational intervention eliminated their very high probability of performing in the borderline or the mentally retarded range themselves, which had a tremendous lifelong benefit for these children. From other research in which we had worked closely with mothers who have intellectual disabilities (IQs below 70 and adaptive behavior limitations), we know that they often face multiple and serious challenges related to providing adequate and appropriate daily care as well as promoting learning and language in their young infants. The quality of stimulation in the home environments for these children whose mothers had low tested intelligence and/or language also were documented in our intervention studies as averaging the very lowest level in the study.

WHAT ARE THE ESSENTIAL PROGRAM ELEMENTS TO PROMOTE SCHOOL READINESS AND ACADEMIC ACHIEVEMENT?

The field of preschool education and early intervention is not without controversy or mixed results. There have been some well-intentioned preschool programs implemented in community settings and funded with public or private dollars that have not been able to demonstrate measurable benefits. Why? We have reviewed and analyzed these studies (e.g., Ramey & Ramey, 1998a; Ramey & Ramey, 2000), as have others (e.g., Haskins, 1989). Here are the most likely reasons that some programs have failed to close the achievement gap. First, many of those programs have not been able to provide the preservice and in-service training needed for their teachers to ensure that the children receive a consistently high-quality learning and language environment. Second, many of those programs are not very intensive; often they are provided after children are four years old, they are offered for just three or four hours per day, or they operate for only seven to nine months. Third, many failed programs have a remedial rather than a preventive focus, making it more difficult to overcome the cumulative toll of limited learning. Fourth, upon close analysis, many of the well-intended programs have primarily supported families and only indirectly tried to help children, while frequently offering little or no direct teaching of important cognitive and language concepts to the children themselves. Although a family's total life situation is undeniably important, high-risk children themselves need to have first-hand experiences with mentoring and appropriate learning experiences in order to progress in their cognitive and linguistic skills. Unfortunately, there are many redundant and poorly coordinated family and early-childhood programs, which simply do not have adequate planning, professional expertise, or resources to deliver a preschool program that will result in major and sustainable cognitive and linguistic gains for children.

Based on reviews of the experimental and quasi-experimental studies about early educational interventions, we have identified the following as major principles or essential features of programs that produce the largest and most lasting benefits for participating children. These are: (1) *the dosage principle:* that is, the amount per day, per week, and per year of the supports provided; (2) *the timing principle:* such that children entering earlier and continuing longer show greater gains; (3) *the principle of academic and language instruction:* children who receive interventions that directly alter their daily learning experiences produce larger positive effects than those interventions that rely primarily on indirect routes (e.g., parent education, family supports) to change children's development; (4) *the principle of continuity of educational supports:* for children who receive educational enrichment prior to entering public school, the quality of their later schooling still matters; if children enter poor-quality schools, this can reduce the measured benefits detected earlier. This latter principle indicates that systematic intervention efforts for the preschool years need to coordinate with and ensure that children enter positive learning situations thereafter (Ramey et al., 2004), essential elements for producing academic and school benefits for at-risk children.

THE QUALITY OF SUPPORTS FOR VULNERABLE CHILDREN AND THEIR FAMILIES: REFLECTIONS FROM OUR FIELD EXPERIENCES

We have conducted many evaluations and reviews of early intervention and preschool programs throughout the United States and in many foreign countries over the past three decades. Although we have seen exemplary programs, and have helped others to plan for implementing programs that incorporate many of the features of the ABC program and aspire to implement evidence-based practices, we have witnessed many disappointing and often short-lived efforts to provide consistently high-quality programs. We sometimes despair that the efforts to provide training and technical assistance appear to be weak and have not been demonstrated to produce gains in the quality of programs. There appears to be a culture of silence about the widespread poor quality that exists in publicly supported and philanthropic efforts to improve the school readiness of at-risk children. We think that professionals and scientists are fearful that acknowledging the poor quality of many of these well-intentioned efforts may lead to decreased overall support for early-childhood programs. To the contrary, we think that allowing poor-quality programs has immediate and even more disturbing consequences: The children and families served by these programs may be harmed or be denied participating in other more effective programs in their own communities, and those policymakers and professionals who also visit poor-quality programs will be distressed that no formal action is being taken to correct the inadequacies. We acknowledge that this is a very delicate situation. What we recommend is that more effort be placed on gathering objective evidence about quality and impact and working collaboratively with funding and monitoring agencies to find effective ways to improve quality of existing programs, close programs that do not demonstrate adequate progress, and stimulate the opening of new programs and supports when need is documented.

Based on the scientific evidence, we offer three major public policy recommendations. The first thing that states and communities need to do is develop strong leadership for a comprehensive early-childhood educational initiative that is linked explicitly to K–12 learning and achievement within each state and community. In developing this initiative, we encourage thinking about the truly high-risk children (who are far fewer than all children in poverty), incorporating the scientific evidence about what really produces measurable benefits, and building upon the resources already available in states.

We also recommend efforts to combine funding streams, to promote innovative partnerships, and to offer high-quality educational supports in ways that build upon local strengths and values. This will help to strengthen existing programs that already are collaborative and can demonstrate positive outcomes; it will also be an opportunity to improve or eliminate those programs that are ineffective or poor in quality. In the future, continued support for preschool programs should be linked to ongoing performance measures of the program's quality and the demonstrated benefits to children in terms of their cognitive, linguistic, and social competence.

Finally, we recommend a system of practical accountability and monitoring that is widely publicized and that parents and the general public can understand and endorse (Ramey, Ramey, & Lanzi, in press). In the past, most early-childhood intervention programs did not have well-designed and practically useful accountability systems. Thus, it has not been possible to characterize the quality of programs or to engage in comparative analysis. This situation cannot continue if we seek to maximize young children's outcomes at reasonable costs. There is much controversy, anxiety, and frank politics surrounding proposed federal guidelines about measuring the development of young children. The fact is there are excellent procedures available to observe and document the quality and amount of preschool education and child care. Child assessments should not be construed as high-stakes testing of children or a disguised effort to diminish public support for early-childhood education; rather, child and program assessments are responsible (and long overdue) for monitoring and evaluation procedures for public preschool services and supports targeted toward our nation's most vulnerable young citizens. The cost of good accountability is relatively small and will not detract from the dollars and efforts available for direct services. To allow interventions and programs to be poorly monitored or not to hold them accountable for their educational quality or child developmental progress would not be in the best interest of our children or our country. Collectively, the well-being and the school readiness of our nation's children needs to be a major priority, so all young children receive the essential transactions and the learning opportunities vital for their brain development and success in school. The past four decades have witnessed remarkable and strong bipartisan support for efforts to serve high-risk young children. It is now time to act upon this knowledge and to provide high-quality preschool programs for all high-risk children. We believe that this is a civil right of all children in a high-resource and ethical society.

It is also time to rethink the research agenda concerning early experience and the modifiability of cognitive development and school readiness for high-risk children. For more than 40 years the predominant research question has been whether or not school readiness could be modified—the so-called efficacy question. We submit that the evidence summarized and referred to in this chapter adds up to a clear and consistent, yes. We believe that the field of child development could make additional useful contributions by focusing on two major issues. First, it would be very helpful to know more about the epidemiology of lack of school readiness. Population-based samples, ideally at the state and community levels of analysis, should be examined on a recurring basis to document the geographical distribution and extent of the school readiness problem. Such research is likely to show systematic concentrations of individuals and their sociodemographic characteristics. Geographical information system mapping can be a useful data display tool to better understand the resulting public policy issues and concerns including where and how large early intervention programs should be to adequately meet the need for service.

Second, comparative analyses of alternative curricular and program features can help to improve program effectiveness by identifying core essentials and to control costs by eliminating weak or ineffectual program features and practices. This refocus would be a sign of the maturing science of human development that increasingly undergirds the provision of services to children and the institutions funded to support the development of individual children.

CONCLUSION

Yes, we now know that we can positively alter the development of young, disadvantaged children through the systematic provision of early-child education. Now the question becomes, "Can we do that better and more efficiently so that we can reach all children who need those services?" We firmly believe that this new focus offers practical promise for children and society.

REFERENCES

Borkowski, J.G., Ramey, S.L., & Bristol-Power, M. (2002). *Parenting and the child's world: Influences on academic, intellectual, and social-emotional development.* New Jersey: Erlbaum.

Bruer, J. (1999). *The myth of the first three years: A new understanding of early brain development and lifelong learning.* New York: Free Press.

Burchinal, M.R., Campbell, F.A., Bryant, D.M., Wasik, B.H., & Ramey, C.T. (1997). Early intervention and mediating processes in cognitive performance of children of low-income African American families. *Child Development, 68,* 935–954.

Campbell, F.A., Pungello, E., Miller-Johnson, S., Burchinal, M., & Ramey, C.T. (2001). The development of cognitive and academic abilities: Growth curves from an early childhood educational experiment. *Developmental Psychology, 37,* 231–242.

Campbell, F.A., & Ramey, C.T. (1995). Cognitive and school outcomes for high-risk African-American students at middle adolescence: Positive effects of early intervention *American Educational Research Journal, 32,* 743–772.

Campbell, F.A., Ramey, C.T., Pungello, E., Sparling, J., & Miller-Johnson, S. (2002). Early childhood education: Outcomes as a function of different treatments. *Applied Developmental Science, 6,* 42–57.

Clinton, H.R. (1996). *It takes a village and other lessons children teach us.* New York: Simon & Schuster.

Donovan, M.S., & Cross, C.T. (Eds.). (2002). *Minority students in special and gifted education.* Washington, DC: National Academy Press.

Haskins, R. (1989). Beyond metaphor: The efficacy of early childhood education. *American Psychologist, 44*(2), 274–282.

Herrnstein, R.J., & Murray, C. (1994). *The bell curve: Intelligence and class structure in American life.* New York: Free Press.

Hunt, J. (1961). *Intelligence and experience.* Oxford, UK: Ronald Press.

Klaus, R.A., & Gray, S.W. (1968). The early training project for disadvantaged children: A report after five years. *Monographs of the Society for Research in Child Development, 33* (4, Serial No. 120).

Liaw, F., & Brooks-Gunn, J. (1993). Patterns of low-birth-weight children's cognitive development. *Developmental Psychology, 29*(6), 1024–1035.

Martin, S.L., Ramey, C.T., & Ramey, S.L. (1990). The prevention of intellectual impairment in children of impoverished families: Findings of a randomized trial of educational day care. *American Journal of Public Health, 80,* 844–847.

McGinness, G., & Ramey, C.T. (1981). Developing sociolinguistic competence in children. *Canadian Journal of Early Childhood Education, 1,* 22–43.

National Institute of Child Health and Human Development (NICHD), Early Child Care Research Network. (2005). Predicting individual differences in attention, memory, and planning in first graders from experiences at home, child care, and school. *Developmental Psychology, 41*(1), 99–114.

Ramey, C.T., Bryant, D.M., Sparling, J.J., & Wasik, B.H. (1985). Project CARE: A comparison of two early intervention strategies to prevent retarded development. *Topics in Early Childhood Special Education, 5,* 12–25.

Ramey, C.T., Bryant, D.M., Wasik, B.H., Sparling, J.J., Fendt, K.H., & LaVange, L.M. (1992). Infant Health and Development Program for low birth weight, premature infants: Program elements, family participation, and child intelligence. *Pediatrics, 89,* 454–465.

Ramey, C.T., Campbell, F.A., Burchinal, M., Skinner, M.L., Gardner, D.M., & Ramey, S.L. (2000). Persistent effects of early childhood education on high-risk children and their mothers. *Applied Developmental Science, 4,* 2–14.

Ramey, C.T., McGinness, G., Cross, L., Collier, A., & Barrie-Blackley, S. (1981). The Abecedarian approach to social competence: Cognitive and linguistic intervention for disadvantaged preschoolers. In K. Borman (Ed.), *The social life of children in a changing society* (pp. 145–174). Hillsdale, NJ: Erlbaum.

Ramey, C.T., & Ramey, S.L. (1998a). Early intervention and early experience. *American Psychologist, 53,* 109–120.

Ramey, C.T., & Ramey, S.L. (1998b). Prevention of intellectual disabilities: Early interventions to improve cognitive development. *Preventive Medicine, 27,* 224–232.

Ramey, C.T., & Ramey, S.L. (2004). Early learning and school readiness: Can early intervention make a difference? *Merrill-Palmer Quarterly, 50,* 471–491.

Ramey, C.T., Ramey, S.L., & Lanzi, R.G. (in press). The health and education of young children: Theory, intervention research, and public policy. In I. Sigel & A. Renninger (Eds.), *The handbook of child psychology.* Hoboken, NJ: Wiley.

Ramey, S.L., Echols, K., Ramey, C.T., & Newell, W.Y. (2001). Understanding early intervention. In M.L. Batshaw (Ed.), *When your child has a dis-*

ability: The complete sourcebook of daily and medical care (rev. ed., pp. 73–84). Baltimore: Paul H. Brookes.

Ramey, S. L., & Ramey, C. T. (2000). Early childhood experiences and developmental competence. In J. Waldfogel & S. Danziger (Eds.), *Securing the future: Investing in children from birth to college* (pp.122–150). New York: Russell Sage Foundation.

Ramey, S. L., Ramey, C. T., & Lanzi, R. G. (2004). The transition to school: Building on the preschool foundations and preparing for lifelong learning. In E. Zigler & S. J. Styfco (Eds.), *The Head Start debates* (pp. 397–413). Baltimore: Paul H. Brookes.

Ramey, S. L., & Sackett, G. P. (2000). The early caregiving environment: Expanding views on nonparental care and cumulative life experiences. In A. J. Sameroff, M. Lewis, & S. M. Miller (Eds.), *Handbook of developmental psychopathology* (pp. 365–380). Dordrecht, Netherlands: Kluwer Academic.

Shonkoff, J. P., & Phillips, D. A. (Eds.). (2000). *From neurons to neighborhoods: The science of early childhood development.* Washington, DC: National Academy Press.

Sparling, J., Dragomir, C., Ramey, S. L., & Fiorescu, L. (2005). An educational intervention improves developmental progress of young children in a Romanian orphanage. *Infant Mental Health Journal, 26,* 127–142.

Sparling, J., & Lewis, I. (1979). *Learningames for the first three years: A guide to parent–child play.* New York: Walker.

Sparling, J., & Lewis, I. (1984). *Learningames for threes and fours: A guide to adult/child play.* New York: Walker.

Sparling, J., Lewis, I., & Ramey, C. (1995). *Partners for learning.* Lewisville, NC: Kaplan.

Walden, T., & Ramey, C. T. (1983). Locus of control and academic achievement: Results from a preschool intervention program. *Journal of Educational Psychology, 75,* 347–358.

Wasik, B. H., Ramey, C. T., Bryant, D. M., & Sparling, J. J. (1990). A longitudinal study of two early intervention strategies: Project CARE. *Child Development, 61,* 1682–1696.

Zigler, E., & Styfco, S. J. (2004). *The Head Start debates.* Baltimore: Paul H. Brookes.

Chapter 13

HEAD START AMBASSADORS FOR LITERACY: PATHWAYS TO COLLEGE

Norman F. Watt and Jini E. Puma

A pervasive problem plagues policy makers in our society. It preoccupies economists concerned with the cost economics of upgrading skill levels in the workplace (Heckman, this volume). It is a primary obstacle to educating the underclass (Duncan & Magnuson, this volume). It complicates our immigration policies (Huntington, 2004) and employment programs (Reich, 2000). It generates heated debates about housing policies (Rusk, this volume) and race relations (Harrison & Huntington, 2001). It challenges affirmative action (Schmidt, 2004) and dictates welfare reform (Sawhill, 1995). The problem is the recalcitrant correlation between employment earnings and years of education completed in the United States. Figure 13.1 plots the average annual earnings by education level attained in the United States. This chart shows a $17,300 difference in the annual employment income of a college graduate

Our introduction to the problem of educating predominantly ethnic minority children from low-income families was made possible initially by two research contracts from the Colorado Department of Education, and much of the credit for successful execution of those investigations must be shared with Irv Moskowitz and David Smith at the Colorado Department of Education and with Maria Guajardo and Howard Markman at the University of Denver.

Extraordinary—even courageous—support for the Resilience Project that by necessity spawned the Ambassadors program originally was provided continuously by Mitzi Barnes, the executive director of the Head Start program in Denver, and Irv Moskowitz, the superintendent of Denver Public Schools when our program was launched.

Inspired community support to raise the funds for the program was provided by dozens of Head Start volunteers, most notably by Marion Gottesfeld, a trustee at the University of Denver for more than half a century, Georgia Imhoff, Susan and Jeremy Shamos, Carol and Kent Johnson, and Helga, Brendan, Douglas, and Kathleen Watt.

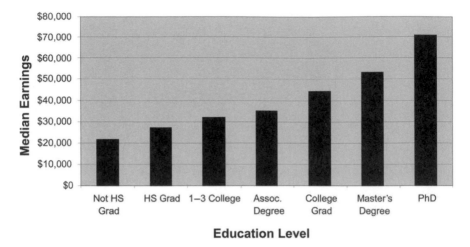

Figure 13.1 Median annual earnings of full-time workers by education level, including all ages, races, and both genders (From "Income in 2002 by Educational Attainment of the Population 18 Years and over, by Age, Sex, Race Alone, and Hispanic Origin," U.S. Census Bureau, 2003)

versus a high school graduate. A master's degree warrants $26,300 per year more than a high school diploma and a PhD degree qualifies for $43,900 more income than a high school education.

If we break these statistics down by ethnicity, we see the same pattern (Figure 13.2). However, we also see that African Americans lag significantly behind whites in yearly earnings, and Latinos lag significantly behind African Americans, even after adjusting for level of education. This trend is troublesome, because Latinos represent the fastest growing segment of the U.S. population and account for more than a quarter of all new entrants into the labor force (Sorensen, Brewer, Carroll, & Bryton, 1995).

These annual differences in income cumulate to very substantial disparities in lifetime earnings attributable to educational attainment. In 1995, the

Generous funding for various aspects of the Ambassadors program was awarded by the Colorado Trust, the Buell Foundation, the Piton Foundation, the Denver Foundation, and the Chambers Family Fund.

Dozens of graduate students at the University of Denver served as mentors for our Ambassadors for Literacy and/or as research assistants for the Resilience Project, most notably among them Peggy Frohlich, Dore LaForett, Nick St. John, Scott Hartman, Jini Puma, Whitney LeBoeuf, Judith McCullough, Laura Diaz, Sandra Barrueco, and Puni Kalra.

Remarkable cooperation and collaboration has been forthcoming at all levels from the Denver Public Schools, the Denver Mayor's Office of Economic Development, the local Head Start centers, and—with the one glaring exception noted—from the Child Opportunity Program.

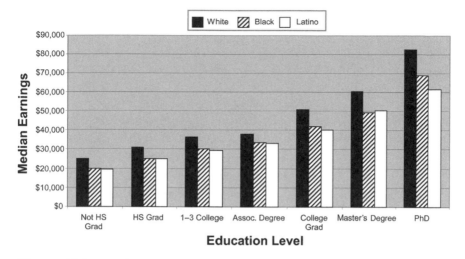

Figure 13.2 Median annual earnings of full-time workers by education level and race, including all ages and both genders (From "Income in 2002 by Educational Attainment of the Population 18 Years and over, by Age, Sex, Race Alone, and Hispanic Origin," U.S. Census Bureau, 2003)

U.S. Census Bureau estimated the premium for a bachelor's degree (over a high school degree) at about $600,000, or 75 percent more in lifetime earnings (Sorensen et al., 1995). A more recent study by the Employment Policy Foundation (2003) estimated the lifetime advantage of a college degree over a high school diploma at approximately $645,000, whereas a master's degree increased lifetime earnings by $140,000 more than a college degree; and a PhD or professional degree warranted almost $600,000 more than a master's degree! Considering that the U.S. population has steadily increased its educational attainment and educational requirements for many occupations, it is clear that a high school diploma is simply not sufficient to ensure opportunity to share in our high standard of living. In addition to the substantial payoffs to individuals for attaining a higher level

Sage advice and occasional discipline have been continuously available from Chancellor Dan Ritchie and the members of our board of directors, currently consisting of Jeremy Shamos (chairman), Vice Chancellor James Moran (University of Denver), Sue Edwards (Denver school board), Al Martinez (Regional Head Start Lead), Susan Shamos (representing donors), Raymond Cordova (representing parents), and Dianne Lefly (Colorado Department of Education).

We are most grateful for the enthusiastic participation of the Ambassadors and their parents, especially Nelson Bock, Flor Amaro, Wendy McCoy, Lorraine Medina, and Raymond Cordova.

The limited dollars in our endowment have been stretched for us by the Marsico Capital Management Company.

of education, there are also societal benefits, because people with college degrees (and concomitant higher earnings) pay significantly more in taxes than those with limited education (Sorensen et al., 1995), which brings to mind a bumper sticker that reads, "If you think education is expensive, you should try ignorance."

It is also well documented that earnings within a family remain relatively stable across generations. Solon (2002) reported that the correlation between fathers' and sons' earnings in the United States is .40 or higher and that no other developed country except the United Kingdom has such immobility across generations. A massive volume of research has established a general consensus that parental intelligence and social class account for approximately half of the variation in the intelligence (Mackintosh, 1998) and social class (Capron & Duyme, 1996) of their offspring. All of these factors create inertia that resists improvement in the fortunes of disadvantaged children.

On the one hand, there seems to be simple Darwinian adaptation in these facts because further education requires great dedication and yields greater skill and productivity for one's employer and for society as a whole. The fly in the ointment is that higher education in our society costs a lot of money and presupposes an appreciation of the intrinsic value of education, both of which are in short supply among our most disadvantaged citizens. Therefore, these predictable regularities conspire to create and stubbornly maintain inequalities of privilege, lifestyle, health, wealth, and even longevity *across* generations, not only in the United States, but also throughout the world (Keating & Hertzman, 1999). This pattern of regeneration is typically referred to as a vicious recycling of poverty. Remedies for this wellspring of inequality naturally gravitate toward education as a cornerstone in our society, though others might take precedence in more primitive societies. There is no surprise here, if one considers the principal sociological components that make up (and measure) social class. Conventionally, some combination and weighting of four family attributes define and reflect the social strata in the United States: occupational status, educational attainment, family income or wealth, and residential location in the community (Hollingshead, 1975). If we wish to conjure up mechanisms for intervention to *change* those factors in order to create the broadest and most sustained impact on all of them, it is logical to attack education (including vocational training) first and foremost. Obviously, residential location and wealth or income are most often heavily dependent on the occupational status and educational attainments of the breadwinners in the family. Furthermore, it stands to reason that the amounts of education and vocational training and preparation (with some rare exceptions) open the doors to future occupational advancement and its contingent benefits in income, wealth, and residential location. We feel that education is the most *seminal* intervention target for improving the quality of life in the United States.

There is abundant literature to support the theory that persistent poverty in the early childhood years undermines later cognitive competence and academic performance (Duncan & Brooks-Gunn, 2000; Linver, Brooks-Gunn, & Kohen, 2002; McLoyd, 1998). Disproportionate numbers of ethnic minorities live in poverty, and they are also more likely to remain in poverty than other Americans (U.S. Census Bureau, 2005) because they underachieve in our educational systems. According to the National Center for Education Statistics (2001), about 28 percent of Latino adolescents, 13 percent of African American adolescents, and 7 percent of Caucasian adolescents drop out of high school. Thus far, few studies have examined why some students from populations considered at risk for academic failure unexpectedly *excel* academically. High-achieving students are much smaller in number than low-achieving students in disadvantaged populations, and these exceptionally talented children can often be overlooked and, therefore, underserved (Robinson, Weinberg, Redden, Ramey, & Ramey, 1998). The Ambassadors for Literacy Program has sought to find and serve these exceptionally bright but economically disadvantaged children in the Denver metro area.

HISTORY OF THE AMBASSADORS FOR LITERACY PROGRAM

The Origins of a Collaboration among Stakeholders in Education

Early in 1992, Norman Watt, a professor of clinical psychology at the University of Denver, called Mitzi Barnes, the executive director of the Head Start program at the Child Opportunity Program (COP), to inquire if there might be interest on her part to collaborate in designing some follow-up research on the subsequent educational careers of the children that had been served as preschoolers by Head Start. She was elated because she had been yearning for years to learn something about the educational fate of the many thousands of children that had been entrusted to her care since she took on the job in 1968. Little did she anticipate the turbulence that was to follow.

The collaboration began with a systematic so-called housecleaning of the totally neglected records on file in the dirty basement of the COP headquarters (which conformed perfectly to the surrounding neighborhood, as described in Vignette 1). All of the available records were reorganized, and the names and critical identifying information about the children and their families were entered into a comprehensive computer file that ultimately numbered more than 17,000 individual children that had been registered for Head Start services since its inception in Denver. Almost three years later, in August 1994, the two collaborators approached Irving Moskowitz on the day before he returned to the Denver Public Schools system to assume the position of superintendent. His announced objective was to make *reading proficiency* the cornerstone of his new administration because he believed that the principal mandate and the principal failing of public education in urban schools was to teach their pupils—especially the disadvantaged ones—how to read English.

Moskowitz had served for two years in the mid-1980s as director of Project 2 + 2 at the Colorado Department of Education. That project was brilliantly christened because it was awarded $2 million each year for two successive years of funding by the Colorado State Legislature for the sole purpose of discovering why so many Latino school children dropped out of school. Moskowitz was (and remains) a dedicated educator, but he was not a scientist. He had previously worked closely with Norman Watt in the early 1980s, so he called on his former collaborator to design a study of Latino public school dropouts in Denver between 9th and 11th Grades, with a comparison sample of Latino classmates who were still enrolled in school. Watt persuaded him that, in order to be fully informative, the research design should include a third sample of Latino children who not only stayed enrolled but also excelled in their attendance and school performance. At that time, it was well known that the majority of Latino school children were demoralized and disinterested in schoolwork, even though they remained in school to the so-called bitter end. Therefore, in order to obtain a full purchase on the dimension of school failure among Latino pupils, a sample of exceptionally *successful* Latino children was necessary to complete the picture. When *two* studies were eventually completed, one in Denver and one in three small rural towns in southern Colorado, the data from the "achievers" proved to yield even *more* insights about the school performance of Latino pupils than did the results for the "strugglers" and the "dropouts" alone.

THE RESPONSE FROM THE DENVER PUBLIC SCHOOLS

Vignette 1: The Setting for the Provision of Head Start Services in Denver

In 1994 Marion Gottesfeld, a Head Start volunteer, invited Bill Coors (a fellow trustee at the University of Denver) and Dan Ritchie (University of Denver chancellor) to visit the Head Start headquarters in Denver. One purpose of the visit was to show Mr. Coors a new playground that he had donated at a cost of $50,000. It was affectionately christened Coors Field II, in honor of the more famous original. While touring the facilities, they asked a teacher if her preschoolers had been exposed to the recent violence in the Five Points neighborhood that was featured in the news. A 4-year-old boy had been killed in his own living room by a random bullet shot to the forehead, and a 15-year-old boy was shot and killed on the street for the purpose of stealing his coveted leather jacket. Both incidents occurred within a radius of three blocks from the Head Start building. The teacher replied with an anecdote. Only last week, an old truck drove past the building and backfired loudly, whereupon a handful of children dove immediately under their miniature tables, reportedly following carefully rehearsed instructions from their mothers. It was a matter of both survival and common sense in the minds of those mothers who, despite their limited education, could and did read the newspapers.

Those were among the most visible and salient threats to the health and future of those Head Start preschoolers. One of the cruel ironies of this most ambitious preventive intervention in history is that it must be delivered for optimal efficacy *on site,* that is, in the ghettos and barrios, which are typically the *least* healthy slums in the entire community. If you are going to lead a horse to water, you do not start the journey at the oasis. This Head Start program was no exception. From its inception in 1968, the headquarters of Head Start was located in Five Points, one of the most notorious slums in Denver. Lack of security and neighborhood safety pose continuous challenges for the provision of child care services to low-income children.

When Barnes and Watt submitted their proposal to track the subsequent educational careers of Head Start graduates in the Denver Public Schools (DPS), Moskowitz was immediately enthused, and, recalling his previous tutorial in Project 2 + 2, he requested that we emphasize foremost studying children that do *well.* We responded that our first investigation would focus on reading proficiency (to honor the cornerstone of his nascent administration) and that our first sample would be Head Start graduates in DPS with consistent Reading Achievement scores on the Iowa Test of Basic Skills (ITBS-R) in the top quartile by national norms. The comparison sample for that first "resilience" investigation would be Head Start classmates who scored in the *third* quartile on reading achievement, that is, between the 25th and the 50th percentiles by national norms. The design of the sampling for the Resilience Project is presented in Table 13.1. Thus was born a collaboration between three educational institutions that eventually coalesced formally as the sponsors of a nonprofit organization now called the Ambassadors for Literacy. (The accompanying vignette describes, however, that *initially* the collaboration appeared *less* than auspicious!)

Vignette 2: The Politics of
Federal Grant Funding Behind the Scenes

Denver Head Start was administered from its inception in 1968 by a scrupulously ethical executive director, but the recurring federal grant (that ultimately exceeded $10 million a year) was controlled by the chairman of the board of directors, a self-described refugee from the streets who prided himself on "packing heat" since he was 14 years old and jealously protected his control prerogatives. A democratically elected board of directors that represents the community must govern Head Start grantee organizations according to parliamentary rules of order. Complaints about abuses of power by the chairman circulated for years and became progressively more extreme, but his leadership became more entrenched, combative, and arbitrary. Eventually, the challenges from community volunteers, investigative news reporters, staff employees, parents serving on the board, and even his own executive director became so intense that every board meeting became a battleground for contesting his authority. Ultimately, enough *responsible* directors took action to remove the chairman from office for several months, but soon thereafter he stacked a board meeting with loyalists of his own race and called in his markers from others beholden to him for special lucrative business favors, and he was reinstated as chair.

That reversal precipitated a spate of resignations by protesting board members, including a respected Latino university professor. He had held out for several years despite the abuses in order to represent the interests of the Latino community. He was bitter because only three Latinos were permitted to join the board (whose by-laws permitted 27 members altogether, including four current vacancies). This rankled because the overwhelming majority of staff members and families served were Latino, yet African Americans loyal to the chairman occupied the majority of seats on the board. When he announced his intention to resign, a volunteer pleaded with the Latino director to change his mind, but he replied, "It will be two millenniums before the Blacks in Denver allow the Latinos to have a seat at the table."

After several months of investigation by the FBI and the Inspector General's Office, the secretary of Health and Human Services ordered a thorough on-site investigation of the abuses at COP. After a week's visit, the investigators defunded the agency because the evidence of fraud and abuse was so overwhelming. During that inquiry, Beverly Turnbo, the leader of the 31-person investigative team, asked local leaders what should be done during the ensuing transition of leadership. One forceful answer was that the new grantee(s) *must* allow full representation of the Latino community commensurate with its majority among the families served and staff employed. "Otherwise, there would be open warfare between the two largest ethnic minority populations in Denver." The matter was resolved by

Table 13.1
Design for the Resilience Study: Frequencies of Head Start Graduates in ITBS Reading Quartiles by Race

Race Group	Reading Quartiles					Chosen for
	76–100	51–75	26–50	0–25	Sum	Embassy
Latinos	122	357	1636	2770	4211	20
African Americans	64	190	962	1180	1902	7
European Americans	38	82	468	315	592	3
Asian Americans	5	21	157	94	150	0
Native Americans	3	12	30	45	79	1
Subtotals	232	662	1636	4404	6934	31

awarding two Head Start grants, one with 57 percent of the new funding awarded to a coalition of agencies under the leadership of the mayor, an African American, and the other with 43 percent of the funding to Rocky Mountain SER, a Latino organization. Transparently, a geographic line had been drawn through the center of the city, partitioning the Head Start program into roughly two halves. Both programs (and a third added since then) continue to function effectively to this day. After decades of frustration—but nowhere close to two millennia—the Latinos had a place at the table at last! Almost 90 percent of Head Start families served by Rocky Mountain SER currently are Latino. More than a third of those children speak only Spanish when they start in the Head Start preschools at age three or four.

At a press conference, Undersecretary Olivia Golden announced the federal decision to change the local Head Start leadership, revealing that approximately 40 federal audits for fraud are conducted every year, and Denver's crisis (assessed conservatively for public dissemination at $800,000 of missing funds in the transition year) was simply the worst of the lot that year. The chairman and his cronies were never prosecuted for wrongdoing, presumably to prevent further tarnishing the reputation of the National Head Start program. The elderly chairman died in 2005 from advanced Alzheimer's disease, which may shed retrospective light on those troubling events.

Glitch in the Resilience Project Sampling

Finessing the suffocating restrictions of the Family Educational Rights and Privacy Act (FERPA), we matched our comprehensive roster of Head Start preschoolers against the Denver Public Schools archives and found 6,934 matches altogether. (Details of the finesse may hold some interest

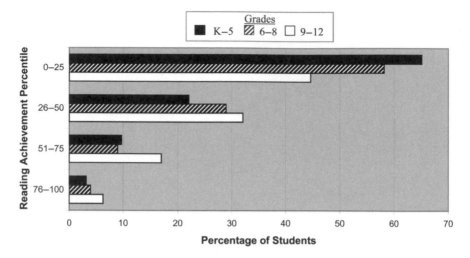

Figure 13.3   Reading achievement of Head Start graduates in Denver schools

for other social scientists, lawyers, and administrators, who are advised to contact the senior author for precise details about how it was done, while still protecting the identities of all the families in the study.) The precise distribution of the entire sample across reading quartiles on the ITBS-R is presented in Figure 13.3.

The extreme distortion in the proportions across the four quartiles, as contrasted with national norms, primarily reflects the well-known so-called poverty penalty and should not be taken as an evaluation of the efficacy of the Head Start intervention. (That evaluation requires much more elaborate research designs.) Several noteworthy observations about the Head Start population as a whole can be seen in Figure 13.3. The most striking, obviously, is the extreme bias at all school levels toward the lower quartiles of reading achievement. However, on close examination, it can be seen that as the Head Start children proceed from elementary school through middle school to high school, their reading disadvantage (relative to national norms) declines progressively, albeit modestly. This could be a reflection of what is referred to as the sleeper effect, meaning that the effects of the preschool program became evident later in the participants' lives, as observed most prominently in the areas of social behavior, self-sufficiency, and moral conduct (Oden, Schweinhart, & Weikart, 2000). On the other hand, especially at the high school level, this trend might reflect a selection bias, in that the least motivated pupils choose to drop out of school rather than stay the course.

Having identified all of the Head Start preschoolers now enrolled in Denver Public Schools, we proceeded to draw the *total* sample of "resilient" children by narrowing the group of 232 with at least one ITBS-R score in the top quartile to those with at least two successive Reading Achievement scores in 1993–1994 and 1994–1995 in the top quartile, thereby adding a criterion of stability in reading proficiency. Ultimately, that procedure yielded an experimental sample of 40 subjects, after dropping 11 children who had already moved outside of the Denver Public School District. (The majority of those 11 had actually moved out of state, which seems remarkable in itself.) We then drew a comparison sample from the total pool in the database that had recorded two successive ITBS-R scores in the third quartile (i.e., above the 24th percentile but below the 50th percentile) in 1993–1994 and 1994–1995. To the extent possible, this control group was matched individually with the resilient group on age, race, and gender.

The considerations that shaped our decisions about the comparison group were as follows. We wanted the controls to be broadly representative of the remaining Head Start population (i.e., not exceptionally proficient at reading but constrained by the matching criteria) and *not* handicapped by the predictable developmental disabilities and intellectual limitations to be expected in the *lowest* reading quartile. Invitations were then sent out to both study groups inviting their participation—in their homes—in a study of Denver Public Schools children that would require about two hours of their time, for which the child and one parent would each be reimbursed $20.

What followed surprised us. Only six of the "resilient" families accepted our solicitation, whereas nearly all of the control families accepted immediately! This caught us off guard since we presumed that the resilient subjects and their parents would welcome close attention because of their sterling scholastic accomplishments, whereas the controls and their parents might plausibly be more reluctant to expose their more mediocre performance at school.

In consultation with the superintendent, we considered several alternative ways to increase the participation of the proficient readers. Finally, we reasoned that these talented children and their parents—still having limited financial resources—might respond to the incentive of having assistance in saving money for a potential college education, so we offered that in broad, rather indefinite terms (in order to avoid promises that could not be kept). The response was explosive: In a few weeks time our experimental sample of 40 subjects was filled. It is interesting, however, to observe that the fresh respondents seemed to have self-selected for older age. On average, the experimental group was now almost two years older than the comparison sample.

The Resilience Study was conducted in 1995 and 1996. We collected extensive data in the homes from the children and one parent, including tests of intelligence, attitude, and opinion, as well as extensive individual interviews with the family members. From the children we obtained nominations of their three best friends at school and of three major-subject teachers (who would see the children at least four times each week in class). We obtained their written permission to review their school records and to track their subsequent performance at school until their secondary education was completed. In the following section of this chapter, we will make reference to some of the results from that investigation but without providing extensive methodological details (to conserve space).

Staffing the Embassy

As the data collection for the Resilience Study was drawing to a close, we appointed the first 23 Ambassadors for Literacy from the pool of "resilient" subjects, with eight more potential candidates hovering near the threshold criterion for qualification at the 75th percentile for career-long average reading achievement. Two years later those eight additional candidates had reached the criterion level, and they were appointed as well. The appointment process was cause for some melodrama.

The school principals for each of those potential candidates were consulted to obtain a character reference. The principals were advised that we were organizing an honorific program to promote opportunity for collegiate education, and we wished to have their assessment of whether these children would be good role models for literacy, school citizenship, and representation of the Denver Public Schools. The principals withheld endorsement for three of the candidates, two for being gang leaders and one for having "drug problems" and being "messed up." The remaining 31 children were offered appointments as Ambassadors for Literacy. They and their parents had participated in the Resilience Study earlier, but, up to that point, none of the children was aware of the plans for the Embassy. Each candidate was called into the principal's office to meet with Jo Thomas, the former DPS director of Bilingual Education, who explained the program in broad outlines and invited each child to discuss the program with his or her parents and then decide whether or not to accept our nomination to serve in the Embassy. During one such encounter, a Latino boy in the 11th grade broke down in tears and confessed that, prior to that moment, he had resigned himself to the virtually inevitable fate that the only way he would ever be able to afford to go to college was to join the Marines. After the invitation was extended, he and his father reevaluated their options and decided they could now afford to apply for admission to the University of Denver, an expensive private university. He has now graduated from DU and is expecting the birth of his first child! It should be noted that two of the candidates for appointment declined our invitation, ostensibly because of their long list of alternative claims on their time but possibly also because their parents already had alternative plans in mind for financing their college education.

Once appointed as Ambassadors for Literacy, we provided expert training for them in emergent literacy and offered several advising seminars to acquaint them with some of the sensitive issues they would encounter with the preschool children and center staff members at the Head Start sites. Not the least of those sensitive matters concerned the disparity between the modest academic credentials of the Head Start teachers and adult volunteers who would supervise our Ambassadors on site and the superior academic credentials of the Ambassadors themselves. Then we turned them loose to serve as community volunteers in their neighborhood Head Start centers, with careful monitoring by the center staff to record their hours and quality of voluntary service.

Ambassadors for Literacy, Inc. (AFL) became a 501(c)3 nonprofit charitable organization in 1999, with formal sponsorship by the University of Denver, the Denver Public Schools, and the Head Start program. The participation by the three sponsors has been quite substantial. The University of Denver provides accounting services and office space on campus at no charge. The Denver Public Schools has accepted the responsibility to cover the liability insurance premiums for the school-related activities of our Ambassadors as community volunteers. And the Head Start programs provide opportunity and supervision at numerous sites throughout the city without charge. The *primary* mission is to enable former Head Start children enrolled in Denver Public Schools to obtain a college education at an institution of their choice. AFL accomplishes this goal by providing the Ambassadors with the opportunity to serve as role models for literacy at Head Start centers throughout the Denver metropolitan region, for which the Ambassadors receive educational stipends that accumulate in their college-saver accounts. Thus we provide financial and social support to economically disadvantaged but intellectually superior students. The goal is to motivate these students and their parents to continue their education and to break the cycle of poverty.

Initially, we were advised by legal counsel to be indefinite in explaining the financial awards for their community service, to avoid raising unrealistic expectations in the minds of the children and their parents, and to avoid conflicts with the Internal Revenue Service about income taxation and child labor laws. That worked until the annual stipends were announced at the end of each year, and the Ambassadors were able to discover retrospectively that those stipends were being awarded in amounts comparable to at least $40 for every hour of volunteer service on site. Since that time we have developed a number of evaluation criteria for the quality of their service in order to avoid violation of regulations under child labor laws.

CURRENT PROGRAM

There are 31 students in the program who range in age from 15 to 24 years old. They are comprised of 20 Latinos, 7 African Americans, 3 European Americans, and 1 Native American. The majority of students have been active in the program and have volunteered a substantial amount of their time at a Head Start site. While in the Head Start classrooms, the Ambassadors promote reading and learning in many ways. These include:

- helping the Head Start children talk and think about things in their world,
- reading about and discussing many different topics with the preschoolers,
- incorporating reading and writing into the children's play,
- exposing preschoolers to the process of reading and writing,
- practicing writing with preschoolers, and
- showing confidence in reading and enthusiasm for going to school.

We are often asked how effective the interventions of our Ambassadors have been at improving the literacy of their preschool charges. We answer candidly that we have never attempted to measure their impact in that way because our sample is still too small to yield definitive and reliable assessments, and the cost for the evaluation would limit the amount of funds available for our primary objective of accumulating funds for the Ambassadors' college educations. However, we have abundant anecdotal and qualitative feedback from Head Start teachers and adult volunteers that resoundingly confirm the value of their volunteer service at the sites, not the least of which is the eyeball evidence of the reception by pre-schoolers when our Ambassadors arrive in the classroom.

The Ambassadors are rewarded for their community service in three different ways. Each year, the precollege students can receive stipends that are invested in individual college-saver accounts. The stipends reflect the extent and quality of their community service, ranging as high as $15,100 in a year, but averaging about $1,000 each year. When the Ambassadors start their college education, they are eligible to earn educational stipends by continuing their community service at Head Start sites during vacation and summer breaks or, if their college enrollment is at a local institution, during the school year. The third reward allows the Ambassadors and their parents to invest up to $200 per month in their college-saver accounts, and those funds are matched dollar for dollar by the program.

Like most nonprofit organizations, AFL has a board of directors. The board of directors comprises seven people, representing all of the constituencies with a vested interest in our program. One person is appointed by each of the three sponsors (University of Denver, Denver Public School District, and Head Start), two people represent the private contributors that donated the funds for the modest endowment, one person represents the parent committee, and one person represents the Colorado Department of Education (which helps to identify candidates for the program). The board meets once each year to formulate program policies and approve annual budgets and personnel appointments.

A unique aspect of the program is the parent committee. The responsibilities of the parent committee members are to promote involvement in the program and camaraderie among the families of the Ambassadors, serve as liaisons between the coordinators and the parents of the Ambassadors, assist the coordinators in planning social events and improvements in the program, and make recommendations through their chairperson to the board of directors regarding any feature of the program that can be improved from a parent's perspective.

PROGRAM BENEFITS

The financial support provided empowers the Ambassadors by raising their consciousness of the feasibility of obtaining a college education. Early, continuous accumulation of money in college-saver accounts realistically improves the prospects of affording a higher education. Low-income parents and children benefit from such encouragement, and attaining a collegiate education significantly improves their prospects for future prosperity. The Ambassadors also receive social support from the program co-coordinators and assistance in planning their educational future. Finally, the Ambassadors receive training in emergent literacy from experts in the field as well as hands-on experience utilizing their training in Head Start classrooms, thus modeling their enthusiasm for reading and learning.

The Head Start preschool children benefit from the program in several ways as well. They receive guidance and support from a caring adolescent or young adult, help in developing emergent literacy skills, encouragement to be curious about the world, support in using their thinking and speaking skills, and exposure to letters, words, and sounds that hold meaning. The Head Start teachers receive aid in the classroom from precocious

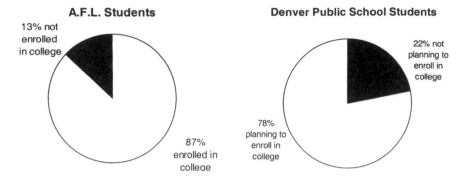

Figure 13.4 Comparison of AFL high school graduates and Denver Public Schools seniors in regard to educational aspirations

students, and our program has sponsored training workshops for all of the Head Start teachers working with our volunteers.

PROGRAM OUTCOMES

Thus far the program has been a resounding success! The Ambassadors have volunteered a total of approximately 13,000 hours, resulting in the distribution of $329,382 in stipends. An additional $67,255 has been given to the Ambassadors in matching funds for family contributions, totaling almost $400,000 of financial support altogether. The combination of financial, educational, and social support provided by the program has resulted in a large proportion of Ambassadors pursuing a college degree (as seen in Figure 13.4).

To date, 87 percent (20 out of 23) of our college-age Ambassadors have enrolled in or graduated from a two- or four-year college or university. It should be noted that these comparisons did not take into account intelligence of the children or income of the family, but this was the only information legally available to us for such comparisons.

The numbers are equally impressive for our ethnic minority students (Figure 13.5). To date, 86 percent (19 out of 22) of our ethnic minority students who have graduated from high school have enrolled in or graduated from college. We have students attending such prestigious universities as New York University, Howard University, Morehouse College, Colorado College, and the University of Denver. Our first college graduate is now attending medical school at the University of Colorado Health Sciences Center.

We feel the success of AFL supports the concept that providing financial and social support for poor students who show exceptional aptitude for reading and hard work is a good investment and a step toward breaking

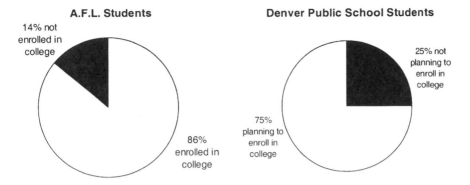

Figure 13.5   Comparison of AFL high school graduates and Denver Public Schools minority seniors in regard to educational aspirations

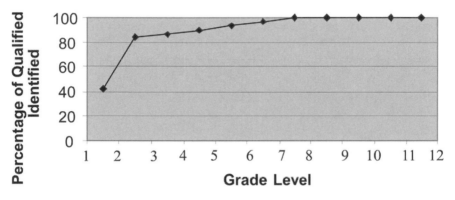

Figure 13.6   Percentage of Ambassadors identified based on reading achievement scores by grade level

the so-called cycle of poverty. The support we have given the Ambassadors has enabled them to continue their education and to make more informed life decisions. This is reflected in the percentage of our students who pursue a collegiate education.

LESSONS LEARNED

Many lessons have been learned since initiating the Resilience Study and the Ambassadors for Literacy program. Perhaps the most important lesson is that almost all of the poor children who will achieve career-long reading excellence can be reliably identified before they complete elementary school. Figure 13.6 shows that 42 percent of the Ambassadors could have been identified by their high ITBS reading achievement scores in first grade. By second grade, we could have identified 42 percent more of the Ambassadors, totaling 84 percent altogether. This percentage gradually increases from grade three through grade six. By seventh grade, our entire population of Ambassadors could have been identified. This leaves a family living in poverty many years to save for their child's college education. Perhaps more importantly, external moral support encourages them to raise their sights for the future.

RESILIENCE STUDY

The results of the Resilience Study gave us insight into what factors are associated with high reading achievement. Demographically, the proficient readers were, on average, 1.7 years *older* than the mediocre readers and were raised in families with *more family income* and *fewer children in the household.* The age difference appears to have resulted from a problem in recruiting the proficient readers. Our solution to that problem (offering support for college tuition) may have attracted older pupils who were closer to graduating from high school, although it should be kept in mind that we solicited *all* of the children in the top reading quartile. The other two demographic differences, we suspect, may *not* be sampling artifacts. It seems more plausible to reason that the parents of the exceptional readers were more *upwardly mobile* than the parents of the mediocre readers, accounting for their differential expansion of income from the preschool years of their children and the smaller number of offspring in the household (4.30 vs. 5.02). We further speculate that these upwardly mobile parents probably possess higher aspirations for themselves and their children and that they pass on this motivation to their children as they grow up. The two groups did *not* differ significantly in the following areas: gender, average age of their mothers at the time they were born, average (measured) IQ score of their mothers, number of years of education attained by their mothers, if their mothers were foreign born, the average age of their fathers, average years of education attained by their fathers, living arrangements of their parents, and if their families were receiving welfare at the time they were born.

After controlling statistically for the age of the child, the family's income, and the number of people in the household, we found several significant differences between the two groups that relate to the child's attitudes and behaviors at school (Figure 13.7).

Teachers rated the proficient readers as more confident and more independent and as showing more leadership, activity, and group-participation skills in the classroom. The extraversion scores show a level of sociability that belies any suspicion that the proficient readers were atypical

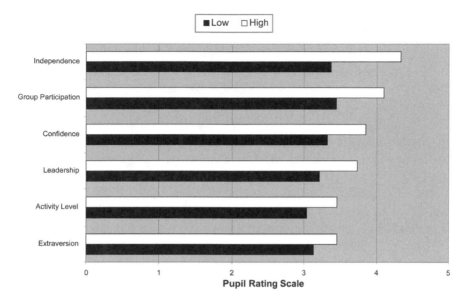

Figure 13.7   Comparison of high and low reading achievers in relation to teachers' ratings of child attributes

bookworms or nerds. Clearly, these exceptional readers were gratifying students for the teachers to teach. The children's self-esteem ratings were consistent with the teacher ratings, showing the highest correlations of reading achievement with scholastic self-esteem, modestly significant associations with behavioral and global self-esteem, but no relationship at all with social self-esteem.

Similarly controlling for the children's age and for the family's income and household size, we found several significant differences between the two groups regarding parenting practices. Parents of the good readers said that they read more often to their children when they were younger. They also reported higher aspirations for their child's future occupational prospects and, interestingly, that they were *less* likely to make their children do their homework before they could play or watch TV. The children corroborated their parents' reports regarding their rules about homework. The exceptional students reported that their parents did *not* make them do their homework before they could engage in other activities. We believe that this finding is related to the fact that the resilient children had higher grade point averages and probably more intrinsic motivation to do well in school, so their parents did not *need* to exert such control over their after-school activities. The resilient children also reported that their mothers enjoyed talking things over with them more and that their mothers were less likely to threaten or make them feel guilty than did the control children.

We were interested in determining how the school behavior and attitudes of the resilient children and three best friends were related to all of the dependent measures of scholastic performance and psychological development. The general premise for the study was that children who excel in reading and graded performance gravitate toward peers of similar ability and orientation to school, thus supporting their own academic performance, self-esteem, and future aspirations. A pervasive disparity emerged between the target children's and the teachers' assessments of the three best friends. In the majority of measures of scholastic engagement, teachers' ratings of the friends were strongly correlated with the reading achievement of the *target* children, indicating favorable appraisals of the *peers* of the most proficient readers. In most cases the respective correlations with GPA were positive and modestly significant. In striking contrast, the target children's ratings of the same engagement behaviors among the peers were *reversed,* showing highly significant *negative* correlations for about half of the variables. These results indicated, for example, that the most competent children made extremely pejorative assessments of their best friends in their dedication to homework, classroom participation, cooperation with others, and how seriously they took their studies, whereas the teachers' collective ratings in all of those domains were highly correlated in the opposite direction. In short, were the teachers' judgments considered accurate and valid, most of the principal hypotheses advanced at the outset of the study would be resoundingly confirmed, but if the children's *own* assessments were accepted as valid, most of the central hypotheses about peer relations would be almost as resoundingly rejected!

AMBASSADORS AND THEIR FAMILIES

We learned a great deal as we came to know the Ambassadors and their families. Here we present several anecdotes about the people this program serves. Besides being exceptional readers and very serious about their studies at school, the Ambassadors are just like most other kids their age. The boys wear their cargo pants at half-mast, and, especially at party time, the girls make eye-catching fashion statements below the neck and above the knees. They will forgo food for a cell phone, without which life is not worth living.

Some of the Latinos encounter conflicts with their cultural norms over their educational aspirations. For example, the mother of one of our most successful students confessed that she did not understand why her daughter wanted to go on to college when she could immediately marry her high school boyfriend and have children. Similarly, one of our Latino boys (with noteworthy talent for working with preschool children) got into serious trouble with the police and school authorities over delinquent activities, especially fighting, at least in part with tacit support from his parents, who bought into the so-called machismo tradition that is prominent in many Latino subcultures.

We have discerned greater distance from our program staff (notably lacking any African Americans) among the African Americans and their parents. This is perhaps also related to three other observations: (1) four of the five African American students (80%) that have graduated from high school chose to attend distinctively African American colleges on the East Coast (Howard University and Morehouse College), (2) one of the seven African Americans declined the Embassy appointment we offered, and (3) the *mothers* in the African American families have exerted strong influence on their children, usually more so than the fathers.

Our sampling procedures were not flawless, or at least one of our intended targets managed to slip past our fishing net, as we discovered at the very first initiation gathering, when we were approached by a self-assured African American mother who startled us with the following question: "Thank you for discovering our daughter, but why did you not invite the best student in our family—also a former Head Start preschooler—to join your program?" We checked out the school records and found to our surprise that the sibling was indeed one of the best-qualified students for our program, so he was added to our list of appointees. Even more remarkable is that there were two such families in our pool with two siblings that qualified for appointment. The base rate of Ambassadors in the total Head Start pool was less than 5 out of 1,000, so the likelihood of finding two Ambassadors in the same family by chance alone would be one in 50,000 trials. The odds against finding *two* pairs of Ambassador siblings, based on chance alone, would be 2.5 billion to one. Therefore it is safe to conclude that there are some (as yet unspecified) nonrandom causes to which exceptional reading proficiency in low-income children can be attributed. Furthermore, there was still a third family in which a younger sister of an Ambassador narrowly missed reaching the threshold for qualification as an Ambassador, and that sibling has gone on to achieve a distinguished academic record at a major state university in Colorado.

In most cases we were impressed that the parents of our Ambassadors were good role models for literacy and academic achievement, albeit not as outstanding as their offspring. However, that was not true in about a quarter of the families, and in a few cases the Ambassadors actually seemed to parent the parents. A case in point will illustrate. At the very beginning of the program, we accompanied one Ambassador with his mother and one infant to the Charles Schwab offices to open a college-saver account. The Schwab agent was very patient in explaining to the mother the various alternative kinds of investments that could be used in a college-saver account, but he was obviously overmatched in that effort. The young Ambassador, just starting fifth grade, interceded to clarify for his mother—in much plainer language—the difference between stocks and bonds, what a mutual fund is, how one can choose to invest for income versus growth, and what special advantages and restrictions apply to college-saver accounts. We should have been taking notes for future reference! Tragically, one of our most exemplary Ambassadors has been called upon in a different quasi-parental capacity: to care simultaneously for her dying mother and her totally disabled, bedridden younger brother, while at the same time pursuing her demanding course of studies at a competitive private university.

We have learned from experience that not all of our Ambassadors are morally scrupulous. One of our most active participants wangled an opportunity to earn some extra money during a summer working in our laboratory. His first assignment was to transcribe some scores from a record archive of graduate students admitted for training in psychology. After several days in the archive we discovered that he had made up all of the numbers on the scoring sheet! Similarly, we discovered that it was necessary to monitor *independently* the reports of community service submitted by most of our Ambassadors, because it was so tempting for these young adolescents to falsify or embellish their monthly service reports. This has not been a source of great consternation to us because we realize that these youngsters had seldom before been exposed to such powerful financial temptations that were so discrepant from their previous experience. We simply took their liberties in stride and built in the necessary safeguards to protect the integrity of our system of rewards.

The average family income in our pool has been approximately $25,000 per year, roughly 40 percent below the population average in Colorado. Our most actively participatory parents, however, reported family incomes at or above the Colorado average of $41,000. Again an example will illustrate. At the first meeting we held in the offices of Charles Schwab, for the purpose of opening the college-saver accounts, we were approached even before the meeting began by one such active mother, who wanted to volunteer to assist us in any way possible. She was also the first parent to buy into the matching program by setting up an automatic monthly withdrawal of $200 from her bank account for direct deposit into her daughter's college-saver account. She has never missed a payment. It was also reported to us independently by our so-called blind home visitors after collecting the interview and test data for her family that the living room in their home was decorated "like a shrine" to their two children. We have come to regard such exemplary parents as major sources of inspiration and aspiration for their children's educational careers and their future lives. Perhaps by coincidence (or perhaps not), all of these families have exactly two children.

Many of the Ambassadors are pursuing academic careers that are not typically associated with underprivileged populations. For example, several of them have chosen college majors in theater, film editing, English literature, architecture, and dance. Their choices seem to be more creative than we had expected.

As a group, the Ambassadors have had their fair share of emotional tribulations. Some have been shuffled, like nomads, among their relatives. One girl had an especially turbulent relationship with her mother, which led her into troublesome peer connections and adolescent debauchery in high school, which eventuated in a suicide attempt and a few years in academic limbo. Fortunately, after emancipating herself from her mother, she was able to get her life together again and is now nearing completion of a successful, self-financed college education.

It is worth noting that, except for the African Americans (as reported above), most of the Ambassadors have been quite reluctant to even consider applying to colleges and universities outside of the Denver area. This obviously refers mainly to the Latino children, many of whom have strong family attachments, but it may also bespeak a certain amount of temerity about their place in the world. For many of them, just getting into college represents their highest aspiration, and nuances of quality or national reputation among their choices hardly come into play. This may reflect an extension of the stigmatizing effects to which most urban minorities are exposed. The educational careers of a handful of Ambassadors have disappointed us, and we strongly suspect that wavering support of their parents for intellectual pursuits may be partly at fault. In a scientific sense, these few might be considered "false positives" for academic success, but only time will tell because other pursuits may also bear fruit.

Most of our Ambassadors have shown remarkable discipline and self-direction in their educational careers and maturity in their personal lives. It has surprised us that there have been no high school pregnancies among them. The majority have found support in a relationship with a person *outside* the family who cares for them. Sometimes that person is a member of our staff. In other cases, it is a coach of athletics or a teacher or a member of a church congregation. Their network of friends and extracurricular activities are extremely broad and diverse, as our frustration in scheduling meetings with them will attest. A very few of the Ambassadors have clearly set themselves apart from the rest as promising superstars, hewing consistently to their academic priorities, and a comparably small number seem to be drifting rather aimlessly through adolescence and young adulthood, leaving difficult pathways for us to track.

AMBASSADOR INVOLVEMENT

In addition to the anecdotal examples of the successes and shortcomings of the program, we studied which personal characteristics of the Ambassadors, as revealed in the teacher ratings and school performance in the Resilience Study, predicted involvement in our AFL program most significantly. We devised a composite index of program involvement that reflected the number of hours of community service, attendance at training seminars and group events, and overall consistency of participation in our program. We found that program involvement was predicted by grade point average and, in *descending* order of statistical significance, the following attributes: orderliness, attentiveness, scholastic achievement, organization, maturity, motivation, reliability, and adjustment. These findings indicate that—*within* the pool of exceptionally proficient readers—the best candidates for future selection as role models for literacy are those whose teachers can single them out for superior scholastic motivation and exemplary character. That knowledge not only improves our understanding of the current cohort of Ambassadors, but it will also inform our selection procedures for the next phase of our program (as described in the following section).

FUTURE DIRECTIONS

We feel this program has greatly impacted the lives of the participating students and families as well as the Head Start preschool children they serve. Therefore, the long-term objective of this program is to promote the image of Head Start as a foundation of literacy for disadvantaged children, while at the same time advancing the educational prospects of uniquely promising (but still quite underprivileged) children. Contingent on future funding, we plan to expand AFL first to other school districts in the Denver area, then to the entire state of Colorado, and possibly nationwide. Overall, we feel that the program has been a success; however, we have failed in one important respect to achieve the original goals of the program, namely, we have persuaded only about 20 percent of our families to take advantage of the matching program to build their college-saver accounts with their own money. Consequently, for future expansion programs we will establish as a prerequisite that the families must *first complete a three-year trial period of college investing* in order to qualify for appointment in our Embassy. Candidates will be selected based on their reading achievement scores (Colorado Student Assessment Program scores) and their eligibility for government subsidized lunches. Eligible candidates will include all students from grades three to five who have three consecutive reading achievement scores in the top quartile (by state-wide standards) and who qualify for free or reduced lunches.

These students and their parents will be invited to open a college-saver account and commit to contribute at least $10 per month for their college savings, which will be matched dollar for dollar by AFL in the first year, 2:1 in the second year, and 3:1 in the third year. In order to ease some of the financial burden families will face, we plan to give each family a free membership to Costco or Sam's Club, thus redirecting $10 per month from their grocery bill to the candidate's college-saver account. Additionally, we will collaborate with Young Americans Bank to elevate the financial literacy of both the AFL candidates and their parents. This will be accomplished by offering additional financial training seminars covering savings, credit, budgeting, and investing, based on curricula developed by the Young Americans Bank. After three years, we will appoint the students whose parents have regularly contributed to their college-saver accounts to the Embassy. This appointment would promise more generous matching amounts and stipends for community services rendered.

Based on our findings from the current program, the effectiveness of any expansion program will be evaluated by the proportion of families who accept the invitation. We now know how important it is *at the outset* to achieve buy-in to the program from both the children and their parents, and the reliability of their monthly contributions to the children's college-saver accounts offers an index of their commitment. We are now convinced that optimum benefit from our program *must be predicated* on wholehearted commitment from both the children and their parents. Ultimately, maximum success would be indicated by the proportion of the new cohort of Ambassadors who will go on to attend a college or university. In the long term, of course, we place the highest priority on the number of Ambassadors that enroll in college and eventually graduate. In our Denver program, the overall results on these parameters have been consistently positive, although the level of participation has varied, as indicated previously. The scope of the future of AFL depends on current and future funding.

A SUMMARY OF SOME POLICY LESSONS LEARNED

From our experiences of the last 13 years we have learned some valuable policy lessons about delivering this unique service to Head Start families.

Some of them are obvious to veterans at providing childcare and educational services, whereas others have, frankly, surprised us. In a nutshell, these are the lessons we have learned

1. Lack of security and neighborhood safety inherently pose continuous challenges to the provision of child care services for low-income children.

2. Good faith and goodwill at the local level are essential requirements for implementing massive federal programs like Head Start, and vigilant oversight is necessary to prevent corruption.

3. The optimal time to initiate merit-based financial aid for disadvantaged children is in elementary school, not only to equalize educational opportunity but also to neutralize the "learned helplessness" that is chronically reinforced in those children and their parents by our society.

4. Within the pool of exceptionally proficient readers, the best candidates for future selection as role models for literacy are those whose teachers can single them out for superior scholastic motivation and exemplary character in elementary school.

5. Recognition and exploitation of economic opportunities came naturally to our Ambassadors and their parents, but budgeting, saving, and scaffolding for the future were far more alien to them, so those deficiencies in financial literacy must be addressed.

6. The prospects for breaking the cycle of poverty in disadvantaged children reflect directly the upward mobility in the aspirations of their parents, which can therefore be utilized as a criterion for cost-economical intervention.

REFERENCES

Capron, C., & Duyme, M. (1996). Effect of socioeconomic status of biological and adoptive parents on WISC-R subtest scores of their French adopted children. *Intelligence, 22,* 259–275.

Duncan, G.J., & Brooks-Gunn, J. (2000). Family poverty, welfare reform, and child development. *Child Development, 71,* 188–196.

Employment Policy Foundation. (2003). *Higher education pays off with higher lifetime earnings: Analysis of March 2003 Current Population Survey data.* Retrieved February 2005, from http://www.educationpays.org/fact5.asp

Harrison, L.E., & Huntington, S.P. (Eds.). (2001). *Culture matters: How values shape human progress.* New York: Basic Books.

Hollingshead, A.B. (1975). *Four factor index of social status.* New Haven, CT: Yale University Press.

Huntington, S.P. (2004). *Who are we? The challenges to America's national identity.* New York: Simon & Schuster.

Keating, D. P., & Hertzman, C. (Eds.). (1999). *Developmental health and the wealth of nations.* New York: Guilford.

Linver, M. R., Brooks-Gunn, J., & Kohen, D. E. (2002). Family processes as pathways from income to young children's development. *Developmental Psychology, 38,* 719–734.

Mackintosh, N. J. (1998). *IQ and human intelligence.* Oxford, UK: Oxford University Press.

McLoyd, V. C. (1998). Socioeconomic disadvantage and child development. *American Psychologist, 53,* 185–204.

National Center for Education Statistics. (2001). *Dropout rates in the United States: 2000.* Washington, DC: U.S. Department of Education, Office of Education Research and Improvement.

Oden, S., Schweinhart, L. J., & Weikart, D. P. (2000). *Into adulthood: A study of the effects of Head Start.* Ypsilanti, MI: High/Scope Press.

Reich, R. B. (2000). *The future of success.* New York: Knopf.

Robinson, N. M., Weinberg, R. A., Redden, D., Ramey, S. L., & Ramey, C. T. (1998). Family factors associated with high academic competence among former Head Start children. *Gifted Child Quarterly, 42*(3), 148–156.

Sawhill, I. V. (1995). *Welfare reform: An analysis of the issues.* New York: Urban Institute.

Schmidt, P. (2004). Federal civil-rights officials investigate race-conscious admissions. *Chronicle of Higher Education, 51*(17), A26.

Solon, G. (2002). Cross-country differences in intergenerational earnings mobility. *Journal of Economic Perspectives, 16*(3), 59–66.

Sorensen, S., Brewer, D. J., Carroll, S. J., & Bryton, E. (1995). Increasing Hispanic participation in higher education: A desirable public investment. In *Rand September Issue Paper.* Santa Monica, CA: Rand.

U.S. Census Bureau. (2005). Current Population Survey, Annual Social and Economic Supplement. Retrieved September 16, 2005 from http://pubdb3.census.gov/macro/032005/pov/new01_100.htm

EPILOGUE

Edward Zigler and Sally J. Styfco

The field of developmental psychology has changed dramatically over time. Just 30 or 40 years ago, child psychologists were defensive about their scientific status. We proved ourselves to be true scientists by developing theories (some very general, some very narrow) and then assessing every conceivable hypothesis to prove or disprove the theories. Great value was placed on methodology and the experimental manipulation of variable after variable. This was carefully conducted basic research, and the prized product was a publication in an esoteric professional journal.

Eventually some brave scholars attacked the artificiality and lack of external validity that characterized developmental research. Urie Bronfenbrenner (1974), for example, argued that the field had been reduced to "the science of the behavior of children in strange places with strange adults" (p. 3). When Urie and other pioneers like David Elkind wrote articles translating the science in the popular media, reaching millions of readers instead of relatively few journal subscribers, they were accused of prostituting themselves and degrading the field. The unwritten rule was that true scientists stayed in their labs and did basic research, whereas only second-level workers did applied research and conversed with the real world. In opposition to this view, Zigler (1980) has long argued that basic and applied research are not different enterprises but are highly synergistic. These decades of rigorous basic research unquestionably expanded our knowledge of human development (Zigler, 1963), but the ultimate purpose of this knowledge gathering should be to improve the human condition.

With the social upheaval in the 1960s and '70s, more and more child psychology students became dissatisfied with the solipsistic laboratory enterprise and wanted to make a real difference in the daily lives of children and families. A major historic event in 1965, the birth of Head Start, was a very visible instance of using the knowledge accumulated in the field of child development to construct program that would change the environment of over one-half million children and their families in that summer before they started school. Three developmentalists served on Head Start's planning committee (Bronfenbrenner, Mamie Clark, and Zigler), along with scholars in other disciplines, including pediatricians, child psychiatrists, early-childhood educators, and social workers. Zigler (and probably the other psychologists) was chastised by senior scholars for forsaking basic research and jeopardizing his career.

Over the next two decades, the disrespect accorded applied work gradually dissipated. Precipitants included pressure on the professional organizations by younger workers and growing demands by funders for investigators to produce actionable results (Zigler, 1998). In the 1970s, four Bush Centers in Child Development and Social Policy were opened at major universities to train scholars to work at the intersect of social policy and the knowledge base in human development. Eventually these changes in attitude and training evolved into a subdiscipline commonly referred to as child development and social policy, or applied developmental science.

Many of the chapters of this book are wonderful exemplars of this discipline. The authors mine the knowledge base to give direction to social policies and actions that will improve children's development and well-being. Several interventions described in these pages are well known and have already had considerable impact on national policies. Although these programs are familiar, it is helpful to have them all in one volume where they can be compared and contrasted. The justification for assembling this particular collection of papers, and what provides their common thread, is well stated in the title of the introductory chapter by Watt and Bradley, *Transforming the Village that Raises Our Children*. Both that title and the contents of the book are reminiscent of Hillary Clinton's *It Takes a Village and Other Lessons Children Teach Us* (1996). Although best known as a politician, Senator Clinton has a legitimate claim for some scholarly proficiency in the area of human development. While a law student at Yale, she studied at Yale's Child Study Center under the mentorship of one of our nation's truly outstanding developmental scholars, the late Sally Provence.

The contents of this book concentrate on child and family policy with a special emphasis on the early years of life, primarily the preschool years. It thus addresses an important segment of our nation's current social policy priority, school reform. During the 1990s, a guiding principle of school reform was Goal 1 of the Educate America Act, that is, all children will arrive at school ready to learn. Early-childhood programs have proliferated since then, and universal preschool is gaining momentum in the states. The famous as well as the lesser-known efforts described in the book remind us of the scientific basis of effective programs and their evaluation.

In the following sections we take issue with some of the evaluations presented in the previous pages, not to discount the studies but to emphasize that ours remains an imperfect science. Not all findings are perfectly clear, not all interpretations are uncontested, and even our best theories are in need of refinement. Without a doubt, however, our knowledge base is sufficient to guide policy in the right direction.

THEORETICAL ISSUES

Our major contention with current interpretations of the intervention literature is the pervasive underemphasis of the nature side of the nature-nurture equation. Interventions structure children's experiences, and changes in expected developmental outcomes are attributed to these environmental modifications. Genetic influences on children's abilities and behavior are typically overlooked. Evidence of this environmental bias is ample, including within the covers of this book. As one example, workers commonly refer to Bronfenbrenner's ecological model, forgetting that its full name is the *bio*ecological model.

Biology is also surprisingly absent in discussions of early brain development. A lopsided emphasis has been placed on the role of environment in shaping the architecture of the brain, even though this development is in large part preprogrammed by biological factors. Indeed, the progression in both physical brain development and the behavior the brain mediates is common to all members of the species. This suggests experience has little to do with it except in extreme cases of deprivation or environmental insult.

This is a critical point and should lead developmental scientists to be modest in their claims. We can not ignore the biological law of human variability. This variability is dictated by the gene pool of the population. Most traits display a normal distribution, with the majority of individuals clustering around the midpoint and relatively few at the high and low ends of the continuum. No program will ever exist that is powerful enough to repeal the law of human variability. We must do more to educate policy makers about this irrevocable fact. The current administration has attempted to legislate child development by demanding that a nine-month Head Start program boost children who live in poverty to the same level of school readiness as more affluent children. Similarly, the No Child Left Behind Act dictates that *all* children read at grade level by third grade. Differences in intelligence and language ability, and disorders like dyslexia, are apparently now illegal.

Our viewpoint does not imply that genes are destiny. What is inherited is a genotype. What is observable is a phenotype, which is the expression of the genes for various traits. A person's height and IQ score are phenotypes, the result of the genetic substrate working within a particular environment. A basic tenet of behavioral genetics is the concept of the reaction range. The expression of the genotype into specific phenotypes is influenced to some degree by the environment, with the influence being greater for some traits than for others. A child with the genes to grow very tall will only attain that potential with adequate nutrition and reasonable health. These same environmental factors will not add height to a child with the genes to be petite. These principles are alluded to briefly in the introductory chapter of the book.

Behavioral geneticists have long pondered how broad the reaction range is and how much can actually be influenced by experiences the individual encounters. Here we will limit our discussion to the trait of intelligence, because this is the trait that has captivated psychologists and policy makers. As much as they would like to hope otherwise, the reaction range for this very important trait is actually quite narrow. The most optimistic estimates of behavioral geneticists is that IQ can be increased by 25 points at most by substituting good environments for bad ones.

A 25-point hike would be quite a feat (almost two standard deviations) for any intervention program. Yet the fact is that after almost a half-century of trying, no intervention ever mounted has permanently improved children's IQs by anywhere close to 25 points. Dramatic improvements demonstrated in some programs were found to be fleeting and have been traced to better motivation and familiarity with the testing situation and content rather than to real changes in cognition (e.g., Zigler & Butterfield, 1968). Indeed, the Abecedarian project is the only intervention that has shown lasting IQ gains, but they are nowhere near the range of 25 points. Nor is the IQ score highly predictive of behaviors important to policy makers such as school performance and criminality.

Believing in genes does not mean being a genetic determinist. Over the past 50 years we have learned a lot about what experiences can enhance or compromise a child's development. The bioecological model, which is currently developmental psychology's major paradigm, indicates that multiple layers of the environment influence the child's innate growth and abilities. Although this approach is undoubtedly correct, the very broadness of the model frustrates workers trying to improve the daily lives of children and families.

What we must do with the bioecological framework is prioritize those social systems that appear to have the most impact and that social policies can realistically address. The chapter by David Rusk, a city planner and former mayor of Albuquerque, New Mexico, illustrates why these choices must be made. Rusk's approach fits nicely into the bioecological model, and his presence here highlights the interdisciplinary nature of both this volume and the policy process. His chapter focuses on the relation between where a child lives and school performance. Using very large sample studies, Rusk makes a convincing case for the value of socioeconomic integration in schools. Concluding that integration greatly benefits poor children and does not harm middle-class children, Rusk has become a champion of eradicating school segregation.

Looking at this goal from a bioecological perspective, integration would require radical changes in multiple layers of the social ecology. Poor families have low-paying or sporadic jobs, so they live in poor neighborhoods that are unable to support high-quality schools for the high-risk, local student body. At the social policy level, Supreme Court decisions against busing and suburban votes against subsidized housing developments are roadblocks to integration. Rusk asserts that "policy makers have it within their power to address the interrelationship of housing and education," which is true but highly unlikely to lead to the massive social actions that will be needed. In the case of school segregation, the bioecological model produces a clear explanatory edifice for the problem but leads to few actionable solutions.

Although we endorse the bioecological approach, it is too broad to be useful in designing intervention programs or guiding social policies. The concept needs to be tamed to a more manageable number of ecological features that programs and policies can actually target. The decades of work conducted by basic and applied researchers lead us to the conclusion that four major systems in the United States are the primary determinants of the child's developmental course. The first and most important is the family. (For convincing evidence on this point, read the excellent chapters by Ayoub and Bradley in this compendium.) The second system (one frequently ignored by developmental psychologists) is the health system. If you can not keep a child alive for the first couple of years of life (the United States is approximately 20th among industrialized nations in regard to this benchmark), the other systems and all of our interventions become moot. The third system is the education system, which in the wake of the No Child Left Behind legislation has become the focal point of U.S. domestic policy. The fourth system is child care, where the majority of our nation's children spend their first five formative years before school entry.

These four systems do not encompass the myriad determinants of child development derived from the bioecological model. One immediately thinks of the media and technology that unquestionably impact children for better or for worse. But these four systems are grounds for intervention, and each and every one of them involves social policies that can influence the nature of the environment children will experience in these settings. The brilliance of the Abecedarian intervention is that it impacted all four systems. The other programs described in this book target one or various combinations of the systems. The editors are to be congratulated for assem-

bling an outstanding compendium of scholarly, and in some cases provocative, chapters, many written by individuals who have become household
names in the field.

Although we have great respect for the scholars whose work and ideas
appear in this book, we will use the pages that follow to take a closer
look at some of their methods and conclusions. Our motive is not to
savor the role of dreaded reviewers but to challenge assumptions about
what features of child development we can realistically expect to change,
by how much, and the types of intervention best suited to accomplish the
task. Our roots are in both child development and social policy, and we
want to take issue with some of the common wisdom emanating from
the early intervention literature because common wisdom *can* lead to
bad social policy. Our ultimate goal is to provoke scholarly debate that
will inform effective policy and programmatic solutions.

RETHINKING PROGRAM EVALUATION

This book contains descriptions of the two most famous and frequently
noted experimental preschool interventions ever mounted: the High/Scope
Perry Preschool and the Abecedarian project. Also included is the more contemporary, mainstream program, the Chicago Child–Parent Centers. These
three programs have had a great impact on public policies and the social
action programs emanating from these policies. Their findings of greater
school readiness, better academic and behavioral outcomes, and especially
the high return to society for every dollar spent on the interventions have pro-
pelled the universal preschool movement. Today two states offer preschool
to all their residents, and 38 have programs for targeted groups.

How did two tiny and one somewhat larger intervention have such great
influence on national and state policies and the early environments of
millions of young children? Evaluations of the three revealed positive but
not particularly large changes in developmental outcomes. What captured
national attention is that the researchers conducted cost-benefit analyses.
The term *cost-benefit analysis* was not even in the lexicon of those who
mounted interventions in the early days. The first such analysis was conducted in-house by High/Scope in 1978 and a second analysis, built on
the first one, was conducted by noted economist Steven Barnett (1985). A
major contribution of this landmark work is that it began to free researchers and commentators from the habit of relying on changes in IQ scores
as the exclusive barometer of program effectiveness.

Head Start, High/Scope, Abecedarian, and the Chicago programs were
all launched at the height of the environmental mystique. Those were
the days when J. McVicker Hunt (1961) was publishing his views on the
plasticity of intelligence, suggesting that IQ scores can be raised by as

much as 70 points if children are provided with the "right" experiences (and that the reaction range for IQ was a full 100 points). These ideas were augmented by Benjamin Bloom (1964), who believed that the early years of life were the magical period for influencing the development of traits such as intelligence. Belief in the power of the environment was cemented when early evaluations of intervention programs showed IQ changes of 10 to 15 points, often after only a few weeks of preschool. When these benefits were found to be short-lived, euphoria turned to pessimism that anything could be done to help poor children succeed in school.

High/Scope and a consortium of scientists (Consortium for Longitudinal Studies, 1983) had the wisdom to look beyond IQ scores and found meaningful, lasting benefits in other developmental domains. For example, preschool graduates had less grade retention and special education placement. Justified in their efforts, interventionists were free to pursue their work of designing programs to impact desired outcomes beyond narrow and unattainable cognitive goals.

However, some benefits so highly valued by developmentalists and mental health experts (social competence, ego strength) are pretty incomprehensible to many decision makers. What, then, is a common language that all decision makers understand and to which they are particularly sensitive? Dollars and cents. Cost-benefit analyses result in clear statements that if you spend X dollars, society will receive Y dollars in benefits. Another plus is that at any point in time, policy makers have a plethora of problems in need of solution and a limited amount of money to allocate across them. The decision-making process is of course influenced by a wide array of factors, including political ideology, the pressure of private interest groups and lobbies, and campaign promises. But cost-benefit analyses can be a powerful aid because they gauge the fiscal value of a program and allow policy makers to compare choices in terms of which would have the greatest societal payoff. Indeed, such cross-program comparisons can now regularly be found in the intervention literature (Aos, Lieb, Mayfield, Miller, & Pennucci, 2004; Reynolds & Temple, in press). This development is pleasing to us because we argued many years ago that such analyses should routinely be used in intervention evaluations (Zigler & Berman, 1983). An important contribution of this volume is that it shows cost-benefit analysis is now firmly entrenched as the ultimate measure of the effectiveness of the programs we mount.

Methodological Concerns

The three well-known preschool programs described in this book were extremely valuable to theory, practice, and policy, but they present problems to the methodological purist. High/Scope and Abecedarian employed a random assignment experimental design (often considered the gold standard), and the Chicago program used a sound quasi-experimental design. Although their research protocols were scientifically excellent, and there are advantages to self-evaluations, one weakness is that all three programs were evaluated by researchers who were very close to the projects. This issue goes beyond questions of self-interest and objectivity, questions we do not believe apply to any of these respected scientists. Our concern is with the Pygmalion effect (Rosenthal, 1987), in which the expectations of investigators are confirmed through a variety of uncontrollable and even unconscious factors. Program designers have a vested interest in their programs and may approach their data with a particular mindset that favors particular outcomes. This effect was avoided in the evaluation of Early Head Start (see the chapter by Raikes and Emde). This relatively much larger federal program was evaluated by a third party at a highly respected research organization, under the leadership of John Love at Mathematica.

Being a methodological purist is one thing, but operating in the real world is another. There are very good reasons why investigators evaluate their own programs. Most interventions are relatively small, local efforts. High/Scope and Abecedarian certainly were. The fact is that early in the history of an intervention, no one other than its creator has much interest in it and is the only one who cares enough to do an evaluation. Only when an intervention is replicated several times and gains visibility in the research community do outsiders become interested in evaluating it.

With this in mind, it is surprising that High/Scope and Abecedarian have had so much influence on national policies. Each was confined to one community at one point in time, and each had a quite small number of participants. Both were internally evaluated, and neither was ever *precisely* replicated. Herman Spitz (1997) raised these and other problems in a scathing criticism. The Chicago program is much larger, more contemporary, and continues to operate so has ongoing replication. Third-party evaluation is possible, although this has not been routinely done.

Efficacy versus Effectiveness

The superb chapter in this volume by Duncan and Magnuson leads us to raise another concern with both the High/Scope and Abecedarian programs. These authors call attention to the difference between an efficacy evaluation and an effectiveness evaluation. Efficacy evaluation is the assessment of a treatment administered under ideal circumstances. As Donald Campbell (1969) taught, if you do not get a positive outcome with your efficacy evaluation, you must try a different or modified program. A successful efficacy evaluation proves the program can deliver its intended benefits and is essentially a go-ahead signal to try the treatment in other sites. If the model travels well and similar outcomes are obtained, this proves its effectiveness.

Thus, a program can claim efficacy without demonstrating effectiveness in the larger world.

The Head Start National Impact Study is a genuine effectiveness study. The results to date show many positive results of the Head Start model as it is delivered in sites across the country (Puma, Bell, Cook, Heid, & Lopez, 2005). Yet even without proof of effectiveness, both High/Scope and Abecedarian have made extremely valuable contributions. Both programs taught developmentalists a great deal about the plasticity of human development and about the lifelong trajectory of psychological growth and social adaptation. High/Scope's evaluators dared to look beyond changes in IQ and discovered the breadth of factors impacted by intervention. Further, these programs demonstrated what is possible if policy makers would spend the money necessary to run high-quality programs and to conduct meaningful longitudinal research.

Like High/Scope and Abecedarian, there is currently no way of knowing whether or not the nurse home-visiting program is effective. Although deserving the high praise it has received, this effort must be understood for what it is. Olds did his original efficacy study in Elmira, New York, and then replicated it in a different locality with a different population. Unsurprisingly, he did not obtain totally parallel findings, although both sets of results were encouraging. To discover if his program could be more cost-effective, he conducted a third trial in Denver, where he employed paraprofessionals as home visitors rather than nurses. However, all three trials were conducted under tight supervision in the demanding manner of his excellent protocol. They essentially are three efficacy studies of variations of his model. Effectiveness studies may be on the horizon, as Olds informs us that 250 communities are considering implementing his program. Future studies in some of these localities will provide the data needed to ascertain the program's effectiveness.

A final point about evaluation that is worth underlining is its timing. The field's methodological mentor, Donald Campbell, wisely instructed intervention designers not to conduct a summative or outcome evaluation until their program "is proud." This is determined by a process evaluation, which essentially assesses how well the model has been implemented and whether or not services are being delivered in the intended manner. More often than not, a number of changes and corrections are required to bring practices closer to the model. Only when process evaluation proves the integrity of the program should outcome evaluation be conducted to assess whether or not participants are achieving the intended goals as well as if there are some unanticipated benefits (including sleeper effects) or negative consequences.

Unfortunately, the wisdom of these sound evaluation practices has eluded Congress, which has become blindly attached to accountability in recent years. As one example, policy makers actually demanded that

Early Head Start be evaluated during its start-up period. Although the early results appear promising, we are not convinced that Early Head Start is yet a finished product. One result strongly relevant to our point is the discovery that the further along an Early Head Start program was in the implementation process, the better the outcomes were.

Although we believe that all programs that consume public funds must be held accountable, it is unwise to expect them to be effective the day they open their doors. Implementation problems are unavoidable, and even the most promising programs will never achieve their promise if their funding is pulled because they were evaluated too soon. The pressures of the political process exacerbate this problem. Policy makers want results they can show to voters by the next election cycle. But as the High/Scope, Abecedarian, and Chicago investigators proved, many of the benefits of intervention do not accrue to society until many years (and elections) later.

IMPERFECTIONS IN THE COLLECTIVE EVIDENCE

A huge literature makes very clear that high-quality early-childhood programs have a stable of benefits. Findings include better school readiness, better school performance and social adaptation, more effective parenting, and significant cost benefits. None of the studies contributing to this evidence was perfect, and critics of the very notion of preschool intervention have relentlessly pointed out their flaws. In this section, we will critique some of the evidence and views presented in this book, not to bolster the critics but to realistically assess the value of the studies' contributions to the knowledge base and to the policies that base supports.

All three of the famous programs discussed previously have been useful in informing policy makers of the academic and social value and cost benefits of investing in preschool programs. High/Scope, Abecedarian, and the Chicago Child–Parent Centers, in conjunction with years of experience with Head Start, certainly helped move the states to begin mounting public prekindergarten systems. However, as we noted, both High/Scope and Abecedarian were hothouse programs mounted by outstanding experts, and convincing replications in many settings will be needed to confirm their value. The Chicago intervention is in the contemporary world, operates in a large number of school sites, and is quite exportable.

The findings of the Chicago study are extremely impressive and deserving of as much attention from policy makers as the others. In comparison to the experimental design used by High/Scope and Abecedarian, the Chicago program is sometimes faulted for using a quasi-experimental design. Yet a very high-quality quasi-experiment like this does not strike us as a great weakness. We do part company with Reynolds and Temple on a couple of points. Although we share with these authors the need for a more intense effort instead of the typical one- to two-year preschool program, they champion intervention from ages three to nine. Much in this book and other sources makes clear the importance of the zero-to-age-three period, and to ignore it is a mistake. We believe that a prenatal to age eight or beyond strategy would be more effective. Zigler's Schools of the 21st Century is a prenatal-to-12 model, with the longer period including after-school care for school-age children.

We also disagree with the handling of the data by Reynolds and Temple on the number of risks families in their program have experienced. The Chicago researchers treat level of risk as a variable to be controlled by statistical means. However, as we have learned from Early Head Start research as well as from the great amount of work done on risk and protective factors, magnitude of risk itself is a variable in determining for whom an intervention works and for whom it does not. (We will write more on this later.) On the other hand, the Chicago researchers deserve praise for the amount of effort they have devoted to discovering what variables mediate the positive effects of intervention.

The Rameys also recognize the variability of outcomes both in their experimental and control groups. To understand why some children benefit more from the same intervention than others, these investigators provide a deep explication of the manipulable factors that could produce this variability. The field is also indebted to the Rameys for their strong empirical support proving the importance of the intensity and quality of a program if it is to succeed and achieve maximum benefits.

A drawback to the Rameys' otherwise informative chapter is that it is peppered with the authors' own very strong, sometimes highly controversial views to which we are sure many readers will take issue. Most evenhanded scholars would take offense with the Rameys' use of the term *controversial genetic influences*. This will be news to the entire field of behavior genetics, in which strong genetic effects have been well documented for intelligence and many other phenotypic traits. Indeed, the Rameys' choice of outcome variables—IQ scores, language, and related academic competence—hinge on intelligence, a highly stable trait clearly linked to inheritance. Although the cognitive approach was popular in the 1960s when the Abecedarian program was mounted, it has long since been replaced by the whole-child approach. The Rameys may be the only major workers who continue to use IQ as a primary outcome measure, even emphasizing the intellectual and academic characteristics of the *parents* in explaining their findings. (The Romanian research reported in the Rameys' chapter is not as well known as their other efforts, but it is encouraging that the evaluation included personality features.)

Our final divergence from the Rameys' views concerns who should be the recipients of early interventions. The Rameys argue that intervention efforts should be limited to children who are at the highest risk among the poor. This suggestion stands in counterpoint to the rigorous Early Head Start evaluation reported in this volume, where the greatest benefits accrued to children who had a modest degree of risk as opposed to those who were at extreme risk. This does not mean that programs can not have add-ons for children at greater risk. France, for instance, allows high-risk children to enter their universal preschools at two years of age rather than the conventional three years.

Like other investigators, the Rameys extol the benefits accruing from participation in their program. Yet a caveat is in order. The findings of many early interventions are impressive when compared to the outcomes of other children who live in poverty. However, in absolute terms, intervention participants end up far from being paragons of society. For example, the Rameys' control group had a 60 percent rate of grade retention, whereas the intervention group had half that rate. Obviously, a 30 percent grade repetition rate is much higher than that found in the general population. Similarly, although High/Scope participants had much lower rates of delinquency and crime than controls, they were still arrested with unacceptably high frequency.

We believe that evaluators should openly discuss base rates for middle-class children in presenting their findings to caution the public about what we can and can not accomplish through intervention. We must make clear that although we *can* improve poor children's developmental outcomes, no intervention program, even one with the quality and intensity of the Abecedarian, can totally offset the deleterious effects of growing up in poverty. We must openly admit that poor children need much more than early intervention programs to be successful in school and later life.

We are surprised that scholars of the Rameys' stature would take such umbrage when confronted with skeptics or naysayers, slipping into such ad hominem terms as *misguided* and *misinformed*. The nature of the scientific enterprise is based upon legitimate skeptics, and methodologists and peer reviewers raise scientific quality by criticizing our work. Any field of study is essentially a marketplace of ideas and debate. As Kuhn taught us, even when we are all comfortable with our consensus, a new paradigm may come along that causes us to rethink everything we believe. In science, this is and should be a continuing process. We agree with the Rameys in believing that scholarly debate should not be tainted with the arguments of ideologues whose primary objective is to champion a particular social philosophy. These activities are far removed from the area of legitimate scholarly disagreement that is so essential to the scientific enterprise. With this belief in mind, we now turn to constructive criticisms of the other chapters in this book.

Head Start and Early Head Start

The questions that animated the FACES study are excellent ones, and the evaluation successfully answered many of them. Because of FACES, we now know that Head Start has an acceptable level of quality and that quality has improved over time. FACES also provides more evidence of the positive relation between the quality of a program and the outcomes it achieves. Whitehurst and Massetti (2004) offered a cogent critique of FACES. Zill and Resnick unfortunately chose to ignore this critique in their chapter, just as the Rameys ignored Spitz's (1997) criticisms of their Abecedarian program.

Despite the relatively broad scope of their evaluation, Zill and Resnick begin their chapter by describing the goal of Head Start as "providing high quality preschool education to improve ... children's emergent literacy." Preschool education is just one component of this multifaceted program, and emergent literacy is just one of a plethora of its goals, which focus on no less than eight developmental domains, including social-emotional development, physical development, parental involvement, and family self-sufficiency. Further, Zill and Resnick define children's outcomes based on the five domains identified by the Goal One Technical Planning Group (1991, 1993) as part of the "whole child" perspective. FACES attempts to measure child and family outcomes in most if not all of these domains. But in this chapter, Zill and Resnick emphasize emergent literacy, language and cognitive development outcomes. This appears to reflect the interests of the current administration, as well as early childhood education researchers. As a consequence, however, the chapter does not tell us about children's social-emotional development in Head Start, although it does provide some indications of change in children's approaches to learning.

The great weakness of FACES is its methodological design, which makes it impossible for this very expensive federal study to show if children who attend Head Start do better compared to children from similar backgrounds who attend no or other programs. The design uses pre-post testing with norm- and criterion-referenced tests but absolutely no comparison group. Norm-referenced tests often have standardization data that can be used as a sort of comparison group to control for the effects of maturation. Criterion-referenced tests offer no such comparison. Alas, all that the FACES findings have shown thus far is that children's performance is better at the age of five than it was at age four. FACES findings *do* show that Head Start children make modest gains toward test publishers' national norms. By using standard scores and complex statistical modeling, including careful analyses to eliminate regression to the mean as a potential confound, the authors conclude that the results cannot be explained by maturation alone. However, since there was no control or comparison group, it is not clear how much of the gains are due to participation in Head Start as opposed to other possible factors. A recent report from the National Head Start Impact Study, which grew out of FACES and shares many of the same measures, revealed that, using random assignment to Head Start or non-Head Start waiting-list controls, some of the gains are indeed due to children's participation in Head Start.

There is a structural deficiency in the $7 billion Head Start program, where there are not sufficient funds for research and evaluation in this, our only national laboratory for early intervention practices. However, it is apparently not just a matter of money. Head Start also does not have enough in-house research expertise to properly direct research expenditures. In the early days, Head Start had a research advisory committee. Today, administrators do call on the wisdom of research task forces from time to time, but not on a regular basis. Instead, they work from a portfolio of studies, each designed to fulfill a niche within the information-gathering, evaluation and performance monitoring functions of the Head Start Bureau. Thus, FACES occupies an important place within a broader portfolio of studies within the Head Start Bureau. The portfolio includes the national Head Start Impact Study as well as smaller-scale random-assignment intervention studies, like those carried out by the Head Start Quality Research Consortium (QRC). The QRC studies make use of many of the same measures as FACES, and the availability of the FACES national sample results has provided a useful comparison point for the QRC studies. However it should be noted that the National Reporting System, one of the most ambitious and promising of those research endeavors, has earned the criticism of Congress's own watchdog, the General Accountability Office (2005).

Another evaluation within the portfolio of research conducted for the Head Start Bureau is the evaluation of Early Head Start, presented in the chapter by Raikes and Emde. Unlike FACES and the Head Start Impact Study, the study was designed early in the program's planning phase, but like these other studies, it was designed by scholars with strong backgrounds in evaluation. The study includes process evaluation, close attention to similarities and differences in Early Head Start models, and looks beyond averages to examine how individual risk factors influence outcomes. Despite these strengths, the Early Head Start study shows relatively small effect sizes (e.g., 10 percent of a standard deviation) and raises as many questions about the efficacy of early intervention as it answers.

Public-use files from two rounds of FACES (1997 and 2000) have been made available to secondary analysts through the Inter-university Consortium for Political and Social Research (ICPSR) at the University of Michigan, demonstrating that the FACES datasets are both robust enough and methodologically sound enough to warrant continuing scholarly analyses. The national representativeness of the FACES samples and the possibility of making comparisons across cohorts are also key strengths in the FACES study design. We await further results focused on outcomes other than literacy and language development.

Ambassadors for Literacy

This intervention is a highly commendable community effort that is not far enough along to merit close scrutiny from the field. The program has a sound rationale: It is a wise investment to identify very bright children who live in poverty and help them even quite early in their educational careers on the road to higher education. It is worthwhile to point out that creating a poverty line does not mean that everyone beneath it has low ability. On the contrary, every level of intelligence can be found in every socioeconomic group. There is a cottage industry among scholars examining the characteristics of children in poverty who, in spite of the odds, show great intellectual promise. This literature shades into the resilience literature of Norman Garmezy and his colleagues, who have identified high intelligence as a characteristic of resilient children. However, the findings are mixed, and the traits of gifted children in poverty are still a matter of dispute (Luthar, 2003).

Evidence of the efficacy of the Denver intervention is seriously wanting. The base rate for college attendance of all children in Denver (or even national cohorts) is a poor comparison group. A more appropriate comparison would be equally capable children who did not experience the intervention. This program calls out for a straightforward experimental evaluation design, but this is not yet possible because the number of participants is still too small.

The Denver group also needs to broaden its probe of outcomes. They rely solely on whether or not the Ambassadors enter college, overlooking the Head Start children who receive tutoring. There is evidence in the literature that both tutors and tutees profit from the mutual experience. Thus it would be informative and not terribly difficult to assess child outcomes.

In this age of stringent accountability, it is worthwhile here to make a simple point. Every intervention with a sound rationale does not have to be rigorously evaluated. Sometimes it is appropriate to take a certain social action because it is the moral and equitable thing to do. We do not bother to investigate the value in feeding a hungry child or providing meals on wheels to homebound senior citizens. Of course, a strong motivator for evaluation is to put a program in a better position when it competes at the social trough that contains limited funding.

Nurse-Family Partnership

The Olds program is much more health oriented than other home-visiting programs, which strikes us as both a plus and a minus. Nurses can speak with authority on health issues, so parents are likely to listen, but their training to deal with non-health-related developmental issues is not particularly strong. Further, the national nursing shortage threatens expansion of this type of intervention. Olds was wise to conduct the Denver trial to compare the effectiveness of paraprofessionals with that of nurses. Yet his interpretation of the Denver findings gives the impression that we must choose between paraprofessionals and nurses. He concludes that the positive effects of the intervention are twice as large for the nurses, but this should not mean the paraprofessionals were useless or that a combination of the two could not promote desired outcomes and be more cost-effective. Clearly, much more work is needed on the staff qualifications and training necessary in home-visiting programs than Olds, or anyone else, has done.

This is not the only place Olds builds his model and his advocacy on principles that are in need of further empirical support. The fact that his program is limited to firstborns requires a much better rationale than assuming that most first-time parents are particularly in need of home visiting. Second children are often quite different in temperament and behavior than firstborn, and the parent now has an older child demanding attention. It is well known that any new birth throws many families out of orbit and is an invariably stressful period (Hopper & Zigler, 1988).

Based on the single Elmira trial, Olds has been clear in asserting that his program target only low-income families. This is dramatically different from the universal approach championed by the Parents as Teachers (PAT) model. There is now general consensus that any intervention will show greater effects with low- as compared to middle-SES (socioeconomic status) populations. However, evidence is accumulating that middle-class families also profit from early-childhood interventions (Zigler, Gilliam, Jones, & Malakoff, in press). Olds's argument against the universal approach is the added cost and resulting dilution of the program. Yet the PAT and Schools of the 21st Century models have demonstrated popularity and effectiveness among middle-class families at far less cost than the Olds program.

These complaints are not meant to detract from the many commendable features in the history of the nurse home-visiting program. Olds has strongly demonstrated his program's efficacy and has conducted an impressive cost-benefit analysis. His willingness to tailor services to fit individual family needs should become a guiding principle for all intervention efforts. On the other hand, we would have welcomed greater emphasis on effect sizes in this report, as he has done in earlier publications, to enable our readers to gauge more accurately the power of the interventions. Finally, other home-visiting programs have been plagued by high attrition rates. For comparative purposes, it would be helpful for Olds to consistently report on attrition in his samples, which has generally been better than the average.

Toward the end of his chapter, Olds cites others' reviews and his own work to question the empirical support for other home-visiting programs. This tacitly implies that their value is questionable because they do not meet his own high standards. Olds has been consistent in this matter and taken his views into the policy arena. While the literature on home visiting is inconclusive, we do not believe that all the other programs are unsuccessful. Stumping for high quality is always good for public policy, but Olds may do a disservice to the field by overselling the weaknesses of other home-visiting programs.

Conventional wisdom already judges home visiting as largely ineffective. For example, Duncan and Magnuson's chapter concludes that most home visiting programs improve parenting but have little effect on children's behavior and academic outcomes. To be even-handed, they do mention the Sweet and Appelbaum (2004) study, to show this is not always the case. At this point in time in the field's development, we feel that conclusions about the value of home visiting should be held in abeyance until much more data are collected. At the logic level, particularly after reading the Bradley and Ayoub chapters in this book, it is difficult to believe that if you change parenting behavior for the better, you do not eventually have a positive impact on the child.

Recent data from the home-visiting model in Early Head Start show benefits to children that are clearly related to later academic performance. Home visiting is essentially a form of family support. The benefits of family support are most vividly seen in the child abuse area, but a large and varied literature supports its effects in many developmental domains (Dunst, 2000). The evidence in favor of family support was sufficient years ago to convince the Missouri state legislature to implement the PAT program statewide. The promising evidence and relatively small cost convinced the first author to include PAT as a component in his school reform model called the Schools of the 21st Century, which now operates in 1,300 schools in 20 states (Finn-Stevenson & Zigler, 1999).

Our hunch is that programs directed at both parents and children will prove to be the most successful. This has been Head Start's model for 40 years, and the Early Head Start data are supporting this approach with younger children. Although methodologically problematic, a large sample study conducted in Missouri (Pfannenstiel, Seitz, & Zigler, 2002) of low-SES children whose parents had experienced the PAT program before they went to preschool found they arrived at kindergarten with school readiness scores approximately the same as middle-class children. The benefits of the combined home-visiting and preschool programs were greater than the benefits accruing from either home visiting or preschool alone.

Logic and the encouraging but tentative findings to date lead us to believe home-visiting components of early intervention are worthwhile. Still, we strongly agree with Duncan and Magnuson that the issue is not a logical one but an empirical one to be ultimately decided on the basis of hard evidence.

Early Language Development

A distinct outlier in this book is the chapter by Risley and Hart. Although these authors do not report on an intervention study, their effort does stem from an early intervention that the first author visited in the 1960s called Juniper Gardens. This program was mounted by a group of radical empiricists from the University of Kansas and was based on the behavior modification formulations of B. F. Skinner. When evaluation of the program revealed minimal effects, the investigators did not even entertain the possibility that the problem was in the underlying theory and the intervention practices it dictated. They insisted the failure had to be due to some set of experiences the children had before they began the intervention. They then undertook probably the most impressive (in terms of sheer time and effort) observational study ever conducted to see what those experiences could be.

Close observations of a phenomenon of interest can only be considered a starting point in scientific inquiry, because the only legitimate conclusion one can derive is a summary of what has been observed. In our opinion, the investigators ascribe much more value to their observational data than its inherent limitations permit. Remember that their study contained a very small sample, only 42 children spread across three SES groups. Risley and Hart found that parental verbalizations were related to children's later IQ scores. This is no more than a correlation that by its very nature can not prove causality. Nevertheless, because the language experiences preceded the IQ test, the authors assert that these experiences determined the children's IQ scores. They also conclude that children's language behavior never rises above that of their parents. This will be news to the countless investigators who have spent lifetimes attempting to unravel the mystery of what determines IQ and to scientists in the large and well-tilled field of language development who have uncovered many complexities that contribute to verbal ability.

The investigators also ignore the undisputed fact that cognitive abilities, including those in the verbal area, have a strong genetic component. It is obvious that children not only get a certain number of utterances from their parents, but even before that, they also get a set of genes from those same parents. Even if Risley and Hart wish to ignore genetic influences, as

Skinner did, there are many other factors known to influence the IQ, such as motivation and physical and mental health.

If one carries Risley and Hart's interpretation to its conclusion, poor children with scant language experience in their early years are doomed. This view gets some tangential support in the findings of the Abecedarian program, in which children did get rich language experience during the first three years of life and later achieved higher IQ scores. However, the Watt and Puma and the Olds chapters partially refute Risley and Hart's beliefs. Both programs had some participants who were doing very well in spite of the adversity in their lives—children with similar backgrounds to the low-SES children Risley and Hart found had experienced insufficient language input in their early years.

These cases underscore a weakness in experimental methodology that makes it easy to ignore variation *within* groups. The intervention field appears to be suffering from the tyranny of the mean. We suspect that many if not most interventions contain off-quadrant cases of children in the experimental group who do not profit from the treatment and in the control group who succeed without the treatment. It is past time for workers to move beyond the question of whether or not high-quality early-childhood interventions work. We must learn for whom they work and for whom they do not. This knowledge will allow us to better target programs.

An effort in this direction is the Early Head Start study, which explored the magnitude of positive benefits as a function of the number of risk factors experienced by the participants. An important discovery was that children with fewer risks and those with a high number of risks displayed a lesser degree of positive effects than those with a moderate number of risks. This pattern of findings is not difficult to interpret. Those with few risks are not in great need of the program and will not accrue much benefit from attending. Those with a great number of risk factors have a true need for the program, but the developmental threats these risks have produced overwhelm the intervention. These children are in need of a more intensive program. This suggests that instead of circumscribed programs, we should be thinking in terms of a family of programs, with the intensity of each determined by the needs of the individual recipients.

Risley and Hart do highlight an important point, namely that SES is not a psychological variable. Although SES is an appropriate variable for sociologists operating at a sociological level of analysis, psychologists should not make the error of using SES as an explanatory variable. A child's behavior is not determined by social class but by events the child experiences as a result of being in that social class. SES and poverty are only shorthand terms for a multitude of factors experienced because of living in a certain general environment. Although we are all indebted to Risley and Hart for directing our attention to the relatively low number of verbaliza-

tions made by low-SES parents, we must be aware that a multitude of negative features common in low-income households can influence both the
number of utterances and IQ scores. Thus, Risley and Hart's recommendations strike us as mundane (just talk to very young children more). In point
of fact, this advice has already been incorporated into most early-childhood
programs following the groundwork laid by Zero to Three (1992), the early
brain development findings, and the current policy emphasis on language
and preliteracy skills.

The Role of Parents

The Bradley and Ayoub chapters have a common thrust: the role of parents and parenting practices in child development. Bradley provides interesting information on the impressive theoretical foundation of his HOME
measure, which has become a common tool for assessing a child's home
environment. His explanation makes clear that parents not only impact
development by their interactions with the child, but they also determine
the environmental context in which the child grows and develops, that is,
the child's daily ecology. This environment can both facilitate and deter
the course of development. In Ayoub's discussion of protective factors, her
points are most relevant for mental health intervention of the sort described
in the Raikes and Emde chapter.

Both chapters are rich scholarly reviews, and both present information
that should be useful in the design of intervention programs in areas like
health, substance abuse prevention, home visiting, and parent education.
Both authors have selected a huge area to cover, so it is understandable
that their chapters devote less attention to policy implications than the
others in this book. That said, these two chapters are certainly more
policy relevant than most of the conventional scholarly papers found in
the *Handbook of Parenting* (Bornstein, 1995), which contains several
volumes. For example, both authors suggest that policy makers examine
practices found in other nations to assist young parents in child rearing,
such as the family allowance being proposed in Great Britain (Huston, in
press) and the children's allowances granted in several countries.

Policy Concerns

The two outstanding chapters by Heckman and Duncan and Magnuson
directly address policy formation and are must reading for everyone
involved in the policy process at the federal, state, and local levels.

Although Heckman is a Nobel laureate in economics, he has become
our nation's most visible champion for preschool education. His chapter
focuses on the most pressing domestic problem in the United States today,

education reform. Unlike the developmentalists whose work appears in this volume, Heckman's goal is not the optimal development of the child but the quality of the future workforce that will secure the national economic system.

Heckman makes two key points that are not currently reflected in education policy. Using cost-benefit analysis findings as his common metric, he demonstrates that investments in skill development in early childhood have much greater payoffs than investments made in the school years and later. His second premise is that an individual's effectiveness in the workplace is not just a matter of smarts or cognitive status but also relies on a variety of social and emotional characteristics. This assertion directly challenges the centerpiece of current domestic educational reform, the No Child Left Behind Act. Heckman draws attention to the importance of the preschool years, which are typically not even part of the K–12 system, and to the vital learning that is delivered through life experiences unconnected to formal schooling.

Heckman is far ranging in the educational factors that take place outside the school building, with a special emphasis on families. His position draws credence from one of our nation's most eminent education experts, Edmund Gordon, who emphasized the importance of what he labeled supplemental education (Gordon, Bridglall, & Meroe, 2005). A factor that Heckman does not consider, and one that has received little attention in this volume, is neighborhood effects. This is surprising in that Duncan is a leading scholar in the study of the impact of neighborhoods.

We do have one criticism of Heckman's curve. The ordinate and the abscissa converge at a point labeled 0. To most people 0 means birth, and Heckman's greatest savings are found a couple of years out from birth. We believe that probably the most critical time in a child's development is the nine months in utero. We have argued that the ideal preschool program should cover the time from conception to school entry (Zigler et al., in press), with the earliest interventions taking the form of good prenatal care and parent education. As a relevant example, the Olds chapter proves the value of an intervention that begins prior to birth and extends to the child's second birthday. Further evidence comes from the evaluation of Early Head Start, which showed that families who participated during pregnancy had better outcomes than those who enrolled later.

Anchoring his views on cost-benefit analyses, Heckman's attitude toward Head Start appears to be ambivalent. This is fair. A prerequisite to cost-benefit analysis is a rigorous evaluation that clearly shows a program has positive effects. As we mentioned previously, Head Start has never had a strong research and evaluation unit. After 40 years, there are still no clear findings that the benefits of the program justify its approximately $7 billion annual cost. The random assignment National Impact Study is now under way and will soon fill some of the gaps in the

Head Start literature and hopefully provide the base on which to launch a cost-benefit analysis.

To derive the most utility from this and other ongoing evaluations, policy makers must commit funding for the long term. Although it is helpful to learn that children have better school readiness at the point of departure from Head Start and that further benefits accrue through kindergarten, significant positive effects may not be evident until children are older. Reductions in delinquency and welfare usage, for example, will not be evident for years. Both the High/Scope and Abecedarian investigators discovered that the value of benefits increases as the participants mature.

The chapter by Duncan and Magnuson is also must reading for developmentalists and policy makers. These scholars have written the best single chapter overview of early intervention programs that we have read. We do disagree with their categorization of early intervention programs into those directed to parents and those targeted to children. Although parsimonious, this dichotomy does an injustice to the complexity of the early intervention field. Along with others (Smith, 1995), we have argued that the most efficacious programs will be those that work with *both* parents and their children. This two-generation approach is often considered Head Start's strongest feature and the major contributor to its success.

One of the great foes of optimal human development is growing up in poverty. Duncan and Magnuson call our attention to the fact that simply providing poor families with money results in better outcomes for their children. Scanning the social policy menu in the child and family area, perhaps one of the most important and effective interventions ever mounted is the earned income tax credit. The credit subsidizes the incomes of working-poor families, often enough to lift them above the poverty line. Many states are copying the idea and providing their own tax credits that low-income families receive in addition to the federal supplement.

This approach to poverty deserves to be pondered by developmental scientists, early-childhood educators, home visitors, and anyone involved in social interventions. Although all of us want to change the world, we must face the harsh reality that our interventions are too limited to have huge effects on parents or their children. Returning to the bioecological model, our programs simply do not impact enough of the child's ecology—housing, health care, the quality of child care and schools, drugs, violence, and a host of modern ills—to dramatically impact a child's life. In addition, we have already pointed out that a child's inheritance has a potent influence on abilities and is a factor we can do little about through our manipulations of child-rearing environments.

The take-home message from this epilogue, then, is one of humility. There is indeed much we can do to help young children who live in poverty do better in school and in life, but there is much we can not do. We must be attuned to the inherent limits not only of what our interventions can accomplish but what public policies can accomplish. This does not mean that dreamers like Rusk should not make their case and share their dreams with us, but we must come to grips with the fact that our very hard work will probably have modest results. Still, we must do everything we can to convince policy makers that even modest benefits are worth the costs because they do improve the well-being and life course of children whose destinies are being woven into the future fabric of U.S. society.

REFERENCES

Aos, S., Lieb, R., Mayfield, J., Miller, M., & Pennucci, A. (2004). *Benefits and costs of prevention and early intervention programs for youth.* Olympia: Washington State Institute for Public Policy.

Barnett, W.S. (1985). Benefit-cost analysis of the Perry Preschool program and its policy implications. *Educational Evaluation and Policy Analysis, 7,* 333–342.

Bloom, B.S. (1964). *Stability and change in human characteristics.* New York: Wiley.

Bornstein, M. (Ed.). (1995). *Handbook of parenting* (Vols. 1–5). Mahwah, NJ: Erlbaum.

Bronfenbrenner, U. (1974). Developmental research, public policy, and the ecology of childhood. *Child Development, 45,* 1–5.

Campbell, D. (1969). Reforms as experiments. *American Psychologist, 24,* 409–429.

Clinton, H.R. (1996). *It takes a village and other lessons children teach us.* New York: Touchstone.

Consortium for Longitudinal Studies. (1983). *As the twig is bent: Lasting effects of preschool programs.* Hillsdale, NJ: Erlbaum.

Dunst, C.J. (2000). Revisiting "Rethinking early intervention." *Topics in Early Childhood Special Education, 20,* 95–104.

Finn-Stevenson, M., & Zigler, E. (1999). *Schools of the 21st century: Linking child care and education.* Boulder, CO: Westview.

General Accountability Office. (2005). *Head Start: Further development could allow results of new test to be used for decision making.* Washington, DC: Author. Retrieved July 2005, from http://www.gao.gov/new.items/d05343.pdf

Goal One Technical Planning Group. (1991). The Goal One Technical Planning Subgroup report on school readiness. In National Education Goals Panel (Ed.), *Potential strategies for long-term indicator development: Reports of the technical planning subgroups* (Report No. 91-0, pp. 1–18). Washington, DC: National Education Goals Panel.

Goal One Technical Planning Group. (1993). *Reconsidering children's early development and learning: Toward shared beliefs and vocabulary.* Draft report to the National Education Goals Panel. Washington, DC: National Education Goals Panel.

Gordon, E., Bridglall, B. L., & Meroe, A. S. (Eds.). (2005). *Supplementary education: The hidden curriculum of high academic achievement.* Lanham, MD: Rowman and Littlefield.

Hopper, P., & Zigler, E. (1988). The medical and social science basis for a national infant care leave policy. *American Journal of Orthopsychiatry, 58,* 324–338.

Hunt, J. M. (1961). *Intelligence and experience.* New York: Ronald Press.

Huston, A. (in press). Connecting the science of child development to public policy. *SRCD Policy Report.*

Luthar, S. S. (Ed.). (2003). *Resilience and vulnerability: Adaptation in the context of childhood adversities.* New York: Cambridge University Press.

Pfannenstiel, J. C., Seitz, V., & Zigler, E. (2002). Promoting school readiness: The role of the Parents as Teachers Program. *NHSA Dialog, 5,* 71–86.

Puma, M., Bell, S., Cook, R., Heid, C., & Lopez, M. (2005). *Head Start Impact Study: First year findings.* Washington, DC: U.S. Department of Health and Human Services. Retrieved August 2005, from http://www.acf.hhs.gov/programs/opre/hs/impact_study/reports/first_yr_finds/first_yr_finds.pdf

Reynolds, A., & Temple, J. (in press). Economic returns of investments in preschool education. In E. Zigler, W. Gilliam, & S. M. Jones (Eds.), *A vision of universal preschool education.* New York: Cambridge University Press.

Rosenthal, R. (1987). Pygmalion effects: Existence, magnitude, and social importance. *Educational Researcher, 16,* 37–41.

Smith, S. (Ed.). (1995). *Two-generation programs for families in poverty: A new intervention. strategy.* Norwood, NJ: Ablex.

Spitz, H. H. (1997). Some questions about the results of the Abecedarian early interventions project cited by the APA task force on intelligence. *American Psychologist, 52,* 72.

Sweet, M.A., & Appelbaum, M.L. (2004). Is home visiting an effective strategy? A meta-analytic review of home visiting programs for families with young children. *Child Development, 75*(5), 1435–1456

Whitehurst, G. J., & Massetti, G. M. (2004). How well does Head Start prepare children to learn to read? In E. Zigler & S. J. Styfco (Eds.), *The Head Start debates* (pp. 379–396). Baltimore: Paul H. Brookes.

Zero to Three. (1992). Heart Start: The emotional foundations of school readiness. Arlington, VA: Author.

Zigler, E. (1963). Metatheoretical issues in developmental psychology. In N. R. Ellis (Ed.), *Theories in contemporary psychology* (p. 344). New York: Macmillan.

Zigler, E. (1980). Welcoming a new journal. *Journal of Applied Developmental Psychology, 1,* 1–6.

Zigler, E. (1998). A place of value for applied and policy studies. *Child Development, 69,* 532–542.

Zigler, E., & Berman, W. (1983). Discerning the future of early childhood intervention. *American Psychologist, 38,* 894–906.

Zigler, E., & Butterfield, E.C. (1968). Motivational aspects of changes in IQ test performance of culturally deprived nursery school children. *Child Development, 39,* 1–14.

Zigler, E., Gilliam, W.S., Jones, S.M., & Malakoff, M. (in press). The need for universal preschool access for children not living in poverty. In E. Zigler, W.S. Gilliam, & S.M. Jones (Eds.), *A vision for universal preschool education.* New York: Cambridge University Press.

INDEX

CONTRIBUTING
AUTHORS AND EDITORS

CATHERINE C. AYOUB, RN, ED.D., a psychologist and nurse practitioner, co-directs a master's degree program at the Harvard Graduate School of Education, holds an appointment at Harvard Medical School and is a senior staff member at Massachusetts General Hospital, where she is the director of research at the Law and Psychiatry Service and at Boston Children's Hospital. She is a co-founder of the Family Connections Project. Her research centers on the developmental consequences and emotional adjustment of children who have witnessed domestic violence or experienced mental illness, child maltreatment, homelessness, chronic illness, or difficult parental divorce. She has special interest in at-risk children of Latin American origin residing in the United States and in their home countries.

ROBERT H. BRADLEY, PH.D., is a professor in the Center for Applied Studies in Education at the University of Arkansas at Little Rock. For over 30 years, Dr. Bradley has been involved in studies of parenting, early education, and child care, with a special focus on children at biologic and environmental risk. He has developed several measures of the home environment and published widely on relations between children's experiences in the family and their adaptive competence. He served on the editorial boards of several professional journals as well as a variety of advisory boards and professional review panels, the Biobehavioral and Behavioral review committee for the National Institute of Child Health and Human Development.

GREG J. DUNCAN, PH.D., is the Edwina S. Tarry Professor of Education and Social Policy at Northwestern University. He has published extensively on issues of income dynamics within and across generations, and on the impact of family, neighborhood, childcare and policy environments on children's development. He was a member of the SRCD Public Policy Committee between 1995 and 1999, the NRC/IOM Neurons to Neighborhoods Committee on Integrating the Science of Early Childhood Development, and the Advisory Committee on Head Start Research and Evaluation. He is a member of the National Scientific Council on the Developing Child and was elected to the American Academy of Arts and Sciences in 2001.

ROBERT N. EMDE, M.D., is Emeritus Professor of Psychiatry at the University of Colorado Health Sciences Center. He serves as Scientific Adviser for the World Association of Infant Mental Health and was previously President of that organization. He was President of the Society for Research in Child Development and Editor of the *SRCD Monographs*. He is Scientific Advisor for the Board of Professional Standards of the American Psychoanalytic Association and is Head of the College of Research Fellows of the International Psychoanalytic Association. Dr. Emde's research interests include early social emotional development and the evaluation of early intervention programs. He served as a national coordinator for a follow-up study of a 17-site national randomized trial of first wave Early Head Start programs.

BETTY HART, PH.D., is Professor Emeritus of Human Development and a former Senior Scientist at the Schiefelbusch Institue for Life Span Studies at the University of Kansas. Dr. Hart's most recent books include: *Meaningful Differences* and *The Social World of Children Learning to Talk* (with Todd Risley in 1995 & 1999).

JAMES J. HECKMAN, PH.D., received his doctoral degree in economics from Princeton University in 1971. He is currently the Henry Schultz Distinguished Service Professor of Economics at the University of Chicago, where he directs the Economics Research Center and the Center for Social Program Evaluation. Heckman's work has been devoted to the development of a scientific basis for economic policy evaluation, with special emphasis on models of individuals and disaggregated groups, and to the problems and possibilities created by heterogeneity, diversity, and unobserved counterfactual states. Heckman has received numerous awards for his work, including the 2000 Nobel Memorial Prize in Economic Sciences (with Daniel McFadden), and the 2005 Jacob Mincer Award for Lifetime Achievement in Labor Economics.

WHITNEY LEBOEUF received her undergraduate degree in Radio/Television/Film from Northwestern University in 2003 and is currently a master's degree candidate in Quantitative Research Methods at the University of Denver. She is working for Ambassadors for Literacy, Inc., a non-profit organization designed to promote literacy learning in younger children and to empower and financially support older children in their efforts to attend a college or university. Additionally, she is a member of the Risk and Protective Task Group within the National Early Head Start Research Consortium.

KATHERINE MAGNUSON, PH.D., received her Ph.D. in Human Development and Social Policy from Northwestern University. Her dissertation research focused on whether children's academic achievement improves when their mothers return to school. During her time at Northwestern, Dr. Magnuson worked on a variety of issues related to family functioning and child development among low-income populations. Dr. Magnuson is currently an assistant professor of social work at the University of Wisconsin at Madison. Her research interests include the effects of poverty and socioeconomic status on children and family well-being and the effects of early childhood and family interventions.

DAVID L. OLDS, PH.D., is Professor of Pediatrics, Psychiatry, and Preventive Medicine at the University of Colorado Health Sciences Center, where he directs the Prevention Research Center for Family and Child Health. He has devoted his career to investigating methods of preventing health and developmental problems in children and parents from low-income families. In recent years, he has begun helping new communities develop the program outside of research contexts, giving emphasis to ensuring quality implementation with fidelity to the model tested in the scientifically controlled studies. Dr. Olds has received numerous awards for his research, including a Senior Research Scientist Award from the National Institute of Mental Health. Dr. Olds obtained his doctoral degree from Cornell University.

JINI E. PUMA, M.A., is a doctoral candidate in Quantitative Research Methods at the University of Denver. She is the co-coordinator of the Head Start Ambassadors for Literacy Program which seeks to promote literacy in preschoolers. Ms. Puma's research interests include longitudinal research on early childhood development in the poverty class and the etiology and intervention in the handicaps of poverty. She recently joined the steering committee for the National Early Head Start Research and Evaluation Study and is a member of the Risk and Protective task group. Ms. Puma received the Gertrude Cox Scholarship Honorable Mention in 2004, given to outstanding women in the field of statistics, and the Ahlborg Scholarship in 2005.

HELEN H. RAIKES, PH.D. earned her doctoral degree at Iowa State University. She is a two term Society for Research in Child Development Executive Policy Scholar at the Admnistration for Children and Families (ACF), and continues to serve as a consultant for the Early Head Start Research and Evaluation project. During the data collection and analyses of the 0-3 and pre-kindergarten follow-up phases of the Early Head Start Project she was a member of the federal oversight team, and participated in data archiving and other research projects pertaining to infants and toddlers. Dr. Raikes also works at The Gallup Organization and the University of Nebraska-Lincoln Center on Children, Families and the Law.

CRAIG T. RAMEY, PH.D., is a Distinguished Professor of Health Studies and Psychiatry and the Director (along with his wife Sharon L. Ramey) of the Center for Health and Education at Georgetown University. He specializes in the study of intellectual development and social competence. He also has used epidemiological methods to investigate distributions of developmental risk in many counties and states. Dr. Ramey has received many honors including the American Psychological Association Award for Exemplary Prevention Research and the Howell Heflin medal for Contributions to World Health and Education. In 2003 he was inducted into the Hall of Honor of the National Institute of Child Health and Human Development.

SHARON LANDESMAN RAMEY, PH.D., is the founding Director of the Georgetown University Center on Health and Education and holds the Susan H. Mayer Professorship in Child and Family Studies. Her primary research interests have included the etiology and social ecology of individuals with developmental disabilities; the social and behavioral dynamics of the modern American family; behavioral teratology and pregnancy outcome studies; innovative treatment strategies for children with neuromotor impairments; and longitudinal studies of the effects of early educational and preventive interventions. Dr. Ramey received the Outstanding Contribution for Research Award from the American Association on Mental Retardation.

GARY RESNICK, PH.D., is a senior researcher in the Child and Family Study Area at Westat, a social science research organization in Rockville, Maryland. He received his doctorate in applied developmental psychology from the Eliot-Pearson Institute of Child Study, Tufts University. His work has focused on the intersection between applied developmental psychology and program evaluation, including the design, measurement and analysis of large-scale national studies of children and families such as the Head Start Family and Child Experiences Survey, the Head Start Impact Study, and the Early Childhood Longitudinal Studies Birth Cohort (ECLS-B).

ARTHUR J. REYNOLDS, PH.D., is a Professor of Social Work, Educational Psychology, and Human Development at the University of Wisconsin-Madison. He directs the Chicago Longitudinal Study, one of the largest studies of the effects of early childhood intervention. A focal point of the 20-year, on-going project is the long-term educational and social effects of the Chicago Child-Parent Centers. Dr. Reynolds is interested in child development and social policy, especially how research can inform public policy. He has written extensively on the implications of early childhood research. He also is affiliated with the Waisman Center and the Institute for Research on Poverty at the University of Wisconsin, Madison.

TODD R. RISLEY, PH.D., received his Ph.D. in Psychology from the University of Washington in 1966. He is a Professor Emeritus of Psychology at the University of Alaska and a former Professor of Human Development and Senior Scientist of the Bureau of Child Research at the University of Kansas. He was a founding editor of the *Journal of Applied Behavior Analysis* and is a Past President of both the Association for Advancement of Behavior Therapy and the Behavior Analysis Division of the American Psychological Association. His work has received many awards including the Edgar A. Doll Award from the American Psychological Association, and the Outstanding Research Award from the American Association on Mental Retardation.

DAVID RUSK has been a speaker and consultant on urban policy in over 120 metropolitan areas. A former mayor of Albuquerque and New Mexico state legislator, he is author of *Inside Game/Outside Game* (Brookings Institution Press, 1999) and *Cities without Suburbs* (Woodrow Wilson Center Press, 3rd ed., 2003). He serves as a national strategic partner of the Gamaliel Foundation and is a founding member of the Innovative Housing Institute. For more information on inclusionary zoning, contact the Innovative Housing Institute (*www.inhousing.org*), Business and Professional People in the Public Interest (*www.bpichicago.org*), or PolicyLink (www.policylink.org).

LAWRENCE J. SCHWEINHART, PH.D., is an early childhood program researcher and speaker throughout the United States and in other countries. He has conducted research at the High/Scope Educational Research Foundation in Ypsilanti, Michigan, since 1975 and now serves as its president. He has directed the High/Scope Perry Preschool Study through age 40, the Michigan School Readiness Program Evaluation, High/Scope's Head Start Quality Research Center, and the development and validation of the High/Scope Child Observation Record. Dr. Schweinhart received his Ph.D. in Education from Indiana University in 1975 and has taught elementary school and college courses.

LOU ANNA KIMSEY SIMON, Ph.D. is the 20th President of Michigan State University. Prior to assuming the role of president, she was provost and vice president for academic affairs at Michigan State University, and Provost of the Michigan State University College of Law. She is regarded nationally as a powerful advocate of a research-active, student-centered university that is an engaged partner with society, in the land grant tradition. Dr. Simon is deeply committed to the development of effective university-community partnerships that focus on solution-based approaches to the problems of children, youth, and families. Most recently, she co-edited with Maureen Kenny, Karen Kiley-Brabeck and Richard Lerner, *Learning to Serve: Promoting Civil Society Through Service Learning* .

SALLY J. STYFCO is Research Associate at the Yale University Child Study Center and Associate Director of the Head Start Section at the Zigler Center in Child Development and Social Policy. She is a writer and policy analyst specializing in issues pertaining to children and families, particularly early childhood and educational interventions. Her work spans the topics of Head Start, child care, children with disabilities, federal education initiatives, the effects of poverty on child development, and the historical progression of government policies in these areas.

JUDY A. TEMPLE is an Associate Professor of Economics at Northern Illinois University. She received her PhD from Michigan State University. Her research interests are in the area of public sector economics, including policy evaluation and cost-benefit analysis.

NORMAN F. WATT, PH.D. is a Professor of Clinical Psychology at the University of Denver. His early research interest in understanding the development of severe psychopathology in young adults has evolved gradually into a preferred focus on studies of children and young families at high risk. Dr. Watt was a founder and Steering Committee Chairman of the Risk Research Consortium and a member of the NIMH Task Force on Prevention. He is now a Principal Investigator for the Early Head Start National Research Study. Most recently, he founded the Head Start Ambassadors for Literacy, a charitable non-profit organization which seeks to promote literacy in preschoolers through a collaborative venture with the Denver Public Schools.

EDWARD ZIGLER, PH.D., received his Ph.D. in Clinical Psychology from the University of Texas at Austin in 1958. Dr. Zigler was appointed by President Nixon as the founding Director of the U.S. Office of Child Development (now the Administration on Children, Youth and Families) and Chief of the U.S. Children's Bureau. Throughout his 45 years at Yale University, he served as Director of the Child Development Program, Chairman of the Psychology Department, and member of the Executive Committee of the Child Study Center. He founded and is Director of the Yale Center in Child Development and Social Policy, and is currently Sterling Professor of Psychology, Emeritus. He helped to plan Head Start, Follow Through, the Parent and Child Centers, Early Head Start, and the Family and Medical Leave Act.

NICHOLAS ZILL, PH.D., heads the Child and Family Study Area at Westat, a social science research organization in Rockville, Maryland. He received his doctorate in psychology from The Johns Hopkins University. He has helped to design, analyze, and report on large-scale studies of children and families for more than twenty-eight years, including the Head Start National Reporting System (NRS), the Head Start Family and Child Experiences Survey (FACES), and the National Survey of Children.